THE GAME OF BUSINESS

JOHN McDONALD gained his reputation as one of America's leading business writers during the nearly thirty years he spent at *Fortune*. He joined the magazine in 1945, and was elected to the Board of Editors there in 1949. While at *Fortune*, Mr. McDonald wrote more than one hundred long stories on American business that emphasized the strategic rather than technical aspects of business. Mr. McDonald is the author of the classic *Strategy in Poker, Business and War*, and collaborator with Alfred P. Sloan, Jr., in the celebrated autobiography, *My Years with General Motors*. He is also a noted authority on sport fishing, which is the subject of three of his six books. Mr. McDonald was born in Detroit and educated at the University of Detroit and the University of Michigan.

The Game of Business

John McDonald

ANCHOR BOOKS
ANCHOR PRESS/DOUBLEDAY
GARDEN CITY, NEW YORK

THE GAME OF BUSINESS was originally published in hardcover by Doubleday & Company, Inc.

Anchor Books Edition: 1977

CONTENTS

Acknowledgments   ix

Introduction   xv

1 Seagrams v. Schenley: A Mutual Interaction   1

2 The Rules of the Game: Finding the Choices   15

3 General Motors v. Ford: A Two-Player Zero-Sum Game   32

4 Corporate Values: A Muted Game   70

5 J. Paul Getty: The Influence of the Values of a Strategic Corporate Player   83

6 Cooperative Games: Chaos and Stability   102

7 Boise Cascade: A Three-Player Bargaining Game with a Failure of Prospects   142

8 Howard Hughes: The Difficulty of Understanding the Values of an Invisible Player   166

9 Walt Disney: Turning a Career of Art and Business Around an Imaginary Game   220

10 Off-Track Betting on Horseracing: The Effect of a New Player in an Old Cooperative Game   246

11 The Communications Satellite: A Ten-Player Co-operative Game   266

12 Sears, Penney, and Ward: One-, Two-, and Many-sided Games   330

13 The Morgan Bank: A Many-sided Game Within a One-sided Game   371

14 Negotiating Pollution: Large Coalitions on Social Issues   386

15 Learning from Games   417

Appendix   428

Index   434

ACKNOWLEDGMENTS

This book is based on several years of research into the concepts of game theory, the modeling of games, and the facts about particular games in the real world. Many people from different walks of life have contributed to its preparation: game theorists, economists, research associates, business executives, editors, and other professional associates and friends.

I mention a number of the specific contributions of game theorists at appropriate places in the text, but that hardly gives the measure of my debt to theorists. Reflected throughout the book are talks about game theory with Oskar Morgenstern, the co-founder with John Von Neumann of modern game theory, which I have had from time to time for more than twenty-five years. He has encouraged my interest in identifying and describing games, in the game-theoretic sense, in the real world.

I have had numerous talks on theory and the modeling of games over several years with William Lucas, professor of applied mathematics and a specialist in game theory at Cornell University, ranging from a few minutes or hours on the telephone to week-long visits to his workshop at Cornell. He also read, criticized, and contributed to the manuscript of the book. There is a lot of Lucas in here. I have had numerous talks with the mathematician-game theorist Lloyd Shapley on the telephone and in his workshop at The Rand Corporation.

These talks likewise covered a wide range from general theory to the art of modeling games. There is a lot of Shapley in here too, in particular games as well as the fabric of thought. And there is a lot in here of the economist-game theorist Martin Shubik of Yale, as a result of talks, letters, and meetings with him. Shapley and Shubik also kindly allowed me to read portions of an unpublished manuscript of their forthcoming book on game theory. I have also had on occasion valued talks on the subject with the game theorists Melvin Dresher of the University of Southern California, and John Harsanyi of the University of California (Berkeley), and with E. W. Paxson of Rand. This book could not have come into being without the discussions mentioned here, along with certain of the papers and books of these theorists. The substance of the games of the real world described here, however, is based on my observations, not theirs, and I alone am responsible for the entire text of the book.

Among other writers who have been concerned with game theory and its applications, I should mention the following whose work I have read: Kenneth Arrow, Robert Aumann, Steven J. Brams, Morton D. Davis, Harold W. Kuhn, R. Duncan Luce, Michael Maschler, Guillermo Owen, Howard Raiffa, Anatol Rapaport, A. W. Tucker, William Vickrey, and John D. Williams.

M. A. Adelman of the Massachusetts Institute of Technology often gave me criticisms from the point of view of classical economics and made suggestions which I have built into the book. For discussions on kindred subjects I am also indebted to Robert Bickner and Alex Mood of the University of California (Irvine), and to David Novick of Rand. Sherman Kuhn, editor of the *Middle English Dictionary* at the University of Michigan, provided learned exercises in early uses of the word "game" and other terms.

One substantial research project for the book consisted of drafting about one hundred questions related to what I view as the description and play of real games, and of putting these questions to thirty-odd executives, mostly chief executives, of corporations whose combined sales in 1974 approached $150 billion. I arranged to do these interviews in order to observe processes of thought that go into strategic decisions in a significant sector of the economy. Culturally, this interview program could be considered research into "establishment" thinking, and in one set of questions I was in fact interested in the response of the executives to changes in social and business standards of behavior. I am indebted to the executives who cooperated; the interviews usually took place over several sessions, with each executive giving from three to thirty hours to the exercise. The results appear in various parts of the book. In quoting from the interviews, I have on occasion taken the liberty of conventional editing.

Still other executives gave much time to discussions of their particular businesses in considerable scope and depth. These discussions, along with other research, provided the basis of the stories of business which occupy a number of chapters. Among them were William M. Batten, then head of J. C. Penney; Robert E. Brooker, head of Montgomery Ward when it was an independent company; Roy and Walt Disney shortly before they died; the late J. Paul Getty at his place in England, and his son, the late George Getty, at his office in Los Angeles; Robert Hansberger, former head of Boise Cascade Corporation; John M. Meyer, Jr., then president of Morgan Guaranty Trust of New York, and also Ralph Leach, now vice-chairman of the bank; and the late Lewis S. Rosenstiel when he was head of Schenley Industries. I received valued assistance from a number of racing executives and horsemen, among the latter especially E. Barry Ryan; and also from Howard J. Samuels when he was head of the New York Off-Track Betting Corporation. I am indebted in a way to the invisibility of Howard Hughes; he provided thereby an ideal game of incomplete information. However, Hughes's representatives and his opponents both gave generously of their time to discussions of the subject. I am especially indebted to the late Raymond Cook, lawyer of Houston, Texas, negotiator for Hughes, for his remarkable insights into the relation of corporate strategy to corporate law; to Chester Davis and the late John Sonnett who led opposing legal teams in their struggle; to New York attorney William Bradner who was present in an early stage of the legal case; and to Charles Tillinghast, head of Trans World Airlines. Franc Ricciardi, when he was a top officer and negotiator for Litton Industries and Walter Kidde & Company, gave many good hours to teaching me dimensions of the conglomerate phenomenon. I am indebted to Peter Bradford, Chairman of the Public Utilities Commission of the State of Maine, for assistance in studying the conflict over oil and pollution in that state, and also to John Cole, editor of the *Maine Times*, Marc Nault of Machias, and the staff of Maine's Department of Economic Development. I doubt that anyone knows the communications satellite business better than Paul Visher of Hughes Aircraft. He was not alone among the executives participating in the satellite game who gave time to educating me in the intricacies of strategic play around the relay signal in space; but with Visher it was not one or a few talks but years of them about this game. What I learned from his naturally strategic mind I have swept into the satellite chapter.

Several institutions gave support to the project. Cornell University and Princeton University, centers of research in game theory, on occasion provided workrooms and other facilities; and there I found teachers and students with open doors. A graduate student in game theory, Pradeep Dubey, who comes from India, one day walked into a room where I was working at Cornell, read the chapter on the General Motors-Ford game, and drew on the blackboard the game tree which appears in that chapter. After viewing his tree, I edited a piece of my text to make it more orderly.

The Rand Corporation, where game theory has flourished for the past quarter century, generously responded to requests for theoretical materials and once provided a workroom for a stretch of two months. Then and on the occasion of other visits, game theorists and others at Rand gave time to discussions of the theory in relation to my interest in real economic games, and so altogether my debt to Rand is considerable.

In 1968 I received a grant from the Rockefeller Foundation for research and writing on the concepts of game theory, for which I am grateful. The work done under that grant forms an important part of this book.

Fortune magazine, where I worked as a member of the staff for twenty-seven years, gave me the time, license, and wherewithal to develop as many suitable articles for the magazine as I could out of the research for the project and allowed me to make use of the material from these and earlier pieces which I published there. I want to thank Hedley Donovan, editor-in-chief of Time Incorporated, for backing the project in this and other ways.

At *Fortune* it is a custom to work in teams: writer and research associate. For the magazine version of various stories in this book, I had the good fortune to work with Marion Buhagier, Lorraine Carson, Carol Higgins, Pat Langan, Edith Roper, and Elizabeth Swayne; and with Ann Tyler on several stories, including those about Howard Hughes and Walt Disney. And there is Ann Hengstenberg with whom I worked on nine *Fortune* stories that formed a good part of the early work on this book, including work on the concepts of game theory. Many of her contributions are represented here.

I am also indebted to *Fortune*'s editors, among them especially the managing editors Louis Banks and Robert Lubar for their encouragement and their editing; and to the executive editor Dan Seligman for extraordinary insights into editorial problems and his confidence in the project. From *Fortune*'s economist Sanford Parker I learned a good deal about relationships between microscopic game studies and the macroscopic economic world. All of this work at *Fortune* provided an important and necessary step toward the book, though of course the book goes far beyond the pieces published there, especially in matters of theory and game modeling and its design as a whole.

For reading and commenting thoughtfully on portions of the manuscript, I want to thank Dorothy McDonald, Joan and Richard Miller, Frederick Moss, Alice Morris, and Christie and Eugene Vance. The chapter on the General Motors-Ford game owes much to earlier work on the subject with

the late Alfred P. Sloan, Jr., and Catharine Stevens, and with
Alfred D. Chandler, professor of history at Johns Hopkins. I
also want to thank the late William J. Eisner and the late
Florine Eisner, H. William and Anita Fitelson, Irving Kristol,
John Kenneth Galbraith, Katherine McDonald, Ronald Nicholson, the late Lionel Trilling, and Robert Penn Warren for
their encouragement and assistance.

I am indebted to Doris Foster, Grace Hagen, Iris Grayson,
Barbara Mullen, and the late Magda Papson for a variety of
editorial operations including valued observations on the text.

And then there is Doubleday, where Samuel S. Vaughan,
publisher, took an interest in the project from the beginning
and backed it with financial and editorial support. I am grateful to him and Nancy Kojima of his editorial staff; and to
Georgiana Remer for her meticulous copy editing of the manuscript. In the end there is a book editor. I have worked on
two earlier books with William Whipple and I was pleased
when he came back on this one. Whipple is in here in a very
important way but he is the kind of professional who leaves
no trace of himself.

John McDonald

New York City
May, 1977

INTRODUCTION

A game is more than a sport, pastime, and amusement. It
is also a model of the real world. For the ancient Greeks a
game provided a liberal education in religion and love. For
the players and spectators of the Middle Ages in Europe it
taught the main elements of the new civilization, chivalry
and learning, which we now call fair play and skill. The
word "game" itself is a deeply rooted native of the English
language. Long before print, the writers of manuscripts used
it not only for the delight of pastimes, but also for amorous
play and pleasant stories; and if one was dealt with severely
in the real world, it was a hard game. A game was also, on
another level, a way of acting by policy or plan, which gave
a hint of a later development. In the nineteenth century, according to legend, a Parisian bookmaker, frustrated in his
efforts to make a profitable odds line on the horse races, appealed to a mathematician who thereupon conjured up the
theory of probability, which became the rationale for predicting the average or expected outcome of the dice and roulette
wheels of the casinos, the spinning particles of modern atomic
science, and common decisions in face of risk.

Thus the idea of real-life games—the subject of this
book—is as old as the hills. What's new in our time is *game
theory*. Its insights into games of strategy illuminate still another aspect of the real world: the free human interactions
that are beyond probability. The main unsettled question in

economic thought—to which game theory is directed—is how to understand the indefinite outcome of interactions among people who can, within limits, make free choices. Freedom of choice defies prediction in the usual sense. The standard doctrine of free enterprise, for example, holds that the parties to it do not influence one another's decisions, though in fact on numerous occasions they do, know they do, and play the game accordingly. Game theory, unfinished as it is, represents the real situation: a game of two or more players is a model of free human interactions, either in conflict or cooperation, and a source of learning about them.

An argument of this book is that such interactions are present, actually or latently, throughout economic life. The demonstration which I shall make is selective rather than comprehensive as regards both game theory and business, and it is not technical. My purpose will be satisfied if I can indicate the presence of games by hint, sign, and description. Real-life games are a largely unexplored field, and the art of modeling them is virtually unknown. Those which I shall describe in precursory fashion are meant to bring some game learning back full circle—real life to game model to real life —on grounds of legitimacy first established by the Greeks and the reasoners of the Middle Ages.

These elevated thoughts may appear to be at some distance from the contemporary games of Alfred P. Sloan, Jr., Henry Ford, Walt Disney, J. Paul Getty, and Howard Hughes; of conglomerate raiders, operators of racetracks and betting parlors, polluters and the polluted; of bargainers and negotiators in and out of markets, and the government in its omnifarious roles. But game models lie close to real life in the plain language of players, rules, values, bargaining, negotiating, threats, bluffs, collusion, coalitions, outcomes, payoffs, solutions.

Modern game theory began in the reflections of the Hungarian-born American John Von Neumann, one of the great mathematicians of this century. He was born in 1903, on the eve of the golden age of science, and bred in the cluster of

Middle European geniuses of whom Einstein is the best known to the world. As a person he was a sort of metaphysical humanist, as a mathematician he was an artist. The criteria of mathematics, he said, are aesthetical. The test is to reduce complexity to simplicity.

Von Neumann left pure mathematics, he said, because he worried about being out of touch with the real world. He came into that world with mercurial wonder and let loose a galaxy of benign and terrifying creations, abstract and concrete, among them a vision of causality in the physical universe; the mathematics of the H-bomb, which he, together with the physicist Edward Teller, designed on the moral ground that technology, though a force for evil as well as good, could not be stopped and others would soon have what could be had from it; the logic of the computer, of which he was one of the principal inventors; the clue to a hidden natural language, neither verbal nor mathematical, in the central nervous system; and game theory. Von Neumann had a passion to unravel distinctions between man and nature. On one occasion, for example, he distinguished sharply between the observable world, the observing instrument, and the peculiarity of the human observer, and then took apart the paradox that if you assigned all of the observing instruments—including the human eye, brain, and whole body—to the universe, you still had to postulate the observer without whom all meaning was lost. He saw in the tradition of mathematics a bias stemming from its empirical origins in mechanics, and he looked for human foundations in games.

As a young man impressing the mathematical world with his genius, Von Neumann amused himself at baccarat and other games and turned this taste for diversion into serious thought. In 1928 he wrote his first treatise on games, which then got little notice. Though it was not the first effort of its kind, it was made independently and for the first time conceptually complete. Traditional games, he saw, had already been cast by unknown minds as models of human interaction. They had invented rules to describe a game and left its solutions to the free will and ingenuity of the players. He found that he could study such games—baccarat, chess, bridge, poker, and the like—for their own sake, as one could study any sort of model, and from them he created the theory of free interactions that distinguished these games from games of pure chance such as dice and roulette. He designed basic models for all games of free interaction and went on to invent sets of rules—i.e., for abstract games not found among traditional games—from selected features of the real world. Thus, he directed his talent first to entertainment games and then to abstract games independent of entertainment games and to the bearing of both of them upon the real world. In 1944 he and the economist Oskar Morgenstern developed the 1928 treatise into their monumental work on the subject, *The Theory of Games and Economic Behavior*. The result was eventually to bring into being a new branch of mathematics concerned with a sort of free-will causality, where many new discoveries have been made by succeeding game theorists. Most of their work has been closeted there, leaving undeveloped the field of direct observation of real-life games—a circumstance which opened the way for this book.

As I am neither a mathematician nor an economist, I owe an explanation for a work which invades their territories. I went to *Fortune* in the fall of 1945 to write about a number of things in the wide range of that magazine, including business, which of course was its main interest. A couple of years later I turned away from the subject of business to write about games. The luck of life then brought the two subjects together more or less as they are to be found in this book.

Fortune had invented a species of writing called "the corporation story" in the 1930s when knowledge of corporations was limited to executives and working men and, rather narrowly, to the financial press. The editors of *Fortune* were always looking for new angles on this form of business, which had become dominant in the early decades of this century. But after a few tries at the genre, I felt that I had nothing new to contribute to it; standard economic theory itself offered no insight into the bargaining and negotiating that, aside from the institutional character of business, seemed to me to be its fascination. I proposed instead to write about games and persuaded the managing editor, Ralph Delahaye Paine, Jr., to run a series on traditional games, one a month for a year, of which I would be editor and sometimes writer. The idea I had then was to do stories about their curious and interesting origins, rules, moralities, and style and to relate these qualities to life at large, that is, essentially to relate the Greek and Middle Ages ideas of games to the pastimes of the present. I drew up a program of twelve games, laid it on Paine's desk, and asked him to pick a game for the first in the series. He ran his finger down the page and stopped at "Poker."

I wrote about the history of poker out of the extraordinary collection of old poker books in the New York Public Library, and though the game was rich in legend, morality, character, and cunning, I had a feeling that the story was nostalgic without drive. I took the problem down the hall one day to a colleague, John Kenneth Galbraith, who was then an editor of *Fortune*—that was before his wide celebrity —and asked him if he had any suggestions. He said there was an eminent fellow at Princeton who had recently written a deep, little read, little understood but important mathematical work on games which contained a chapter on poker. That of course was John Von Neumann and the work he had produced with Oskar Morgenstern, *The Theory of Games and Economic Behavior*. I got a copy of the book and turned to Chapter 19, entitled "Poker and Bluffing." Enough of it was written in English for me to get the idea that this was the solution to my poker story. The difficulty was to get at the rest of the treatise which was in the, for me, impenetrable language of mathematics. I made a preliminary sketch of the story and got an appointment with Von Neumann.

As I walked through the main hall in the Institute for Advanced Study on the way to his office, a wave of white hair passed and said good morning. It was Einstein, dissolving the exotic into the familiar. Von Neumann's opening gambit was who knows if I'm any good or a bum except another mathematician? I brushed that off and said what chance have I of getting through this stuff on poker? About the same as reading Persian poetry, he said. It's a theory of everyone's games, I said. What about expressing the ideas in the vernacular? Von Neumann was a game fellow, and I think that got him. He was also interested in how actual games players at poker, bridge, chess—and always baccarat—would take to the theory. We talked about games, particularly poker, which was the object of my mission, and found that the problem of bridging the gap between the mathematical and verbal language was not so difficult in so common a human affair. Along with his mathematical skill, it was also in his style to have grounded his thought in the force of ideas.

To cut this narrative short, the meeting started an association, joined later by Morgenstern, which resulted in a poker piece in *Fortune* in 1947, largely the history of the game with a promise of more to come; fifteen months and fifteen drafts later, a piece on the theory of games; and in 1950 the book *Strategy in Poker, Business and War*. Meanwhile, since game theory had everything to do with bargaining and negotiating, I went back to writing about business with a new emphasis on strategical interactions. But it was a long time before I could get any distance into the description of real-life games.

Von Neumann died in 1957, and game theory, which had received wide notice in the 1950s, disappeared into mathematics. A new generation of brilliant game theorists, working in obscurity on its considerable unresolved theoretical problems, in time crystallized new discoveries, especially in the field of cooperative games. In 1967 I began to study their creations and received from them—particularly William Lucas, Lloyd Shapley, and Martin Shubik—as I had earlier from Von Neumann and Morgenstern, the kind of help that made this book possible.

The legacy of the origin of game theory in the study of parlor games, though important, has been to some extent misleading. It is important, as noted, because it provides roots in a model of human conduct. But the idea of finding a rationale of significance among poker players—to which I made the contribution mentioned above—was so delightful to a wide public who heard of it that unfortunately it stuck in the mythology of game theory as what the theory was really about. Without discounting the significance that belongs to game-theoretic insights into poker and other parlor games, this bit of myth became particularly misleading. For much of the theory differs from poker both in its divestment of the sporting associations of that game and in the nature of most of its models. Bluffing, for example, is examined in the theory not for its psychological drama, but as a means of controlling information by not disclosing a strategy to an opponent. Furthermore, poker belongs to a class of games known as "zero-sum" games—the gains (plus) and losses (minus) of the players sum to zero—and as it is a game of pure opposition of interests, with each player according to rule playing on his own, it excludes cooperation. Even in learned circles, this limited type of game and Von Neumann's solution of it came often to be taken as the whole of game theory. The myth then took the form that economic game theory, like poker, deals with the redivision of established wealth.[1]

[1] Typical casino games—dice, roulette—are not strategic like poker but mechanical, with the odds set to favor the house by statistical probability. There is no honest strategy readily available by which the player can beat these games. The trend, however, is a wavy line which may favor the player in the short run. The dice may "pass" many times in a row; and in roulette red or black or certain numbers may come up for a while more often than the odds dictate. Hence, with the trend against him, the player's only "rational" hope, if the word serves, is that the drift will briefly favor him. Physical systems, however, have a bias if one can find it. A computer, for example, should be able to find the bias in a roulette wheel—and one has seen players copying down sequences of numbers in a notebook for this purpose. To circumvent this, casinos are known to switch tables. J. Paul Getty, asked if he liked to gamble, said if he did he would buy a casino; he liked to gamble with the odds in his favor. The best explanation for gamblers playing against casinos lies elsewhere than in concepts of rationality. There is a lot of luck in life and one gives Fortune a chance to

Game theory in its early years in fact emphasized problems of conflict. Four fifths of Von Neumann and Morgenstern's great work deals with zero-sum games—including, however, cooperation in coalitions—and only the last fifth deals with the productive games of economics. This is not surprising since they were pioneers working from traditional games, which are typically dominated by situations in which the interests of the players are purely opposed. The value of analyzing conflict can hardly be overestimated, but in economic life conflict is only one side of the story. There is conflict in dividing the wealth, but there is also cooperation in determining how much wealth there will be to divide.

So many meanings cling to the word "game" from time immemorial, including its corrupt use for covering up cheap learning and dishonorable conduct, that it is not an easy one to keep clearly defined. Game theory is important only incidentally as the theory of entertainment games. And it gives one no license to make a sport of the real world or to play entertainment games for real—either of which could be perverse indeed, if not pathological. Having drawn certain concepts from entertainment games, it moves so far away from them to other spheres that the theory could as well be called by some other name having to do with the structure of human interactions. But *game* theory it is, and so one needs to bear in mind that its aims are not trivial. Nor does it take account of the pleasure of playing a game except as it may affect the values of the players. Some people, for example, enjoy taking risks, some do not, and their preference will have a bearing on the description and play of a game.

Game theory peels off most of the metaphors surrounding the word "game." A few remain on the fringes. A strategy is

---

shine on one for a little while—but Dostoevsky is the classic authority on what moves a casino gambler.

The games in this book are not games of the casino type, that is, they are not chance games, though chance usually comes into them as it does into all life and is dealt with either as statistical probability or subjective guesswork.

a central game concept, and a strategy may suggest a deception. Game theory actually may be useful on occasion in penetrating acts of cunning. But the main line of game theory is straightforward. The main line of economic game theory, for example, is the main line of economic life. Its concepts are particularly appropriate for the formal aspects of that life: markets—whether or not they live up to ideal standards—publicly owned goods, pollution, discrimination, consumerism, antitrust policy, corporate raiding, transactions over and under the table between economic and political agents, and the like. The scope of game theory in these matters is always determined by how much free choice the players actually have.

Theories remind one of the fallibility as well as the strength of human thought. One of their virtues is that they lay down explicit assumptions; if there are always further hidden assumptions in a theory, they can be ferreted out in the contests of criticism between theories. Game theory, for all its discipline, is a plastic art; its end product is a model. It is no monolithic system of thought. It is not formed like a building and may never be, though in its central concept of free human interaction it has a dome that sets its unity and reach as firmly as the Pantheon's. It affords room for all sorts of speculation on games. It contains within itself many different points of view. It stands as a criticism of other theories of human conduct, but game theorists also look for its links with other theories. When it comes to real-life games, the case for this plural spirit is not merely greater; it is a necessity. One seeks refuge in it. At present, one can usually only talk around and about real-life economic games, a circumstance that conditions the plan of this book.

As there is no precedent for it, I should explain the plan. I have taken a group of basic ideas from game theory and arranged them in a design that moves from the simple to the complex and, I trust, back to the simple again; and I have illustrated these ideas, along with others that came along with them, in games actually played in the real world. Observation and cataloging have been the first business of Western thought since Aristotle; and so with that apology I set forth the following concepts concerning all games, which I shall employ as a guide to the labyrinth of real-life games.

Divide a game into two parts: its description and its solution. The description is the rules. The solution is what the players do or can do within the rules.

Divide all games into three kinds, according to the number of players in the game: one, two, and three or more.

If there is only one player in the game, he is playing solitaire or Robinson Crusoe against nature or suchlike. He does not worry about nature on the other side making willful decisions similar to his own. He controls his own situation as well as he can to get what he wants out of nature. If it rains, it rains; but he calculates how many inches a year and in what season and what the chances are tomorrow, next week, or next month. It is a classic game of chance for which the theory is probability. Lacking human interaction, it is not a game-theoretic game in the modern sense. It is, in a word, one-sided.

A game-theoretic game begins with two players. They form the minimum condition for human interaction. That's obvious, but distinctive.

If three or more players come into a game, they may form groups or coalitions, the phenomenon of society.

Divide all games into two: on the one hand, those in which the gains and losses sum to zero (what one player wins, another loses) or any constant sum; and on the other hand, those that offer a collective gain or loss to the players for playing it. Many traditional parlor and field games, as noted, are zero-sum games. In the real world, political voting games are often zero-sum—winner take all. There are also economic games that have a constant sum, as when parties play for equally valued shares of a market, or divide the proceeds of a bankruptcy. But economic games are typically gainful; everyone gets something, or expects to, for playing.

A market game, for example, is a game of consent; if buyer and seller fall out, each keeps what he's got. That's the worst that can happen until something better happens—an exchange.

Divide solutions to games into two kinds: cooperative and non-cooperative. If a player chooses to play non-cooperatively, he takes a one-sided view of the prospective interactions and, seeing the actual strategies available to the others, seeks a course of independent action that brings him the best result regardless of what the others do. If, on the other hand, he chooses to cooperate, and can, he looks to the value of potential coalitions over and above the value of going alone. Most traditional parlor games have rules that require playing non-cooperatively, as in poker. In the real world, political games are the epitome of cooperative games conjoined with conflict. Economic games may be played either way, depending on the rules, what is to be gained, and the inclination of the players. If there are more than two players, it usually takes a rule to prevent them from cooperating—and it is not easy to write a rule that ingenious players cannot to some extent get around.

At the center of Western thought there's that bedeviled word "rational." What's a "rational" player in a game? Game theorists make up their own definition. A player in a game is rational when he seeks *more* of something, quantitatively a higher number. So stated, this idea looks simplistic and hard-boiled. But "more" may mean not only more marbles, money, or power, but also, for example, more clean air and water, more space, more time for meditation, more sleep, more jobs for one group or another, more assurance of survival, more value of any kind in one economic exchange than another. The term fits the assumption in game theory that each of the players in a game seeks a gain of some sort. This does not imply that gain is in fact what people want or should want. It is an assumption and when it does not materialize, the game of game theory does not exist. Likewise, the theory does not say how one should value anything; nor does it provide any means to measure values, such as the intensity of a player's preference for one thing over another. Knowledge of the players' values, if any, comes from outside sources. In their abstract models, game theorists assume that the players have preferences and that they have numbers that "mirror their choices." In the real world, as we shall see, measurable values are not easy to come by. But real players have the same problem about themselves and one another, and one can make plausible observations of their preferences.

With the concept of rationality so defined, divide it into three kinds, that of the individual, the group, and the whole society.

The rationality of the individual is said to be gauged by how well he alone fares in a game, irrespective of how any one else fares.

The rationality of the group is said to be represented by what a coalition can gain over and above what its members have or can get as individuals: it is the act of getting the maximum amount available to the group.

The rationality of society as a whole is said to be represented by the total benefits that the society can get. Standard economic thought looks for the optimum efficiency of a society made up of atomized individuals. Economic game theory recognizes groups as well as individuals in the make-up of the society, and looks for the optimum state of affairs, in which all are satisfied that they have done the best they can.

The mark of a game is uncertainty. Divide uncertainty into two kinds: chance and choice. How the dice will roll is a very different question from what another player may do if he has a strategic choice. Either or both uncertainties may be present in a game. If only chance is present, the game is, as noted, a one-person game and not a game-theoretic game. A game-theoretic game is distinguished by an uncertainty situated in the free will and choice of the players, albeit within limits. The prototype of such a game, without chance, is chess (Bobby Fischer's antics introduce chancy behavior into the environment of the game but not into the board). Stud poker has chance in the deal but is otherwise strategic: a player may bet a little or a lot, but whether he has a high or low hand is hidden in the down cards and the possibility of a bluff. Many parlor games contain both chance and strategic choice; when the players want to increase the uncertainties, they add more chance elements, such as more cards or wild cards. Most real-life games contain both elements. Where is the gold in the hills? Which way will the economy go? How will a million consumers behave if you raise or lower a price? These are chance questions, with answers in probabilities, usually guesswork, narrowed perhaps by research. But, for example, if you raise or lower a price, the question of whether your competitor will choose to follow is strategic. He has the choice. The important thing about game theory is that it distinguishes sharply between uncertainties of chance and choice and pursues as a specialty the study of the uncertainty of freely chosen interactions.

This leads to distinguishing two kinds of players: strategic and non-strategic. A strategic player is one who has a free choice; a non-strategic player has none beyond take-it-or-leave-it, though he is in the game and may receive a payoff. Typical non-strategic players in economic games are consumers, diffused shareholders in a corporation, horseplayers. Strategic players typically have a bargaining or negotiating position. Who knows what they will do? If you know, forget game theory.

These concepts, which are sufficient for a start, make distinctions with interconnections. If two persons, for example, play a zero-sum game—chess, poker, etc.—the conditions dictate independent play, for with their interests completely opposed and only two of them present, they have no ground for cooperation. If, on the other hand, it is a gainful game with two players—a buyer and a seller, for example—they have both common and opposed interests, common in their desire for mutual gain, opposed in how they will divide the gain:

and so they at once cooperate by proposing to join in a deal and dicker over the terms of the exchange.

But take a zero-sum game with three players. Their interests are opposed, and yet not entirely. Any two of them may cooperate by forming a coalition in opposition to the third player, as in a political game.

Now consider a gainful game with three or more players, the typical situation in an economic game. Each player may choose to regard the others as the environment and play independently, taking account of strategies available to all. Or they may cooperate by forming coalitions to divide the gain among all or some of them. Game theory views such coalitions from two angles: Which is the most beneficial in some sense to the players? and Will it stick—that is, will the members of the coalition withstand offers from outsiders? These and other such related distinctions begin to transform the catalog of ideas into the structures that form the design of this book.

It is a remarkable fact that a game is played largely in the mind. Only a small part of the play appears in overt action. Its full scope and depth lie in the players' looking backward and forward and running through their minds their alternative moves and countermoves or choices among coalitions before taking action. A player may reject dozens or hundreds of potential coalitions before adopting one, and the rejections are as much an inherent part of the play as the action taken. In an abstract game, it is the game theorist who does this, usually on the assumption that he possesses complete information about the rules of the game. The practical problem of setting forth a real-life game takes in not only the rules—about which the information is usually incomplete—but also the play, the larger part of which is submerged. The problem is not much different for the players in real-life games, and as they walk where angels fear to tread, one may learn something from observing them.

A real player may understand his own situation; but he may not. The main problem of a team playing the game of bridge is how to signal the information within the rules of communication. Likewise, a corporation, although it has a chief executive, has division heads and numerous other members who may have different information; hence a corporation is likely to have incomplete knowledge of itself as a player. And of course, an individual person may be of two or more minds. Nevertheless, a real player has an obvious edge on the outside observer as far as his own position in the game is concerned. In other respects both player and observer have the same problem: limited visibility. To get an image of the game, each has to resort to guesswork, hypothesis, and inference as well as observation. The only test of the validity of the image is its plausibility. If it appears approximately complete, one has a model of sorts, from which one should, in principle, be able to work out possible ways of playing the game. That, again, is something of an idealization, because even if one has a complete description of the rules of a real-life game, it is likely to be too complex for anyone, in the present state of the art, to work out all the possible strategies or coalitions that it contains. Here the observer, game theorist, and real player are all in the same boat.

It takes a good deal of narration and description to bring a real-life game into being and a good deal of reduction to bring its structure sharply into view. To have carried each game through to this end would have been beyond the scope of this book. Hence I have made three approaches to the games here. In the simplest of these I narrate a sequence of events—not itself a game—and with mere touches, point to the signs of a game and comment on them. In another I model, as it were, in words the structure of general and continual gamelike situations in the economy (for example, the corporation viewed as a game model). In the third, I rough-model specific games to the point where they represent approximately the first stage of a formal model of game theory. In one instance, the satellite game, which I have carried furthest in this direction, I turn the model over to game theorist

William Lucas, who carries the analysis through as he would if it were a formal model.

Although few of the real players described in this book know game theory, their conduct I submit is game theoretic; the theory offers an understanding of what they are already doing. Readers may find in this a honing of their natural intuitions, which is quite enough for most of us. Those whose interest is in theory, however, may also find here some good examples, even empirical verifications of it; and also perhaps some new questions of interest.

I believe it was Stendhal, writing on the theory of love, who said that after theory comes the novel. I draw that line, some will say with a vengeance, and never go near it. I make no effort to describe these real strategic players beyond features sufficient to the game, which for other occasions would be the merest sign or caricature. But I always give them their essential imagination and freedom to choose their acts.

My descriptions of specific games are as relaxed, I trust, as the design of the book as a whole. My object in this respect has been to keep the book within the range of the "common reader," where as author I, too, am situated. The stories here, though they embody a train of ideas about games—some of which I have taken the liberty of repeating when the occasion required—can also be read independently of one another.

THE GAME OF BUSINESS

1

SEAGRAMS V. SCHENLEY:
A MUTUAL INTERACTION

Game theory stakes out its territory distinctly as the mutual interaction of two or more players in a game. The action is always an interaction, at very least in the sense that each player in his decisions in a game takes account of the strategies of the other players. In an economic game the interaction is usually directed at creating and dividing wealth. On occasion it may have the narrower purpose of dividing a fixed sum, such as the shares of a market where a percentage point for one player is a percentage point less for another. The outlines of such interactions emerge in strong relief in a game between Seagrams and Schenley at an important moment for them in 1948. The results of this game have been felt in these companies ever since.

THE PLAYERS

- Samuel Bronfman for Distillers Corporation-Seagrams Limited
- Lewis S. Rosenstiel for Schenley Industries, Incorporated
- Emil Schwarzhaupt of Schenley

Samuel Bronfman, chief executive and principal owner of Seagrams, for several decades of this century was the nearest thing to a whiskey king in North America. His chief rival in the United States was Lewis S. Rosenstiel, long the chief ex-

1

ecutive and principal owner of Schenley. Each of them controlled and personally guided his company. Between them they dominated the liquor industry for many years after the repeal of prohibition, alternating in the No. 1 position as measured by the number of cases of liquor they sold.

Bronfman, a small man, hid his intense competitiveness behind the placid demeanor of the cat who swallowed the canary and quietly laid down his strategical plans. His style, which was somewhat affectedly ornate, he himself described as a policy of "the silken gown." He liked to drink his own V.O. Canadian whiskey. His public relations theme could be stated in one word: respectability. That was not just to offset the fact that a lot of his liquor had been poured in speakeasies in the United States in the 1920s. It was the style of the entire liquor industry after repeal, out of fear of a return of prohibition, at least in spots, through local option. Everyone in the industry adhered to norms of respectability, which set limits on their struggles.

Everything about Lewis Rosenstiel was in contrast to Bronfman. He was a big man whose weight, like Bronfman's, seemed to be part of his character. In the liquor industry, he was impetuous, passionate, and colorful, and though not a drinker, he promoted bourbon like a fire-eater. He ran his company in detail, down to the price of a pint of I. W. Harper in Tampa, and his flamboyance got into his strategies, which were often spectacular.

Not only did Bronfman and Rosenstiel for a long time vie for leadership of the liquor industry—in cases sold—but going back into the mists of the whiskey-making past, they were goaded by a legendary personal feud. They never revealed what it was about, but it was bitter and unrelenting. To what extent this colored their values in the game to be described here is difficult to say. Doubtless, each wanted to be No. 1 in the industry, which could only be scored win, lose, or draw. But they were also businessmen who rationalized their motives with the hard and conflicting economics of short- and long-run profits. Both were dedicated to the disciplines of their business and to their work as a way of life. And the liquor business, by its nature, fostered rivalry.

The size of the American liquor market is not much influenced by innovation or anything that a liquor company can do. It varies mainly with the level of the economy, changes in age groups, and the like. There is not a great deal of difference in the ways of making whiskey and other spirits and there hasn't been a really new recipe in the art in a hundred years, except for the recent light, or "white," American whiskey made for the first time in used cooperage (as whiskey is made outside the United States), and no one has an exclusive on that. Liquor, especially whiskey, is often traded among liquor companies as a commodity before it is put into bottles. That is to say that distillers—Seagrams, Schenley, and the others—whose main business is to make whiskey and other spirits to sell in bottles under their own brand names, also trade whiskey and other spirits in bulk to adjust their inventories to their sales. In mixing whiskeys from different distilleries, they of course have to take care to maintain the taste and quality of their brands. Only when whiskey is "Bottled in Bond" must its label tie it to a particular distillery.

Hence the action, and the interaction, in the American liquor industry centers on who can best sell an array of products that for the most part are available to all contenders. Their competitive problem is to divide the available business. Their big gambles and great strategies are in distribution: promoting the product that catches on, or the one that doesn't; adding new lines (vodka, tequila); packaging; getting a position in wholesaling; side payments to store owners to feature a line or to bar owners or bartenders to pour one's liquor; and above all, winning the brand loyalty of consumers. Even acquisitions and mergers which are rampant on and off in the industry are often related to strategies of distribution. Brand loyalty is somewhat mysterious. Advertising may stimulate it and liquor companies spend from $1 to $3 a case in that effort. But sometimes a company will spend millions on advertising and promoting a brand and not get it.

Then a small company comes along and captures favor at no cost—merely by word of mouth or some other magic: Beefeater, J & B, Jack Daniel's, Wild Turkey, and numerous other premium spirits—now big moneymakers—came out of obscurity in the American market to popularity. The label is everything. A big company buys a small company at times to get its whiskey stocks as a commodity, but more often to get its label, that is, its brand loyalty.

The decisive game between Seagrams and Schenley in 1948 began when neither company could gain in both brand sales and profits. Their choices were interlocked. The conditions at the starting point of this game were established by the results of previous games, notably the fact that Seagrams had just regained, in 1947–48, the coveted No. 1 position in the industry, well ahead of the major contenders, Schenley, National Distillers Products Corporation, and Hiram Walker Incorporated. A question in the game would be who would be No. 1 in the future.

This was not the first time Seagrams had been on top. It led the industry from 1938 through 1943, at which time Schenley seized the No. 1 position and held it during the rest of World War II and through 1947. Bottled-whiskey sales by all producers in the United States then fell about 25 percent, while Seagram's sales, moving against the trend, rose 53 percent. The effect of these inverse movements suddenly gave Seagrams about 30 percent of the total whiskey business in 1948, and Seagrams passed the declining wartime leader, Schenley. But Seagram's newly won position was shaky. Fast brand sales drain slowly built inventories of whiskey. Seagrams did not have much whiskey left. Schenley, on the other hand, had possession of most of the aged whiskies in the United States.

This peculiar circumstance was no accident. It came about as the result of the broad strategical policies of Bronfman and Rosenstiel, together with some trends in the industry.

In the brief fifteen years of the industry's existence since repeal, the intensity of brand competition had resulted in a measure of concentration familiar in many American industries. Ten brands in 1948 were doing the same proportion of business (60 percent) that fifty brands did a decade earlier. Of these ten it appears that Seagrams had three (7 Crown, Calvert Reserve, and Four Roses), and Schenley three (Schenley Reserve, Three Feathers Reserve, and Golden Wedding). The five leading brands, which before the war did 20 percent of the total U.S. business, after the war did 50 percent of that business. The Big Four distillers got about 75 percent of the business, made about half the whiskey, and held about 60 percent of the inventories. Thus the distillers met each other warily in a small world, and as this world was a cage of relatively fixed consumption, their strategies were very interactive. Seagrams' 1948 gain had been a loss to some of the others, particularly Schenley.

These companies were not only in the liquor business but also necessarily in the banking and inventory business: banking, because of the enormous federal taxes prepaid to the government when whiskey is removed from bond; inventory, because one year's crop of whiskey is produced for sale four or more years in the future. This time lag ties up capital and entails the risk of production in one economic climate for sale in another climate. A company therefore is usually restrained by its discretion from getting too far ahead of or too far behind its rivals in inventory. What "too far" is, however, remains the question.

Thus the two basic elements in the game at this time were brand sales and inventory, with Seagrams, as noted, enjoying rising brand sales and Schenley holding the strategic inventory of aged whiskey. National Distillers and Hiram Walker were present, too, in no inconsiderable way, but because of the peculiar situation between Seagrams and Schenley, they broke off, as it were, from the industry game as a whole to play a game of their own.

The postures Seagrams and Schenley took toward one another were conditioned by their style of play in previous games. Bronfman's approach to the whiskey business derived from the manner in which he entered the industry in Canada

5

back in 1916. Pre-prohibition distillers in the United States, who were later to return and revive the industry in 1933, learned the trade as bulk-whiskey producers. They sold whiskey in barrels direct to their customers, and if it was to be blended or bottled, this was done in a separate branch of the industry by rectifiers and local merchandisers. Bronfman, however, starting in the wholesale end of the business in Ontario, was able under the Canadian liquor laws of the time to sell bottled whiskey by mail order from one province to another. Thus he learned the package liquor business, the form the business was to take in the United States increasingly during prohibition—legal and illegal—and entirely after 1933. Success came early; Bronfman built up a mail-order business that had more geographic coverage than that of his principal competitor, the old Hudson's Bay Company. When in the early 1920s the provincial governments took over the distribution of liquor, government dealers bypassed the wholesalers to buy direct from the distillers. Bronfman responded in 1924 by taking his mail-order earnings and putting them into the distilling business as Distillers Corporation Limited.

This private company in 1928 became a public company, Distillers Corporation-Seagrams Limited, and for a while Bronfman and the British scotch-whiskey trust shared its controlling ownership. The company prospered in the Canadian export trade during the prohibition period in the United States. Without admitting any liability, the company in 1936 settled for $1.5 million claims by the U. S. Treasury for duties on liquor allegedly shipped into the United States during prohibition. Similar settlements were made by other Canadian distillers. When Seagrams branched into the U.S. after repeal, the scotch-whiskey trust, attending to its world interest in scotch, kept clear of the whiskey scene in the United States by selling its interest in Seagrams to the Bronfman family. Samuel Bronfman thus entered the golden era of the liquor industry in complete control of his company.

When Bronfman came down from Canada after repeal, he was, as noted, an experienced merchandiser of packaged whiskey. Because of his background in the Canadian and scotch whiskey tradition, he was committed by tradition to blended whiskey. His presence in the United States set off a struggle between representatives of two tendencies in the whiskey market, the backers of "straights" against the backers of "blends."

Blends, the combination of whiskey and neutral spirits in roughly one-two proportions, were not unknown to drinkers in the United States before 1933. In fact, before 1900 blends were the dominant form of whiskey in many parts of the country. Thereafter, for a period, it is said, straights dominated, though it is argued that blends were returning when prohibition ended the industry. Many distillers, however, abhorred blending and took pride in distinguishing themselves from "rectifiers." Julian ("Pappy") Van Winkle, proprietor of the Stitzel-Weller Distillery, maker of a good Kentucky bourbon, Old Fitzgerald, translated "straights and blends" as "whiskey and compounds" and regarded blenders as "chemists." Most of the American distillers entered the repeal market without experience in blending, bottling, or merchandising. They loved the peculiarly American straight and strong ryes and bourbons and knew nothing about Bronfman's light and mild blends.

Bronfman then taught the American companies a new lesson in merchandising liquor. He initiated and led a trend to the milder-tasting blends. Mildness and uniformity in taste were his formula, following the standard estimate of the dominant American taste developed in the 1920s by merchandisers of ham and cheese and cigarettes. The result: first 5 Crown, then 7 Crown led the field and 7 Crown is still in the 1970s the biggest selling whiskey in the United States.

But the extent to which Americans prefer blends was still in doubt in 1948. Bronfman's competitors debated whether the popularity of the blended taste was real or just a quirk in whiskey labeling—a quirk that first established the blend market. The straight ryes and bourbons that old-time distillers liked to make and savor and sell had by law to report on the label "rye whiskey" or "bourbon whiskey." The "Bottled in Bond" label, as noted, went even further in specifications, with a printed record that the whiskey was distilled by a certain plant (limiting any individual B.I.B. whiskey to production in one plant). When whiskies were blended with equal amounts or more of neutral spirits, however, they could no longer be labeled as "rye" or "bourbon," but only as "blended whiskey." This was a penalty that the old-timers induced the government to levy against the blenders. After a while the old-timers began to see the light of modern merchandising. When Seagram's 5 Crown, a blend, became the first big seller in the United States, they fumed in their own trap. For they could not at that time sell much bourbon in the East nor much rye in the West, and so establishing a truly national brand of straight whiskey was a difficult proposition. People demanded rye here and bourbon there—but "whiskey" all over. The old-timers sold many brands in many different places. Seagrams campaigned nationwide and sold its product as just "whiskey, blended." This was the first big play and it ended in 1938 with Seagrams, carrying relatively few, well-liked, well-established brands, on top of the industry.

The second big play on the consumer end of the business took place several years later, during World War II. With more money around, fewer things to spend it on, and a great many uprooted people finding sociability in bars, the demand for whiskey went up enormously. But the production of both whiskey and grain neutral spirits was shut off for a time during the war and converted to industrial alcohol for various war purposes. The lack of whiskey production caused no immediate actual shortage but it did cause distillers to stretch their stocks to cover the lost inventory years. They retreated from their straight whiskies to spirit blends to conserve their stocks of whiskey. Bottled output of spirit blends then rose from 30 percent of the market in 1941 to 87 percent in 1946. Meanwhile, the shortage of grain neutral spirits became the focal point of the crisis. Distillers had the choice of adopting substitute neutral spirits—for example, spirits made from potatoes—or of declining to meet fully the increased demand.

Schenley elected to substitute and expand; Seagrams elected to slow down.

These were momentous decisions for the companies. By its decision Schenley took the leadership it had lost to Seagrams in 1938 and held it for four years, through 1947. Schenley reached about 20 percent of total case sales while Seagrams dropped to about 17 percent. This outcome resulted directly from strategies relating inventory to brand sales.

Bronfman had always held his inventories at some level below sales and relied upon purchases in the bulk-whiskey market to close the gap. As a blender he held to the inviolability of grain neutral spirits as the base of the blend. Finally, he had then kept almost entirely to the whiskey trade, with only minor forays into gin, rum, and brandy.

Rosenstiel on the other hand had aggressively built inventories for the future on the basis of complex calculations of the national income, estimates of "jingle money," the rising population curve, and optimism. No whiskey in the United States, he observed, had ever been sold at a loss—excepting occasional small distress sales. He had followed the trend to blends but straddled the taste issue with a straight-whiskey business. In his blends he had not always been committed to grain as the base of his neutral spirits, which led to trouble, as we shall see. Rosenstiel also diversified his business with beer, wine, and brandy.

Such policies brought Bronfman and Rosenstiel into the industry's wartime crisis in different circumstances. When production of beverage alcohol was stopped in October 1942 and the industry had to rely upon its existing stocks, Rosenstiel had larger inventories of whiskey on hand than Bronfman. Both of them then went out to buy all the whiskey they could, even buying up independent distillers. But while Bronfman had relatively less whiskey, Rosenstiel had relatively less spirits for the blending.

During the war, Bronfman gave up potential sales by restraining his use of his grain neutral spirits, and he used no other. Rosenstiel seized the opportunity. Long on whiskey but short on grain neutral spirits, he looked around for substitute neutral spirits with which to meet the wartime demand. Two other kinds could be had, namely, potato spirits and cane spirits. It is conceded in the industry that potato spirits are a proper base for good whiskey, though in the United States distillers have generally followed the public preference for the idea of grain spirits. Cane spirits inadequately distilled abroad carry over distinct traces of rum flavor. Rosenstiel went to Cuba—it is said he beat the others there—and bought the less expensive cane spirits. Later he decided to make potato spirits in the United States at considerable expense. Then with grain, potato, cane, and some fruit spirits in hand, he went into the market full tilt. He gained a large and profitable business, providing the wartime public with what it wanted. But the public did not long thank him after the war.

That, of course, was not in accordance with Rosenstiel's plans. He had tried to produce whiskey in quantity and at the same time preserve the integrity of his brand names. To do this he had, first, reserved his dwindling supply of grain neutral spirits for the traditional Schenley brands of blended whiskey. Second, for the principal marketing of the cane spirits he created a subsidiary company, with new brands, which, if they had been clothing instead of whiskey, might have been called "Victory" brands. Third, he finally used part of the potato spirits in the production of his very popular Three Feathers brand, which, of course, had formerly been made with grain spirits. As it turned out, it was not the new brands that caused difficulties, but Three Feathers. This brand had sold so well before 1947 that it accounted for a good part of Schenley's prosperity. But during the war the public read "potato spirits" on the back label and was often reminded of it by competitors. Bronfman advertised "Seagram's superb neutral spirits" to the trade. Despite a return, after the war, to grain neutral spirits in combination with fine aged whiskey, Three Feathers fell precipitously in sales and accounted for a good part of Schenley's decline in 1947–48. Rosenstiel argued that by supplying the wartime demand, and incidentally taking the industry leadership in sales and profits for a few years, he had forestalled the rise of a black market in whiskey. To Schenley's dealers he said, "We kept you in business." He was surprised, then, when a good share of the public demand turned to Seagrams, which had sat out the boom aspects of the war. But Rosenstiel was still in possession of the largest stock of aged whiskies in the industry, while Bronfman by 1948 had depleted his more modest inventory.

The wartime liquor game had been played largely along the lines of one-sided decision theory, each party making his own decisions according to his interests and in light of how he viewed the economic environment as a whole, which was made up of inventories, brand sales, labels, consumer tastes, and the presence of other parties with their strategies. The interactions had revolved largely around Bronfman's conservatism creating larger opportunities for Rosenstiel's aggressive decisions. Now with the starting positions described above, the more interactive game of this story began.

Again, it should be remembered among the important facts of this game that it takes four years to mature a standard American whiskey. Thus, any interruption of production leaves its mark four years later. The war stopped all production of whiskey for almost two years, 1944-46, except for a few brief periods, and this put a high premium on scarce whiskey stocks at the time the game started. Some whiskey could be bought wholesale at a price from professional whiskey traders and distillers, and some was actually traded in 1947-48 at $11 a gallon. At this price, the buyer would take a loss of 25 to 35 percent when he marketed it in bottles. The seller, if he also had a bottled whiskey business, thus sacrificed brand sales for profits, and the buyer sacrificed a large measure of profits for brand sales.

Bronfman's problem was that he could not maintain the high level of his brand sales without buying whiskey. Deals were possible only at a high price, and there was no given market price for large quantities of bulk whiskey. Price would have to be negotiated. And for aged whiskey that meant that

Bronfman would have to try to negotiate mainly with Rosenstiel.

The game now can be reduced to its bare essentials, or ultimate rules.

Bronfman had just two principal choices. He could offer a high price for Rosenstiel's whiskey and maintain Seagram's brand sales at low profit. Or he could let his brand sales decline and maintain a better profit.

Rosenstiel also had two choices which were the opposite of Bronfman's. He could sell his whiskey to Bronfman at a high price and take a big profit while his own brand sales continued low. Or he could keep the whiskey, forgoing the big profit on a bulk sale, and put the whiskey into his brands to increase their sales, which would be a more costly enterprise.

Neither could maximize both brand sales and profit. If Bronfman got his brand sales, Rosenstiel would get the profit. If Rosenstiel got his brand sales, Bronfman would keep more profit. Their choices thus were completely interactive and interdependent.

These observations describe the game. How could the players resolve it?

Clearly much would depend on how each valued the profit and the brand sales. As it was a one-shot game which would be scored with a payoff, each party had to combine these values, including prospective profits in the short and long term, and his feelings about being No. 1 in the business, to reach his choice. If the combined value of less money and more brand sales was high for Bronfman, while the combined value of more money and less brand sales was high for Rosenstiel, they could cooperate in an exchange of money for whiskey which would bring them a mutual gain. Precisely how they would divide that gain would depend on how they came out in their bargaining over the price of the whiskey.

But if Bronfman preferred to keep his money and take less brand sales, or if Rosenstiel preferred to keep his higher brand-sales prospects and take less money, then there was no basis in their values for a deal. Each would play a more or less non-cooperative game to get or keep as high a share of the market as he could; and National Distillers, Hiram Walker, and others would join them in this game.

As it actually happened, both parties gave a lot of thought to their alternatives, going over them and imagining the potential outcomes. The overt action came when Bronfman in 1948 bid a high price for a lot of Rosenstiel's whiskey. Rosenstiel was prepared to reject the deal and take the noncooperative solution. He preferred to take his aged whiskey, bottle it with the age on the labels, and put on a selling campaign for Schenley brands of straight whiskies and for blends with a proportion of aged whiskey—both strong selling points with consumers. The campaign would be risky as well as costly.

But before Rosenstiel made a decision, he listened to Emil Schwarzhaupt, his second-largest shareholder. Schwarzhaupt had become a shareholder in Schenley when he merged his own Bernheim Distilling Company of Louisville, Kentucky, into Schenley in 1937, giving Schenley its celebrated I. W. Harper bourbon. He was one of the most experienced whiskey traders in the business and, in semiretirement, kept an office at Schenley. Schwarzhaupt's preference was to sell Bronfman the whiskey and use the money to set Schenley up in a strong financial position for brand-sale battles in the future. But he succeeded only in opening up this alternative for exploration. In the end, Rosenstiel rejected Schwarzhaupt's view and so rejected Bronfman's offer.

It is worth noting that their judgments of value were decisive and it was precisely because their judgments were similar that they did not cooperate. Both preferred brand sales to immediate profits. It takes a difference in judgments of value to make a cooperative deal. Thus the game ended there.

The immediate consequences were that Bronfman had to tide himself over with the purchase of some young whiskey and probably did not do as well in the next couple of years as he would have with Rosenstiel's whiskey. Rosenstiel put on his age-label campaign at substantial cost and certainly did not do as well in profits as he would have with Bronfman's money. Beyond that, one cannot read too much into the effect of that game on subsequent games in the liquor industry, except for an impression that the games beginning in 1943 and concluding with the game of 1948 established the positions of the major companies in the industry.

The dynamics of the industry, including the changing preferences of consumers, brought the rise of the lower-cost white liquors, gin and vodka ("you make it in the morning and sell it in the afternoon," said a whiskey man), which altered the spirits market. In case sales, blended whiskies during the next two decades dropped steadily to about 23 percent of all spirits sales. Straight whiskies leveled off at about 24 percent, but bonded whiskey dropped to about 2½ percent. Canadian whiskey rose to 7 percent, scotch to 11 percent. Altogether, whiskies dropped to about two thirds of the spirits market while the white liquors came to occupy almost a quarter of it. In that changing market, all liquor companies had to do some fast footwork, and yet the Big Four kept their styles and remained in remarkably stable positions.

Until his retirement from Schenley in 1968 Rosenstiel featured his age-labels as the "image" of his company, and the Bourbon Institute which he promoted gave bourbon an international popularity. Bronfman, until his death in 1971, continued to stress blends but also diversified his lines. Seagrams, moving the most cases, stayed on top of the industry with National second, Walker third, and Schenley fourth.

2

THE RULES OF THE GAME:
FINDING THE CHOICES

The rules of a parlor or field game are usually written in a booklet or on a box of equipment. The rules of a real-life game, if not routine, or formalized as in the stock market, usually have to be discovered. Rough-modeling a real-life game is thus largely a do-it-yourself affair. Skill is needed not only to play a real-life game but also to construct one.

The rules of a game are commands, "absolute, inviolable, and above criticism," in the unequivocal words of the founders of modern game theory, John Von Neumann and Oskar Morgenstern. This declaration is not empirical but purely logical. Rules may in fact be criticized, violated, and abolished, but a change in the rules by definition changes the game. The existence of a game implies the acceptance, or recognition, of rules commanding the obedience of its players. A significant change of rules signals the end of a game and perhaps the beginning of a new one. Games players have understood this from time immemorial.

A game contains two parts: the rules, which describe it, and the play of the game, which is concerned with possible solutions. Solutions are what the players do or could do within the rules to attain their ends. As solutions make no sense without rules, one has first to understand the rules in order to get to the action.

In parlor and field games, where the theory of games and much of its terminology originated, the rules typically are set down with great clarity. Describe such games and you find yourself saying what the rules are: deal from fifty-two cards, ace takes king, etc.; in bridge, four players divide into two teams seated North and South, East and West; a baseball team has nine players; chess has one player on each side, white and black. The rules usually say who moves first (decided often by a random chance), when the game ends, how to score it, and so on. The peculiarity of play games is that the game is the model, constructed of rules, and the model is the reality.

Game theorists likewise invent game models, taking from real life certain of its features for their materials and blotting out the rest. The rules of these games, as in play games, are rigorous and precise and tend to be even more abstract. Since the rules set the limits on free choice in the playing of the game, they ultimately may be reduced simply to the choices available to the players.

Thus the description of a game by its rules may range widely in the amount of detail that is included. But some of the general rules, common to all games, have a special significance.

The number of players is an important rule, since it affects the number and character of the player's choices. Indeed, the number of players is a basis of classifying games, for the addition of one player to a game, when the numbers are small, radically changes the game. A one-person game is a game against nature and in modern game theory is not ordinarily considered to be game theoretic since nature, as opponent or collaborator, is not considered to be capable of making free choices. The human player chooses; nature is represented by physical "laws," determined, probable, or unknown. A two-person game is profound in human interaction but lacks coalitions. The latter appear in games of three or more persons and give rise to a complex society of groups.

So the rules must say how many players are in the game. The preferences of the players, based on their values, also set limits on the play of a game (in theory, the players want more of something, or, as theoreticians put it, prefer a high number over a lower one). And so the preferences or values of the players must be worked into the rules. The concept is not so esoteric as it might appear at first sight. One player, for example, does not have a choice of buying another's land below the value the latter puts on keeping it.

A number of such general rules for all games have been discovered, as we shall see; on the other hand, of course, one has to recognize that particular games also have their particular rules.

In any case, when one gets down to a pencil-and-paper game model, the players' choices will be explicit. They fan out like branches of a tree with alternations in the moves of the players at each fanning point. As Von Neumann and Morgenstern codified it, "The game consists of a sequence of moves, and the play of a sequence of choices." As the game fans out, each choice of a player sets up the occasion for the move—or countermove—of another player who will choose among his alternatives. At some point the game terminates and is scored.

The choices available to the players here constitute the rules of the game as they are described in a basic game-theory model (called picturesquely the "extensive form" of a game). In theory, this model gives a panorama of all the possible moves and countermoves, from which the players can derive their detailed strategies. Unfortunately, it is so realistic—so extensive—that in a complicated game the tree becomes the jungle. Before that happens, however, game theorists obtain a great deal from it about the nature of games. From it also they extract another model with fewer rules, called the "strategic form" of a game (sometimes known as the "matrix" or "normal" form).

In the strategic form, instead of describing in detail each move and the information it is based on, game theorists set forth a picture of all the strategies—complete plans—available for playing the entire game, with the players making decisions in advance for meeting every possible contingency. We still want to know the number of players and their values, but each player now needs to make only one choice: his strategy embodied in a complete contingency plan. The number of complete strategies available in a complex game will be very large, and so a complete strategy resolving every move in advance is likely to be impractical. In chess, for example, the number of possible strategies for playing the game from the first to the last move goes out of sight; even the computer cannot spell them out, and the complications of chess are often exceeded in the real world. But in devising the strategic model, the theorists stated that their purpose was not practical but conceptual.

The generality of the strategic form of a game is exceeded in still another basic model designed exclusively for cooperative games. This is the coalition model. It leaves behind the strategic details and reduces the game to the values of all the possible coalitions of the players. By cutting through the complexity of strategic interactions between numerous players, the model gets to the nub of the matter of coalitions with an economy that even players in the real world may need when they are committed to somehow resolve a game with many players.

The rules of the game in the real world are usually vague by comparison with those of play games and the abstract games of theorists. Play games presumably derive from real life and are themselves quite abstract. The rules of game-theory games are expressly abstracted from life. Turning to the games played in the real world, one reverses this direction. That is, one takes the knowledge learned in games and returns to the real world to design concrete games. To describe them even in a casual way, one has to include much that has been left out of abstract games. As there is no substantial precedent for doing this, one can expect to do some groping among a motley lot of perceptions of the world to find the rules of a game.[1]

[1] Martin Shubik broke ground here in his book *Strategy and Market Structure* (John Wiley, New York, 1959) and various papers.

Imagine an economic agent—the chief executive of a corporation—who is likely to be engaged in one or more games. Say he is in a fairly common problematic stage in his business—in doubt about the future of his present markets and his position in them, under some pressure from inside and outside the corporation, and wondering what sort of business the corporation should be in and what changes he should make. Let us say he scans a check list of elements of his business, such as products, production, services, markets, prices, supply and demand, vertical and horizontal expansion (or contraction), the scope of his lines of business (e.g., automobiles or transportation in general; movies or entertainment; telephones or communication); his plant, equipment, and inventory; other resources and resource structures (cash, receivables, debt-equity ratios, etc.), advertising, accounting, his corporate organization and its outside links, values, goals, and the like. Outside, in the economy at large, he also looks over the gross national product, money supply, interest rate, movement of the price level, the consumers' cost of living, the balance of payments, employment rate, wage level, the aggregate plant, equipment, and inventory of the society, and in general questions of inflation, deflation, and the recent "stagflation," and the direction in which such things seem to be going. He also looks over the state of the technologies that he is in or that could affect his business, the laws of the country and perhaps some international laws, the social standards, the politics.

It's a big order but one he is used to. If he correlated such elements, he would have a model of some sort. He might look at it as a one-person game, like solitaire, in which he wants to maximize some objective function, say profit and survival. This is the common "decision model" which almost everyone uses for a systematic attack on an economic problem: the basic assumption made is that the world it describes will respond to the decisions of the player in some sense predictably—a good chance that this or that will happen, a better chance that something else will happen, with some things as good as certain for all practical purposes, by guesswork, or according to the record. If he has reliable data and makes good guesses and calculations, and is lucky, he will, like Robinson Crusoe, get out of his world what he wants to get.

But of course, even though he may view his model as a one-person game, the chief executive is not alone in his world. Others like him are also making similar decisions and the paths of at least some of their decisions are likely to cross. A corporate buyer negotiates with a supplier; the supplier also negotiates with another buyer and is looking for the most profitable deal. There may be no established market price. The world of business is full of situations, in and out of markets, that require dickering, bargaining, negotiating, and other such interactions whose mark is the free choice of the actors and the indeterminateness of their outcomes. When he comes to make decisions about the elements that involve the decisions of other executives, who unlike nature have free choice, he can no longer maximize the outcome. Nor can they, for, to take the simplest example in economic logic, a buyer cannot get the lowest price while the seller gets the highest price. Each is free to try to get the best price he can, or other compensations, free to give premiums or rebates, make threats—credible to incredible—pull out of a deal and go somewhere else or sit tight, and the like. With these interactions and thoughts about them going on, standard decision theory is no help. The executive is in a game in the game-theoretic sense. He may still try to play it one-sidedly, taking account of the strategies of the others and making his own choices independently. But if there are two or more players in the game and they can do better by getting together, the standard decision model crumbles. It has no place for players who cooperate.

So the executive needs a game model or some semblance of it in his thought, and for that he needs the rules of the game. Getting to know the rules of a game in what appears to be a diffused and disorderly real world may be so challenging as to take a large part of a player's time and creative talent, especially since he may have some control over rules.

The difficulty is not only in primary perception but also in getting a grip on the concept of the rules of a game.

Much of the difficulty in describing a real-life game would disappear if one could say unequivocally what a rule is. But most of the elements in the check list for the decision model above are not themselves rules, though they—or at least some of them—must be brought into the rules of an economic game. The rules of a game are not things floating loose in the world. They are always tied to the actors. Indeed, a game theorist would say that a rule implies an actor. It is related to his behavior. A rule is what an actor in a game obeys.

Two elements seem prima facie to qualify as rules of a real-life game, namely, the number and character of the players and the laws of the country. The number of competitors, rivals, or buyers and sellers, together with their interests, values, goals, preferences, and resources, clearly shape the choices available to the players and thereby form part of the rules of any game. And the laws of the country are invented and invoked by the actors in society very much as rules for play games are created and expected to be obeyed by their players. Of course, a rule of law in life may not have the quality of absoluteness demanded of a rule of a game. Obviously, almost any legislated law can be broken, and even the penalty—a secondary rule of law—may be escaped; and so, since a rule of a game must be absolute for the duration of a game, one has to judge whether a law is really working in a game. If it is not, it's not a rule.

While in our society we may be struck by the number of departures from the law, on the whole we operate within it. We can see that most of the conduct of most of the people in our society is obedient to the law. It controls a massive amount of daily activity, from the guidance of traffic to the payment of debts. This is an important fact about the rules of an economic game. But it is also important to notice that strategic players, moved by strong economic forces, will often press around and against a law, finding what they can do that it does not seem precisely to forbid. Think of the laws against coalitions in markets, where coalitions are not sharply defined (game theorists observe that coalitions are shadowy in theory, too). Prices cannot legitimately be fixed by agreement, but what is the concerted action known as "price leadership"? Actually, the leader is not always followed and there is another kind of game there whose character—cooperative or non-cooperative—has never been adequately described, and which has stumped theorists and enforcers of antitrust law. Laws in general at their boundaries are never firm. A good deal of business behavior is on the margins of the law—whatever the prevailing width of the margins—where efforts are made to rewrite the rules of the game. Politicking the rules of law is a prime sideline of all economic activity.

Another difficult problem in observing the presence of a rule of law in a game is to distinguish it from a custom. When a custom has the force of an effective law, it must of course be counted as a rule of the game. A custom that does not have that force is regarded in game theory not as a rule but as a solution of the game. That is, it is part of the play of the game, something the players in common are doing but don't have to do. A law that is weakly supported or widely flouted—like the prohibition law or gambling laws—has to be gauged for whatever residual force it has in a real-life game, but it is likely to be a sign that its supporting custom or social norm is also ineffective. Many economic issues are legislated into laws which fail for lack of understanding of the underlying economic game that gave rise to them.

With these ambiguities in rules of law as rules of the game perhaps cleared up, the aspiring modeler of a real-life game can try his hand at the "laws of nature." Obviously, a real-life game is replete with "laws of nature." A game, like society, rests on a physical foundation. "Laws of nature" in modern science are often if not usually viewed as probabilities. On the assumption of free will, the actions of games players are not predictable by probability because they can *choose* what they are going to do. But nature may be imagined to be a predictable player with chance moves, that is, with odds as in the roll of dice. In general, the "laws of nature" may better be seen not as a rule in the game but as opportunities, perhaps for disasters, in sum as "the physical consequences of decisions."[2]

Technology, which rests on nature, is a bugbear to the modeler. It is always there threatening to change the rules of a game. An important aspect of the physical facts of a game is that they indicate whether a given choice is possible or im-

---

[2] Modern game theorists make this distinction between rules of the game—which in real life include human laws if they are obeyed —and "laws of nature" as consequences of the decisions of players. The English words and phrases for these matters seem to have been formed in early times by analogies that blur the distinction, though their meaning in usage is clear enough. Sherman Kuhn, editor of the Middle English Dictionary, writes (in a letter to the author):

The Medievals thought about the "laws of nature" but usually called them the "law(s) of kind" or "kindly laws," where *kind* means the same as *nature*. The earliest references to "law(s) of nature" seem to be in John Gower's *Confessio Amantis* late in the fourteenth century (e.g., Bk. 7, l. 5375). References to laws of *kind*, etc., appear as early as about the beginning of the thirteenth century. These are references to a principle or principles controlling the behavior of material things, physical law(s), etc.

The earliest reference to anything like rules of a game seems to be *the laue of the feld* ("the law of the field"), meaning the rules governing a tournament. This is found in a religious writer about 1340.

The English knew about Roman law, which they called *Emperoures Laue* or *Laue of the Emperour* . . . [but] were more concerned with church law (or canon law) and the codes of the various English kings (statute law) and the Common law. They could have reasoned analogically from statute, canon, or Common law to natural law more readily than from Roman law to natural law, I think. However, the idea of natural laws was already present in Medieval Latin, ready to be taken over bodily into the vernacular. The *lex naturae* ("law of nature") seems to be commonest in the Latin saints' legends, where we might expect it to derive from the idea of canon law.

Game theorists want to avoid the possible inference that a "law of nature" is obeyed in the sense that a "rule of the game" is obeyed. The distinction was noticed by Shapley in connection with the modeling of games where it becomes operationally important.

possible. The big thing about technology is that it makes things physically possible that formerly were not. Certain technologies—most of those that large corporations work on—merely extend development in a given direction, with more or less foreseeable results (in some spheres the progress of technologies can be measured in advance by the number of man-engineering hours to be put into them). These can be worked into the rules as they affect the choices of all the players. But technology in general has no such direction lines. Two companies had a lock on the steam locomotive business and General Motors came up with the diesel locomotive. Such innovation is not common among large companies, except for AT&T's Bell Labs. Important new technologies usually come as bolts from the blue. Computers came from outside the calculating-machine business; rocket and communications-satellite technology came from scientists funded by the government—the source of so many modern technologies. Many new technologies came from small, unknown entrepreneurs, like Xerox. The list is long and spectacular. There are theories for such dynamic changes but they are not yet well developed. And so when one is modeling a game of business, one has to keep an eye on what may happen outside the model which may affect it.

The contrast between the typically static character of abstract game models—in the temporal sense—and the typically ongoing character of economic activity in the real world forms one of the big gaps between the present state of game theory and any attempt to describe and rough-model real-life games. But the gap needn't stop one from proceeding. Building patchwork bridges is an inherent part of the modeling art.

A game-theory game, as noted, has a place where it starts (with a rule for who moves first or for moving simultaneously) and a place where it stops and the payoff is scored. The game ends there, while in the real world life flows on. However, a game theorist doesn't altogether accept Heraclitus' metaphor of the flowing river as a different reality from moment to moment. There are "steady-state" games—games over time with repetitive activities. Numerous real-life games are played this way, with a policy guiding detailed repetitive moves over time—the price policy of a J. C. Penney store, for example. Chief executives usually don't play steady-state games, but they make the policy that results in the repetitive activity. They do play one-shot games—mergers or acquisitions where the game stops when the deal is settled.

A steady-state game presumably maximizes a stream of income, a one-shot game a definitive outcome. In between, the question is what one is playing for. In the typical ongoing game of business the payoffs are spaced out intermittently along the way, with no given end points for scoring.

So a game modeler, with his problems of avoiding long unwieldy sequences of moves and qualitative changes in the rules, has to question whether the changing world will sit long enough for it to be described in a model. The business executive has the same problem. He wonders whether a situation will hold long enough for him to analyze it and make a considered decision. Numerous economic games—steady-state, one-shot, and others—can be found in which the essential rules will hold for a space of time and give a score. Furthermore, games of business can sometimes be tied together in a sequence, with the end of one giving the starting position of the next game. Thus at present dynamic changes complicate and restrict the modeling of real-life games, but do not prevent one from proceeding with a fairly realistic design of a game.

With the guiding principle that rule and actor are inseparable, one can gather the known facts about a game and transform them into the rules of the game. Take the money supply and interest rate, for example. The government has the power of decision and the means to influence money and interest. What the government does about them becomes a fact of life which may be among the facts that describe a game. As facts, then, but not as rules, they may come into the decisions of a corporate executive. Say he is in the housing business where the number of housing starts in the country is affected by both the supply of money and the interest charged for it. In view of these facts he has to decide whether to expand or contract his business. The rule of the game, then, is that he has a *choice* of expanding or contracting. Likewise price, which plays such a central role in classical economic theory, is not a rule of an economic game, but may come into a rule as it affects the choices of the players. The transformation to a rule is always from fact to choice.

It is apparent that the word "rule" in play games has a sharp edge that it may not have in real-life games. This is further evident in the way players in the real world handle the rules. Say a real-life game is under way and there is a change in the rules, perhaps a new alternative introduced by one of the players. By formal definition the game is over, and some other game, described in part by the new rule, is under way. It should be clear that a change in a significant alternative will in fact change the game. If the game has one seller and two buyers and one buyer drops out and leaves the game, the seller has lost an alternative deal with all its implications of change in the relationship of the remaining buyer and seller. The three-person game has ended; a two-person game is under way. The change is about as radical as is possible in an economic game. But in the case of some other alternative being added or taken away, there may be no significant change in the game; or at any rate, it might be unreasonable to interpret the game as ended. This involves a judgment about the importance of any particular piece of information.

It is typical of real-life games that the players have incomplete information about the rules of the game, particularly the available alternatives. A game may be played on the assumption of incomplete information, with no further question raised about trying to complete the information or any way to get more of it. Games may be played that way if not too much information is blanked out. But before corporate executives get to that stage, one is likely to find them exploring for new information in the form of new alternatives. This showed up as one of the most striking results in the interviews with executives for this book. Exploring a game for alternatives is a creative activity which may be viewed simply as learning the game. It may not really change the game, for one reason, namely, that there may be either an explicit or implied rule which indicates the *kind* of alternatives permitted, even though they are not all known. There may be large classes of alternatives that the executives know exist but have not worked out until intuition somewhere along the way prods them into working them out. Many executives say they find this to be the major part of their activity. They don't seem to feel that they are expanding their game. They are merely filling it in, and at the same time finding out just how incomplete their information is.

Modeling a real-life game, even tentatively, engages one as intimately with the subject as playing a game does, and with its own disciplines. One should in the end be able to say about a model that its rules are approximately correct. In sum, that means to a game theorist that one should be able to describe a set of players, a set of possible outcomes, a set of ways of proceeding, and be able to place a limit on the available choices of the players, the number of complications, and in general on the elements one will consider to be in the game—all of course matters of judgment. For the occasion of the game, then, you have excluded most of the world; you close up the model and play the game within it. You no longer speak of the rules of the real world but only of the rules of the game in the model.

With the concept of the rules more or less in hand, one can sketch a small economic game—the relations of a few players negotiating some interest or other in or around a market—or a large game, taking in as players the government, producers, consumers, the society as a capitalist democracy. That is to say, there is a game-theory way of looking at these things.

Corporate chief executives, who are situated in the midst of both small and large games, have, in fact, a model that covers the spectrum, which a person with game-theory eyes would describe as a game model and they call the corporation. For each chief executive, his model is his organization, tailored to his world.

To see this, divide the corporate world into four parts (games) in ascending hierarchic orders of magnitude and complexity.[3] The rules set the levels.

At the first level, place the day-to-day business of buyers and sellers in regular consumer and supplier markets.

At the second level, expand the model over time.

At the third level, expand the model in scope.

At the fourth level, expand the model beyond economics to society and its rules.

At the first level the players on the selling side are typically store managers, branch managers, dealers, and the people who work at the point of sale. The rules are the rules of particular markets together with the rules established for particular enterprises. Chief executives—or the controling person in any business, corporate or non-corporate, if he has employees—largely delegate the game at this level to subordinates. A general merchandise chain, for example, might have a policy—i.e., a rule—that it is not a price cutter, or that it is. If it is not, the rule might be explained on the grounds that the company's prices are already low across the board, and expressed in a corresponding advertising policy. Local managers then play the game day by day according to this policy which for them is a rule. Perhaps there is another rule that if the store is getting hurt on some occasion by a discounter, the manager has the option of meeting the other store's price temporarily, after which he must revert to the no-price-cutting rule. The overwhelming majority of transactions in the economy, billions of dollars' worth every day, take place in line with such rules. They are well known and, day by day, fairly well established.

At the second level, where policy for the first level is made, the rules just described are not rules but strategic vari-

---

[3] This model, together with the general concept of the corporation as the executives' model of a game, grew out of discussions with Shapley.

ables. The policy maker lays down the rules for the first level as part of a strategic plan for one industry over time. Here typically are merchandisers, manufacturers producing a single line of products, or a service or transportation company operating in one kind of market. For the chief executive, setting rules on price policy is of course only one of several variables under his control. He can also, for example, vary his budget; it will normally last for a year but can be changed from year to year; and he will normally expect to modify his corporate long-range plan from time to time. But the rules at this level, too, may be controlled at a higher level.

At the third level the model stretches out over more than one line of products and so over more than one market. This extension in scope introduces a new situation in the rules. Each product line (and correspondingly each market) at the second level becomes a submodel of the model at the third level. The rules of the second level do not hold at this level but are again strategic variables in the hands of the one who is making decisions at the higher level. This third level is the location of those participants who hold strategic control of diversified companies, including conglomerates.

At the fourth level the model transcends economics. Here the rules of all economic games, except the physical constraints of technology, are variables in the hands of the powers that be in society who make the rules of law. The rules are political rules, which form a very different kind of game. It is the game of games, which for the players of economic games consists of efforts in the political arena to get the rules of their games changed. Here individuals and economic groups—farmers, labor, industries, etc.—employ a variety of means to prevail upon the government to alter or create rules favoring them in relation to other individuals and groups in society—electing sympathetic officials, lobbying in legislatures, making institutional and personal alliances between themselves and government agents, playing arbitration games, and the like, down to common bribery.

This four-level model has the merit of envisioning the corporate world in terms of the actors in and around a corporation. It shows who makes strategic decisions and what kind. It shows that a new product, by opening new markets, means new players to cooperate or compete with. In the succession of levels it shows how firm rules keep you in a game and how you may break them by going to another model; that is, how in real life there is a way to understand rules as fixed or variable without having to declare open season on all of them.

This four-level model is extremely simplified; there is room for an infinity of games at each level. A particular corporate player will be influenced by his own model which he tailors to his conception of his industry or industries.

But the general model has room for such central questions asked in contemporary corporate business as "What business should I be in?" It has a place for the so-called "production function"—i.e., so many inputs, so many outputs. At the first level—the short run—you take what you have. But at the second level—the long run—you may choose to build new factories, install new machines, and the like, restricted only by what is available and what you might get out of research and development.

The model also has room for the consumer, who typically is a passive player in a game. He has no strategies but receives a payoff. This is of particular interest when one goes over to the fourth level where coalitions are prevalent and paramount, and the government (or a Ralph Nader) may play on behalf of the consumer.

Likewise, one can put the general public interest in at the fourth level to measure, for example, the effects of various concentrations of industry, with a view to resolving antitrust problems. This is not to say that anyone can model the whole political process. Game theorists like Steven J. Brams have taken it on in pieces, and with discipline.[4] Game theorists are

[4] Steven J. Brams, *Game Theory and Politics* (New York: The Free Press, 1975). Brams and his associates have also modeled various legal games, for example, the jury selection system of the United States, showing that it does not do what it is purported to do (Brams and Morton D. Davis, "A Game-Theory Approach to Jury Selection," *Trial Magazine*, December 1976). Also he and

the first to say that no game model is useful if you go too far in political depth or try to model too far into the future. But one may get a look at the outlines of an economic problem, and perhaps at what could be done about it by those who have an interest in it.

Douglas Muzzio have modeled as a game the historic Supreme Court decision, *United States v. Nixon* (1974). ("Why the Supreme Court Was Unanimous in the White House Tapes Case," *Trial Magazine*, May 1977.)

3

GENERAL MOTORS V. FORD:
A TWO-PLAYER ZERO-SUM GAME

For about one month beginning April 6, 1921, Alfred P. Sloan, Jr., and a management team in General Motors engaged in imagining a game between General Motors and Ford. Their objective was to invade the low-price car market that Ford then fully occupied with the most celebrated automobile ever produced, before or since—the Model T. The lines of strategic thought set forth by Sloan's team foreshadowed the way the game would actually be played in the auto industry and influenced the present shape of that industry in the United States.

Although the players were real and their model was a model for action, the April game was imaginary in the sense that all of its events were mental events. It guided the actions of General Motors during the following two years—despite an internal conflict that inhibited some of its projected moves—and by the late spring of 1923 the game in real life was concluded and scored. A second game then began, based on the outcome of the first one and pursued along similar strategic lines; it was concluded in 1927 when the Ford Motor Company collapsed for the better part of a year and lost its dominance of the industry to General Motors.

As the game here contains only two corporate players playing for all-or-none stakes, it is conceptually simple, though it had considerable depth in action and reaction.

THE PLAYERS

■ Henry Ford, Sr., for Ford Motor Company

■ Alfred P. Sloan, Jr., and Pierre S. du Pont for General
   Motors Corporation

Everyone knows the corporations in this game in their present state. General Motors produces more than half the cars
made in the U.S., Ford about a third, in a more or less stable
ratio year after year. In 1921 their circumstances were the
reverse. Ford was No. 1, with more than half of U.S. car production. General Motors was No. 2, with only about one
tenth, or a somewhat larger fraction if one averages a number of earlier years. These rankings, however, did not quite
measure their strengths in the game. Their assets were comparable; and in dollar sales for the previous year General
Motors, selling higher-priced cars than Ford, was a close second to that company. The two were far ahead of the field, together accounting for about two thirds of all the cars produced in the United States. The rest of the market at that
time was divided between many well-known cars produced
by other companies: the Dodge, Essex, Franklin, Hudson,
Hup, Maxwell-Chalmers (later Chrysler), Nash, Packard,
Paige, Reo, Saxon, Studebaker, Willys-Overland, and others.
None of these cars figured directly in the games described
here, which included just two players, Ford and General
Motors. Ford then had only one car, the Model T. General
Motors had several ranging from a medium-priced Chevrolet
to the high-priced Cadillac.

Thus, before the game began, General Motors was not in
competition with Ford. The game was conceived when the
management of General Motors decided to invade Ford's monopoly of the low-price car market. It promised to be an
eventful decision not only because Ford was dominant and
seemingly unassailable but also because both parties were
agreed that the big payoff in the auto industry in the foreseeable future was in the low-price field.

So much has been said in retrospect about the flaws of
Henry Ford that one could easily imagine that the players in
1921 should have known all that is now known about him.

Of course they couldn't, but what did they know? He was then the outstanding businessman in the world, though he had not quite yet reached the zenith of his success in the auto industry. He was a hero to a wide public for his promotion of high wages and low prices, a villain to a few among his erstwhile stockholders who believed, erroneously, that he cared nothing for profits. ("If you give all that, the money will fall into your hands: you can't get out of it," he said.) Owing to his spectacular pacifism—the "Peace Ship" with which he proposed to stop World War I—and occasional pronouncements on subjects on which he was not well informed, he appeared to be eccentric. But in business he had a strategic mind.

Ford had recently demonstrated this talent in an internal corporate game with his minority shareholders. Ford owned about 58 percent of the Ford Motor Company in 1919, Dodge Brothers, Incorporated, about 10 percent, and a few other shareholders the remainder in substantial pieces. From 1916 on, the company had made enormous profits and Ford wanted to reinvest them in further expansion. The Dodge brothers wanted dividends. They sued to force Ford to declare dividends and in 1919 won the suit, as a result of which the Ford company was required to pay out about $20 million in cash. Ford then threatened to leave the Ford Motor Company—he actually resigned as president—and go out and start a new company with a new low-priced car that would compete with the Model T. At the same time, he offered to buy out the minority interests in the Ford Motor Company, providing that he got all of the outstanding stock. In face of the prospect not only of a Ford Motor Company without Henry Ford but also of competition from a new Ford car, the minority shareholders chose to sell their stock. Thus Ford that year obtained complete family ownership as well as control of the company and proceeded to expand as he wished.

As the company's sole ruler, Ford called all the shots, and his domineering style of management resulted in some good executives leaving him. Norval Hawkins, for example, who is credited with building the Ford sales organization that put over the Model T, switched sides and was sitting on the General Motors executive team that in 1921 planned the game against Ford (switching sides is as common in the auto industry as in professional sports). But the shot that Ford had called again and again since 1908, namely, the simple, light, uniform, durable design of the Model T, offered at the lowest price in the market, had earned him his pre-eminence in the automobile market. He had resisted advice to make basic changes in the design of the Model T, and if sales are the measure, he had proved his case and was still in the course of successfully reiterating it. With high volume for only one chassis, he had achieved low unit cost, and by passing on a good part of the benefits to consumers in the form of the low price, he had got the allegiance of most of them. When another car approached the Model T in price, as Chevrolet once did briefly in 1915, before it became part of General Motors, Ford ran away from it with a still lower price. No contender could stand the gaff. In retrospect, it is said that Ford came to regard the Model T as "immutable," that he became "fixated" on his mechanical creation. But the question for the game in 1921, as we shall see, is whether anyone thought less then of the Model T's basic design and its foreseeable prospects than Ford did; and furthermore, whether those who would oppose him would assume that they could *predict* how Ford would respond to the invasion of his market.

The auto industry in 1921 was a small world in which most of the participants knew one another quite well. General Motors for a dozen years had been a turbulent part of that world. William C. Durant, prophet of the industry, wizard in corporate finance, and founder of General Motors, had once negotiated to buy out Ford and is said to have missed only by a failure to raise some cash. R. E. Olds, producer of the Olds (later Oldsmobile) in the early part of the century and the first to demonstrate the value of a simple design and quantity production, left the Olds company to start Reo. Durant put the Olds company together with Buick—then the largest U.S. producer—in 1908 to form General Motors, and the following year added Oakland and Cadillac and a number of other corporate entities to the ensemble. Henry Leland, one of the organizers of Cadillac and its president, came along into General Motors; some years later he left and started the Lincoln company which he was to sell to Ford. Durant lost control of General Motors to a group of bankers in 1910, and while out of power there he started the Chevrolet company which won instant success. Inside General Motors during that time Walter P. Chrysler became president of Buick, succeeding Charles Nash who became president of General Motors. Under their guidance Buick provided most of General Motors' profits, a fact of the patchy corporation that was to go on and make the game of 1921 possible.

Durant maneuvered the Chevrolet company into control of General Motors and through this medium recaptured the big corporation in 1915–16. (In a financial juggling act, General Motors later absorbed Chevrolet.) About this time Pierre S. du Pont, head of the du Pont chemical company, became chairman of General Motors (he was the compromise candidate during the final conflict between Durant and the bankers). He stayed on when Durant resumed control. At Pierre du Pont's behest, the du Pont company—in perhaps the biggest financial parlay ever executed—subsequently invested in General Motors a substantial piece of the large profits it made from the sale of munitions in World War I. The du Ponts thereby came to share with Durant the control of the corporation with the understanding that the du Ponts would take care of General Motors' financial affairs while Durant took care of its operations.

Chrysler, Nash, Leland, and other luminaries were gone from General Motors when the corporation met a new crisis, internal and external, in the national economic slump of 1920. General Motors then made seven cars (eight, if one counts two Chevrolets, each with a different engine, as two cars): Buick, Cadillac, Chevrolet, Olds, Oakland, Scripps Booth, and Sheridan, each of them produced by an independently operated division. The last two hardly counted, but all of the others had sold well in the middle- and upper-price regions during the inflationary boom that followed the war, giving General Motors about 20 percent of the car market, in units, in 1920. The corporation had been expanding rapidly when in the summer of that year prices and production suddenly fell, bringing chaos to the divisions and financial trouble to the corporate office. The stock market also fell, taking General Motors shares down from about $35 to $13 in a few months. Durant, the largest shareholder in the corporation, personally went under. The day came when he could not meet the margin calls from his brokers, who threatened to dump his vast holdings on a weak market. What he was trying to do, speculating so heavily on margin, he never made clear, but it appears that he and J. P. Morgan & Company were operating separate pools in the market in support of General Motors' stock. Morgan objected to Durant's second pool as being, in effect, non-cooperative. Perhaps then they traded against each other. In any case, something went wrong with Durant's market operations and he got knocked out.

At the conclusion of this episode, Durant lost his part in the control of General Motors. The du Ponts, aided by Morgan, bought out its failing founder and the du Pont company came out of the deal with a good part of Durant's shares along with those it had previously acquired, giving it altogether about 36 percent of the outstanding General Motors stock, not counting that held also by individual du Ponts. The du Pont company thereby took absolute control of General Motors. Durant resigned in December 1920, and Pierre du Pont, then a sort of leader of the du Pont clan, took over as president and chief executive as well as chairman of General Motors. Thus, after the conclusion of many earlier games, the situation inside both the General Motors and Ford companies was considerably simplified with each of the imminently opposing sides represented by just one principal strategic player.

One might suppose that the most influential executive in

the century-old du Pont company would have a conservative cast of mind toward risk in handling the company's $75-million investment in General Motors. But soon after taking control of General Motors, he revealed himself as willing to bet the future of the corporation on a one-shot gamble. He directed his executives to consider a radically new engine as the prime mover of a new low-priced Chevrolet design and to put the new car into the market against Ford's Model T.

The new engine, air-cooled but called "copper-cooled" because of the copper fins that dispelled the engine's heat, had been developed by the practical inventor and promoter Charles Kettering. He had brought his research organization with its ideas and inventions into General Motors a few years earlier. The new engine promised to be lighter, to contain fewer parts, and to cost less and perform better than the industry's conventional water-cooled engines. As a revolutionary prospect in the auto industry, the new engine also promised to be a devastating threat to the Model T. Early in 1921 Pierre du Pont ordered the Chevrolet division to prepare to bring out a new car with this new engine; and he would soon extend the order to other divisions of the company.

These sweeping decisions were set forth by a four-man executive committee that consisted of Pierre du Pont, two other du Pont men, and Alfred P. Sloan, Jr., then a vice president of General Motors. The presence of Sloan on the committee indicated a significant difference between Pierre du Pont and Henry Ford in the way they conducted their organizations. Ford, by all accounts, took little advice from his management, whereas du Pont, lacking operating experience in the automobile industry, and perhaps also as a matter of inclination, listened to his advisers and made or allowed compromises when he adopted the position of one executive against another. Du Pont put Sloan on the ruling committee because he respected him, and he needed someone with automotive experience at the top corporate level. Most of the other senior executives in the corporation at that moment either had no such experience or were division heads without corporate experience. Sloan, with his past as entrepreneur and executive in auto parts and accessories, had been close to auto production, and in proposing plans for the management structure of General Motors he had demonstrated a talent for corporate organization. Sloan's personal fortune, such as it was then—several million dollars in General Motors stock—and his future in the corporation were at stake in the game against Ford, and it was the biggest game of his life.

A compromiser but not a yes man, Sloan opposed Pierre du. Pont's decisions on the copper-cooled engine. He did not oppose experimenting with the new engine but opposed absolutely an all-out gamble on the air-cooled design before the new engine was proved out. He proposed a new conventional design for Chevrolet, which, though it would entail the risk of an uncertain reception in the market, represented little or no technological risk. His power to oppose the majority in the ruling committee was limited to persuasion and the nominal power of the highest management man, outside the du Pont group, in the organization, but these powers proved to be not inconsiderable. Sloan's interests, values and skills formed an important, even decisive, part of General Motors as a corporate player in the game.

Sloan had a ruling passion for success in the world from early youth. With the aid of his father, he got into a small business making roller bearings in the 1890s, and so success came to mean success in business. He preferred organization and operations to distant financial manipulations. He would interest himself in microscopic detail if he thought it necessary but his inclination was to look for a policy. He had no taste for taking any chances that could be avoided; he preferred the strategic move to the dice roll. He trusted economics and distrusted politics; if he could have modeled the world, he would have made it a world of business, with as few politicians as a philosophical anarchist would tolerate. He was an emotional man who did not trust his emotions. Any decision he reached while in an emotional state he would reconsider later; and he did not hesitate to revoke a decision. He would try to reach around a problem with such fluidity that in speech or memo his last sentence might contradict his first one. He has been tagged the "organization man" par excellence—yet, paradoxically, on the personal side he upset the stereotype. Except for the functional relationships of business and corporate life during the business day, he was a loner by preference, with few if any intimate friends. He was as austere as a monk, eschewing pleasure trips and taking them only to oblige his wife; shunning parties, perhaps in part because, with his defective hearing, he could hear nothing at their noise level. He played no games except the game of business. He got much more kick out of making money than he did out of spending it. He was perhaps as close as anyone has come in real life to the nineteenth-century ideal of "economic man." His feeling for style in automobiles was eclectic; he would have been glad to make Stutz Bearcats if people would buy them in volume. "All that volume," he used to say with relish about the car business. In his single-minded and consuming passion for the strategic approach to making money out of producing automobiles, he had some of the qualities of a genius.

Sloan developed his minuscule Hyatt Roller Bearing Company into a supplier to the automobile industry when that industry began and saw his business grow mainly with the growth of Ford. He came personally to know Henry Ford—they used to lunch together in Detroit, and though he had a healthy respect for Ford he was not in awe of him. Sloan also knew well a number of key members of the early Ford organization. But, in part because he sold half of his volume to Ford—a situation he regarded as strategically vulnerable—Sloan accepted Durant's offer in 1916 to take his company along with several other auto suppliers into a new company called "United Motors Corporation." As president of United Motors he participated in merging it into General Motors in 1918, became a vice president of General Motors, and began worrying about and working on the problems of its management. And so in 1921, after Durant left, he emerged in the new ruling group.

• • •

Sloan's resistance to the new engine program brought out a basic disagreement in General Motors' councils on how to plan the invasion of Ford's market, with du Pont preferring the technological (chance) approach and Sloan preferring a strategic approach. They reached a compromise which was to be worked out and represented in a plan. Hence it was that on April 6, 1921, four months after the du Ponts had taken power, the ruling executive body of General Motors, by formal resolution, declared its intention to invade Ford's market and at the same time appointed an ad hoc advisory committee, a sort of task force, to draw up the plan. The task force consisted of a number of the corporation's executives headed by Sloan. The plan would in its largest aspect express a comprehensive new product policy for the corporation. The game on General Motors' side thus began with the complexity that its plan of invasion had also to resolve an internal conflict on the way to go about it. During the next month the task force worked on the product policy. On May 4 they submitted it, and on June 9 the executive committee adopted it as the policy of the corporation.

GENERAL MOTORS' APRIL 1921 PLAN TO INVADE FORD'S MARKET

Let us assume, they said, that we are just starting in business with a capital of $600 million and that we are making preliminary decisions about the lines of cars to be manufactured. This is not actually the case, but we are charting the true best course for the future with policy standards. Hence we should consider first the controlling purposes of the organization and its operations and draw the whole picture in relation to the chief objectives of the corporation. We presume that the first purpose in making a capital investment is setting up a business that will pay satisfactory dividends and preserve and increase the capital value. The task force then set down an explicit and precise formulation of the nature of the corporation's values: the primary objective of the General

Motors Corporation, they said, is to make *money*, not just to make motor cars.

There are advantages in covering the market for all grades of automobiles that can be produced and sold in large quantities. No monopoly is intended. There will always be competing cars.

Having established their values and the principle that the scope of General Motors' market was to be guided by the economies of quantity production, the task force set forth a fine theoretical distinction concerning General Motors' products that had implications for the copper-cooled venture. To gain the advantages inherent in being present in all quantity markets, they said, it is not *necessary* to lead competitors in design. It is sufficient only to be equal to the best competing car in any grade. Of course, they expected General Motors' cars to be pre-eminent in all grades; the corporation could afford to buy the required technical talent. But General Motors can lead by other means than running the risk of untried experiments.

The corporation must coordinate its line of cars—a reference to the prevailing chaos of its independent car divisions, each going its own way. That means an ordering of car designs by price classes. In accordance with an instruction of the executive committee, the task force proposes that General Motors design a car to sell for not more than $600. That would be the one that would compete with Ford. They also have an instruction to design a car to sell for not more than $900. They approve of this but they go further. They propose dollar measures for each car in General Motors' line of cars. To this end they create a model of the entire quantity car market, dividing it into six parts by price classes. The dollar numbers are not immutable—though they roughly corresponded to what was practical at the time—but they give the ordering and the spacing. Starting at the bottom, the first class ranges from $450 to $600; the second, from $600 to $900; the third, from $900 to $1,200; the fourth, from $1,200 to $1,700; the fifth, from $1,700 to $2,500; the sixth, from $2,500 to $3,500.

It is necessary to understand this model of the car market if one is to form a picture of the strategy that is to emerge from it. These are imaginary price classes, each of which contains subclasses. Each class and subclass impinges on the classes and subclasses above and below it. The concept— basic to all of Sloan's conceptualizations of the car market— requires that dollars be taken to measure the basic design of automobiles. The task force explains this concretely.

General Motors actually has no car in the first class. That class at present is monopolized by Ford. Now imagine a move. Chevrolet invades this market. But Ford sells at the lowest price in this class and they reject any attempt to build and sell a car at the Ford price. Instead, they will design and market a much better car at a price at or near the top of the first price class. This car, while not competing directly at the Ford price, will be so near in price and so superior in design, that it will draw demand from Ford among those who are willing to pay a little more for a better car.

Conversely, the new car will exert an influence on the demand for cars in the next higher class. A car selling at about $600 will draw demand from cars selling at $750. The demand will come from car buyers who for a saving of $150 are willing to yield the comparatively slight preference they have for the design in the higher class.

The task force now bows to Kettering, who was one of its members, and to the wishes of the corporation's chief executive. The car for this low-price class will be a new Chevrolet designed on the foundation of the copper-cooled engine. They concede tactfully that the copper-cooled engine will probably be successful, but just in case it doesn't stand up technologically or in the market, the engine will be so designed that it can be replaced in the new car at no great cost with a water-cooled engine.

So, air-cooled or water-cooled, Chevrolet will enter Ford's market with a car priced at or near $600, and the Chevrolet division of General Motors shall make no car in any other price class. Meanwhile, the present water-cooled Chevrolet should be sold as hard as ever, in case the new engine does not make good. Chevrolet is now making cars out of its prescribed price class, a failure that should be corrected as soon as possible.

The task force supplements these directions for maneuvering between old and new car designs with some observations on Henry Ford. The longer the low-price class is left solely to him, the more entrenched he will become in the advantages gained. There will never be a more opportune time to oppose him. Ford's dominance of the lowest price field has been gained not by underselling alone but by all-round superiority in marketing and service. But the Ford dealer organization is disorganized (the task force's diagnosis presumably of the effect of Ford's having required his dealers to help him financially in the economic slump). The task force believes the public is growing away from Ford cars and that the new Chevrolet design will not only draw wide user demand but also a number of Ford dealers. Ford, they said, is vulnerable today, as never before, to such a car as General Motors proposes to put into the first price class.

Each of General Motors' cars likewise shall have a prescribed place in the price-class spectrum. The spectrum contains no wide gaps, yet limits the number of cars to the smallest number sufficient to cover the whole range of the market for quantity production, with each car exerting its drawing power upon the areas of demand above and below, in the manner described for Chevrolet. Coordination of engineering, production, advertising, selling, and service should be introduced to serve the principal purpose of making money by making automobiles.

Although the task force devised the plan to sort out the whole General Motors' line of cars in rational fashion by price classes, the main force of the plan then lay in its proposed invasion of Ford's market, the only price class in which General Motors then had no car. For simplicity I shall speak of the task force's plan as the "Sloan plan." I shall view it as an important part of the evidence that a game was taking place between General Motors and Ford. To give a wider perspective on the game, including the interactions of both players, I shall move now from General Motors' view as a player, as expressed in the Sloan plan, to my view as an observer.

THE GAME INTERPRETED

The Sloan plan indicates the existence of a game between General Motors and Ford but does not completely describe it. What's missing is Ford's strategic choices and what General Motors will do about them. The omission is not surprising. It is a rare thing in real life to find a game complete and open to the eye, even from the point of view of one of the players. Commonly, one finds only fragments. In the formalities of corporate life, long chains of complex reasoning are normally summed up in a relatively small number of observations, conclusions, and decisions.

The omission cannot be taken care of satisfactorily by going on from the plan to narrate what actually happened, even in the form of a sequence of the moves and counter moves of the players. For to describe a game *one needs to know what didn't happen*. Actions conceived by the players, or seen to be available to them, but not taken, in the concept of a game, have a bearing, even, in a peculiar sense, a causal bearing on the actions taken which we know as the actual external events. This universe of imagined events—the options considered, possible interactions, dormant threats, and other potentials—contains not only the larger part of the content of games but also, in the theory of games, the decisive part, whether the game is an entertainment, an abstract model, or a game in real life other than an entertainment.

But Sloan's vision of a market divided into price classes was a strategic concept. It is true that he predicted the behavior of consumers in relation to the prices and related this to the technical functions of quantity production. But this field of prices was populated not only by passive consumers but also by other actors among the producers who were as free to move as Sloan was. Anyone who made a move—a price cut, for example—influenced not only his own outcome but also the outcomes of others. Sloan might attribute this freedom only to General Motors and see the car market as the environment; nevertheless, that market would be an environment of players with actual strategies. And so the game of price classes was inherently interactive.

It is important to note that if Sloan had assumed he could *predict* Ford's reaction to General Motors' invasion, with whatever kind of standard guesswork, there would be no game here in the game-theoretic sense. Nor would there be such a game if Pierre du Pont's preference for gambling exclusively on the copper-cooled engine prevailed. These would be the foundations of one-sided decisions with uncertainties in the one case about how well they understood Ford's behavior, in the other the chance uncertainties of technology.

But in his plan Sloan does not attempt to predict what Ford will do. Nor does he give any sign of belief that Ford is stupid, compulsive, or fixated on the Model T. He confines his predictions mainly to the nature of the car market and to a side mention of the consequences of supposed disaffection among Ford's dealers. The copper-cooled engine he buries as a chance move inside the strategic plan—if the engine worked, so much the better; if it did not, the strategy could proceed without it. Only equality in engineering was required.

Thus all of the uncertainties of games were implied in Sloan's plan—the natural and unavoidable uncertainties of the economy and the market, the introduction of the chance device of a new engine, the move to invade Ford's market, and the strategic uncertainty of Ford's counteraction against invasion, to be followed by further possible interactions on both sides.

Ford, for his part, as the greatest price cutter in history, had based his position on strategically controlled prices. It was a pure strategy well known to both sides. With it he had long divided the American car market into two classes, his and the others. From Sloan's point of view, Ford had designed and priced his car for the wide base of the "pyramid of demand." Sloan's price classes therefore begin with Ford's price and taper upward to the smallest demand at the highest price. As Ford's car occupies the bottom of the pyramid, no one threatens, or can threaten him from below. But Sloan proposes to redivide the market by attacking Ford from above. Various counteractions—not just price cuts—were available to Ford. Sloan was fully aware, as we shall see later, that his own strategy could be turned against him by Ford. For his part, Ford composed no known verbal record of how he imagined the game, but we can infer a good deal about how he could have imagined it from the choices available to him and make some observations on him as a strategic player.

Although at the outset of the game both players had confidence in the long-run future of the economy and of the automobile industry, neither quite envisioned the Roaring Twenties. Both believed, however, not only that the United States was a car-oriented country but also that the prospect of a big payoff was in the low-price class. The approximate equality of their financial resources was an open book. But their preferences concerning possible outcomes of the game take some reflection.

General Motors' formulation of its primary value as that of making money, not just motor cars, presumably would satisfy the shareholders. It would also satisfy the dominant norms of society at that time. Ford, on the other hand, as the sole proprietor of his company, could, within limits, exercise any personal values he chose to. He, too, apparently wanted to make money and was demonstrably a master money maker. But as noted, he also spoke of his role as a social one, advocating high wages, promoting the Model T as the liberator of the farmer from the farm, and so on. If in pursuit of these social values, Ford was willing to take less money, these values would complicate the game and could lead to outcomes different from those stemming solely from a desire to make money. But if we take him at his word, he believed that with his views on wages and prices "the money will fall into your hands."

One has also to take account here of another question of values. That this was a two-person game—confined to the low-price market with no other contenders—does not necessarily mean that the interests of the two players were entirely opposed. Although the outcome of the game could be scored in shares of the low-price market—a fairly clean-cut basis for opposition—one would want to know how each of them valued these shares. If they played for shares and valued them equally, their interests would be entirely opposed—a share for one being one share less for the other—and that would go a long way toward defining the kind of game it was and the way it should (logically) be played. But if they valued the shares differently, their interests would not need to be entirely opposed. An outcome in shares, when valued by the players, would give each of them different payoffs. They might, in that case, conclude that it paid each of them better to find a means to divide the market between them. It would be no less a game if they willingly shared the market, but it would be a different kind of game.

Dividing the car market by some sort of coordination of strategies (collusion was illegal) would not be a far-fetched solution to this game. The classic distinction made between the old Ford company and General Motors has the former interested in a static utility car and the latter interested in upgraded annual models, that is, it has each company carving out a separate piece of the market. The Sloan plan itself contained the seeming paradox that General Motors would "invade" Ford's market but "not compete" with him at his price and corresponding design. General Motors would yield to Ford the low end of the low-price class but that was only in recognition of his current strategic power in that area.

There is another point that we must remember, too, and that is that the issue of a static utility car versus upgraded annual models was not part of the game of 1921–23, even as an anticipation of the future market. The auto industry made a number of detailed improvements in car design after the period of this game and the great step in upgrading cars also came later with the development of low-priced closed cars.

Both parties here were talking not only about low prices but also about open cars—touring cars and roadsters. Closed cars, only 17 percent of the market in 1920, were lodged in the higher price classes, far above the purview of the price class of this game; and neither party included in his calculations any forecasts of the future status of closed cars in the market. The demand for basic transportation in the relatively new automobile system was still far from satisfied; used cars were not yet a large factor in satisfying that demand. To put a wedge into this market in opposition to the Model T, Sloan proposed only to offer Ford's customers a little more car for a little more money, a fine distinction which was to acquire further significance in dynamic developments of later years.

Here we are in 1921 at the start of the modern automobile market, before the historical events had taken place in which the producers resolved their division of the market. Chevrolet will invade Ford's market. Is there some sort of bargaining solution for Ford, some mutually recognized balance of threats, which would satisfy both parties and relieve them from the direct costs and risks of a collision in the market? Ford conceivably could choose to see the outcome not in shares of the market but in terms of his general dominance and allow Chevrolet to pick up some of the increment of prospective growth in the market. The difficulty with this approach is that if he allows Chevrolet to become viable at a low price, there is no clear way under the prevailing conditions to stabilize the shares of the two competing companies at any particular level. They cannot make binding agreements even if they wanted to. And with each gain in volume over its minimum level of viability, Chevrolet becomes a greater and greater threat to Ford's strategic price position; indeed, if Chevrolet got enough volume, it could compete head on with Ford on price.

Thus, before one can see very far into this game one has to settle the question of how it might be played and scored. Is it a bargaining game to divide the market or a game of pure opposition? As a bargaining game it would seem to have no stable outcome in view of the future threat of a viable

Chevrolet. Chevrolet's viability appears to be the key to any solution.

Shares of the market cost money. But it was not difficult for General Motors' executives to see that they would make more in the long run if they could gain a position in the prospectively fastest-growing car market. Viability for Chevrolet at its newly assigned low-price level required it to obtain sufficient volume to bring its unit cost below that selling price. Eventually, General Motors would want to measure the resulting profit against some desired return on investment, but for the occasion of this game, winning a foothold in the low-price class would appear to satisfy its minimum objective. The actual figures for Chevrolet's break-even points at that time are not available, but one can make a useful guess that the number of cars Chevrolet needed to sell at $600 would very likely not exceed a range of 150,000 to 200,000 at the prevailing costs. (A hint of this comes from the fact that Chevrolet lost a million dollars a month for several months in 1921 selling cars at a rate of 70,000 units for the year.) And of course, if Chevrolet lowered its price below $600 with the same costs, it would need more volume to remain viable.

Translating this goal into shares of the market for scoring purposes brings a curious question to light. One has to determine the size of the market. At the beginning of the game in 1921 the actual low-price market—all in Ford cars—was about one million car units. Roughly, let us say that Chevrolet would need to gain 20 percent of a one-million low-price market, 10 percent of a two-million low-price market, and, as noted, still larger percentages if they cut the price with the same costs. Thus we have two steps in scoring Chevrolet: one, a certain number of cars at a certain price, the other, the translation of that number into shares of a market. A block of shares of the required size wins for General Motors; substantially less than that loses for General Motors.

A simple way to score Ford would be to reverse that. But before settling on it, we must get over one more hurdle.

Sloan's concept of the low-price class was a novel insight into the nature of the car market. It was a conceptualized space above Ford and below the next higher price, to be filled by drawing consumer demand from both directions. In drawing demand from above (conceived here not as a strategic contest with another player in the game but as a sort of market mechanism), Chevrolet would create new volume in the low-price class—not then obtained by Ford with his combination of price and car design—and so would enlarge the low-price class beyond that represented by Ford alone. The amount Chevrolet would draw from above would be the smaller since in the pyramid of demand the higher price class offered less volume to draw from at the time of the game, but it would not be insignificant. Call it one fourth of the total volume Chevrolet expected to get in the game. That would mean that Chevrolet would have to take three fourths of its expected volume away from the market that would be Ford's if Chevrolet were not there. Here in this large fraction, assuming they are playing for shares, the interests of Ford and Chevrolet are directly opposed. To complete the scoring, then, it seems reasonable to say that if Chevrolet gains its required block of shares, Ford loses; if it does not, Ford wins.

So defined, this is not the most common kind of game in economic life, but it is a good one for observing in isolation the individualist, non-cooperative way to resolve a game. No force inclines them to coordinate their strategies. If Ford gives General Motors an inch it could take a mile. Each cares only about his own payoff, and it's all or none.

THE GAME ROUGHLY MODELED

To model this game one has to station oneself at its beginning and imagine all of the possible strategic interactions of the players to their conclusion. The duration of the game is not given on the calendar. It ends when Chevrolet secures its prescribed aim, with a win for General Motors; or when Chevrolet fails decisively enough to call it a win for Ford. In this sense—and on the analogy of a plus one and a minus one equaling zero—the game is zero-sum. Anything one player gets will be at the expense of the other. They are totally opposed.

It helps to begin by distinguishing chance from the free strategic choices of the players. Chance governs the outcome of the technologies, the reception of car designs in markets, and the direction of the economy. Should General Motors, for example, come up with a copper-cooled engine that lives up to its hopes, and the economy holds up, and Ford does not respond in kind, then Ford very likely has lost the game to chance. Ford, of course, has the option of a similar move with a radically new Ford engine and should take it. In general, the greater the uncertainty of chance, the less the role of strategic uncertainty. A focus on new engines by either player would overshadow the strategic moves. But if both of them tried and failed or tried and succeeded with new engines, they would be even Stephen on their dice rolls and the game would turn on their strategic play.

Similar chance moves with conventional car designs might have considerable though less drastic effect on the character of the game. A brand-new water-cooled Chevrolet, for example, would have the prospect of competing with greater strength against the Model T, if Ford did not match the improvements. He should match them. To get a comprehensive model, one would have to put all of these moves into it; but for simplification I set them to one side.

I am unable, however, to set aside certain elements of chance that are outside the will of the players. One can say, in a manner of speaking, that "nature" makes chance moves. In this game the future direction of the economy is one of nature's moves. The players must take this direction into account because it is linked to and gives different outcomes for the strategies adopted by the players.

Chance is assumed to have four possible moves over the span of the game: (1) the economy declines (a low probability); (2) the economy stays level (a fairly low probability); (3) the economy rises steadily (a high probability);

and (4) the economy booms (a low probability). The probabilities are assumed to be estimates made in 1921 at the start of the game when General Motors planned its long-term strategy; they are consistent with the general point of view on the economy held by Henry Ford and the executives of General Motors. There is no way they could foresee the boom of 1923.

Nevertheless, despite the inclusion of these complications, the game is predominantly strategic. General Motors can only control its own moves, not Ford's; and Ford likewise can only control his moves, not General Motors'. The potential outcomes will depend upon how they interact.

General Motors makes the first move, placing Chevrolet at the upper end of the low-price class.

It is Ford's move. He has four major options.

1. He may stay put for a spell and wait to see how chance deals with the economy and the threatening Chevrolet and reserve his strategic moves to be made later and contingently on the basis of Chevrolet's fortunes.

2. He may immediately cut the price of the Model T, widening the price gap between the two cars.

3. He may offer a counter-car against Chevrolet—a companion to the Model T, comparable to Chevrolet in price and design—thereby aiming to share the top of the low-price class with Chevrolet and so to block it from attaining viable volume.

4. He may combine a counter-car with a price cut in the Model T.

Each of Ford's moves is followed in sequence by either a chance move by "nature" or a strategic move by Chevrolet. The simplest way to see the play of the game is to follow through to their outcomes the sequences resulting from Ford's moves.

1. If Ford stays put, he faces a low probability that the economy will decline. If it declines, Chevrolet will not get its viable volume, and the game is over. Ford wins. He also

faces a high probability that the economy will do one of three things: stay level, steadily rise, or boom. If any one of these things happens, Ford has one option left: a belated price cut. Now, if the economy declines, Ford wins. But if the economy levels, rises steadily, or booms—a combination with a high probability—Ford's belated price cut will not avail because Chevrolet will have had enough time to make gains in volume toward its modest goal of a viable volume; Ford's belated price cut is a weak move against a stronger Chevrolet. In the event that the economy then leveled, Chevrolet could cut its price along with Ford and hang on to its gains. And a continuously rising or booming economy would promise still more volume for Chevrolet regardless of Ford's price cut.

Thus as seen from the beginning of the game, if, when Chevrolet makes its first move, Ford stays put, he could win, but there is a high probability that Chevrolet will win. Needless to say, Ford should reject the option of staying put.

2. Ford's second option after Chevrolet's opening move is an immediate price cut (or series of them) which would counter Sloan's price-class strategy by widening the gap between the new Chevrolet price and the Model T price.

It is then General Motors' move with Chevrolet and it has two options. One is to stay put with Chevrolet's original invasion price. The other is to cut its price further with each Ford cut, following his price downward while always remaining just above the Model T price. There are consequences for either course.

If Chevrolet holds its price while Ford cuts his, Chevrolet could expect to pick up some business from the price class above it, perhaps a fifth or a quarter of its required volume. But by failing to maintain a close ratio of difference in price between the Chevrolet and the Model T, it would be offering a little more car for a lot more price—not a very good prospect for taking sales away from Ford.

Nature now makes a chance move. Either of two things may happen. A boom may take place in the economy—it's improbable but not impossible—in which case Chevrolet, despite its relatively high price, gets its viable volume. General Motors wins. Or something less than a boom may take place, which is highly probable; Chevrolet then fails to attain the desirable volume. Ford wins.

General Motors' other option in response to Ford's price cuts—to chase them—has better prospects. If the economy rises steadily or booms, the highly probable combination, Sloan's strategy will work: Chevrolet will draw business away from the Model T. General Motors wins. In the unlikely event that during the game the economy levels or declines, however, chasing Ford's price won't help. Ford wins. This outcome needs some explanation.

At each lower price level, Chevrolet needs a larger volume to become viable. Until it achieved that volume, Chevrolet would be selling below cost and taking large losses. Meanwhile Ford, with his enormous volume, would be taking less profit, but he could cut his price without going below his break-even point. It should be noted that although Ford can make the contest costly to General Motors, there is no reason to expect either party to make cuts so extreme as to threaten mutual bankruptcy. The difficulty for General Motors is that although it has financial resources comparable to Ford's, it does not have a comparable position in the low-price market —indeed, as noted, it has no position at the start of the game. General Motors is willing to pay a price for a foothold in that prized market, but the question is how much. If it chased the Ford price cuts in a level or declining market, Chevrolet would gain volume but need ever more volume at the lower prices to reach the elusive viability, while General Motors' resources were draining away. Allowing for some unknowns, one can say the chances of Chevrolet's success are very small. Ford wins. On the other hand, if the economy rises or booms, as is most likely, Sloan's strategy would result in Chevrolet's picking up business on the downward price path sufficient very likely to attain the desired volume. So General Motors wins.

Thus, viewed from the beginning of the game, and taking

account of the chances, even an immediate price cut by Ford in response to Chevrolet's invasion is bad for him, if he assumes that General Motors will follow with its best move.

3. If Ford takes his third option in response to General Motors' opening move—a counter-car to Chevrolet—a quite different set of interactions takes place. Several ways of going about this are available to him, none of them easy in view of the lead time needed to get out a new car; but he has the essential dealer organization ready to sell one. There appear to be three possible ways for Ford to come up with a counter-car. One is to design an improved version of the Model T, a sort of Model TT, which, with many common parts, would share in the economies of the Model T's large volume. Such a car would have one drawback. Owing to the peculiarities of the Model T—its planetary transmission operated by foot, for example, as compared with the standard stick shift—a similarly designed companion car would not be closely comparable in design characteristics to the Chevrolet. But the car was imaginable and would in some measure share with Chevrolet the high end of the low-price class. It was also possible to design a new car from scratch for this purpose. That would be a fairly big order but entirely feasible for the 1923 model year. A third route to this end would be to buy a car from among many makers of cars then in the business and market it at Chevrolet's price.

This last course would not have been unprecedented at the time. General Motors had absorbed Chevrolet, along with Scripps Booth, in 1919, and purchased the Sheridan car in 1920. And it was in 1921, not long after the start of this game, that Henry Ford began negotiations to buy the Lincoln, which with its very high price would have no bearing on the game. He could also have bought a counter-car to Chevrolet ready made; the cars were there and he had the resources.

The difficulty lay not in the cost but in the side-effects. A counter-car competing with Chevrolet would also—as the Sloan strategy suggests—compete with the Model T on the top side of its market. By joining Chevrolet in taking volume from the Model T, it would raise somewhat that car's unit cost, hence its price. The move thus would conflict with Ford's prevailing strategic price policy, and so would require a modification of that policy. The question was whether it was worth it. It was worth it if it split the Chevrolet market—the upper end of the low-price class—between two cars to the extent necessary to block Chevrolet from gaining a foothold in that price class.

If Ford makes this move, nature again makes its move. If the economy booms—the least likely event—it is nip and tuck whether Chevrolet survives. One can't say who wins. But if the economy declines, stays level, or steadily rises—a combination with a high probability of occurring—Chevrolet will almost certainly not gain its aims. Ford wins.

4. Ford's fourth option after General Motors' opening move is to combine a counter-car with an immediate price cut. General Motors then has two choices: to hold Chevrolet's price or to chase Ford's price cuts.

If Chevrolet stays put, it does not matter what chance move nature makes: in a declining, level, steadily rising, or booming economy, Ford wins.

If Chevrolet chases the Ford price, the assumption of the counter-car strategy is that Ford would keep its price in line with Chevrolet. Nature then moves. In the unlikely event that the economy booms, it is again nip and tuck whether Chevrolet can reach its goal; and one can't say who wins, except perhaps to note that an early boom in the time span of the game would favor Chevrolet, a late boom, Ford. But in the very likely event that the economy declines, levels, or rises steadily, Chevrolet can't make it. Ford wins.

In sum, the model points to the strategy of a counter-car along with a price cut in the Model T as the best one for Ford, and most likely the winning one regardless of what moves General Motors makes thereafter.

The line drawing here shows at a glance the entire GM-Ford game as it may be seen from its beginning. This is the "game tree" of game theory. It contains the possible moves and countermoves of the players described verbally in the text. It also contains the

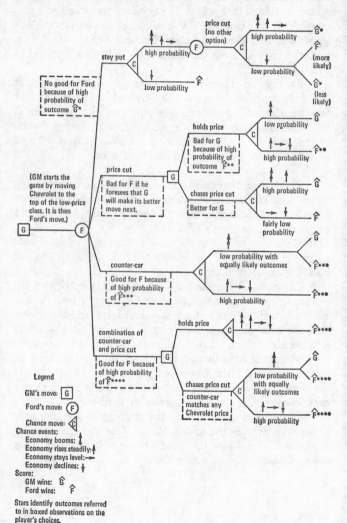

Legend

GM's move: [G]
Ford's move: (F)
Chance move: ◁C
Chance events:
Economy booms: ↑
Economy rises steadily: ⤊
Economy stays level: →
Economy declines: ↓
Score:
GM wins: Ĝ
Ford wins: F̂

Stars identify outcomes referred to in boxed observations on the player's choices.

chance moves of the economy (for simplification, I have omitted the chances associated with new car designs—they had no actual effect on the strategical game).

The game tree above is rooted at GM's opening move (G): Chevrolet to the top of the low-price class.

The first fanning point is Ford's move (F). Its four branches represent Ford's four choices, which as noted are to stay put, cut price, put up a counter-car, or combine the last two.

The consequences of the moves of chance (C) likewise are given on the branches of fanning points.

From the beginning, each branch and its succeeding ones may be followed to the end points which give the possible outcomes of the game. The sign $\hat{G}$ indicates that GM wins; the sign $\hat{F}$, that Ford wins. Stars identify the most likely outcome for a player. The boxes placed after each of Ford's major choices contain comment on the merit of each choice as he might have been able to appraise it at the beginning.

Start, for example, with Ford's choice to stay put. The next move belongs to chance: which way the economy will go. Arrows indicate the possible directions: double arrows up indicate a boom; a single arrow up, a steadily rising economy; a flat arrow, a level economy; an arrow pointed down, a declining economy.

If chance "chooses" a declining economy (a low probability), the game is over forthwith.* The outcome: Ford wins. If chance chooses anything else (level, up, or boom), Ford has another move. But his move contains only one option: a price cut. Again, chance moves. If chance has it that the economy now levels, goes up, or booms (a combination with a high probability), the game is over with the outcome that GM wins. (If the economy should level here, GM has a choice to cut price with Ford and should take it—a move that is not shown in the tree above.) But if chance

* The probabilities are assigned on the basis of estimates that could be made in 1921, when the game started and both parties wanted to plan long-term strategies. There was no way either of them could foresee the boom of 1923. Often two or three moves of chance are lumped together here and shown as one move, because each leads to the same subsequent moves and outcomes. On occasion a single move of chance is split into two, one favorable to GM, the other to Ford, when it might thus go either way; for example, the chance of a declining economy after Ford's delayed price cut.

has it that the economy declines (a low probability), then either of two things may happen: Ford wins (most likely) or GM wins (less likely).

Each of Ford's choices at his first move may be followed in the same way. If, for example, he chooses to make an immediate price cut, the next move is GM's, with two choices: hold price or chase Ford's price cut. In either case, chance then moves and the game ends with one of the four possible outcomes indicated at the end points.

If Ford chooses to put up a counter-car, the next move is up to chance, as indicated.

If he chooses to combine a price cut with a counter-car, it is GM's move, as indicated. If GM chooses to hold Chevrolet's price, Ford is the winner no matter what move chance makes thereafter. But if GM chooses to chase the price cut, chance moves with the possible outcomes indicated.

THE ACTUAL GAME (1921–23)
NARRATED AND SCORED

Three months after they adopted the plan to invade Ford's market, the management of General Motors made its move with Chevrolet. The prices of all cars continued to fall in the economic slump that began in 1920 and extended into 1921, but by the sharpness of their cut in the price of Chevrolet, General Motors created the desired new situation in the low-price class. At the beginning of the year, they had sold the Chevrolet touring car at $820. Ford sold the Model T at $415. In September the price of the Chevrolet was cut to $525, the price of the Model T to $355. But when adjustments are made for Chevrolet's demountable rims, self-starter, and other standard items not carried in the Model T's price, the two cars on a comparable basis were then only about $90 apart. The game had begun as planned.

At the same time, however, the management of General Motors split on the issue of technological risk. Their adopted plan, as noted earlier, contained two voluntary chance moves, the radical, untried, copper-cooled engine, and the alternate new conventional water-cooled design, more or less riskless technologically. The conflict in General Motors reflected different estimates of the risk in the copper-cooled engine and also different attitudes toward the risk. The new engine, the plan had said, was to be adopted if tests proved it out; otherwise, the new lower-risk conventional design was to be adopted. Both programs were to be developed in parallel. As it turned out, however, Pierre du Pont was persuaded by Kettering that the new engine was a fairly sure thing and he used his authority as chief executive to try to impose his views on Chevrolet, to the extent even of appointing himself manager of that division. He ordered Chevrolet—and later Oakland and Olds—to adopt the new engine, and—the crucial issue for Sloan—he also ordered Chevrolet to cease both the development and the production of Chevrolet's conventional water-cooled engine. In other words, du Pont reduced the entire strategic plan to a gamble on the new engine. If chance favored this engine, General Motors would gain a smashing victory over Ford. If it failed, Chevrolet failed.

As a one-shot gamble, it may have carried the implication that du Pont thought Ford was unbeatable in any way other than technical innovation. In any case, Sloan and the division managers balked. With his lack of faith in an untried engine and his aversion to high risk, Sloan, as the top executive for operations, maneuvered to keep alive the old water-cooled Chevrolet and the strategic plan. Du Pont did not block Sloan, as he had the power to do, but allowed a cloudy situation to develop in the corporation while he awaited the outcome of the new engine. The upshot was that General Motors eventually put a copper-cooled Chevrolet on the market alongside the standard Chevrolet. It failed and was recalled. Chevrolet survived. The conflict left its mark on the game, however, by blocking the development of a new standard Chevrolet. General Motors thus took the riskier of its two chances on technology and lost, not altogether harmlessly. The strategic game proceeded on the basis of the old Chevrolet design which Sloan had kept in production as a back-up.

Ford also took a gamble on a new engine but in a less

risky way. He started work in his laboratory on what he called "Engine X," but never brought it out. Like General Motors, he held to his old car design throughout the game.

The immediate results of Chevrolet's price move in the fall of 1921 were not indicative of much. Chevrolet, as noted, sold only about 70,000 cars in 1921 and lost a lot of money. Ford sold almost a million cars. But the economy began to turn up in the fall of 1921 and Chevrolet's new price should have been the signal to Ford that he was being challenged. It was time for Ford to consider his reply. Perhaps he did not then sense the threat; doubtless he was unaware that it represented an elaborate plan to invade his market. Perhaps he sensed it but, not being able to gauge it, decided to chance living with it. He shaved the price of the Model T from $355 to $350 and then waited. The economy continued steadily upward in 1922 and Chevrolet began to pick up some volume in the spring and summer of that year. Ford's sales were rising strongly again, but he sensed something that made him move. In September of 1922, belatedly but with a grand flourish, Ford cut his price to $300, taking the Model T far below Chevrolet and opening a wide gap in the middle of the low-price class. It was Chevrolet's move.

The conditions had changed. After a full year within range of the Model T, Chevrolet was in business with fairly good sales. Having the choice of holding its price and taking less future volume or following Ford down, Chevrolet chose then to hold. This move was favored, and presumably motivated, by the rising economy. Ford that year sold about a million and a half cars, but Chevrolet, with sales of a little over 200,000, had reached its viable level at its selling price. Thus in 1922 a novel event had occurred. General Motors and Ford divided the low-price class 87 percent for Ford, 13 percent for Chevrolet. The new year would be decisive.

As it happened, the economy continued rising to the middle of 1923 and the automobile market rose with it to its fabulous first four-million car-and-truck year. Ford made minor improvements in his car design for that year. Chevrolet also made minor but important changes in the Chevrolet design, altering its radiator, cowling, and headlights and raising and straightening its hood, thereby further differentiating its appearance from the Model T's.

It was clear by late spring of 1923 that General Motors had won the game. Although Ford set a record that year with sales of more than two million cars—more than half of the total car market—Chevrolet, with a now expanded dealer organization, sold 450,000 cars, or about 18 percent of the low-price class—a niche from which it would be difficult to imagine Ford ever dislodging it.

Could Ford have done better, and if so, where should he have reacted?

Compare his actions with the model. After Chevrolet's move into his price class in September 1921, Ford had only a few months in which to make an effective move before chance made its move. He had the option, which he took, of letting the chance of the economy determine whether Chevrolet would become a serious threat in the spring and summer of 1922, after which, if necessary, he could make a sharp yet strategically weaker price cut and again wait on chance.

Alternatively, Ford could have moved ahead of this chance no later than the winter of 1921–22. A substantial price cut then—before the usual spring buying season—would have given General Motors a tough choice of counter-replies. With Chevrolet then in possession of no significant actual volume but only of expectations, General Motors would have had to choose whether to hold its price at $525 or to cut with Ford. If Chevrolet held its price against a Ford cut, it would, according to its own price-class analysis, probably fail to draw enough business from Ford to gain viability, though the amount it would draw would depend on which way the economy went. General Motors could chance it as the model shows. Alternatively, if they cut the price and kept the Chevrolet-Ford price ratio intact, the cost would have been great and so would the risk of failing to attain the much greater viable volume entailed by the lower price. Chance would decide the matter and chance favored a rising economy in which Chevrolet would pick up sales.

With so much at stake, Ford might also have looked at his less chancy, more strategic option of meeting Chevrolet with a counter-car as a companion to the Model T. He had just enough time to carry out such a move for the 1923 model year. Chance would of course have played a role in determining how the counter-car actually divided the market above the Model T with Chevrolet. But if the counter-car did as well as Chevrolet, or even somewhat less well, only a boom in the car market could have saved Chevrolet, and not for sure at that.

Thus, Ford's best strategy appears to have been a combination of two simultaneous moves: an immediate substantial price cut and preparations for the counter-car for 1923. Chevrolet might still have been saved by the unexpected boom of 1923, but coming off a lower base in 1922, it might have failed. Ford's strategy of belated price cuts gave him only a slight chance to win against Sloan's strategy. That Sloan's strategy could have been beaten is no knock against it. It was a game of skill and Sloan was a more skillful strategist than Ford in this particular game.

THE SECOND GAME (1923–27) NARRATED

The outcome of the first game in 1923 gave General Motors and Ford new starting positions in their next game, which took place between 1923 and 1927. An important part of that outcome was the effect it had in resolving the conflict inside General Motors. In the spring of 1923, when his hopes for the copper-cooled engine had collapsed and Chevrolet was victorious without even the benefit of a basic new conventional car design, Pierre du Pont resigned as president and chief executive of General Motors—willingly, of course, as he was still the sole strategic shareholder. In recognition of Sloan's role in designing and carrying out the winning strategy, du Pont arranged that Sloan should become president and chief executive. Du Pont remained as chairman and took responsibility for financial policy, but Sloan thereafter was in charge of operating the corporation.

Sloan restated and pursued an extension of the main lines of the strategy of the first game. He unified the corporation and designed its organization to obtain "decentralized operations with coordinated control," which enabled it to act as a single player. Ford, on the other hand, with his personal rule, came into increasing conflict with his organization.

In the new game, Chevrolet could hardly be dislodged except by some big mistake on Sloan's part. Ford's realistic aim now had to be not to shake off Chevrolet but to dominate it.

Both players also now faced a radically changing car market. For one thing, it had reached a plateau at the four-million level where it would remain for the rest of the decade. With the forecasting art of the time, they could hardly have predicted that, but they could guess that it was one of the possibilities. In fact they would now be playing in a closed arena.

In the early stages of this game, things did not go well for General Motors, and Ford looked better than ever. The booming economy with which the first game ended receded after the middle of 1923. Chevrolet's sales in 1924 fell to 290,000, off 37 percent from 1923. Ford's sales fell only 4 percent. In view of the fact that the sales of the car industry as a whole fell 12 percent in the recession, Ford made a strong relative gain: his sales of two million Model T's represented well over 50 percent of the whole car market. The antagonists were back to the positions they held at the end of 1922, with Chevrolet having not much more than a foothold.

To the casual observer, Ford's dominance of the industry was still impregnable. But other forces were at work. The most important technological and market change in automobiles in that era was gathering force. That was the rise in the proportion of closed cars sold and coincidentally the decline in the cost of producing them and in their market price. Although the first game had begun with 22 percent and ended with 34 percent of the market in closed cars, those cars as noted had remained in the upper price classes. In 1924, despite the recession, the proportion of closed cars rose to 43 percent of the market and the trend was clear. In 1925 the big event took place. The price of closed cars dropped suddenly and demand shifted to them that year to the extent of 56 percent. At the same time used cars from the upper price classes came into the market in volume to compete with new low-price open cars. The position of the Model T as the provider of basic transportation was thus undermined.

Sloan was prepared for the change. While General Motors' sales were declining and Ford was riding high during 1924, Sloan had his engineers working on a new water-cooled Chevrolet design, called the K model, for the 1925 model year. The K model was a much improved car and was flexible as regards open and closed bodies, whereas Ford's Model T was not. The Model T was essentially an open-car design; with a closed body it was a patchwork.

Ford thus in 1924 and 1925 had his last good chance to do something to preserve his dominance. Without parity in engineering design, his old strategic price policy would be powerless. A new Ford design timed to supplant the Model T with uninterrupted momentum in the market was all he needed to stay far ahead of the then struggling Chevrolet. No longer was it a matter of putting up a counter-car to keep the Chevrolet off his back, as it had been in the earlier game. It was now one of being present in full force in a new kind of market, the low end of which though still ample was destined to shrink, and the upper end of which was growing with the rise of the closed car.[1]

[1] That Sloan was fully aware of the possibility of a counter-car strategy he made clear in 1925. Roy Chapin of Hudson Motors that year led in reducing closed-car prices. He surprised the automobile world by bringing the price of the Essex coach down to the bottom of the second price class—as defined by Sloan—just above the Chevrolet. This move threatened Chevrolet in precisely the way Chevrolet had threatened Ford. Sloan responded by putting a counter-car opposite the Essex. That was the Pontiac, which he brought out the following year. It had common parts with the Chevrolet, which gave it shared economies; and it was priced just

When again in 1925 Ford had not begun a new design, he was no longer making strategic sense. For the first time in either game, Sloan made the observation, "We expected Ford, generally speaking, to stay put." Ford had become predictable. That meant that the contest was no longer game theoretic.

Nevertheless, Ford again, for the third year in a row, sold two million cars in 1925. Chevrolet's new Model K sold about 480,000, however, and the end for Ford was near. The substance of the so-called "upgrading" of cars in the 1920s was contained in the relentless movement of the market to closed cars, from 56 percent in 1925 to 73 percent in 1926 and 82 percent in 1927. Ford could not keep pace with his Model T. His sales fell off to about a million and a half cars in 1926, and only about half of them had closed bodies, while Chevrolet's sales rose to a phenomenal 700,000, about three fourths of them with closed bodies. Chevrolet performed this feat by making the final move that was implicit in the strategy of 1921. Having widened its niche and attained the essential volume, Chevrolet brought its closed-car price down approximately to Ford's, with the power now to stay with him, and so destroyed the pricing strategy on which Ford had relied. Having no effective reply and at last seeing the end upon him, Ford shut down his factories in 1927, for the better part of a year, to design the Model A, successor to the Model T.

While Ford was substantially out of the market in 1927 and 1928, Chevrolet sold about a million cars in each of those years, representing about two thirds of all of General Motors' car sales. Then and thereafter General Motors had in Chevrolet its largest and most important division, and Ford lost his dominance. Neither Sloan nor Ford had expected such a radical outcome.

---

above the Chevrolet. It completed the filling of the price-class spectrum called for in the April 1921 plan. The car line, running in ascending order of price from Chevrolet through Pontiac, Oldsmobile, and Buick to Cadillac, consolidated General Motors' strategic position throughout the car market.

In the aftermath Ford came back to life again with the Model A, one of the best little cars ever made, smart on the street and a goat in the mountains, which again proved his genius for making a basic car for which millions of people could feel an aesthetic affection. It had its moment, out-selling Chevrolet in 1929, but as a four-cylinder job at the beginning of the six-cylinder age (the next new low-price Chevrolet), it could not, like the Model T, divide the market in two—Ford and the others—nor could it outsell Chevrolet in the long run.

The Sloan concept of price classes won out. Walter Chrysler adopted a version of it for his new company in the late twenties, and so eventually did the Ford company. These three went on to subsequent games, in which they were the survivors, sharing most of the car production in the United States in fairly stable proportions for the next few decades.

Looking back over both games, it is hard to say precisely when Ford became "irrational" and what sort of irrationality it was. One interpretation, as noted, has his mind tied not to the market but to the Model T as an object. But if he had a blind passion for the Model T in the first game, he must have only recently developed it, for he didn't have it in 1919 when he threatened to abandon the car along with the Ford Motor Company in favor of another car and another company if his minority shareholders did not sell him their stock. If that was a bluff, the other shareholders certainly took it as a credible one. Furthermore, as it happened, it made no difference whether he was "fixated" on the Model T in the first game. Its design was at least as good as Chevrolet's, and it had a big market; indeed, it would have been irrational for him to change its basic design over the span of that game. His failure, as we have seen, was in strategic skill—a price cut made too late to be effective and his neglect of the strategy of splitting Chevrolet's market with a counter-car.

The second game took a different kind of turn. Sloan adapted the Chevrolet to changes in technology and the market. Ford waited too long to change. Strategically, he stopped playing the game; so after 1925 the question was no longer one of strategic skill but of a failure of perceptions. He had lost track of the rules of the game. The theory of games gives a measure of his irrationality.

4

CORPORATE VALUES:
A MUTED GAME

The inside of a corporation contains a nascent game which on occasion erupts into a visibly active one. This happens when the values of the inside players—shareholders, directors, the chief executive, management, and other employees—are not satisfied. In normal circumstances, it falls to the chief executive to keep the game inactive by satisfying the players' values, a responsibility that uniquely defines his role in the corporation. The chief executive combines these values into a formal expression of objectives and policies which he expects will lead to satisfactory outcomes. When he fails, the players go to their corners and the game is on, as when a takeover impends.

A game has two results, outcome and payoff. The outcome is what happens as anyone might describe it. The payoff is what the outcome is worth to the player. The outcome of a game may be the winning of fifty dollars, but one player may light his cigar with the money, another pay his rent with it.

Whether the payoffs of real-life games, and even on occasion the outcomes, can be described in numbers is a subject of contention, but because numbers are useful if not essential in the description of real-life games, I shall open this Pandora's box a crack and hope for the best.

A satisfactory description of complex human values in numbers awaits a complete number theory of value, which may be awaiting the millennium. But real-life games can't wait. In modeling economic games, theorists make the simple but sweeping assumption that numerical values exist, in money or on an imaginary single scale of "utility" combining different values often including money. In the real world, people do in fact value their choices every day, with and without numbers; and when corporations are in a game, the numbers, or quite a few of them, get fairly hard in money, though with qualifications. It is the qualifications that pose the interesting questions.

Values limit the choices of the players. In a bargaining game, for example, the object to be traded is worth something to the seller if he keeps it or eats it and is presumably worth something more than that to the prospective buyer. The difference in their values makes the game. They can make a beneficial exchange somewhere between the two numbers expressing these values, customarily in the measure of money.

Money has served the purpose of measuring economic values for three thousand years; its invention set off the phenomenon of widespread trade among human beings. Yet for all its remarkable powers, money does not completely satisfy the purpose of measure. It isn't only that "money isn't everything." For the measure of money is itself conditioned by the worth of money. As anyone who has thought about risking his last dollar to get another, is aware, money is not always measured evenly in proportion to the amount of it. For a rich man, does an additional dollar have the value of each of the dollars he already has—that is, is the value of money linear? Even more curious, a player in corporate business may reject the best deal on the odds because he doesn't want to risk what he's got, thereby refuting the notion that his purpose is to maximize an expected gain in money. And to complicate matters further, money of course isn't everything. If money is present, the situation is certainly economic, but the situation may also be economic without money.

At the risk of opening the troublesome box another crack, I offer the following standard observations on the vagaries of an individual trying to settle on his preferences.

Logically, if you prefer A to B and B to C, you should also prefer A to B. But it may happen, contrary to this logic, that at the end of that sequence you prefer C to A. The inconsistency may not be irrational and it is certainly common. Time may have passed and in the interval you may have forgotten your previous choice—sometimes a blessing; or you may have changed—perhaps also a blessing; or you may have learned more about yourself or the world; perhaps someone persuaded you to a different view, or your mind works in compartments or by impulse; and so on. Furthermore, a group of individuals, say the members of a corporation, may be inconsistent because the organization is not acting as one: individuals down the line may be making choices different from those above.

All this has to be coped with in some fashion in real-life games by calling upon all sorts of knowledge, except game theory. Game theory itself is not a theory of value but assumes that a measure of value exists. Indeed, a game could hardly be played without measure. For the duration of a game one wants players who can order at least a pair of preferences; better a sequence; and at best one wants players who can say *how much* they prefer one imagined event to another.

The question of "how much" had been abandoned by economists as hopeless when Von Neumann and Morgenstern made a passing try at reviving it. In their work on games they accepted the established opinion that if a person was presented with a choice of three definite outcomes, A, B, and C, the best you could hope for was an ordering of that person's preferences: first, second, and third. Which, of course, lacks the scale of how much he prefers one to another. But they then showed that if A, B, and C were not definite outcomes but risky combinations, such as a fifty-fifty chance of B or C, the presence of such probabilities would result in a system of preferences across the array of possible outcomes, which could be described in cardinal numbers. That is, a person could say how much he preferred one choice to another.

Von Neumann and Morgenstern pursued the workings of this remarkable observation for fourteen revolutionary pages, but then they too shied away from further entanglement with the subject, making no claims for value theory as a practical art. To divide the difficulties in coping with both values and games, they went back to plain money for their countable values.

If ever one is to find anything approaching cardinal numbers for values, however, it should be in the corporate world. To this end I propose to make some limited observations on corporate values.

In the aggregate, especially to consumers of its products, a corporation appears monolithic. But economic games are played by real actors who have their own values as well as values common to the corporation. Setting aside the vending machine, a corporation typically is represented in a market by a personal agent. The agent may have some scope for decision, hence for personal preferences, but these will either agree with or be restricted by corporate policy. The standard assumption that the corporation seeks a profit in money seems a valid enough measure of "its" values at this level—the market—and in general for routine decisions. But linear money—money whose worth is proportional to the amount of it; that is, the worth of every dollar is a dollar—or even money alone, cannot be relied upon for understanding how strategic corporate policy is made or how deals out of the routine are made by negotiation and bargaining. For these one has to look inside the organization where the corporation itself is the game.

For the players in a corporation game—shareholders, directors, the chief executive, management and other employees—the profits at the level of the corporation's markets only describe an outcome of the business. As outcome, the profits look the same from anybody's point of view. They do not represent the payoff to anybody; for the payoff is not to the corporation but to someone in it. To reach the payoff you have to go to the personal players and see how they measure the worth of corporate outcomes, of which profit, however prominent, is only one. Thus, despite the prevalence and apparent simplicity of the measure of money, the question of combining and measuring values, so obscure in theory and practice, must be and in some fashion is met in corporate as well as personal economic life.

Some corporations are controlled by a single shareholder whose values are dominant—J. Paul Getty and Howard Hughes in their corporations, for example. Many are controlled by a group of substantial shareholders; many by fairly small shareholders or their coalitions—as no particular percentage of shares determines control, the tail may wag the dog; and large investment or trust funds may have strategic influence over a nominally independent chief executive.

But let us take the situation of a person who, whatever the source of his power, dominates a corporation, say under the title chief executive. For him in normal times—call them normal—the corporate game is muted. In times of internal crisis —a merger, proxy fight, or struggle for control—he and the other players go to their corners and pick strategies or join coalitions. But even the muted game is real enough underneath if one wanted to see it that way—that is, as a many-sided interactive game which in normal moments has been resolved to everyone's satisfaction in a core of stability.

It seems reasonable again to "divide the difficulties." Let the interactive game be stilled and view the situation as a one-person game of decisions. Gone are the free-choice assumptions of an interactive strategic game. The only active player—here the chief executive—will try to predict the behavior of the other parties and to resolve their conflicts and common interests in his decisions. We need a model for this person who makes decisions on behalf of others as well as himself.

The model is simple. As the only strategically active player, the chief executive links control with judgments of value. The other players—mainly shareholders and management—have no control but receive a payoff. The shareholders are diffused in relatively small holdings and are strategically passive. On the operating end, the management, also strategically passive, is tied to the chief executive's decisions in which they may participate as a team. Other employees are likewise non-strategic, except as they may be represented by unions, which are not strictly part of the central corporate structure. The uncertainties of chance in the world at large—which way the economy will go, the surprises of technology, etc.—come in through their influence on the outcome. The market game, with its consumers and competitors, in this arbitrary view, is also part of the natural environment and comes in as part of the outcome.

Thus, with strategical uncertainties set aside, the chief executive can start to build his model with three elements: decisions, outcomes, and payoffs. Having the values of the inside players in mind, he formulates the corporate objectives, some of which he quantifies as goals: earnings per share, return on equity, return on capital employed, net worth, growth of sales, dividends, etc. Such targets make up the shareholders' scorecard. Somewhere he also suggests the prospects, tangible and intangible. Having thus codified the values as general objectives and specific goals, he can make policy decisions without always having to go back to the values. He releases the actual outcome in the conventional quarterly and annual reports. The players gauge the payoffs to themselves according to their lights and the cycle is complete.

Thus expanded, the corporate executive's decision model looks like this:

Values of the players
Objectives (derived from the values)
Policies (derived mainly from the objectives)
Outcomes
Payoffs (the outcomes valued)

Two events jolt this routine. One occurs when the chief executive makes a mistake or fate goes against him and he doesn't make the expected score in the prevailing values of the players. Corporate inertia may save him, but his control may be threatened. The other occurs if the values of the players change, as they have in recent years. When this happens, the chief executive may be hard put to resolve the new values before he is drawn into an open game for control.

But the point of the model is that there will be no confrontations so long as the chief executive satisfies the passive players with the outcomes. As fiduciary agent, he follows the values of the shareholders as well as his own; it is a vaguely defined obligation but he doesn't want to turn them against him. As head of management, he rules its members and takes care of their interests, too. To satisfy all parties he internalizes their values and tries somehow to blend them in a non-crisis mode of thought. Money of course is a common element in most of his decisions, but money has different dimensions and is often alloyed with other values. Ideally, he would distill out some sort of single line of value which would enable him to make "rational" decisions by choosing the largest number among the numbers associated with his alternatives.

Making judgments that combine a variety of values emanating from a variety of sources could be said to be one reason for the chief executive's existence, and he is usually experienced in making them. Chief executives say they seldom make routine decisions; they make the decisions that become the routines, steering their corporations over time with periodic payoffs to the shareholders who are on for the ride and to management which is more or less there to stay. Satisfying the players with his decisions takes skill in sensing the differences in their values.

THE PLAYERS AND THEIR VALUES

Shareholders. Their desire to gain more money—a return on investment reflected in dividends or the price of the stock or both—is not simple. For they want the chief executive to make money now and in the long run, that is, in two dimensions of time; and they also want it qualified as to risk, another dimension: he is not to lose money in unacceptable ways.

Shareholders also may influence executives in their choice of lines of business. Wall Street fashions, at one time or another, have decreed that the best prospects lie in cement, public utilities, electronics, airlines, computers, nursing homes, and whatnot.

Management. The relationship of management to the shareholders is financial: their interests in the profit outcome are parallel. The members of management want money and the positions that make money; and their salaries and side benefits, rationalized as beneficial to morale, are usually accepted by the shareholders. But the interests of management extend beyond profit to power, prestige, enjoyment of the work, way of life, continuity, security, and the like, which are tied to the one outstanding unique management value, namely, the survival of the corporation as an institution.

Shareholders and management part company here, for survival of the institution and survival of the assets—which the shareholders care about—are not the same thing. Survival of the institution cannot be described in money or expected money; it is a non-economic value. Large shareholders often identify themselves with a corporation's economic power and place in the economy, and even some small shareholders may share vicariously a feeling for the organization. But typically, the small shareholder lacks the motive for such loyalty. Rationalizing the survival of the institution and the assets as overlapping makes a certain kind of sense for very large corporations whose economic and political power is translatable into money. But often the assets would have a better chance to survive if the institution were shrunk or even dissolved; or the shareholders might think so. Agents of a group of shareholders in the United States Steel Corporation at one time years ago set forth the thesis that its shareholders would benefit substantially by the voluntary dissolution of the corporation, so that its inefficient parts would not burden its efficient parts. Needless to say, the management did not agree. The issue, in less drastic form, is a permanent one in the corporate world. Decisions on whether to expand or contract are always before a chief executive, to be measured in the values of more than one set of players. The urge to get bigger for the sake of being bigger may not originate only in management. As an organism, the corporation has a peculiar tendency to grow with a seeming purpose of its own, apart from the motives of specific individuals and groups.

The values of the managers play an important role in operations throughout a corporation, especially under a decentralization which necessarily leaves sets of decisions to be made down the line; one could not adequately model a game with a corporate player without taking the managers' values into account. But at the level of the chief executive, the conflict lies between the values of management as a whole and those of the shareholders as a whole. It is these that the chief executive attempts to reconcile.

The chief executive. His values are typically the same as management's, plus more of the same and the power of control; and of course, he may also be a shareholder himself as well as a fiduciary for the others. Since he makes the decisions, his desires, style, and personal objectives—not necessarily expressible in terms of earnings and assets—can also be expected to play a part in his judgments.

COMBINING VALUES

The act of combining values is not abstract. Policy is formed concretely out of combined values and, once formed, becomes a routine. One doesn't like to think about trading lives for money, yet engineers in their highway designs do it every day routinely. The chief executive of a corporation, having in mind the monetary values of the shareholders and the survival values of management, has also to ask himself what they will think about other not easily monetizable things such as the value of corporate prestige, politics, law, the welfare of the employees, and the social role of the corporation.

The effect of corporate prestige on the stock market,

though real, is vague, and so it is not clear how much the chief executive should pay for it in the manifold ways by which it is attained and preserved. Politics, which affects the rules of the game, is an ever-deepening and hazardous subject in this era of intimate government-business interactions; some of its effects, monetary and other, are clear in the present, some stretch into a future that is dim for all. Businessmen have reason to worry that a government that does favors may discriminate. Legal decisions—crowding the law, risking antitrust, and the like—also have long-range effects difficult to measure. The welfare of employees obviously bears on morale and so on the quality of the employees and their productivity and has links with the prestige and social role of the corporation. It costs money and has an outcome only partly measurable in money. The social role of the corporation is critically involved with the standards of behavior of society, which do not rest on individual judgments of value; but in fields where such standards do not exist or are breaking up, the chief executive has to make a judgment, which he may impose on the corporation as an act of citizenship. One chief executive will rationalize it as paying off vaguely in money; another as essential to survival. Both wonder what the shareholders will accept.

It seems hardly possible for anyone to combine all these values in a single scale of numbers such that when confronted with a choice of alternatives he could pick the one whose outcome represented the highest number on the scale. But this ideal concept, which provides numbers for abstract games, serves as a criterion for wonder about what happens or doesn't happen when one makes a complex choice in the real world. The fact is, when all the caveats are taken, that several of the corporate values mentioned above push the players toward cardinal numbers. Combining money with money in dimensions of time—for example, today's money with tomorrow's money—is not simple but leads toward measure. Trade-offs of long- and short-term gains in the absence of risk are fairly standard and can be reduced to borrowing money. You invest the money for the future and pay a current rate. But the dimension of risk is hardly avoidable when the subject is future prospects, and risk, too, leads to numbers. Choosing between alternative risks, as noted, tends to require one to say how much one prefers one alternative to another. Small risks can be insured, but a large risk—a new product, a new business—calls for a judgment of value. Executives often use cut-off points, with piecemeal decisions in a series of steps instead of one-shot risks, and make an irrevocable commitment only when the outcome seems to be a sure thing. There are notable exceptions: the Edsel car that the Ford company produced and that failed at a loss of hundreds of millions; Sewell Avery's contraction of Montgomery Ward in the expectation of a depression after World War II, which didn't materialize; William Zeckendorf's opposite gamble in the early sixties that inflation was coming soon—it came too late (had they won their gambles they'd be superstars of business). Such gambles are common enough in the business world, yet typically executives of large companies are averse to large risks if they are avoidable—excluding for the moment the big merger in which the parties to it necessarily bet their whole companies.

The observations of the head of a multibillion-dollar oil company suggest a common way of thinking about risk. In a conversation with the author he declared that the objective of his company was to make money, but he immediately qualified that by saying that he was not prepared to take a good gamble if its magnitude was unsuitable. "You ask in particular how I would feel about investing $100 million of the corporation's money with a fifty-fifty chance of losing it or making $500 million? Well, as it usually goes, there would be some chance of making less than the maximum, maybe $200 million or $300 million. But if it were a case of $500 million or broke, I would seldom elect to take it even at fifty-fifty. . . . I duck first of all because of the uncertainty regarding the numbers. . . . In the end, how much gamble we would take depends on how much money is involved—$25 million is one thing, $250 million is something else. I would risk the smaller number but not the larger one, which would, if lost, mar the earnings."

As I understood the complexity of his thought, he observed that in his world gambles do not usually show up so starkly as a fifty-fifty chance of a definite outcome; it would be more realistic to expect a range of possible outcomes. But though he had the resources to take a big gamble, he would not take it even if he were certain about the probabilities, because he also put a high value on the assurance of maintaining the earnings record. That would be, at least in part, a question of what gambles the shareholders would accept. In the end, he was able to suggest a magnitude of $25 million which he would risk on a fifty-fifty chance of getting back $125 million. Thus, despite some skepticism about cardinal numbers as a description of realities, he worked his way through the problem without leaving them.

Other forces, too, push corporate values into cardinal numbers. A large number of transactions tend to result in linear money. Corporate routines, set by policy, introduce repetitive transactions, and these lead to the same end. Bargaining, as noted, elicits both a range of numbers and a precise point of settlement. And not least, the fiduciary relationship of the chief executive to the shareholders leads him to treat the value of their money with definite measures. All these things —risk, time, trade-offs, numerous transactions, routines, bargaining, and the fiduciary relationship—reinforce one another to give the corporation a main line of values in hard numbers. And with all the inherent difficulties and their doubts concerning numbers, executives use them amply in making decisions.

Then there's the outcome, which is not a single number but an ensemble: survival, profit, prospects, and "another day went by."

Then comes the quantum jump from manageable to not-so-manageable decisions, which used to come up only on rare occasions. But for the chief executives of thousands of corporations, the one-sided game of combining the values of quiescent players ended in the mid-1960s. For a long time share-holders had been satisfied to look at the scorecard and read how the corporation was doing on return on investment, growth of sales, and dividends. But in the stock market boom of the sixties, shareholders changed their way of valuing corporate outcomes. They began scoring a chief executive's performance mainly on the performance of the stock in the market and on intangible prospects and growth of earnings per share as determinants of market price.

Numerous chief executives found that they could not increase their earnings per share fast enough in their existing markets to satisfy their shareholders. So, led by the conglomerators and in part in defense against them, they turned to acquisitions. Fictional numbers came into the scoring with juggled accounting and "funny money," a magicianship not altogether new but more flamboyantly employed, which made the outcomes difficult to measure. But the game broke out everywhere. And with outsiders, friendly and unfriendly, coming into corporations to negotiate mergers and bidding for control of corporations in the stock market, each set of players inside corporations consulted their own values and looked for the most profitable deal they could get. Even those corporations that were not directly threatened felt the tremor. The rise of the conglomerates in the late 1960s thus shook the traditional stability of corporate business, and the subsequent fall of so many of them did not quite restore it. What sort of game business was to be with corporations interacting more freely posed an unresolved question. At the same time changes in society were erupting all around. Confronted with takeovers, the threat of a consumer revolution, and awareness of new issues of pollution, discrimination, and the like, the corporate executive's one-sided model fell apart. To deal with this situation, he needed to turn to the concept of a many-sided game with its interactive strategies and values.

5

J. PAUL GETTY:
THE INFLUENCE OF THE VALUES
OF A STRATEGIC CORPORATE PLAYER

The fantastic Argentine poet Jorge Luis Borges wrote a story of a man who so identified himself with Cervantes that he wanted to write *Don Quixote*, not another *Don Quixote* "but the *Don Quixote*," and embarked on the project of writing it. There is evidence to suppose that J. Paul Getty similarly wanted to be John D. Rockefeller, and not just the man but his works. Rockefeller's works are well known: the Standard Oil Company, a billion or more dollars, the richest American. As to Rockefeller's true purpose, his grandson and companion Fowler McCormick observed to the author, "I suppose he wanted to make a fortune." Two generations later Getty's works are almost equally well known: the Getty Oil Company, a billion or more dollars, the richest American (richer than the other contemporary candidate, Howard Hughes, according to *Fortune*). He, too, wanted to make a fortune. One expects a few personal differences. Rockefeller stayed in the United States. Getty is an expatriate. And Rockefeller would not have written for *Playboy*, as Getty did. But these are minor differences. Getty performed Rockefeller's works, all but the last chapter, the creation of an oil company whose service stations appeared from coast to coast. He gave up in the course of the game that would have made that possible, which is the subject of this chapter.

Getty was not prepared to reveal his eminence as the richest American. *Fortune* discovered it a number of years ago when he was living in obscurity in the George V Hotel in Paris. Getty was irked by the discovery. Everyone began to expect him to pay more for personal services. He rejected progressive taxation by waiters at the dinner table, moved to England, bought a country estate, Sutton Place, outside of London, and took up residence in its seventy-three-room manor house. The rooms were originally designed in proportions suitable for visits by Henry VIII. And so Getty, a lone bachelor after several marriages, moved into a corner of the great house and employed the rest of it as a museum for his collection of paintings. In a hallway outside his apartment sits the famous pay telephone booth for visitors (another minor difference from the dime-dispensing Rockefeller).

A small, somewhat frail, gaunt, gentle-speaking man, he takes a pastoral walk on the grass and through the garden outside his corner, putting one foot before the other in short staccato steps. Over tea late in the day he speaks of his business in maxims and aphorisms that have specific tangible reference. "Don't get too widely spread out. Don't try to advance too rapidly. The thing in business is to distinguish between the possible and the impossible and stick to the possible." In these words he described what may have been the most important business decision of his life.

From his corner of the great house, with the aid of a few secretaries, and more by mail than telephone, Getty directs his one-and-a-half-billion-dollar world-wide oil business (as measured by its 1973 sales), which includes oil and gas fields in the Middle East and North America, an international fleet of tankers, refineries, and gas stations.

Getty won his empire largely in a running contest with the Standard Oil Company of New Jersey. His goals of fame (of a certain kind) and fortune then came into conflict in a key game in California in the 1960s, when he got into some interactions with several oil companies larger than his and had to choose between his ambitions. As the game was played, it showed the decisive influence of the values of a strategic corporate player in a struggle between corporations. The story is based on interviews with J. Paul Getty and his executives, including his late son and executive vice president, George F. Getty II, and on other interviews and observations.

THE PLAYERS

- ▣ J. Paul Getty
- ▣ George F. Getty II
- ▣ Standard Oil Company (New Jersey), now Exxon
- ▣ Several major oil companies operating in California

Jean Paul Getty made his first million as a wildcatter in 1916 at the age of twenty-three, working in partnership with his father, George F. Getty, a Minneapolis lawyer who had gone into the oil business in what is now Oklahoma. His father died in 1930, leaving an estate of about $15 million, part of which became the Sarah C. Getty Trust. This trust was worth about three-quarters of a billion dollars in the late sixties and was by far the largest single shareholder in the present Getty Oil Company.

Both J. Paul Getty and the Getty companies were able to raise cash after the 1929 crash, and so for them the depression was an opportunity. He kept a diary then, from which he later wrote his autobiography (*My Life and Fortunes*, Duell, Sloan & Pearce, 1963). In it he set down the objective that he would pursue for thirty years, as follows: "In 1932, many oil stocks were selling at all-time lows. They were spectacular bargains. . . . The more I thought about the matter the more convinced I became of the feasibility of putting together a completely integrated and self-contained oil business, one which engaged not only in oil exploration and production, but also transportation, refining and even retail marketing. . . . This was the goal."

To this end he studied the seven integrated oil companies in California, and picked No. 7 in sales, called Tide Water Associated Oil Company,[1] as the one he would try to gain control of. The company had what he regarded as a good marketing organization, and as it produced only about 50 percent of its crude requirements, he could integrate his own oil production into its operations. He bought his first shares of Tidewater in March 1932 at $2.50 a share. (By the sixties the value of each share had multiplied more than a hundred fold.) Throughout 1932 and 1933, he and the Getty interests acquired about 700,000 shares of bargain-priced Tidewater common stock.

Getty then collided with the Standard Oil Company (New Jersey), which in 1930 had divested itself of working control

[1] This was later changed to Tidewater Oil Company, the name used hereafter for convenience.

of Tidewater by selling its approximately one million shares
to a holding company, Mission Securities, Limited, on a time-
payment plan. In 1934, when Getty had his campaign for
control under way, Mission failed in its payments. Jersey
Standard took back the stock and, with it, control of Tidewater. Getty says that the Tidewater management, backed
by Jersey Standard, then tried to block his campaign for control. Getty wrote a letter to Jersey Standard which suggested
that the social norms concerning competition might be in his
favor. "My contention," he said afterward, speaking of that
letter, "was that a large corporation such as Standard should
not have a controlling interest in a smaller competing company such as Tidewater."

Subsequently, Jersey Standard put its Tidewater stock in a
new company, Mission Corporation. Jersey Standard, among
its many possessions, then owned a controlling interest in the
Skelly Oil Company, which operated in the Midwest, and it
also put this interest into Mission. Getty with his usual ap-
lomb then set his sights on gaining control of Mission Corporation, with a view to taking both Tidewater and Skelly away
from Jersey Standard. The big oil company apparently didn't
or couldn't try too hard to thwart his intentions.

By persistently buying up its shares, Getty got control of
Mission in 1937. That did not give him sole control of Tidewater, since Mission's holdings, even combined with Getty's
holdings in Tidewater, still fell short of a majority interest.
But after a complex series of corporate maneuvers over many
years, Getty finally, in 1951, gained "clear-cut numerical
control" of Tidewater and in 1953 elected all of its directors.
In these maneuvers he also got control of Skelly.

That same year, 1953, Getty struck oil in the Middle East.
In 1949 Getty Oil Company had obtained a sixty-year con-
cession from the king of Saudi Arabia to extract and market
Saudi Arabia's 50 percent interest in the crude-oil products
from the 1,800-square-mile coastal Neutral Zone. (The emir
of Kuwait awarded the concession for the other 50 percent to
Aminoil, a consortium formed by Signal Oil, Ashland Oil and
Refining, Phillips Petroleum, and other oil companies; Amin-

oil and Getty Oil operated together in the area.) The first strike proved to be low-gravity, low-grade crude—i.e., heavy oil with high sulfur content. Such oil requires special refinery equipment to reduce the sulfur and to get high yields of gasoline. Although the quality of the oil was disappointing, Getty began developing what he hoped was a big field.

The year after its first strike in the Neutral Zone, Tidewater began to close down its old refinery at Bayonne, New Jersey, and to build a new and efficient one at Delaware City, Delaware, with a capability for efficient handling of Getty's Neutral Zone high-sulfur crude. It was completed late in 1957. Mainly to get funds to build the new refinery, Tidewater went more than $300 million into debt. To bring in foreign oil the company also assembled its own tanker fleet. All this gave Tidewater a much heavier debt load than is customary in the oil business. Nevertheless, the future seemed promising.

In that same period Tidewater sold off its modest marketing organization in the Midwest—where it was competing with Skelly—and expanded its marketing on both coasts. Between 1954 and 1960 its service stations grew in number from about 1,900 to 3,900; the investment outlay for them came to $120 million. Much of this expansion took place in California. To back it up, Tidewater spent $60 million modernizing its refinery near San Francisco, and in that market, where Tidewater had choice sites, it was probably No. 1. But in California as a whole, in 1961 it was still No. 7.

With Tidewater expanding its refining and marketing in the eastern and western United States, Skelly Oil entrenched in the midcontinent, and Getty Oil tapping the Middle East for crude, Getty's grand design, more or less as he had conceived it at the outset in 1932, began to take shape. The setup suggested a great new integrated international oil company with nationwide retail marketing throughout the United States. And indeed, early in 1959, two of the Getty companies, Tidewater and Skelly, began to negotiate a merger. It was not far-fetched for Getty to imagine the name "Getty Oil" becoming a household word like "Standard," "Gulf," or "Shell," which was the kind of fame he aspired to.

But now Getty ran into unexpected trouble. When he began expanding Tidewater in 1954, he gambled that foreign oil would be freely marketed in the United States. That prospect dimmed in 1957 when the federal government established voluntary oil import restrictions. Getty was hopeful either that they would not be made mandatory or that he would get special consideration for Tidewater's new Delaware refinery. But two years later, in 1959, the government set rigid import quotas, which changed the direction of the oil industry for years to come (imports were not decontrolled until 1973). One reason advanced for the quotas was national security, based on fear of a Middle East cartel (a version of which came about anyway). But there was also another side to it. In most oil-producing states of the United States, authorities limit production of crude oil on the basis of estimated consumption, and prorate the market among the existing producers. The price of domestic oil thereby is kept up. Domestic producers feared that substantial quantities of imported foreign oil would break down these arrangements. Getty felt that he had been outplayed by the powers that be. The quota system reduced the market for his Middle Eastern crude and restricted the inflow of oil that Tidewater's new refinery was mainly designed for and for which Tidewater had gone into debt. These debts now played a part in blocking the Tidewater-Skelly merger negotiations; their managements, of course, had fiduciary obligations to their public shareholders,[2] and they were unable to agree on estimates of the relative value of the two stocks.

---

[2] Getty Oil, Skelly, and Tidewater were public companies, with their own boards of directors and many public shareholders, and were subject to the laws and conventions of control that apply to such companies. J. Paul Getty himself was not even a director of Tidewater, much less an officer, though his son George F. Getty II was its president. Yet people in the industry naturally thought of the potential merger of these companies in terms of the older Getty and his empire, and one is inclined to speak of all the big decisions about them as his decisions. There is no doubt that he had effective control of all three companies.

These setbacks did not necessarily mean that Getty's goals had become unattainable. Oil is a dynamic business and luck or strategic advantage could again turn his way (the boom in domestic off-shore drilling, the Alaska prospect, the end of quotas, the price rise set by the international oil cartel and the resulting energy crisis, for example, were still to come). He still had in Tidewater and Skelly two of the essentials of a nationwide Getty Oil Company. It was only in part, however, his taking of chances that decided matters. Even more decisive was a new game in which Getty and others had a part in making strategic choices.

Tidewater, with its debt and altered prospects, was not in the best of shape—it was at any rate far from what Getty had planned—when a new game started up in California, its major market. The California retail gasoline market—especially Los Angeles and Orange counties, which accounted for more than half of it—was an extraordinarily big and growing one. The main question for its participating oil companies was how they would divide it. As George Getty, who was stationed there, remarked, until the end of the fifties, a number of major companies, among them Tidewater, had long been in the market and saw it "like the Mediterranean, a Roman lake." Then Gulf and others moved in, and in the early sixties several major oil companies made the strategic decision to do something to protect or increase their shares of the market. Shell, for one, had dropped from 12.4 percent of that market in 1958 to 11 percent in 1961 and was inspired not only to recoup its lost share but also to get a lot more. Shell and Texaco battled with Gulf; everyone was drawn in and, of course, anything that anybody got had to come out of someone else's share. In the struggle that followed, the aggressors employed four principal means: upgraded refineries with new economies of scale, improved and relocated service stations, new service stations at new locations, and price cuts—indeed, what was known as a "price war."

Getty was pessimistic about Tidewater's position in this game. As he himself would say later:

> It looks like the industry in the U.S. just evolved into a pattern of practically everybody except the market leaders losing money on downstream investments [i.e., refining and marketing]. I don't think it's hurt the market leaders. Marketing is one end of the business where they that have shall be given.
>
> The point I'm trying to make is this. You've got a well-run company. You buy oil land as efficiently as anyone, have surveys, drill wells, build tankers with maximum efficiency—you do all these things and you won't feel handicapped because you're smaller than other companies. But, when you want acceptance in the marketplace, you find there is a very definite handicap in being low man on the totem pole [i.e., Number 7]. And there isn't much you can do about it because those companies fight desperately to maintain their position. You advertise, they advertise more; you build filling stations, they build filling stations. Everything the smaller fellow does, the competition does double. So where do you go from there? It's one of the things that's a fact of business life, that you're more or less frozen in that situation. It's not one of those deals that if you come out with a new invention, you build up a large volume of business almost immediately. You're not selling something that's revolutionary. You're selling gas—and the public apparently doesn't think there's too much difference in the various brands of gas. I don't see particularly that it's in the interest of the company or the industry to have four different brands of gas on practically every intersection. You'll see Shell on the first corner, Mobil on the second, Standard on the third, Texaco on the fourth. There's no doubt that from the standpoint of efficiency there's too much duplication in filling stations in America.

Getty's remarks need a word of interpretation. There is no necessary handicap in being "low man on the totem pole" if a company has sufficient size to get economies of scale. To the classical economist M. A. Adelman, Getty's observation suggests that Tidewater may have been a high-cost operator which lost money when the others at least broke even. It seems that Tidewater on the whole was in fact less efficient than others or than others were becoming in the California market at the time. Adelman's and Getty's views may be reconciled by viewing the issue as a game. If Tidewater is falling behind in a contest for shares of the market, owing to the fact that other companies are spending to become stronger and more efficient competitors in that market, Getty has a number of choices of response, and his judgment will be influenced by his values as the dominant strategic shareholder in Tidewater.

Getty had four principal options in the game.

One was to have Tidewater fight back in kind, paying the price in risky capital expenditures and low or zero profits for the duration of the game.

The second was to retrench and wait for the market to stabilize.

The third was to sell Tidewater's refinery and marketing assets and organization and get out of the West Coast gasoline market.

The fourth was to study the question of whether the others were breaking the rules of law and, if he thought so, to take action outside the purely economic game in a legal one.

These options raise questions about price wars, stabilization, and rules of the game.

Getty analyzed the price war in its relation to the rules of the game and, as we shall see, reached some decisive conclusions about the situation. But as the concept of a price war implies some sort of stability at higher prices before and after the price war occurs, let us look first at these boundaries. How one looks at them may depend on one's theory.

The price of anything in the standard version of classical economic theory is based on supply and demand and so is automatic. This theory cannot easily explain prices that to some considerable extent have been willed by the competing producers.

In game theory there is a way of looking at a stable market which has a kinship with classical economic theory. Assume that each producer is viewing the market independently, despite the fact that what each one does has some influence on what the others do. Each puts the strategies of his competitors into his calculations. Let us say, then, that each producer refrains from charging "too high" a price because he knows that others can profitably undercut him. Likewise, each refrains from charging "too low" a price because it is unprofitable. They seek an equilibrium that expresses a composite of their independent decisions.

It is easier to say this than it would be to model the game in California where there were perhaps sixty identifiable players, of whom seven were doing about 80 percent of the business. To present a game-theory model of the interactions of this large group would be an elephantine task. I do not have a picture of an elephant, however, because it is much too big. I do have a picture of a much smaller animal, say an amoeba, for comparison, which illustrates the desired principles. These principles are shown by game theorist Martin Shubik in a simple model of two producers, each with a choice of two strategies.

In the Shubik model, if the first producer chooses his first strategy, he gets either a medium-sized payoff (if the other chooses his own first strategy) or a somewhat better payoff (if the other chooses his own second strategy). If the first producer chooses his second strategy, he gets either a zero payoff (if the other chooses his own first strategy) or a large payoff (if the other chooses his own second strategy). The second producer is in the same predicament in reverse.

The reader is probably already aware that, even in so simple a model, a condensed verbal description of interacting strategies is difficult to follow. The following diagram may help (the first number in each box is the payoff to the first producer, the second number to the other):

SECOND PRODUCER

	Strategy 1	Strategy 2
FIRST PRODUCER Strategy 1	5, 5	7, 0
Strategy 2	0, 7	10, 10

The first thing to notice is that both producers can get their maximum payoff (10, 10) if each adopts his second strategy. But if they are competing, each runs the danger that if he chooses his second strategy and the other chooses his first strategy, he will get zero. On the other hand, if either of them chooses his first strategy, the worst he can do in any event is get a medium-size payoff (5, 5), and he might get more. Shubik's argument is that rational *competing* producers in this game should choose their first strategy. If both do, each gets a payoff which is relatively modest but guaranteed. Shubik further argues that if, in fact, both of them choose their second strategy and take their maximum payoffs, they may be colluding, for it would not be rational for them to do so without some sort of agreement, understanding, or trust.[3] If there were a rule against collusion in the market,

[3] Understandings need not be formal. The game theorist Anatol Rapaport has described how two players may arrive at a sense of trust by repetitive action. In the example diagrammed above, one player could go for a payoff of 10 with his Strategy 2 and repeat this a couple of times. If the other player goes along, they both stay there and take the maximum payoff. But if the other one insists on playing his Strategy 1, the first player reverts to his Strategy 1.

A much-discussed game model of the problem of mutual trust

such as antitrust rule, it would at least be a sign that the rule may have been violated. Contrariwise, if both were choosing their first strategies and so getting the medium payoffs, that would be a sign that they were playing as individuals, non-cooperatively.

Shubik's matrix model above illustrates the principles of cooperative and non-cooperative strategies. Game theory diverges at this point into two quite different approaches to a game. In theory, one can expand the above model to include any number of players, each playing independently against the strategies available to all of the others. In the absence of contrary information, a plausible case could be made that that is how the oil companies in California played the game. But when a game has more than two players, it is also possible that they will cooperate by forming coalitions.

From the cooperative point of view, in the California oil game one may look beyond the firm, cartellike agreements that are forbidden by law in such a market to hazier alignments. One may look, for example, for the group that is hovering around a profitable price level in the market—the Roman lake—to their satisfaction and without disruption from any other group. Now if the group members get into a price war, one may see them as just bumping against each other in a transitory way to readjust their division of the essentially stable collective profit. Economist M. A. Adelman, however, has pointed out that independent gasoline sellers in California have different costs and different incentives, and so tend to stay out of even the most tenuous of alignments and threaten to break them up with lower prices. If, however, the independents' threat is only a modest one, though it has to be recognized by the others, one could consider whether there is not a business norm operating that allots a place in the market and a payoff to the independents. If one could

is "the prisoner's dilemma," attributed to A. W. Tucker. Anatol Rapaport and Albert M. Chammah have written a notable book on the subject: *Prisoner's Dilemma: A Study in Conflict and Cooperation* (Ann Arbor, Michigan: University of Michigan Press, 1965).

model a game of this magnitude, with the non-strategic consumers in it for their payoff, one should be able, by varying the conditions in the model, to get some idea of who gets what under those different conditions. Or, leaving the consumers out except as the providers of the potential gains in the market, one should be able to glean something about the payoffs to the producers and the stability of their alignments.

The practical difficulties of observing and interpreting such interactions and weighing the outcomes were in fact precisely the difficulties that Getty tangled with. How long would he have to wait for the "normal" market to return? What would the bumping around cost him? What would his payoff be when the redivision of the market was resolved? What strength did he have to influence the outcome? Thus, although he had the usual risks of chance to wonder about, the principal uncertainty he faced lay in what the other oil companies would choose to do in response to his response to them.

Recall that Getty's options were to fight, retrench, sell, or sue (or some combination of these moves). If he saw the situation as one of bumping around for a while with an eventual return to the profitable clustering around a higher price in a core of stability, he could choose either to fight hard or to retrench, depending on how he gauged his strength and how much of his fortune he was willing to stake. Other companies had resources greater than Tidewater's. The cost of fighting hard for shares of the market would be high, both in refining and marketing. Retrenchment—essentially scaling down the scope of his operations to its strongest elements—would be moderately profitable but would end in a smaller share of the market. He had to judge the value of these alternatives.

Getty's remarks quoted earlier indicate his belief that there was an inherent handicap in Tidewater's being No. 7 in size in this contest. He also, as noted, could not see the value of four gas stations on a corner, which suggests a view of the marketing game different from those who put four on a corner. George Getty observed that his own marketing people favored a fight but that they were not profit-minded. "They would like to see a gas station in the middle of the Pacific. We [Tidewater's executives]," he said, "could afford to think only of profit and it was nominal. The big companies are spending the small ones out of business with $100,000 gas stations. If one does it on a corner, the other three have to do it, and for the extra $50,000 you don't get more gallonage. You only hold even. If we put that extra $50,000 in a service station, that's one well we are not going to drill. If you love to sell, you can build service stations until you are bankrupt. I had to keep in mind the whole company, a balancing act, a lot of things. The profit motive comes first. When you make a profit you can do things. Otherwise, oblivion."

Needless to say, these judgments of value made by the Gettys, father and son, and Tidewater's executives, led to their rejection of the first option. No matter what else they thought of doing, this judgment drove them to the second option, retrenchment. As a result, Tidewater's share of retail automotive gasoline sales sank from 6.9 percent in 1960 to 5.7 percent in 1963, and it was still pointed downward. On the other hand, Shell, for example, by that year had pushed its share up to 14.6 percent, and its share was still moving up.

In November of 1963 Tidewater moved to its third option, namely, to get out of the West Coast market. The company agreed to sell its West Coast marketing, together with its refinery and five tankers, to Humble Oil & Refining Company (a wholly owned subsidiary of Jersey Standard, Getty's old adversary from whom he had captured Tidewater). The Department of Justice, however, blocked the deal, and Tidewater went on retrenching.

The following year, 1964, Tidewater's executives studied their fourth possible option. They concluded that their major competitors were violating the rules of law and that they had grounds for turning from the purely economic game to a contest over the rules of the game. Tidewater sued Richfield Oil

Corporation, Shell, Socony Mobil Oil Company, Standard Oil of California, Union Oil Company of California, Texaco, and others, who as a whole represented a little more than 75 percent of the California market for taxable gasoline. Tidewater charged them with selling gasoline below cost for the purpose of injuring Tidewater and other competitors, contrary to California law.

For this contest over the rules, Tidewater executives and lawyers made a model, as follows: The California rule of law stated, "It is unlawful for any person engaged in business within this State to sell any article or product at less than the cost thereof to such vendor . . . for the purpose of injuring competitors or destroying competition."

Tidewater's complaint, despite its legal jargon, put its central matter simply:

> Beginning on or about September 13, 1964, and continuing to and including the date of the filing of this Complaint, service station dealers supplied by defendants, and each of them, were engaged in selling gasoline to the consuming public at the following locations and at the following retail pump prices, which prices are being charged at various service stations supplied by defendants throughout the area.

Supplier of Station	Location	Regular Gasoline Price per Gallon
Richfield Oil Corporation	Atlantic and 4th St., Long Beach, California	23.9 cents
Shell Oil Company	Willow and Santa Fe, Long Beach, California	23.9 cents
Socony Mobil Oil Company, Inc.	Pacific Coast Highway and Santa Fe, Long Beach, California	23.9 cents
Standard Oil Company of California	Daisy and Willow, Long Beach, California	23.9 cents

Supplier of Station	Location	Regular Gasoline Price per Gallon
Texaco, Inc.	Cherry and Spring, Long Beach, California	23.9 cents
Union Oil Company of California	Willow and Santa Fe, Long Beach, California	23.9 cents
Wilshire Oil Company of California	Fourth and Alamitos, Long Beach, California	23.9 cents

Said prices include State and Federal gasoline taxes totalling 11.00 cents per gallon. Plaintiff is informed and believes and upon such information and belief alleges that said prices also include a dealer "margin" or "mark-up" of a minimum of 4.5 cents per gallon, and that hence defendants' sales prices for sales directly to their service station dealers are no more than 8.4 cents per gallon based on the above retail pump prices. Plaintiff is informed and believes and upon such information and belief alleges that certain defendants distribute their gasoline products to their service station dealers by means of either "commission" or "purchase and sale" wholesale distributors, and that in such cases the sales price realized by such defendants is even less than in the case of sales made directly to their service station dealers.

In addition, plaintiff is informed and believes and on such information and belief alleges that defendants, and each of them, use various and elaborate systems of discounts and rebates in the sale of gasoline to their dealers. In such cases the sales price realized by such defendants is even less than the price of 8.4 cents per gallon as set forth above.

Plaintiff is informed and believes and on such information and belief alleges that defendants cannot manufacture and deliver Regular gasoline to their service stations in the area at a cost of less than 11.00 cents per gallon.

> As a proximate result of defendants' said conduct, plaintiff and other competitors of defendants have been injured in that they have suffered losses in profit per unit of gasoline and other petroleum products sold. Competition has been and is now being destroyed and said injury to competitors and destruction of competition will tend to create a monopoly in the manufacture, distribution and sale of gasoline and other petroleum products to the detriment of the general public in the form of higher gasoline prices in a controlled market. Unless defendants, and each of them, are restrained and enjoined from selling in the aforesaid area at a price less than the cost thereof to defendants for the purpose of injuring competitors and destroying competition, plaintiff will and other competitors of defendants will suffer irreparable damage and injury.

Thus Getty contended that the major companies were selling gasoline at least 2.6 cents per gallon below cost. And he contended also that they were doing this "for the purpose of injuring competitors of said defendants or destroying competition" contrary to the rule of law. He asked the court to stop the defendants from selling regular gasoline below 11 cents per gallon. The complaint was signed by Tidewater's lawyers and by George Getty, as president.

It is noteworthy that Getty did not charge an antitrust conspiracy against him, but only that the companies he named were clustered at a price below cost. But the rule of law had two parts; Tidewater had to prove both that they sold below cost *and* that they did this for the purpose of injuring competitors or destroying competition. This was surely a game played in a shadowy area of business interactions. For if each company individually strove to increase its share of the market, it would necessarily be to the "injury" of anyone who had to yield a share; and if they did not individually strive to increase their shares of the market, they would have to divide the market in some other way, perhaps cooperatively. It is not surprising that a seller of standard gasoline charges the same price as a nearby competitor. Getty's contention, it seems, came down to his judgment that with his weaker resources he could not meet the alleged below-cost competition without suffering financial injury, nor could he stay out of it without suffering a loss in Tidewater's share of the market. Either way, Getty could not see a satisfactory resolution of the game for him.

In denying Tidewater's charges and asserting that Tidewater had not proved its case, the defendants emphasized the essential link in the rule of law between the price and the purpose. The essence of their affirmative defense, as stated by Texaco, was that "the prices which it charged for gasoline . . . were established in an endeavor in good faith to meet the legal prices of one or more competitors selling similar products in the area of Los Angeles and Orange Counties in the ordinary course of trade."

When Getty filed the suit on September 18, 1964, at Los Angeles, a formidable confrontation loomed between him and the major oil companies in California. But in a surprise move, one year later, on September 3, 1965, Getty relented and requested the dismissal of the suit, and it stopped there. George Getty explained rather anticlimactically that Tidewater anticipated that the Federal Trade Commission would issue regulations covering gasoline marketing, including industry-wide guidelines to determine the cost of gasoline.

The following July, the Gettys closed a deal with Phillips Petroleum Company to sell Tidewater's western refining and marketing facilities for about $110 million and abdicated the West Coast market.[4] In 1967 Getty arranged to merge what remained of Tidewater into the Getty Oil Company.

[4] The government sued to dissolve the deal on antitrust grounds, but it was completed anyway. In November 1973 a federal court decided in favor of the government and ordered Phillips Petroleum to divest itself of former Tidewater properties. The U. S. Supreme Court declined to hear an appeal and so in 1975 Phillips Petroleum was working out how to do it.

Getty Oil signs now appear on about 2,500 eastern service stations. In the Midwest, Skelly Oil Company remained Getty-controlled but unintegrated with Getty Oil Company's operations. Thus did Getty fail in his ambition to build a nationwide Getty oil company at the retail level. Instead, he went for the money as he saw it; that is, to the making and conserving of money, and in that he succeeded. The present Getty Oil Company prospers.

Getty of course believes his was the wise decision. But not all oil men make the same judgments. A corporate institution controlled by a management bureaucracy might have been expected to act otherwise, basing their decision on other values—the survival of the institution and all that would mean for jobs, power, status, etcetera. Not long after Getty left the California market, the late William K. Whiteford, once chief executive of Gulf, made this observation to the author: "J. Paul Getty was always a production man. If he had stayed in California, he would be okay now. There was a fight for gallonage and he miscalculated future prices. He always made money in crude oil."

Thus the professionals disagreed on what was the best course to take in the game. The story shows, however, that to understand a corporate game, one must start with the values of the strategic players. If they played cooperatively, they needed to understand one another's values. But if any one of them decided to go his own way, as Getty finally did in selling out, he needed only to consult his own values and the strategies on all sides. He could be indifferent to how they made out with their values.

6

COOPERATIVE GAMES: CHAOS AND STABILITY

A cooperative game is one in which the players have common interests and are allowed to get together and act jointly. Although in the real world there are some rules limiting cooperation, economic activity is at root cooperative; hence cooperative games are at the center of economic life.

In their search for solutions to cooperative economic games, John Von Neumann and Oskar Morgenstern came to focus their attention on the role that society plays in bringing about the division of its wealth. It is thirty years since they published their great work, and during this time other game theorists, working intensively on economic games, gradually shifted the focus of their solutions from society to the sheer economics of cooperation. As a consequence, one of the most important new developments in economic game theory, and by the same token one of the hopeful developments in contemporary economic thought, is the solution called the "core." The term is an invention of game theory—there is no commonplace word for its logic of pure cooperative economics—and it has the right connotations. Its principal feature is that it is as quintessentially economic as classical economic theory and yet has the realism, absent in classical theory, of recognizing the centrally cooperative character of economic life. The core of a game is, as we shall see, a measure of stability in society.

Wrestling with the dragon of free will in cooperative games, Von Neumann and Morgenstern employed social standards to explain how players achieve stable solutions in these games. One might expect anything to happen when players have a free choice. But by invoking the standards of behavior or norms of society—custom, convention, tradition, mores, habits—the theorists narrowed the outcomes, an insight with some remarkable dimensions. In applying this insight to economic games, they perceived but left latent and undeveloped the related sphere of purely economic interaction which contemporary game theorists have now differentiated as the core of the game. The latter, putting their results together with those of Von Neumann and Morgenstern, have set forth some intriguing and not at all self-evident observations. One of these is that whereas political games tend toward instability, economic games tend to be stable and market games are always potentially stable, though this condition may not prevail over the contrary dispositions of society. The role of the social norm and the nature of the core, and the insights they give into cooperative games, will take some explaining, which is the aim of this chapter.

From the time of his earliest writing on games in 1928, Von Neumann showed his talent for understanding them in the skill with which he distinguished the uncertainties of free strategic choice from those of chance. He managed this simply by assuming that the players possessed complete information about the rules of the game, including the role of chance. The assumption, of course, was not realistic, except for games like chess—a strategic game with complete information.[1] But by making the assumption, he isolated and set up for exploration the kind of uncertainty that arises solely from the free choice of the players, the largely unknown world which became the special province of game theory. Likewise in his earliest writing, when he came to games with more than two players, he brought out their characteristic

[1] In chess, at the beginning of a game, each player knows all the rules of the game and in principle the strategies that derive from those rules. As play proceeds, each knows in principle all the previous moves that have been made or could have been made, that is, he knows where he is in the game tree.

feature—namely, cooperation in the form of coalitions—by suppressing or overlooking, for the occasion, the strategic details of move and countermove between the players. To do this he reduced the description of a cooperative game to the values of the coalitions that potentially could be formed in it and named this model "the characteristic function" form of the game. When the players form coalitions, he wrote, "a new element enters, which is entirely foreign to the stereotyped and well-balanced two-person game: struggle." "Struggle" was a strong word, but not for zero-sum games where, he noted, if there were three players, two could get together and "rob" the third. On the other hand, in the gainful and constructive games of economics, where the players would have both opposed and parallel interests, their interactions would take the form of contact between players milling around in search of membership in what might be for them the best and most stable coalitions. Then—remarkable discovery—in his search for the source of stability in coalitions, Von Neumann glimpsed the nature of its complement, chaos.

Understanding the relative value and stability of coalitions became the principal objective of the theory of cooperative games, or more precisely, of cooperative ways to resolve a game. After Von Neumann and Morgenstern together published their work, it became clear that their cooperative solutions to games distinguished, in effect, the different societies in which a game might be taking place—that is, the standards of behavior that are characteristic of the economies of different societies.

Real-life games are not always open to the eye, either in society at large or in the detailed operations of business. One's image of the structure of a real-life game may be obscured by a multiplicity of perceptions and by hazards built into the observable world which often block the view of actual or potential forces at work. The role of coalitions in real markets, for example, is partly obscured by antitrust law which, when effective, suppresses them. This, of course, only emphasizes the potential force of coalitions that in the absence of a rule of law would be expected to form. Yet even with this restriction, such as it is, the economy of the United States may be seen to be honeycombed with socially approved and legal group formations, not to mention those that are not approved or not legal, some shaped by hard economics, some by social norms or political intervention.

What game theorists see in their models may be seen in the real world in the newly active issues of pollution, discrimination, consumerism, and the like. It seems worth while to quote the remarks on this subject of a few chief executives of large corporations—made to the author in writing or interviews—because they give some idea of how economic agents in this age are dealing with the problem of reconciling their hard economics with changes in the large lines of society.

In 1921 Alfred P. Sloan, Jr., could say the primary objective of the General Motors Corporation was "to make money, not just to make motor cars," which contrasted with his chief rival Henry Ford's doctrine that making motor cars with a social purpose would result in a profit in money. Sloan could put the emphasis where he did because he took his social environment for granted. It was not necessary for him to say more than he said, and in saying it so precisely, he codified the dominant consciousness of business executives for much of this century.

The reflections of most executives today differ sharply from Sloan's doctrine and cut a wider swath than Ford's. Their key word is "issues." Take pollution, for example. The chief executive of an automobile company, talking in his Detroit office about having to redesign his product around antipollution devices, repeated the question I had asked him: "Why wasn't all this anticipated?" After a few moments' thought, he said, "Issues don't get dealt with until they become issues." A few miles away, on the shore of Lake St. Clair, the owner-president of one of the country's largest marinas sat in his office by a window brooding over the empty pleasure boats rolling in their wells and the deserted expanse of water condemned for a time for its mercury-poisoned fish. "We sell enchantment," he said. "I'm going to survive, but a lot of people around the lake aren't. Now we are trying to do something about it politically and perhaps legally, but why, you ask, didn't we do something before to prevent this from happening? I don't know. What could we have done? Who's used to coping with problems like this?"

Elsewhere across the country other chief executives made similar observations of which these are characteristic: "In the interests of stockholders and people in the organization, executives must concern themselves with public affairs and with social change—equal rights, equal opportunities, hard-core unemployed, the whole bit. Today these matters are equal with the obligation of making a profit, in contrast with former times when the businessman was only interested in profit." / "We have got to be engaged in social matters. Some businessmen say this is not true or even that it is a dangerous view, but it has come to just that." / "I got over a long time ago the feeling that business exists only to make a profit. . . . The social rules have changed." / "In the fabric of society, unless you make a contribution to enhance human values, your institution is in danger." / "We are being pushed, not reluctantly, into taking a wider role in the progress of society. We are putting our noses beyond the factory wall." / "There is more to social responsibility than economic gain in the short run. Short run is poor. We have to be in it because of the long-run effect on the company's profits." / "There are things you think you should do . . . which from a strict monetary approach would not appear to be good decisions. But you rationalize them to the ultimate spirit of the corporation." / "The knowledge of how to assume social responsibility is not there. It is a new problem."

Anyone bred in conventional economic thought might say that the words quoted above, if they may be taken at face value, sound more like the expressions of political animals than of executives doing billions of dollars' worth of business. The executives appear to meet the changing customs in a surprised sort of way, as unfamiliar subjects. Consciousness of issues is the central new event in their decision making at the policy level. Their remarks about wanting to go along with society, however, would have been just as valid in 1921, except that in the absence of issues they would not have seemed worth making on other than ceremonial occasions. The social standards for business then were stable enough to be hardly noticed operationally. Sloan's policy-making assertion simply instructed his executives to forget about everything but making money because every other relevant social condition then was stable. The game at large, in Von Neumann-Morgenstern language, already had its established broad "solutions" in the prevailing social standards and Sloan could get on with a narrower game with Ford.

How it happens that certain general ways of dividing the spoils in society are stable for periods of time and yet vulnerable to upsetting pressures, as in so many present instances, and how this vulnerability is related to stark economics, are as much the objects of wonder in the world of theory as in the real world. The standard mode of economic thought called classical economics, in which most business executives and other interested persons are trained, is not set up to understand them.

Classical economic thought is a story of the individual and of society as a whole, but not of intermediate groups. Its standard model, like all theoretical models, is an imaginary construct made of selected features of the world it is meant to represent. It describes economic society as large numbers of small decentralized units, each pursuing its own interests, and all governed by an impersonal price mechanism which automatically regulates supply and demand, thereby clearing markets of their goods. This is the well-known "free market" or perfectly competitive price system which always finds its point of equilibrium. The chief claim made for it is that it is efficient, that is, no one can get any more out of the system without taking something from someone else. If it results in socially unacceptable differences in income, these can be adjusted outside the model by taxing and redistributing the income (a rather casual way of referring to a complex political game on the side to satisfy economic dissatisfaction). The theory is highly developed—more than two centuries of work have gone into it—and its elegance and power of generality are widely acknowledged. It serves as an analytical tool of professional economists and probably always will; no other theory can safely go altogether against it. It is also a myth, and a reference point to which one can relate the contrary realities.

In the real world the classical model bears some resemblance to the clothing industry, stock markets, banking, hotels and numerous other service industries, and a multitude of detailed everyday transactions. One does not, of course, expect to find exact representations of an ideal model in real life; but the awkward thing about the classical model is that it forces one to contend with a vast region of exceptions. The theory, consequently, has its nether world where it attempts to account for the vagaries of reality. This world is occupied by intensely cultivated subtheories, or categories set up for investigation, each representing an effort to contain in a single useful and related concept what happens in the real world that does not happen in the standard model. These have been designated variously as "imperfect competition" (where, for example, the numbers of economic units are small and their sizes large), "externalities" (economic activities or their consequences, desirable or undesirable, outside of markets, e.g., pollution), "public goods" (air, water, what the government owns and operates, etc.), "transaction costs" (markets inhibited or blocked by the costs of their operation), and "market failures," a catch-all category.

The enormous scope of market failures in the real world is, of course, neither a fall into chaos nor a transformation into socialism but only one of the realities of a relatively free-exchange economy in a pluralistic society. Nor is it new. Air, water, public land and forests, dams, streets, police, schools, libraries, government research, money controlled by the Federal Reserve Board and the Treasury, and the like, throughout the large public area of the economy, represent goods that long ago were consciously plucked or unconsciously kept out of putative markets. Some of them—turnpikes, armies— are known to have had a pre-existence as markets. A water commissioner of ancient Rome, Frontinus (c. A.D. 100), wrote a book about the tradition of public aqueducts going back centuries before his time, with much concern about all sorts of illegal private schemes in his own day for purloining the water, schemes he thwarted by ingenious measurements and metering. The roads of ancient Rome, too, were public goods. In the decline and fall, some became local, private, and entrepreneurial; and turnpikes continued to be private enterprises until the nineteenth century when they went broke.

The standard market fails notoriously in the presence of pollution—the production and forced distribution of un-desired products—and also when economic activities external to a market are positive and benign. Much thought has been lavished on the beekeeper and orchardist exchanging pollen-izing services for nectar, usually without a market; and not trivially, for the economy blooms with beneficial exchanges outside of markets. And, of course, unrecorded billions of dollars' worth of economic values are produced communally in families, which a branch of women's lib would like to con-vert to a market.

But economic activity in the absence of any sign of a market is only the extreme phase of market failure. The standard market may also fail when an actual market exists, as when the number of traders on either side is small. Mar-kets may be thin, as when only a few shares of a stock are available for trading. The technology of a production line, giving increasing returns to scale, may reduce the number of sellers to a few—the typical situation in many industries. Groups of buyers or sellers may form to reduce the number of traders on either side of the market. In some markets the government itself may be the overwhelming buyer or seller.

The surprising thing about the events in the oil crisis of the 1970s, for example, if viewed as the play of a game, was not that the producing nations put up the price of oil and ran off with all the money. That was one of the things that could have happened anytime over a number of years. The surpris-ing thing is that the consuming nations were surprised. They put a high value on oil and took no strategic or coalitional measures in advance to protect themselves from the power and free choices available to the potential and ultimately real cartel.

When actual markets exist, the standard market within a country may also fail owing to manipulations of the rules. Getting the rules changed through law is a political act—a game on another level. Some of these manipulations may originate in society at large, but more striking is the phenomenon that many participants in markets—notably major corporations—are not always satisfied with the results of a free market. Members of the oil industry, for example, prefer production control, quotas, and subsidies to a free market and lobby for the view that the market in oil should be made to fail in the public interest as well as their own. They are not alone in their success in inducing a failure of the standard market. The failure of markets has been sought and welcomed not only by oil men but also by textile manufacturers, publishers, farmers, organized labor, and almost everyone in and around business. Markets have been attacked, bent, twisted, and molded into multifarious forms: government-regulated private monopolies, unions, trade associations, "fair trade," patents, copyrights. There have been labyrinthian alterations of almost every market by means of taxes, government expenditures, subsidies, quotas, tariffs, corporate structures, conventions of business behavior, professional ethics, and discriminatory standards. Often these arrangements have been secured by appeal to some public principle—national security, trade balance, education, employment. Some groups negotiate prices collectively in Congress by sheer political power. A good deal of the redirected money passes through to local economies and the general economy but not without marked effect on who gets what. To all this one should add the side payments, sanctioned and unsanctioned, on the table and under the table, made by economic agents to political agents here and abroad, and the quid pro quos, specified and unspecified, that are expected to complete such transactions.

•   •   •

Game theory is designed to comprehend any kind of economy, and it is particularly suited for analyzing a mixed economy with its social-political surroundings. Indeed, when the standard market fails, the situation becomes game theoretic. The point at which this happens can be identified quite precisely. The standard market, a game theorist will grant, is a satisfactory way to run the economy—until you make a judgment of value outside the price mechanism. The judgment becomes the basis of circumventing a market. A favorite example is the lighthouse. One does not now think of marketing the light from a lighthouse, but at one time presumably someone thought about it. Why was the judgment made that it would better serve society as a public good than as a private business? Reconstructing, baffling questions appear. How could the proprietor appropriate the light and exclude non-paying ships from using it? And if the intrinsic difficulty were surmounted, how would the buyer and seller bargain and what would be the cost of such bargaining? The economist Kenneth Arrow has conjectured that transaction costs— in the end the costs of running the economy, including the essential element of risk bearing—account most generally for the failure of markets to exist.[2] It is possible, in the instance of the lighthouse, that no one could be found willing to go into the business. But other questions are asked about other

---

[2] A condensed yet comprehensive and mainly verbal exposition of Arrow's view of transaction costs is given by him in a remarkable paper written for the U. S. Congress. See "The Organization of Economic Activity: Issues Pertinent to the Choice of Market Versus Nonmarket Allocation," *The Analysis and Evaluation of Public Expenditures: The PPB System*. A Compendium of papers submitted to the Sub-Committee on Economy in Government of the Joint Economic Committee, Congress of the United States. Vol. I. U. S. Government Printing Office, 1969, pp. 47–64. In line with his theory of transaction costs, Arrow criticizes economic game theory for not taking into account the costs of bargaining. This seems to be true of many economic game models but does not seem to be a necessary limitation. It does not contradict Arrow to observe that real players do not overlook the cost of playing a game. But it suggests an interesting problem for the modeling of real games, about which there should be more discussion.

public goods: could an entrepreneurial operation take good care of the multiple uses of Yellowstone National Park, including the protection of the headwaters of the great central and western river systems? Can a particular commodity be divided up, measured, or metered? Who could raise the private capital to go to the moon? What would the consequences be of commercializing the public schools? The presumption about all public goods—apart from ideological pros and cons—is that at least in the beginning they were preferred to a market because for one reason or another the prevailing powers judged that getting around the market with some other means seemed to represent a greater benefit to society.

A judgment of value enters into any species of market failure because it departs from and is essentially different from the automatic behavior prescribed for the traders in a standard market. Making such judgments is an event; automatons cannot make them, particularly when they involve the collective worth of things. Judgments of value, therefore, at once mark the end of the standard market and the beginning of a game. This is the meaning of the point made earlier that when the standard market fails, the situation becomes game theoretic. It holds, whether or not a market even exists. When no market exists, the economic situation can still be analyzed and played as a game.

Many institutions that reflect market failures—roads, schools, armies, parks, and the like—with origins in some earlier judgments of value, have become stabilized on a different basis. They are now taken for granted as the natural order of things. The distinction, which has not been greatly explored, is important for the understanding of a game. A judgment of value is made by individuals. The social norms that institutionalize the collective conduct of a society are a quite different phenomenon. In abiding by a social norm, orthodox individuals make no individual judgments about it; they act, in a sense, unconsciously or indifferently. Their freedom is the freedom to be a heretic (with the hope, perhaps, of becoming a heresiarch). The members of a society—

the players in its games—may be torn apart when they attempt to revert from social norms to judgment of values, as in the stresses today around the active economic and political issues.

Neither myths nor theories, of course, are troubled so much by realities as by other myths and theories. Economic game theory is designed not only to study the real economic life that falls outside the standard classical vision, but also to serve as a criticism of the classical model itself: model against model. Like classical theory, game theory, too, is an artifact (with its own problems), but one that makes some fundamentally different assumptions about the nature of economic life. The buyers and sellers of the standard model, as noted, are robots responding to a price mechanism. Game theory takes account of prices, but its focus is on compensations. It centers not on mechanisms but on human actors endowed with free will.

In the concept of a game, a new story emerges. Players with values and the capability of making free choices come together by their own consent to divide the proceeds of an economic activity. Their futures are joined, inasmuch as the choices made by one influence the outcomes and choices made by another. Their interests, as noted, are not exactly opposed: each would like to get all he can, but there are benefits to be created and shared, and if there are more than two players, they may form into groups. In this story, the individual would remain alone with what he had if he gained nothing more, in some sense, by cooperating with others. That is, he will join a coalition if he gains by his membership in it. The members of a group, in turn, must be satisfied that there is not another group that is more satisfactory. A set of groups may form which prefers that set to all others that could be formed. When all groups are satisfied that they are doing the best they can in the circumstances, the whole society is said to be satisfied. Its wealth should not be distributed in such a way that the whole society gets less than the total that is potentially available. But getting all it might get depends upon the peculiar fact that a society can create, on a given physical base, varying amounts of wealth in production and exchange. With free choice, within limits, granted to the players (though not necessarily to all of them: a game may also include passive players), the amount of wealth they create, as well as how they divide it, depends on the relations between the individuals, their groups, and society.

The wealth to be divided in a game is not something identifiable as industrial or pastoral, or even as a concrete thing, though of course most economic goods and services have fairly solid identities. But as game theory rests on values, it is how the players value things that counts. Game theorists do not provide the values or even espouse any particular theory of value. The values of the players are part of the description of the game; they belong to the rules, as it were. Game theorists hope that the description will include values that can be counted in cardinal numbers. To simplify matters in an economic game, they often take the lead of Von Neumann and Morgenstern and work with money. It is the easiest thing to work with—not surprisingly, as its qualities of measure and transferability had something to do with its invention. There are the well-known qualifications that money isn't everything, and that even when it is the only thing one has in mind, different amounts of it may not have proportional value to a person. The value of money, for example, can go up astronomically when one is short of it. Also there are varieties of near-money (commercial and bank paper, IOUs of various kinds, bonds, even stocks). To get a more comprehensive measure of values, some game theorists have invented an imaginary thing of value called the "util," an awful term with an etymological relationship to another awful term, "utility," which sank the whole theory of economic value in the nineteenth century. But none of the hundreds of more felicitous words for it in the English language alone—pelf, lucre, wampum, token—satisfactorily meet the criterion that it must combine all the values a person brings to bear on the act of choice in one transferable number. It is not a bizarre quest. People do combine values, though not always consistently, and though combining values is a subjective act, it may exhibit itself fairly clearly above ground.

The remarkable thing about wealth in cooperative games is that it varies with the coalitions that are formed. This corresponds to the remarkable fact that economic life is inherently cooperative. A coalition of buyer and seller is always constructive (though of course they may fail to find the best available deal). Each party to the exchange is in the deal by his own consent. Each gains by it. If one did not think so, he could withdraw and keep what he started with. When they have made the transaction whereby each has gained, the "society" of the parties has created more collective worth than existed before. Contrariwise, an exclusive coalition of all sellers in a market would be destructive; if they withheld their goods, they would injure themselves as well as the buyers by failing to make the trade by which they would gain. The same goes for the buyers; if all consumers, for example, broke off trading, they would starve.

The contrast between the standard model and game models grows even wider. The behavior of the participants in the standard model is pristine. The players in a game model are earthy and so is the theory. The theory looks for whatever might happen under any rules or lack of them. Its language comes directly from life. The struggles of the players take the form of cooperation, collusion, coalitions, contracts and understandings, threats (if only to join another group or to retire), double crosses, questions of credibility and trust, fairness and equity, the orthodox versus the heretic, competition, monopolies, oligopolies, cartels, favoritism, discrimination, quid pro quos, premiums, rebates, kickbacks, bribes, finders' fees, and other side payments, playing politics, manipulating the rules of markets, and more. Lurid as this list is, it represents what, to a great extent, is really going on or might go on if not constrained by some other force. Thus game theory is a theory of social strength and human frailty. It is hard-boiled analysis, but because it encompasses cooperation, the economist Paul Samuelson has called it "love in economics."

A MODEL OF CHAOS

Von Neumann and Morgenstern caught their glimpse of chaos in a model which they created of a "constant sum game" in which three players could gain a certain amount (call it $100) if any two could agree on a way to divide it among them. Coalitions were permitted. That is all one knows about the game except that the money is equally valued by the players and each of them wants to get all he can. How can they resolve the game?

The thing immediately noticeable about the possible outcome is that any coalition of two players can take all the money, leaving the third player with none. If, for example, two players get together and split 50-50, they have it won. The trouble is, however, that their coalition is not stable. The player getting 0 can come back with an offer to either of the others to split 60-40. A player with 50 will take 60 and give 40 to the one who had 0. Then the one who is left out of this distribution can offer 50 to the one who has 40 and these two now have a split of 50-50. And so on in the following manner:

PLAYERS	1	2	3
	50	50	0
	60	0	40
	0	50	50
	25	75	0
	0	80	20
	50	0	50
		to	
		infinity	

There is here no one coalition that does best and is unassailable, and nothing to tell anybody what to do about it. There is only an endless forming and re-forming of coalitions in a round-robin circularity in which every coalition is unsatisfied. On paper, this was chaos.

Reflecting on the fact that societies with all their groups

do nevertheless attain stability, Von Neumann and Morgenstern theorized that some barrier to this flux must exist in real life and that they should be able to find such barriers to resolve the game. They observed that the actors themselves, sensing the endless rigmarole, could collectively stop it—either through express agreement or some form of coordination, alignment, or concerted conduct—by invoking some standard of behavior that would either limit the freedom of some of the actors to negotiate with the others or limit the number of ways of dividing the benefits. This led to no single outcome, but it raised the possibility of a *set* of outcomes which could handle defections. A standard of behavior, or social norm, could do this, and so it became their solution. They came up with three broad standards.

One was discrimination. This solution says that two of the players agree to exclude the third from the negotiations, though not necessarily with no payoff at all. But the two discriminators would establish the payoff to the third player and proceed to bargain between themselves over the remainder. The significant thing was to diminish the negotiating power of the third player so that he would not be able to invite a defection from the coalition of the other two and so bring about a distribution more favorable to himself.

In simple numbers out of the above game model, a discriminatory solution could look like this:

PLAYERS	1	2	3
	10	10	80
	10	20	70
	10	30	60
	to	to	to
	10	80	10

Thus Players 2 and 3 in coalition have, in some way, agreed that they will allot $10 to Player 1, and they have a bargaining problem over how to divide the other $90. But in any case, there is no new coalition forming.

Von Neumann and Morgenstern were astonished to discover discrimination turning up in the game as a solution, despite the fact that under the rules all players were alike. Discrimination in game theory is not part of the rules of the game but a solution that may be found in it. The solution in the model is interpreted as a social standard, and it must always be a class or group rather than an individual who is discriminating (if it were an individual, it would belong to his personal values and therefore to the description, rather than the solution, of the game). The theory shows how the discrimination occurs and why it persists. Once formed, the discriminating coalition maintains itself because by excluding certain players from free participation, it assures itself of a collective gain. The coalitions in being, therefore, have the loyalty of their members and so are stable. Just how much each of them gets, as noted, is not determined here but will depend upon how the discriminators conclude matters with each other. The theory suggests how in these circumstances discrimination can be stable.

The second standard of behavior that would resolve this game, Von Neumann and Morgenstern discovered, was to divide the gain in a prescribed way among all the players without saying which ones will actually receive the gain. For example, they might follow a mode of division in which two players split the $100 equally without knowing which two of the three will split it, as follows:

PLAYERS	1	2	3
	50	50	0
	50	0	50
	0	50	50

This standard of behavior stops the infinite run of coalitions by not allowing anyone to offer anything to anyone else. It doesn't say where any player will land. It just regulates the players by saying that to be stable their whole set of distributions—potential coalitions—should form in this symmetrical pattern of equal splits.

Thus the discriminatory solution states the coalition that

will form but not the division; and the non-discriminatory solution states what the division will be but not what coalition will form.

But there is no prediction here either of the social standard that will be chosen or of the outcome when one is chosen. The topic is stability: whether the solution is stable. One can see in the model what this means.

Before a standard was prescribed, no form of distribution could resist change to another one; none was stable, hence the chaos. But when, for example, the non-discriminatory 50-50 standard came into being, it could resist change in the following way. We are considering, one will recall, not a particular distribution but a stable set of distributions: three of them, each an equal split. The whole set is stable within itself because only the player with zero in each distribution would want to change, and he cannot find a partner to form another coalition with him. So, since no particular distribution in the set dominates another one in the set, the solution is credited with internal stability.

Since the standard is, by interpretation, "the established order of society," it raises the question of how its followers will deal with heretics. In theory, if a heretic tries to dominate the arrangement from the outside with some other arrangement—as he is free to do—there will always be an effective counterobjection inside the established arrangement—short, of course, of a revolution which changes the standard. Again, look at the model. Any distribution other than the three 50-50s prescribed by the standard would give two players a payoff of less than 50. Since they prefer the distribution that gives each 50, they could be expected to turn back the heretic's proposal to go to some other distribution outside the set. The solution therefore is also credited with external stability. The standard thus keeps the solution stable both internally and externally.

One would like to know which coalition will actually form, but the solution goes no further than to describe the set. It has reduced the possibilities to a few and excluded all others for the duration of the standard. Coalitions must form—in fact or imagination—to realize the distributions. In the example, a particular 50-50 split would take place of course when two players form a coalition against the third.[3]

The game in this model has the peculiarity that the sum of the gains to the players remains constant no matter how they divide it. The arrangement of payoffs thus is always symmetric: more here, less there. Such a game has only the two types of Von Neumann-Morgenstern solutions which I have described. Furthermore, this game is not typical of economic life, where the payoffs are not symmetric. The total payoff of the typical economic game is non-zero-sum: it varies with the coalitions that are formed. And so Von Neumann and Morgenstern devised a third solution for productive economic games, which takes the form of side payments between certain players in a bargaining pattern established by a standard of behavior. A different model will demonstrate this and also lead to other solutions, notably the "core."

THE FARMER GAME

The game here is an old one of auctionlike bidding which, with variations, has served for almost a century to illustrate both a classical approach and a number of game-theory approaches to a non-standard market—that is, one with only a few buyers and sellers. The fact that it is an extremely simple model, of a market whose outcomes are open to common sense, allows one to put the emphasis less on the results than on different ways of thinking about reaching them.[4]

[3] Later theorists of bargaining—R. J. Aumann and M. Maschler, for example—identify distributions with coalitions. For convenience, I often speak of one or the other as if they were identical.

[4] The auction model goes back to a now obscure branch of classical theory developed by Eugen Böhm-Bawerk and Karl Menger in the nineteenth century. They gave it a non-cooperative interpretation. Von Neumann and Morgenstern, in 1944, interpreted the same model with their cooperative solution. Lloyd Shapley and Martin Shubik recently recast it as the "farmer" model and gave it the further interpretation of core theory. D. B. Gillies and Shapley introduced core theory in the early 1950s in relation to

The market has three traders—one seller and two potential buyers. The seller has put up one indivisible object, on which he has a reserve price, below which he won't sell. One buyer is prepared to bid higher than the other. There are too few traders, of course, for the ideal classical model, but a price analysis makes the obvious prediction that the stronger buyer will get the object at a price somewhere between the most that the weaker buyer is able to bid and the most that the stronger buyer is able to bid. But this is only one possibility.

Von Neumann and Morgenstern chose this model to show that there is another possibility, as follows. Social conditions permitting, the stronger buyer could make a side payment to the weaker buyer to get him to withhold his bid. The price range on the down side then would extend all the way to the seller's reserve price. The outcome, that is, could be different from the "classical" price.

Von Neumann and Morgenstern give the following interpretation of these results: "The two buyers have formed a coalition, based on a definite rule of division for any profit obtained, and are bargaining with the seller. . . . No bargaining can depress the seller under his own limit [his best alternative use instead of a sale of the object]. On the other hand a price above the limit of the weaker buyer would exclude him from any possibility of exerting influence. . . .

---

the solution of Von Neumann and Morgenstern, and Shapley developed it as an independent solution. Shubik later discovered a similar concept in a work by F. Y. Edgeworth in 1881. Thus, schematically, the model and its treatment have this lineage:

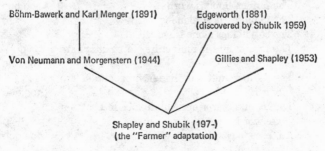

Böhm-Bawerk and Karl Menger (1891)   Edgeworth (1881)
                                       (discovered by Shubik 1959)

Von Neumann and Morgenstern (1944)   Gillies and Shapley (1953)

Shapley and Shubik (197-)
(the "Farmer" adaptation)

Thus it appears that the classical argument—at least in the form used [here]—gives the first possibility only, disregarding coalitions. Our theory, to which the coalitions contributed decisively from the beginning, is necessarily different in this respect: It embraces both possibilities, indeed it gives them welded together, as a unit, in the solutions which it produces. . . ."

The model has been a magician's hat from which even more has been conjured. Lloyd Shapley and Martin Shubik, in their forthcoming landmark work on game theory, picked it up to draw forth a display of their ideas. They tell a story. The object for sale is a farm. The farmer considers that its worth to him as a farm is $100,000. The first buyer is a manufacturer who considers the land worth $200,000 to him as the site for a new plant. The second buyer is a subdivision developer who, for his purposes, considers the land worth $300,000. Either buyer, of course, will have to pay more than the farmer's fall-back value of $100,000, and if both bid, the subdivider will have to pay more than the manufacturer's highest bid of $200,000.

Shapley and Shubik see two great and quite different coalitional powers at work here: on the one hand, the force of straight cooperative economics, and, on the other, the bending force that society may exercise on the game. Each has its province, as it were, and the way in which one or the other may prevail is a pivotal question. They describe the values of the coalitions in this game as follows:

The farmer alone is worth	$100,000
The manufacturer alone is worth	0
The subdivider alone is worth	0
The farmer and manufacturer in coalition are worth	200,000
The farmer and subdivider in coalition are worth	300,000
The manufacturer and subdivider in coalition are worth	0
All three in coalition are worth	300,000

Thus, this market offers the traders a potential gain of $200,000 over the present worth of the farm. Neither alone nor together, in the absence of the farmer, have the manufacturer and subdivider anything to gain. If the farmer joins in a deal with the manufacturer, however, the gain to be divided between them would be $100,000 (the difference between the farm's present worth and its worth as a plant site). If the farmer joins with the subdivider, the gain to be divided would be $200,000—which is the most that the game is worth. No coalition can get more than this amount. Thanks to the manufacturer's presence in the market as a bidder—which pushes the price over $200,000—the farmer is assured of getting at least $100,000 of the total potential gain. The actual price should be in a range between $200,000 and $300,000.

So far, this model has brought out little that is new. The outcome is the common-sense one, the classical one, and the same as the first of the two possibilities pointed to but unemphasized in Von Neumann and Morgenstern's treatment of the auction model. But consider now what it is that makes the farmer-subdivider arrangement a stable coalition in its own right.

Take note first that as long as the farmer and subdivider are dickering to settle on a price somewhere between $200,000 and $300,000, their coalition cannot be upset by any other offers. They are going to make a joint gain of $200,000 over the worth of the farm as a farm, and divide it between them. In the presence of the manufacturer's bid, the farmer will get at least half of that gain and will divide the other half with the subdivider. If, however, for any reason, at some stage of the negotiations, they happened to dicker below a price of $200,000, say $150,000, the manufacturer would be able to give the farmer a better price and the farmer-manufacturer coalition would dominate the farmer-subdivider coalition, with the manufacturer making a profit. On straight bidding and overbidding, however, the price would be driven up to the $200,000 mark, where the farmer-subdivider coalition takes over and cannot be dominated by any other coalition. By themselves, the farmer and subdivider cannot improve their joint position. That position is represented only by the wide range between $200,000 and $300,000, that is, it is indeterminate as regards the point within that range at which they will finally settle. The solution has narrowed the outcome. It will require some further means, presumably bargaining, to reach the actual price which will serve to divide the gain.

This is the "core" of the game. It is what one would expect to happen and what logically should happen if that is all one knew about the game; if, that is, one knew only its straight economics and nothing about the society in which it is taking place.

We have so far ignored the possibility raised by Von Neumann and Morgenstern that the game may be taking place in a society where it is considered proper to make side payments to anyone who can lay claim to them, such as rewarding a potential bidder for not bidding. Consider that possibility.

The coalition of the farmer and subdivider, as we have seen, does better if there are no side payments outside their coalition, since any side payment would cut into their mutual gain. But the manufacturer, who is getting nothing, might under certain conditions be able to get into contention. We have seen that if the dickering is below a price of $200,000, the manufacturer could bid and make a profit. He could see, however, that persistent bidding and overbidding would soon land them at the $200,000 price where he has to stop and get nothing. He could also see that since his highest bid would not represent the full potential value of the game, the bidding forces would naturally tend toward the realization of its full potential. So instead of bidding any further when the dickering is at, say, $150,000, he could—according to the standards of his society—offer to refrain from further bidding on condition that the subdivider make him a payment.

The subdivider and manufacturer are now enveloped in a complex of economic pressures. Let us say that the sub-

divider proposes to pay him $15,000 and to buy the farm for
$150,000. The manufacturer could do better by entering his
own bid for $180,000, for a gain of $20,000. That bid would
drive the subdivider to overbid $180,000, say with a bid of
$185,000. That leaves them only $15,000 below the manufacturer's maximum potential bid; so, for the manufacturer's
agreement not to bid, they have only $15,000 left to work
with. If the subdivider offers $5,000, the manufacturer could
still bid $190,000 and gain $10,000, and so on, as any given
side payment is dominated by smaller side payments. The result is that the actual traders—the farmer and subdivider—
together always get more. If both realize this, they will give
the manufacturer nothing.

Imagine, however—odd as it would be—that the manufacturer got the farm for his bid of $180,000, which would give
him a profit of $20,000. The outcome of the game then
would be inefficient. The farm would not be put to best use,
according to the values in the game, and the players as a society would fall short by $100,000 of realizing the potential
gain available in the game. Thus, at any price below
$200,000 there are additional ways to resolve the game, in-
volving other coalitions of two or three players. It would be
better then, for example, for the three players to get together
and allot the $20,000 to the manufacturer. Given the general
standard that allows side payments, and let us say, for example, a particular business standard that says the subdivider
and manufacturer split evenly whatever extra gain they can
take from the farmer, the total distribution would be as follows:

Farmer:	$180,000	(a net gain of $80,000 over the value of the farm to him)
Subdivider:	110,000	
Manufacturer:	10,000	

The subdivider thus gets the farm and the three as a
group make the full possible gain of $200,000 over the

farmer's reserve price of $100,000. Contrary as this three-way split is to the pure economic logic of the core, it is a possible solution when one considers the dictates of society.[5]

So, in sum, the coalition of farmer and subdivider, which represents the core solution of the game, prevailed so long as social affairs were not considered. But it failed to dominate all of the other possible arrangements outside itself, as when the subdivider and manufacturer followed the side-payment standard of the society of the game, an event that takes us to the center of cooperative game theory, namely, the kinds of stability found in different solutions.

To see the difference in stability between the core and the social standard, let us begin with the last example of a side-payment arrangement and retrace a few steps. The arrangement:

Farmer:	$180,000
Subdivider:	110,000
Manufacturer:	10,000

Alone on its own merits, without the support of a standard of behavior, this solution is unstable (as is any other particular three-way split). It leaves unsatisfied potential coalitions which have the power to intervene and upset the arrangement. The farmer and manufacturer, for example, could improve their lot by forming a coalition to make another deal, leaving the subdivider out and dividing the gain as follows:

Farmer:	$185,000
Subdivider:	0
Manufacturer:	15,000

[5] In the old language of game theory, Von Neumann and Morgenstern called their solution of the game "*the* solution." In the new pluralistic language of the theory, their solution is called a "stable set," that is, any set of arrangements stabilized by the standards of society at large or a subsociety. Other solution concepts, such as the core, are distinguished on an equal footing by their own names. I have followed current practice.

But this coalition leaves the game $100,000 short of its potential worth of $300,000. The farmer and subdivider can do better to form a coalition to divide the additional $100,000 as follows:

Farmer:	$200,000	
Subdivider and farmer:	100,000	(to be divided between them by bargaining)
Manufacturer:	0	

Now, of course, they are back in the core and within the province of this distribution no further coalitions can form to upset it. No other deal can better reward the farmer and subdivider as a group. It is proof against collusion. It thus has very strong stability within itself. Call it internal stability.

Yet something may happen outside the province of the core which it cannot prevent. The question then is, when an arrangement is outside the core, what accounts for its stability in the presence of the unsatisfied groups which, as we have seen, could form to upset it? And furthermore, what kind of stability does this arrangement have?

The three-way split that cuts the manufacturer in is, of course, just as good for society as the two-way split in the core: both arrangements realize the full value of $300,000 which can be obtained in the game.

But within the province of the three-way arrangement, some new force must arrest the power of the unsatisfied groups to upset it. This force is the standard of behavior.

A word about standards of behavior in this game. The general standard—side payments—is not stable until it is expressed in a particular standard which sets the division of spoils between the two buyers. That would be a ratio such as 50-50, 75-25, and the like, of which there are an infinite number.[6] So the players here take three steps to reach this

[6] The stable set we saw earlier in the three-person constant-sum game had only three distributions of 50-50 each, but that

solution. First, they accept in principle some broad standard of behavior, here side payments. Second, the coalition that forms picks a ratio for settlement between its members. And third, the coalition as a unit bargains with the third player.

Let us say, then, that the two buyers who form a coalition in this game settle on a standard that says they will divide equally what they can jointly take from the farmer. This, or any other standard, will be stable both internally and externally.

Look at it internally. What they can jointly take from the farmer will range between nearly $100,000 (if they can bargain him down close to his reserve price) and nearly zero (if the farmer can bargain them up close to the manufacturer's cut-off price, above which the latter has no influence).

If they settle at a price of $180,000, the coalition through its own power will have taken $20,000 from the farmer, and so the division set by the 50-50 standard will be the now familiar:

Farmer:	$180,000
Subdivider:	110,000
Manufacturer:	10,000

And if they drove the farmer down to a price of $160,000, they would divide as follows:

Farmer:	$160,000
Subdivider:	120,000
Manufacturer:	20,000

The internal stability of the arrangement is fairly obvious. Neither of these apportionments dominates the other; nor would any one of any number of them dominate any other. The whole infinite set of apportionments is stable at the ratio of a 50-50 split of the take from the farmer. The standard

---

was unique, belonging only to that game. All typical economic games have an infinite number of stable sets, each equivalent to a standard of behavior.

does it. If it were not for the standard the farmer could intervene with offers and take them around in circles, as we have seen when a standard was absent.

The test of the external stability of the solution by standard is the heretic. Suppose they are about to settle for this arrangement:

Farmer:	$180,000
Subdivider:	110,000
Manufacturer:	10,000

And let us suppose the subdivider turns heretic and proposes this arrangement:

Farmer:	$185,000
Subdivider:	115,000
Manufacturer:	0

How is the standard to assert itself against the heresy? The manufacturer, for example, could counterpropose the following:

Farmer:	$190,000
Subdivider:	105,000
Manufacturer:	5,000

Now they are back in the standard, with the subdivider and manufacturer dividing equally what they get from the farmer. The heretic-subdivider can't oppose this since the farmer and manufacturer can get $200,000 by themselves. Their counterproposal thus dominates the heretical one. So the standard of behavior is externally as well as internally stable.

This game is really an abstract one slightly clothed with identified actors, their values and intentions, and a particular social standard. Strip some of these clothes away and we have the old abstract model we began with: one seller of one indivisible commodity, two potential buyers one of whom is stronger than the other. From this any number of plausible stories could be told about the actors and any number of standards of behavior could be introduced to get distributions of the available benefits. However clothed and whatever the story, game theorists wring from the game a virtual litany of observations and inferences, as we shall now see.

THE CORE OF THE GAME

The core expresses the three types of rationality found in games.

It starts with the individual. As the players are in the game by consent, each can choose to stay out of any coalition if it offers no more than he can get by going alone. That is his "individual rationality."

Each individual can also freely join a group if he finds that he can do better there than he can alone. That's the beginning of "group rationality," which generalizes "individual rationality" to the group. But there are likely to be many possible groups that could form, and so the players look for the one (there could be more than one) that gives the best payoff and at the same time is resistant to any other arrangement. "Group rationality" thus also represents the unwillingness of the players to accept one group arrangement if there is another where all the members get a better payoff.

When all the groups in a game are satisfied that they have done the best they can, the whole society of the game is said to be satisfied. For want of a better term, theorists call that "societal rationality." It corresponds to the optimal society envisioned by classical economists, where no one can do any better except at someone else's expense. But in classical theory this is accomplished by a society of atomized individuals. In cooperative game theory it is accomplished by groups. Society is envisioned as the group of groups.

The core in game theory thus emphasizes the intermediate groups between the individual and the whole society. Two traders, for example, see an attractive deal for making an exchange; if the market as a whole offers nothing better, they can secede and trade among themselves. If it is not profitable for any traders to secede from their coalition, free as they are to do so, they are in the core.

The most remarkable thing is that there is always a core in a market. That is because a market is a gainful game in which there is always a way of distributing the gains such that no subgroup can do better by withdrawing. That is to say, in every market game there is potentially a set of outcomes that satisfy every coalition, not in the sense that all the appetites or desires of the players are fulfilled, but in the sense that they are doing the best they can in the economic circumstances.

The agreement reached in the core may only be an agreement to bargain. If there are only two traders in the market, they of course know that it is they who will bargain. If there are more than two, they have to find out—perhaps by negotiation—who is going to do the bargaining and within what range. To find that, the players look at the total potential worth of all coalitions. In the three-cornered farmer game, only one coalition formed in the core. The presence of the outside player, the manufacturer, determined the range of payments between the other two; but once two actual traders got into the core, the loser had little or no effect on their bargaining. This is understandable, since the farmer and subdivider together got a more favorable result if there were no side payments. Thus they dominated any other coalition so long as they were not considering the norms of society.

Finding the value and power of coalitions takes one to the end of the core analysis. It has performed an essential service in narrowing the field, but that may not be sufficient to the occasion. The core may be too large for the final purposes of the players. They will have to complete their business by some other means, such as bargaining. In the instance of the farmer and subdivider, if between them they change the price, one gets more, the other less. That defines their joint stability in the core. Whatever their settlement price in the core, they share the $200,000, which is the most that can be gained in the game.

A further remarkable thing about core theory is that it provides a link between game theory and classical economic theory. In all market games with small numbers of traders, the core has the kind of wide range indicated in the farmer game. But as the number of traders in a market grows large, the pressure of alternative coalitions upon one another—different deals—reduces the range in the core until it approaches a single point, corresponding to the price in the classical competitive equilibrium of supply and demand. Thus, under these conditions, game theory and classical theory agree on the outcome. The agreement between the theories implies that if the number of traders in a market is large enough, it does not matter whether you are considering them as forming coalitions or as acting individually. As game theorists put it, the classical economic solution is in the core.

When you examine any economic game, it is worth while to look first for the core. For the core can also be viewed as an independent solution. If it is there, it tells you something about the inherent stability of the economic situation. If it has not been realized but could be, it serves as a sign that economic stability is possible. By the same token, if it is not realized, it tells you of the existence of unsatisfied coalitions. If it is not there at all, even latently, that finding is also important: for something else then is needed to inhibit coalitions from forming and reforming without end. In that case, a social norm will be the only other hope for stability. For if society has no norms operating beyond physical rules and there is no core, the whole situation will be chaotic. As one theorizer put it, the place where the core should be is "the eye of the storm." It is in this sense that the core is the measure of stability in society—the society, that is, of the game.

The location of the core in an economic game is clear. It is a most profitable deal in which the parties to it can block any other deal. In the hurly-burly of the real world, the core is not always easy to conceive, even though it is doubtless present at least potentially in all markets and most economic situations. To trace the precise outlines of a core in a real-life game would require sophisticated mathematical calculations. However, the possibility of a core, when one has learned the concept, is open to intuition. It is likely to be surrounded by or buried in the social way of doing things. And yet as a concept, it is asocial; it does not take account of society. Consequently, if one is looking at the social structures of any particular society, the core will have an elusive, almost diaphanous quality. You have to shut your eyes, as it were, and imagine it. Having imagined it, you can see it, devoid of the social props. It is not really difficult to understand, but to grasp it requires this condition, that one excludes society from one's vision of it. You can't tell from seeing it what society it is in. It is a conceptually isolated economic force that occurs in any society.

Imagine, for example, a number of people brooding over their pond which they have polluted. Where's the core? It had been the norm to pollute, but there has been a revolution around the pond and the norm is no longer holding. Everyone is dissatisfied. It's a relatively simple situation. A pond has no upstream-downstream problems, which in most pollution situations eliminates the consent essential to a core: upstream has no interest in downstream, and downstream gets the pollution without consent. Here the players control the whole pond, and, let us say, there are enough benefits, in relation to the costs of cleanup and abstinence from polluting, to buy everyone off if they can all agree. The different players have different problems, but say each of them wants clean water, each is polluting, and each is capable of not polluting. Some are big polluters, some small, and so the costs vary. Forget, for the moment, about society and about passing laws, which would be an attempt by some to impose a solution on the others. Can they examine their interests, make compromises, and get an agreement? That is to say, in a game sense, can they find the coalitions that could form, and take account of their influence and values? If they can imagine them and see the arrangement that "satisfies" them with no effective coalitions remaining outside the arrangement, they have found the core. It gives them the best possible result and it is stable. They have a clear-water pond and a satisfactory arrangement for paying for it.

Thus, the solutions described by the core and the social norm work not only for a market but also for any economic situation, whether or not a market even exists, a latitude denied to standard economic theory: the whole gamut of market failures, from non-standard markets to public goods is open to scrutiny as a game.

The significance of the core, which has been emphasized here, by no means downgrades the significance of the social norm. Indeed, as noted, the norm contains the core if there is one. Furthermore, games outside of markets are often coreless, and the range of such games covers the landscape of both economics and politics. It was in these coreless games that Von Neumann and Morgenstern made their first discoveries. They explained why a game can have a particular outcome despite the fact that it could be overthrown.

One needs to be wary of what any model teaches one about real life, since the modeler has selected some elements for study and blotted out the rest. But by the same token, a model may give rise to insights not otherwise attainable. The following examples suggest the significance of the core and the norm, either or both, in real-life games.

Not many events are more important to a corporation than a change in the parties who control it. Let us say that several corporations, in the persons of their controlling managements, are considering mergers. The situation can be very complex, as it involves both active and passive shareholders and professional managements. Each corporation has possible alternatives. To simplify, let us assume that each would like to find the most profitable deal. Essentially, they have to consider all potential coalitions that are practical and put a value on them that expresses the combined mutual gain that each will yield. When they find the best one and stop looking around, they are in the core. Now we find perhaps two of them at the bargaining table. The range over which they will bargain has already been set by the rejected mergers. The question then is how they will divide the gain, or the prospect of gain, which is embodied in the merger.

But this may not be all. The interests of professional managements may have an influence on the outcome; managers are concerned with how they make out after the merger. The principals may have to pay them off with job commitments, salaries, bonuses, stock options, etc. So far as the basic shareholders are concerned, the solution may no longer be in the core. It may be in the field of the Von Neumann-Morgenstern norm of side payments.

THE NORMS OF BUSINESS

In the real world of societies within societies, the corporate sector contains a number of powerful business norms. One might suppose that if a corporation is not doing well, for whatever reason—poor management, feathering the bureaucratic nest, bad luck—it will be subject to takeover by another corporation. The rise of the conglomerates in recent years encouraged this notion. There is nothing in the rules to prevent takeovers if antitrust law is not violated. And yet the conglomerates were widely condemned by business executives, and not only because of their financial gimmickry but also because of a tradition against forced takeovers. It's "raiding." Raiders are upstarts, predators, outsiders. But they had the freedom to do it; it was a choice they could make under the rules, and they did it as heretics. Sensing retribution they preferred the traditional negotiated merger. But they edged over the line with offers that amounted to threats if they were rejected. The stockholders, whose preferences in the stock market made the movement possible, wouldn't easily stand for a management that blocked their getting a higher price for their stock than the prevailing one in the market. In the end, the band of "raiders" grew larger and less inhibited as the force of the pressure for continued "growth" seized them. They bought control of companies in the open market without negotiations. A revolution seemed to be in the making. The orthodoxy then found a voice.

In 1968 James J. Ling chilled the steel industry with his "friendly" offer to buy control of Jones & Laughlin Steel Corporation, and the reverberations ran through the managements of all corporations who for one reason or another could imagine the possibility of a takeover happening to them. In Ling's imagination, not even Westinghouse or General Motors was sacrosanct. The government, then, in the person of Richard W. McLaren, then assistant attorney general in charge of antitrust, rose in defense of the orthodoxy. As there was no apparent rule of law against takeovers, providing there were no conflicts between merging companies in their markets, McLaren appeared to see in Ling a test case for a new theory: that the intent of antitrust law was to prevent concentration of industry, and if he could not persuade the courts of this, he would go to Congress to get a law. He seemed to be going all out against Ling,[7] but the government settled for a consent decree by which Ling divested some companies while keeping Jones & Laughlin, though with only qualified power over the steel company.

The government's action blighted Ling's dreams of capturing a Westinghouse or General Motors and, along with concurrent difficulties, was a major factor in his downfall. Other conglomerators got the message that even if there were no clear rule of law against "raiding," the government would in one way or another attempt to reinforce the business norm which said that corporations do not buy control of large established corporations in the open market or by threat. In the early 1970s, after the original conglomerate movement had collapsed, McLaren seemed about to make another test case, of ITT, but called it off. This gave rise to the well-known scandal involving political pressures on antitrust administration and allegations of side payments (a different kind of

[7] Ironically, McLaren, who seemed to be counting more on social norms than existing law for his case, subpoenaed the author for his work papers and a deposition in connection with a story about Ling in *Fortune*—one of the Nixon administration's early heretical breaks from the norm that, along with the First Amendment, traditionally protected the press from invasion by the government.

game). It appears in retrospect that though many conglomerators fell in the fray, they succeeded in making a revolution, though a qualified one. The old norm against raiding has weakened. Forced takeovers go on, but they are selective. Resistance in the traditional quarters of corporate business is still strong. One does not yet know where the revolution will end. It is still being tested, as in the instance of Mobil's recent takeover of Marcor, the holding company for Montgomery Ward and the former Container Corporation.

It seems reasonable to interpret the opposition to raiding as the norm that maintains the prevailing structure of corporate life. With control of large corporations growing increasingly tenuous, with traditional pools of capital representing smaller percentages of the total shares of particular corporations, and with control in the hands of strategic shareholders with marginal positions or in the hands of professional managements, open season on them has meant insecurity for each of them and the threat of instability for the whole system. One can imagine an infinite series of coalitions—one actually got a glimpse of it in the conglomerate outbreak—with corporations forming and re-forming by merger and spin-off without end. The point here is not to hazard a judgment about the potential outcome of open season on corporate control, which would take considerable information and theorizing from several points of view. (Classical theorists, for example, usually favor takeovers as healthy for the economy.) It is only to observe that there is a powerful business norm still at work against raiding. The norm does not say which particular corporations or corporate or industry alignments will prevail but that the alignments of corporations and their managements, which will divide the spoils, are to be found in the set described by the norm against raiding. It is the corporate set that has the stability, and the status-quo norm collectively enforced it until the revolution came.

Business has few explicit ethical codes comparable to those of the professions, but it has various norms of conduct that shape its activities. Some of these save a lot of effort that otherwise would get into rule making and haggling, reducing large areas of indeterminacy to manageable proportions. Businessmen get much of their work done by knowing whom to trust, making oral agreements without a contract, talking the language peculiar to markets. The chief executive of a very large though still not dominant oil company described a special but not unusual cautionary standard: "Don't challenge the giants," he said. "They have an awful kick. But if you don't challenge, they don't kick. So stay decent and play the game."

Some business standards have been formally institutionalized. The one that says that an advertising agency gets 15 percent is, in game-theoretic terms, a "discriminatory" standard—that is, it prescribes a fixed payoff to one player—and has long been a stable solution to the game (along with some bargained flat-fee variations based on dollar volume rather than percentage). Excluding the ad agency from participation in the dickering simplifies the coalitional possibilities and thereby reduces the number of ways in which the total worth of the game can be distributed. The other players —client and media—are able to enforce this allocation in the game so long as they hold to this norm.

The "martini norm" is often influential in allocating business between corporations. It requires that the agents of two corporations—perhaps buying and selling or perhaps doing some other business—drink martinis together repeatedly over time, so that dynamic changes in their respective corporate situations get washed out or overlooked and their trading situation could be said to be in a steady state. One corporate chief executive described it as follows: "If you assume there's no difference in the quality offered, or the service, or the substantiality of the companies, then you get to personal attitudes. You like him and you don't like me, so you buy the stuff from him and not from me. That's a fact of human nature and one of the selling tools we use—you're always aware of it when you transfer a salesman to another district. When there's no difference between two suppliers, this is a factor.

That's why so many martinis are drunk, why there are so many trips to Miami Beach."

The chief of a high-technology company whose profits depend largely on new products finds the martini norm his main obstacle. "The market is made up of human beings with allegiances and alliances—there's no question about it. As for the personal relationship, if two things are of absolutely equal value to you and you're the purchasing agent, you'll go with who you trust more. But you damn allegiances when you're coming in with a brand-new product and trying to unseat someone, and that's the kind of business we're in." But such allegiances are also formed even when there is in fact an economic difference between suppliers. A chief executive observed: "The martini norm is our problem in selling the railroad industry and all old, established industries."

One sees, of course, that discrimination in real life occurs most readily when there is some means of identifying the excluded party. For about a century after the Civil War, Negroes were generally kept out of the main line of economic dealing, and the norm in the South permitted black workers to rise only as high as foremen supervising other blacks. The effect was to distribute economic benefits in favor of white workers. Similar arrangements were common in business and industry throughout the whole country.

Discrimination in game theory does not necessarily have a pejorative meaning—ad agency men and martini drinkers are quite satisfied with their lot.

Now that the black revolution has overturned the old norm, U.S. society has been trying to accommodate the change. Many corporations, by helping black businesses and engaging in "hard-core unemployment" programs and programs for the "affirmative" employment of all minorities, are trying to bend markets in ways to overcome their former bent. What we see here is an old discriminatory norm being replaced by a new one. The women's revolution is also overturning an old discriminatory norm. In these large areas as well as many others, plain hard economics has been superseded by the Von Neumann-Morgenstern "standards of behavior."

Consumers typically have adhered to the individual, passive, decentralized conduct prescribed for all participants in the standard market. The great body of legislation put on the books in their behalf has been prompted largely by the sensitivity of professional politicians to unorganized consumer interests. The movement called "consumerism" proposes to change that tradition. In certain respects—boycotts, class actions, and other concerted acts—this movement can be interpreted as an effort to convert the non-strategic consumer into a strategic force; and Ralph Nader often singles out weak norms for reinforcement in a rule of law. If the consumer movement should succeed in its aims, it would have an impact analogous to the establishment of organized labor as a major institutional force in both markets and politics. From the point of view of standard economic theory, this would be an aberration. In game theory it would be what people do or try to do in gamelike ways with cores, norms, and rules.

In the search for new solutions where old norms have weakened, it is possible to imagine new norms emerging from the old ones. But as a social norm is an unthinking kind of thing, thinking about adopting one would be contradictory. Yet one supposes that there could be transformations in which an old norm was substantially qualified; not quite a revolution. There is another possibility. People may actually be searching for cores in the economics of pollution, discrimination, consumerism, and the like. Hardly anyone, however, is giving any thought to whether they accept government control of money, public roads, the legitimacy of trade unions, or the barring of children from the labor markets—all present-day social-norm solutions to economic problems which were contested issues before they became institutionalized. A description of all the social norms we take for granted would be a description of our society and the way it allocates its benefits. But with revolutions overturning certain norms, if that is what is happening, game theory suggests that stability will be restored only if people find the cores of these economic games, if indeed they have cores, or new social norms. Certainly, in this theory, as we have seen, where long-standing norms are absent, any solution outside the core will be unstable, even if adopted into law. Unsatisfied groups will move to the political games and get the laws changed. Judgments of value are being made which point to a search for those areas of greatest collective economic gain, here called cores, where people can settle down to bargaining. If society finds them, as it apparently has on past occasions, they will be the starting point of new norms, which gather their stability as they are practiced over time.

7

BOISE CASCADE:
A THREE-PLAYER BARGAINING
GAME WITH A FAILURE
OF PROSPECTS

The managements of Boise Cascade Corporation and Ebasco Industries, each having set its sights on rapid expansion, were in the market for a merger with another corporation. They concluded that among the alternative deals they perceived, the best was to merge their two companies. Their agreement upon this signified that they had probably found the "core" of the game, i.e., the best possible deal with a gain for both of them to be divided. The measure of the division of gains would be expressed in the ratio of the exchange of stock between the two companies, over which they would bargain. Thus the game here is one of bargaining within the core to reach the final precise settlement. The game was enlarged when a minority of Ebasco directors entered the bargaining as a separate force to alter the settlement. But all parties bargained within the basic deal. Subsequent disaster, not being perceived, was not part of this game. It was the surprise outcome of future games.

THE PLAYERS

- Robert V. Hansberger, chief executive of Boise Cascade Corporation
- The management and majority directors of Ebasco Industries

■ The minority directors of Ebasco Industries

When two players in an economic game get down to set-tling a deal with one another, undisturbed by other players in the game, one may assume it to be likely that they have already resolved the larger game, formed a coalition around its core of hard economics, and are now dividing the gains. If there had been only one other player, they would somehow have rejected three of the game's four potential coalitions: 1-2, 1-3, 2-3, 1-2-3. If there had been ten players all to-gether, they would somehow have rejected 1,012 potential coalitions before arriving at theirs. Though their agreement may be only an agreement to bargain, it is reasonable to as-sume that their coalition had appeared to them to be the most profitable one and that no other player or group of players had anything better to offer either of them. Now that they have narrowed the field to themselves, the big work in the game is done and they are in the mysterious arena of bargaining. Their mutual gain, which they are to divide, is measured by the range between their respective fall-back values, that is, the value of not making any deal, and also by the values of potential alternative deals. With good, reliable communication, both parties may know the range within which they are bargaining. It is to their interest to reach a final point of settlement.

This was the situation of Boise Cascade Corporation and Ebasco Industries Incorporated, two large and prosperous companies whose joint assets totaled close to $2 billion, when they met in 1968–69 to settle the terms of their proposed merger. Ebasco had cash, Boise, prospects of putting the cash profitably to work. Before the deal was settled, a third force emerged in their midst, complicating matters and alter-ing the first settlement point to another one. The game that brought about the bargaining and the bargaining itself were, of course, based on values that included the future in the form of prospects.

• • •

It was twelve years since Robert Vail Hansberger had become chief executive of Boise Cascade. He had quietly built a record of growth in sales and profits that was worthy of the envy of the most flamboyant conglomerators, and unlike many of them, he had emerged in 1969 stronger than ever. A "congeneric" rather than sheer conglomerate expansionist, he had extended a business that began with the log in the forest into tangibly related areas. When he took over at the beginning of 1957, Boise Cascade's sales were $35 million. In 1968 its sales passed $1 billion and were still climbing. This represented an extraordinary twelve-year annual growth rate compounded of 33 percent.

If Hansberger had sought this growth only for growth's sake, his performance would have been one of the foremost among modern empire builders. But in the contemporary style, Hansberger professed to disdain mere growth in sales, regarding it only as an instrument for reaching his primary goal of increased earnings per share. On this score, he had moved Boise Cascade from 34 cents a share in 1956 to $2.38 in 1968, a sevenfold increase. In the previous five years, while Boise's sales tripled, its after-tax earnings increased 514 percent.

This record had been very nice for both shareholders and executives of Boise Cascade. Some forty of the company's executives had each made more than a quarter of a million dollars in stock options, and a few of them were millionaires. Hansberger himself had gone into debt to buy Boise Cascade stock in 1957, and he also received his first stock options then. Taking into account splits, his stock had cost him $3 a share. In September 1969, with the market price per share around 70, his total personal holdings, including subsequent stock options, were worth about $20 million, which was quite a bit above par for present-day chief executives.

Hansberger put an intellectual stamp on his company. A star graduate in a celebrated class at Harvard Business School (1947), he had been a recruiter of M.B.A.s and a believer in trying new tools of analysis and decision. He and his top executives made annual three-day pilgrimages to

Stanford University where they submitted to the scrutiny of M.B.A. candidates in seminars—as a result of which Boise Cascade, Hansberger believed, had become the subject of the largest university case study ever done on any company. He had also recently invited a group of M.B.A. candidates from the University of Washington to conduct a detailed study of the company's operations in various locations, after which he and other key executives subjected themselves to their critique of the operation.

Yet Hansberger deliberately kept his corporate headquarters in a "relatively primitive area of the United States" —Boise, Idaho (1968 population about 73,000). "There's a studied informality in what we do," he said. "We don't compress people. We don't insist they do what they do in an environment of rigid procedures or too many formalized policies." He believed that these humanist manners were nurtured in Boise's relative isolation, and found no difficulty in conducting from there a business that had grown to be nationwide. "We are heavy users of the airplane and the telephone," he said.

Boise Cascade, of course, started in Boise. It had been called the Boise Payette Lumber Company for forty-four years up to the time Hansberger became chief executive and began its expansion. In what was then a fractured industry, it was natural for him to take the route of merger and acquisition to strengthen and widen the company's position in wood products and related areas. His first mergers were with other lumber companies, laying the base for borrowing enough money to build a pulp mill and get into the paper business in 1959. From paper he went into packaging. In time he expanded in timberland, lumber, paper, and packaging and also into the distribution of these products and other building materials and office supplies all the way to the retail level. He later moved into housing: factory-built houses, on-site houses, and mobile homes.

Now he was taking the company further out along the branches: building "leisure-living" communities, industrial parks, mobile-home parks, and apartments. He had also started in urban development. Two thirds of Boise Cascade's business was in housing and associated fields and one third in paper and packaging.

Altogether, Hansberger had made about thirty-three mergers and acquisitions in twelve years. He estimated that the total annual sales of all the enterprises merged or acquired were about $600 million at the time they came into Boise Cascade. This represented about half of the company's 1969 sales rate.

But Hansberger differed from the conglomerators in three significant respects. First, he had made his acquisitions in accordance with a clearly defined pattern, whereas most conglomerators are uninhibited about acquiring a wide variety of unrelated industries. Second, he was an operating as well as a financially oriented executive, unlike, for example, James J. Ling, who acquired companies for the purpose of managing their assets from a largely financial point of view. Third, Hansberger had never made tender offers. He made cooperative deals with the strategic controlling managements of other companies.

He was actively in the merger game in 1968 and, among various possible deals, came to prefer the big one with Ebasco Industries. Ebasco likewise was in the corporate market for a deal and came to prefer the one with Boise. Ebasco, once the world's largest utility system and a holding company—a sort of traditional conglomerate—contained such disparate components as a lot of financial paper from the sale of utilities in South America, some remaining operating utilities in Ecuador, Guatemala, and Panama, three engineering and construction subsidiaries, and a $65-million portfolio of marketable U.S. corporate securities. Thus their merger would be a conglomerate-like departure for Hansberger, but his past suggested that he would tailor the assets he acquired to his operational pattern.

They merged on August 31, 1969, after several bargaining sessions over several months. Shortly thereafter, Hansberger described the bargaining to the author, along with his general corporate strategy and objectives which they had discussed earlier.

McDONALD: How did you get interested in Ebasco?

HANSBERGER: *Ebasco could be characterized as a closed-end finance company. It had a large portfolio of domestic securities and foreign bonds. It had a few operations, but they were small ones—the company had a value of $680 million in assets and sales of only $176 million. But they didn't have the opportunity to invest their cash resources at the good rate of return that we have. This is what provided the motivation for putting the two companies together. We have a large inventory of projects that involve the prospect of high return—and that require large amounts of cash. We can use that money, especially in this tight money market, at returns well above what they can achieve. We felt that in virtually every dimension the companies were compatible. Merging with Ebasco is a sophisticated way of selling stock to the public.*

Q: Where did the stimulus for the merger originate?

A: *David Mitchell, the New York representative of the investment banker S. G. Warburg, became acquainted with the management of Ebasco and thought it would be a logical merger. He was quite familiar with Boise's appetite for cash, and on Ebasco's side, he was aware of their ability to generate cash. He saw that in partnership we'd be able to do each other good. So he simply called us and arranged the first meeting. That was in the Ebasco offices in October 1968.*

Q: How many meetings did you have with Ebasco?

A: *As far as the actual bargaining sessions go, there were maybe ten over three or four months. During the prebargaining period, the management of Ebasco insisted that they see what investment opportunities were available to their funds. In these discussions we convinced them that we had these opportunities.*

147

We provided each other with information on request. The investment banking house Lazard Frères looked us over carefully for them and reported to their directors. We used each other's outside auditors for certain information. It was a pretty thoroughgoing exchange of facts, figures, futures. As important as anything at a bargaining session is this homework you do beforehand, the careful evaluation of alternatives.

Q: How did you go about evaluating the merger?

A: *We think we're unique in having devised a mathematical way of analyzing the price we should pay for a company. It shows the values put in and taken out by the shareholders. Suppose, for example, that our price-earnings ratio was at 25 and the company we were going to merge with was at 10. As we are the surviving company, with our image we will stay at 25. So there will be an increase in values there in the merger, along with synergistic values in operations. The model shows the participation in the gain by both parties. It gave us the basis for setting the range of price within which we could bargain.*

Q: What in your experience are the principal difficulties inherent in bargaining? What makes a good bargainer?

A: *The question is how to prorate the mutual gain—that's bargaining, isn't it? A most important ingredient is judging the end point of the other side and being willing to take a tough risk on your own end point.*

Q: How far apart were you when you first began talking?

A: *Not really too far on price or value, just method. After some preliminary skirmishing, we felt, going into the formal sessions, that we were close enough to a price. I can't tell what theirs was exactly. We knew we'd have to pay 10 to 15 percent over the market. The question then is how much beyond that have you got to go. Ranges become somewhat fluid in hard bargaining. The evaluation of things changes.*

For example, we considered leaving with the Ebasco share-holders their Latin-American portfolio while merging the remainder of the company with Boise. We decided that this was excessively complicated.

We presented our proposition at the final bargaining session on March 11. That was the first full confrontation of the two managements and their investment bankers. Their side told us categorically that our first bid was too low. I think it was in the area of a ratio of 1.1 shares of Boise Cascade common stock to one share of Ebasco—maybe a little below that. There were a number of figures floating through the oxygen at that time. I think the top figure they threw out was in the area of 1.3 to 1.4. There were a few caucuses for each side to re-examine its position. And then both sides agreed to take a 1.2 figure to the respective boards. An alternative was provided for their shareholders. They could take it as .65 of a share of our common and .4 of a share of our convertible preferred carrying a dividend of $2.50.

Both boards voted for it, but theirs was only by a majority. We were aware during the bargaining sessions that there was likely to be a minority of their directors who would not favor the merger. I think that this was a factor that both managements kept very much in mind.

Merging or acquiring public companies is a harsh discipline. Bargaining in this kind of situation is really a process of looking over each other's shoulders at each other's publics. We realized that they had a divided board to contend with and a large group of shareholders. We also knew there was outside competition in this—either active or semiactive. I think it had a bearing on the negotiations. It may have had an effect on the timing of the negotiations, the speed at which we worked.

Q: What about personal values that came into the Ebasco negotiations? For example, what about the effect of the merger on Ebasco executives?

A: *Yes, that was involved. I spent a considerable amount of time with the president of Ebasco discussing the key members of his organization. I was aware on my part that there might be less than overwhelming enthusiasm for the merger on the part of some of their people because Boise would be the survivor. We had a series of meetings to look at the things these people might do in the combined company. I talked with them and tried to give them the best understanding that I humanly could as to what the consequences would be in terms of their own futures.*

Q: What was your impression of the attitude of the Ebasco directors who voted against the deal?

A: Four or five of their directors, I think, felt two things. One, that really Ebasco should do this kind of thing itself—that is, go out and acquire other companies. They did not like the company to be sold. And second, they felt the price—the 1.2 ratio—was not high enough. These two were related. As for Ebasco's survival—there was no way I could make the merger and do anything about that value. All I could do was be awfully sure that down the road there would be no suitable grounds for criticizing our price.

Q: There was a change in the price. Why?

A: After the first agreement on the ratio and their board had met and voted, the discussion continued, and a strong effort was made by the Ebasco management to make an upward adjustment in the ratio. Then their first-quarter earnings were announced, and they were better than had been anticipated, and we acquiesced and did make an upward adjustment of approximately 4 percent. That's not a big percentage, but it's a lot of money. What we did was raise our part of the ratio from 1.2 to 1.25 shares. That was close to the high end of our range. And as for the preferred-stock alternative, we increased the dividend on that to $3. That was on the twenty-fourth of April. That final negotiation was brief—there had been a lot of homework beforehand. We actually agreed on the telephone.

Q: Mr. Hansberger, you have talked about how Ebasco

fits into your operating objectives. Could we turn now to the over-all objectives of your company?

A: We have spent a lot of time on this subject in our company. Our objective is to increase the shareholder's value, and the best way to do that is consistently to increase the earnings per share by 20 percent compounded annually. This concept avoids overstressing the price of our shares in the market, which would suggest a short-term view. We are much more interested in consistency and permanence. If the basic value is developed by the company, in the long term the price of our stock should reflect it. We want a high but not delicate price-earnings ratio. Up to 30 is good. Between 30 and 60 would be fragile. We don't need that. The price itself is a short-term thing and not in our control, but earnings are. This concept of consistently increasing earnings on a long-term basis is one that we use universally throughout the company, and all of the subordinate objectives of the company obtain their relevance from this basic objective.

Q: How have these objectives changed?

A: I joined the company at the beginning of 1957. When I arrived, I found that the company had a written statement of corporate objectives, consisting of a two-page list of fine things like early spring and motherhood, to which no one could object. These objectives included fair wages, sound prices, adequate profits, high returns on investment, outstanding relations in communities in which the company operated, etcetera. But if pursued to the ultimate, each would have conflicted with others. We sensed that what we needed was an over-all kind of pinnacle objective from which all of the other objectives could derive relevance.

At that time we had only 308 shareholders, as compared with about 60,000 now. We were practically a private organization. As we evolved into a public corporation, we felt a need to modify our pinnacle objective in order to reflect more accurately the attitude of public shareholders. Accordingly, we changed our objective; it became "consistently to increase our shareholders' value." The important word here is "consistently," and the measure we adopted was earnings per share.

We still use return on investment as an operating tool in allocating funds on a divisional and group basis inside the company. We do use variable standards of return on investment in allocating capital to reflect differences in risk. For example, if an investment action is reversible, that is, if we can liquidate the investment virtually dollar for dollar, we will accept a lower return. However, a paper mill, for example, has value only in one location. If this location turns out to be wrong, much of the investment value is gone. But if the investment is in a merchandising operation such as building materials or office supplies, these investments, being largely working capital, can easily be liquidated almost dollar for dollar.

We do not measure the performance of individual units of the company in terms of earnings per share, but we measure their performance in terms of increases in profits over the preceding years in total dollars for each unit. But our operating units are asked to make an appropriate contribution to the over-all corporate target of an increase in earnings per share of 20 percent year after year. We realize that for the long-term future this is a very difficult target. Obviously, if you extrapolate an annual improvement by 20 percent over a long enough period, the magnitudes become absurd. Eventually, as we become larger, the target is going to slip a little. But that doesn't mean that we won't still use it internally as a target for our people. So far, over the past twelve years, we've beat it a little, even though inside that period there were two times when our earnings actually dropped. These were times when we were a weaker company and much more vulnerable to cycles in our business than we are now.

We are now favored by being in a balance of businesses with contracyclical movements. Basically, this is housing versus paper. When the economy is up, more paper is used and mortgage money dries up as the money flows elsewhere. Then the reverse is also true. This is our theory. The merger *with Ebasco does not alter this balance, but is going to result in domestic growth and growth overseas with the same underlying balance.*

Q: How have your recent gains affected your discipline?

A: You ask whether the company is more lenient when it is affluent? We are more affluent now but still improving our earnings per share. We have a tough objective—20 percent compounded—and it keeps us lean and hungry each year. Our fellows are working harder than ever before. Our earnings per share were up 49 percent last year. So now this year we must try to go up 20 percent on a bigger base; thus, the more we make, the tougher the job.

Q: How do you relate such elements as earnings, dividends, growth, and survival in the process of making a decision?

A: Growth in sales is not our basic objective, but one of the best ways of increasing earnings per share can be to grow. We have deliberately kept a low cash-dividend policy since we have so many opportunities inside the company to invest funds at very high returns. We think maximum earnings per share and high-dividend payouts are incompatible. The ability to borrow is a real asset and we have maximized the use of debt, keeping a safe balance between debt and equity to increase earnings per share. Like most other timberland-owning companies, our assets are substantially understated, and our lenders know this. Accordingly, we have been able to maintain a fairly high debt-to-equity ratio.

Q: When you make a decision that involves a significant portion of your resources, how do you take into account the relations of the stakes to your total resources?

A: We consider this question all the time. We think in terms of the probability of being wrong, and the worst impact being wrong might have, and what we could do to offset it. If the alternatives in a decision were, on the one hand, a sure thing with a modest return and, on the other hand, a much better bet on the odds but with the chance of ruining the company, I would choose the first alternative. The company is not yours as an individual to gamble with. But if it were a case of risking 5 or 10 percent of the company, I would choose the second alternative. Of course, there is a damage factor to be considered even if it is not outright a question of survival. Our mission is to consistently increase the shareholders' value—consistently, that is, with safety, security, stability, and stability of earnings growth. So we don't say only that we are maximizing earnings but that we are doing so continually.

We have taken some risk in areas of uncertainty that almost bet the whole company. But the advantages if we won were so important that we felt we had to take the chance. For example, back in the late 1950s, when we were tiny and only in the lumber business, we borrowed a lot of money to build a mill to go into pulp and paper. We needed to do this to make use of the waste wood we were generating at our sawmills. We were in the midst of the project when our internal cash flow dropped because of a slump in the housing market. We had to make a decision: whether to shut off the project or borrow more money. If we shut it off, we would lose two years' time and we felt that then we would have to meet higher costs and maybe it would be too late for us to get into the business. It meant almost extinction of the firm if we were not in pulp and paper. A company with two products can afford to sell either product cheaper than the company that has to spread its log costs over a single product. On the other hand, to borrow more money was very risky and made our debt-to-equity ratio very high. So there was also a possible extinction problem there. The question was which way do you want to risk extinction. We thought this risk through and decided to take it. The worst happened. We hit a recession and lost $14 million of expected cash flow. We went back to our lender, John Hancock, and, fortunately, they gave us the additional money. The fact that we had told *them of risk beforehand, I think, made it easier for us to get the money.*

Lately we had another such big decision. This was to enter the South on a $200-million gamble, right in the peak of the 1966–67 money crunch. We knew that if we were ever to enter the South, it was then or never. For the property offered was the only major timber reserve still available. Timing was critical. We had to go then or forget it. It was a big bet, but it was not betting the company. But we had to scramble. If the project did not come up to expectation, it would be a drag on the company. We went ahead with it.

Q: What risk did you recognize in the Ebasco merger?

A: *Well, the risk was zero in taking over $137 million in cash and prime U.S. marketable securities. On the other hand, some risk had to be recognized in their $191 million of foreign bonds and their $97 million of investment in their Chilean subsidiary. But for these investments they have reserves on the books of $52 million. We took a hard look at the figures and decided that they were a pretty safe gamble. There was a loss in contracts on nuclear plants but that had already have reserved for on the Ebasco books, so we didn't have to take it.*

Q: What does the term "calculated risk" mean to you?

A: *To me it means a mental try to establish a risk or a situation where you know your chances, that is, the probabilities. We sometimes do this explicitly for acquisitions. And we use numerical risk-analysis procedures to test major capital expenditures. We try to break down a problem into areas of risk in the marketplace, the start-up problems, etcetera. We assign a probability to each area and try to get an overall probability. I don't think we are very scientific about it.*

Q: Do you ever put a number on a subjective probability —like "I think the chances of such and such taking place are fifty-fifty"? Or do you express yourself qualitatively in likelihoods or comparisons in which you think one event is simply more or less likely to happen than some other event?

A: *Yes, we do this sort of thing at the top corporate level. We do it as individuals but more often in groups. We raise the question, what are the chances of a price decline versus price maintenance or improvement. We argue and perhaps come up with something like fifty-fifty or sixty-forty. There are several types of price situations in our business. For example, the lumber market, like agricultural markets, is highly volatile in its pricing. No one producer influences the market. There are tens of thousands of them and they act on the basis of what looks like mob psychology. An example of another kind of situation is kraft paperboard or newsprint, where one, two, or three companies can drive the price down by cutting the price and do so when they have excess of unused capacity. The price goes up when all are filled up. Somebody sticks his neck out by raising the price and hopes the others will too. Otherwise, he has to go back.*

When you try to analyze the lumber market, you think first of the supply and demand situation. There is just so much timber. So the question is how much demand is there. You look at the housing industry and then at the money market. There will be building when mortgage money is available. So we ask: What is the probability of enough mortgage money for 1969 to build 1,500,000 or 1,600,000 housing units? Say we think the chances are 80 percent of the number being 1,550,000 units. We then say, in the light of supply and demand history, that if that happens, the price per 1,000 board feet of lumber will go up $5. That figure in turn tells us what to build into our budgets and cash flows. When we are thinking out five to ten years in the same way, it tells us what additional productive capacity to build.

Q: Apart from stakes-to-resources problems, what situations do you meet in which the immediate dollar values are clear but not adequate for making a choice among alternatives?

A: *One example comes to mind. Out of cash flow we recently had so many dollars for capital expenditures in the paper group. We had two alternatives. One was a number of projects which would return 50 percent before taxes and interest. The other was a group of projects returning 35 percent before taxes and interest. We took the second alternative because we had only one shot at it. If we had not, a competitor would likely come in and take that market. We took this alternative to protect the market. It was a matter of timing. We may very well go after the higher-return projects later. I would be surprised if any company can make selections solely on return. We say that a certain course is important to a product area and is part of our total strategy.*

Q: Would you describe in a nutshell the basic elements that go into the strategies of your industry, that everyone works with?

A: *Forest-products companies have to get the most value out of a log. It is a kind of rule of life. We are dealing with a limited resource. In pulp and paper, location is a strategic factor. We have to compromise among access to water, timber, and transportation. Proximity to markets is less important. But with corrugated boxes that contain lots of air, you don't want to ship very far, so you locate close to the markets. With newsprint, you want to be close to the forest and water. You can ship thousands of miles.*

We have choices to make among products using the same raw material. It is a kind of strange business in timber. If you're a company planning to be in the tree business forever, you can only harvest as much timber as you grow annually. Therefore there's a basic limit on how much timber you can take to market. So you've got the responsibility to make choices between the kind of products that can be made from those resources. For example, out of a given tree we could make lumber, plywood, paper, particle board—or we could sell the logs overseas. The Japanese, for example, are buying logs like crazy. Personal decision making does not give us the best selection of these complex choices. We have to program

157

the tree and log into the computer, which can then select the best combination of choices reflecting instant market changes.

Q: How do you relate these elements to your corporate strategy?

A: *We have the basic objective, as I have said, of consistently increasing the owners' value. Our strategy is the blueprint for what we do, the how, the procedures we use to accomplish that. Our strategy sessions are very thorough. We have a strategy committee that sits and hears operating management review its plans for the next five years and takes a deep look into the coming year. The basic question is how will you make your contribution to the company's basic objective—both for 1970 and over the next four years. Our strategies involve not only an analysis of our own actions within our present environments, but also an analysis of the reactions of others to our own actions.*

Suppose, for example, you are thinking of building a paper mill near timber that you do not own—government or private timber—and suppose you know that this timber is within economic reach of an existing competitive mill that is currently working another timber source nearby. I would think long and hard about pre-announcing that I was building a mill in that area. I would think about what action a competitor might take and what total mill capacity could result available to the over-all timber body in the area. And what I thought his long-term plan might be. We recognize that he might say to himself something like this: "I can expand capacity more quickly than they can put a new mill into production. So I'll enter that unworked tract by leasing or buying sites for log-gathering depots, or make a start at buying the timber, if possible, and announce an expansion without necessarily intending to go through with it and thereby chase him off." This happens.

In this situation we weigh all the things he can do. We try to decide what the chances are that he will do any one of them—recognizing that each may not be equally available.

We consider his position, his balance sheet, his psychology, his gutty or conservative nature as an individual, and the past patterns of the corporation's behavior. We also have to recognize his motivation. For example, getting additional wood in the area might be more important to him if he had in mind a long-term expansion. We have to decide what we would do if he goes through with one or another of his alternatives, while still being uncertain of which one it is.

If it would be okay for us to build while he expanded too, though not so attractive to us, we would go ahead and buy the site and equipment, move in and establish our own depots, accelerate and make hard moves and announcements of plans and progress. Since the one who acts first has the advantage, we would hope in view of our moves that he would decide not to expand.

But if his expansion would be fatal to our plant, we would need to know how critical to him it was to expand. In that uncertainty we would try to smoke him out while remaining flexible in our options. It is not so risky to move into raw material as it is to start building a mill, and so we might buy our equipment on option and our site on option and announce our plans for a mill. But we would not be committed and would wait for our competitor to make a decisive move before we made a further decision. If he went ahead with expansion and we believed he needed it, we could retire, or better, perhaps, instead of building the paper mill, which is extremely expensive, we could shrink back to building a plywood, particle-board, or lumber mill.

Q: In what other kinds of matters do you find it advisable to observe as well as you can what the competition is doing?

A: *I am concerned about the financial competition and with our competitive position in the marketplace. And I take an over-all look at our price-earnings ratio, growth in earnings per share, return on investment, and return on sales, as compared with similar or competitive companies.*

Share of market is one of the key things we look at. If I

detect a decrease in market share, I bring it up at the top executive council meeting. Or talk to the manager in charge of the operation. I ask why. The answer is usually one of three things. A newcomer may have entered the field, or our product quality has slipped, or somebody has cut prices in order to increase his market share. We act accordingly.

In the case of a newcomer, we have the choice of whether to take action to regain the amount we've lost or to content ourselves with what we have left. There's often a trade-off— short- versus long-term—but you might argue for the short- term and be content with reduced volume. If it is a quality problem, we may have to spend money to improve. It is expensive to increase quality, and the question is how fast so as not to lose position. If it is price, we have to make a decision whether to meet competitive prices and maintain volume or keep prices up and take a reduction of volume.

There is no predetermined answer. Usually, it is a question of a short- versus long-range criterion. No matter what you do it will affect what your competitor does. We try and think what our action will do to his actions. We know our competitors by pattern and often can predict their reaction. I can almost guarantee that if we take an account away from company X they will cut the price to another of our accounts.

Q: Well, to turn from specific strategies to your general plan for Boise Cascade, do you think you can maintain any reasonable approximation of your past growth rate without maintaining the same pace of acquisitions?

A: *Yes. As of today, we have a new ingredient in the company that we've never had before—and that's a lot of cash. The cash resource that Ebasco has given us is new and it makes possible exciting opportunities for internal growth. They have it now invested in what we consider low-return projects, whereas we have a huge inventory of high-return projects that we've been waiting for cash to go into. We also feel that there are some acquisition opportunities in foreign countries where Ebasco has cash resources, and in some related domestic fields.*

We could use some cash to pay off some high-interest debts that we have on some of our land-development interests. We have the opportunity to build a pulp mill that will cost about $40 million but has a high return associated with it. We're planning on investment in additional capacity for factory-built homes, including mobile homes. We want to expand our distribution centers for building materials. We want to expand our capability to produce shelter—to get in position for the housing boom that's got to come eventually. We're interested in packaging abroad. We want additional plywood plants—we need one in Idaho, one in the upper Midwest; we'd like one in the South. We'd like to look abroad in office supplies.

Also we wanted the Ebasco expertise in operating in some of the foreign countries that we're thinking of moving into. The skills they had in operating in foreign countries was attractive. They're more experienced than we are in operating in Latin America. And their construction and management consulting activities fit naturally into our pattern.

In sum, we have these two huge areas for investment. One, internal development, and the other, foreign acquisition. In the foreign area we've just scratched the surface. Because we are an operating company, we've got exportable skills, we have knowledge in an industry that has tremendous possibilities for growth abroad—housing, packaging, forest products, in Latin America, Central America, Indonesia. These are basic industries, and just as important in foreign markets as they are in the United States. We want to be as involved internationally as we are domestically.

Thus Hansberger concluded his remarks on the Ebasco merger and on his executive style, in which he set forth an almost perfect guide to modern corporate management and also provided an illustration of the kind of activity that takes place in bargaining inside the core of a game. The core gave the players the range and they bargained over that range to reach a point of settlement.

THE BARGAINING

The game thus concluded between Boise and Ebasco is a remarkable example of how neat bargaining can be for very high and complex stakes. When two players bargain over the range between their fall-back values, the outcome is so indefinite that one might call upon anyone to say what could happen, linguist, arbitrator, consultant on business procedures, novelist. Game theorists, having established the range, usually observe that the rest is up to the personalities and their innate and inscrutable bargaining ability. That is, having found the shape, size, and location of the bargaining area —the core—they back out of the end game that takes the players to the specific point of settlement. In real life, players willy-nilly find a way to settle, as Boise and Ebasco did with such precision.

The appearance of the minority directors of Ebasco as a third party in the bargaining gives a flicker of suggestion of the start of a new three-person game. But as they apparently drew into the game no third economic force—shareholders or competitors—they appeared for all practical purposes to stay within the bargaining range, where they succeeded in getting Hansberger to move from a ratio of 1.2 to 1.25. How did they do that? By word play, perhaps, or a show of emotion? They convinced Hansberger that to minimize present and future complaints about the price, he should move the ratio of exchange in Ebasco's favor. All parties apparently were satisfied that that was the best they could do. What happened after this game had nothing intrinsically to do with its conclusion.

THE FAILURE OF THE PROSPECTS

Although the game was played well and with no error in perceptions, its prospects, which gave value to the game, did not pan out. They failed in an unpredictable way in the play of a subsequent game that followed immediately after the merger.

The first jolt to the prospects came the following year. Hansberger opened his report to the shareholders with the observation: "Boise Cascade had a very disappointing year in 1970." Although the company's sales had held about even at $1.7 billion, net income was down 55 percent, and earnings per share were down 55 percent. The next year was worse. Hansberger observed: "Boise Cascade's performance reached a low point in 1971 . . ." Sales still held even, but the company's net income was a minus $85 million, with about half the losses in operations and half in discontinued businesses, and, of course, earnings per share were below zero. The report to the shareholders for 1972 was written by a new president and chief executive, John B. Fery, and a new chairman, Stephen B. Moser, who had moved up inside the company. Their report began: "This has been a time of dramatic change for the company." And it was indeed. Sales were down to $1.1 billion, net earnings down to a minus $170 million, despite about $40 million in operating profits. The company had been to the brink of insolvency and had been reorganized with vast write-offs and sales of assets. Its stock had dropped from a high of $80 a share in 1969 to $10. Hansberger had resigned.

The fine details of Boise Cascade's descent from the heights of the corporate world are not germane to this story. The disasters included some of the former Ebasco companies in South and Latin America and some in the United States in construction, a Boise foray into "black capitalism" in Harlem. But the company very likely could have suffered these and other setbacks without shock, despite their convergence in one brief period of time. What rocked the company was its failure to understand a real-estate development game it had entered before the merger, which ended in 1972 with a dead loss of about $250 million. Boise was defeated by failing to meet the large social issues known as environmentalism and consumerism.

A word about this game. Boise had entered the field of

recreational communities in 1966 and had hundreds of millions of dollars invested in the development of twenty-nine such communities in 1970. By mid-1972 it had sold to the public about $350 million in recreational lots, mainly in California. Consumer groups attacked these sales for misrepresentation in the sales talk and advertising. Through class-action lawsuits, with the State of California among the plaintiffs, they piled up claims against the company of about $500 million. Although Boise settled these claims in 1972 for a little over $50 million, the adverse publicity had put a damper on the sales of lots. But the decisive blow came from environmental groups who attacked the projects for damaging the natural environment. The State of California then imposed stricter environmental specifications on the developments, which raised Boise's costs higher than they could raise the selling price. At mid-1972 Boise began to liquidate its realty projects and wrote off a loss of about $200 million. Boise then was in default on its loan covenants and was forced to reorganize its finances. To get straightened out, they sold off timber assets and a number of operating companies, altogether about a quarter of the company's assets, and started over again from a lower base in assets, sales, and income, and with the old momentum gone.

WHAT FAILED

How does one account for this debacle? Hansberger was not a romantic businessman like William Zeckendorf, Sr., or James Ling, both of whom had a meteoric rise and fall. In the interview above he professes the highest order of standard modern business management philosophy and method. He designed a contracyclical set of diversified operations, centered on, if not altogether closely linked to, forest products. His aim was "consistency and permanence." His "pinnacle objective" was to increase the shareholder's value consistently. He set the ambitious target of increasing the company's earnings per share by 20 percent a year and met it for twelve years. Such a target may put pressure on a company to take on risky projects, but Hansberger had buttressed this principle with other restraining measures, such as return on investment and unit increases in profits. He thought in terms of both chance and free competitive interactions. He held advisory staff strategy sessions and opened the company to scrutiny from the outside. When he negotiated with Ebasco, both sides and expert outsiders evaluated the "facts, figures, futures."

And yet it didn't work because of a failure in dealing with a major aspect of cooperative games. In the chapter on cooperative games we saw two basic solutions to these games, the hard economic core and the social norm. We saw a number of chief executives worrying for the first time about the effect of changing norms on their business operations. Boise Cascade is an example of how these large social issues can affect the fate of billion-dollar corporations. The fact that the actors representing consumers and environmentally oriented people went to politics and law for their solutions does not alter the underlying economic character of the game. Real-estate developments until recent years only needed to carve up land and sell the parcels. In that norm, the social costs of damaging the environment—whether by pollution or development— were not counted in the costs of production. That norm changed, and since the upset, the question of the allocation of these costs between producers and consumers of pollution is unsettled. Now nothing in this sphere can be taken for granted. It is a matter of judging the values, an unstable situation unless you can find the cooperative economic core. Hansberger's investment was committed at a certain environmental level when the judgment, different from his, came from unsatisfied economic and social groups, and they proved to have the power to prevail. The economic consequences were concrete: they got the specifications changed. The risk of this happening to Boise Cascade was not the standard risk of chance. It was a very game-theoretic affair involving the changing social standards in economic life.

8

HOWARD HUGHES:
THE DIFFICULTY OF UNDERSTANDING
THE VALUES OF AN INVISIBLE PLAYER

The picture of a game in the real world which a player forms in his mind usually contains a number of blank spaces. If too many of them remain unfilled, there may be a question of whether one can play the game. This problem of incomplete information is recognized in theory as well as practice. Real players resolve the problem as well as they can through guess-work, hypothesis, and even through negotiating and bargaining which tend to bring out needed information. Classical game theory, as noted, rests on the assumption of complete information about the rules of a game, but contemporary theorists are working to break away from this restriction, and we shall see something of the direction they are taking. Three types of information are critical. In a strategic game played non-cooperatively, the players want to know the rules and the strategies; in a cooperative game, they particularly want to know the values of the players.

The invisible Howard Hughes provides a good game of incomplete information. This is not the "Howard" of the anecdotes—aviator, moviemaker, lover, and eccentric of the night—but the Hughes who works at making money, an amount sufficient to account for a substantial part of his fortune. The game takes place in and around Trans World Airlines (TWA), of which he was once the principal owner. The game is dominated by uncertainty about the rules as well as the strategies, and the ambiguity in the values of the player who cannot be seen. The purpose here is not to unmask Hughes in the sense that inspires the large and growing literature of his legend, but to describe what it is like to play an interactive game with him fully masked. The other players, of course, want to read the mask, but their purpose is circumscribed by the game. It does not matter who or what "the real Hughes" is outside the game. If he is, as one of his old associates remarked, "a litigious Athenian," it matters only to the extent that it affects the game. Even the roughest model of a game contains only what is inside the game; anything outside is irrelevant. The difficulty will, of course, be to determine what belongs inside.

The game is better seen as two games, with a connection between them. The first is economic. The second, which follows in direct sequence, is played on two related levels—economic and legal—that is, the players struggle both within and over the rules.

THE PLAYERS

- Howard Hughes and the Hughes Tool Company
- Trans World Airlines (TWA)
- Three major insurance companies: Equitable Life Assurance Society of the U.S., Metropolitan Life Insurance Company, and the Prudential Insurance Company of America, led by Equitable, TWA's historical lender
- Two major banks: Bank of America, major bank for Hughes Tool, and the Irving Trust Company, lead bank for TWA and a lender to Hughes personally as well as to Hughes Tool
- Manufacturers of jet airliners: mainly Boeing, Convair (General Dynamics), and Lockheed; and their lenders
- Investment bankers and brokers
- Individual agents for these institutions and for Hughes

THE PRELIMINARIES

The first signs of the biggest game in the history of commercial aviation came in the early 1950s when the airlines faced the prospect of converting their fleets of propeller aircraft to jets, which they could not afford. In 1952 and 1953 the English aircraft maker de Havilland tried to get the jump on the commercial jet era by delivering its first Comets to the airlines and taking orders for delivery of later models through the decade. The potential change in air travel was then seen by some as being as radical as the change from sailing vessels to steamships. By being first to market, Great Britain hoped to rule the air as it had the sea under the first Elizabeth—that was the story, and as 1952 was the accession year of the second Elizabeth, the Comet was celebrated at the same time as a patriotic event.

But technical and strategic uncertainties then dominated both the airframe and airline industries in the United States and led them to wait. The financially shaky airlines were heavily committed to new piston props not yet delivered. Jet speed had not yet proved it could reduce operating costs and to some it appeared as a luxury. Others—C. R. Smith, president of American Airlines, was one—doubted both the economy and the safety of the jet. If jet propulsion was the prime mover of the future, a jet-driven propeller plane (turbo-prop) was seen as promising less speed but more economy than pure jets.

For airlines and manufacturers alike, the crux of the matter was timing: to avoid being too early for adequate performance or too late to capture the market. Two of the aircraft makers expressed the problem from opposite poles:

> Timing is a vital factor in producing a new aircraft and it is often better to produce a slightly inferior aircraft at the right time than a perfect one at the wrong time. —C. T. Wilkins, designer, de Havilland Aircraft Company, Ltd.

> In our business, the race is not always to the swiftest or the first to start.—Donald Douglas, Douglas Aircraft Company, Inc.

The Americans—Boeing, Douglas, and Lockheed—in the early fifties measured the time, as they saw it, for jet development. An engineering executive would lay a ruler across his desk, its units the years of the fifties, and lay over it explicit stages in sequence: preliminary design (1952–53), certification and operational tests (1955–58), construction of production aircraft (1956 onwards), scheduled deliveries (1958 onwards). There was room here for different choices. Bereft of position in the piston-propeller plane market, but experienced in making jet bombers (the medium bomber B-47, and big bomber B-52 then in prototype construction), Boeing had little to lose and much to gain by moving first. With jet engines of commercial quality under development by the military and expected in 1956 or 1957, Boeing designed the 707 jetliner, timed it for production in 1958–59, and soon started talking to the airlines. Douglas and Lockheed, who dominated the big piston-prop market, also talked jets (both pure jets and turbo-props). But rich in contracts for piston-prop planes, they were not in a hurry and made plans to bring out more advanced jets after Boeing. So the timing moves were laid down, with the Comets flying and the Americans counting on the developing state of the art to give them higher performance at later dates.

All were conscious of the possibility that history might repeat itself. In the thirties Boeing designed the first monoplane liner, the B-247, only to have Douglas come out a year later with the DC-2 and sweep the market for decades with a succession of DC designs. History did repeat itself, but with variations. The early Comets failed for being too early for the state of the art, and England lost a gallant gamble for which test pilots, engineers, and eventually passengers died. The airlines began signing up with Boeing.

No one knew the aviation business better than Hughes, and he too, in TWA, was caught up in the swirl of uncertainties of the early fifties, one of which has not yet been dealt with in this story, namely, finance. The airlines had to raise the money to finance a changeover costing hundreds of millions of dollars, which would stretch their resources and credit to the limit. They would get it from lenders, of course, and lenders tie strings on their money. Here was the issue that especially differentiated Hughes from all the other players and set the stamp on his game. The American aviation business was pioneered, appropriately, by tough romantics like Eddie Rickenbacker of Eastern, William Patterson of United, C. R. Smith of American, Juan Trippe of Pan American. And Hughes. The difference between Hughes and the others was that they were managers who owned little equity in their companies—none more than 5 percent—whereas Hughes owned most of the equity stock in TWA and alone governed its policies.

Hughes, through his corporate creature, the Hughes Tool Company, bought into TWA in 1939 and had obtained a substantial position in it (almost half the stock) before the end of the Second World War. He participated with its then president, Jack Frye, in tying Europe into the transcontinental run, giving the airline two long hauls that would pay off tremendously in the future. At the same time, the equipment problems, in part related to routes, were continuously pressing as aircraft designs moved rapidly from DC-3s to DC-4s to DC-6s and the Lockheed Constellations (which Hughes is said to have had a hand in designing) and their later hot-rod versions (the DC-7s and "Superconnies"), the controversial turbo-props, and pure jets with their enormous financial requirements. TWA, like all airlines, was always looking for money.

In 1946 TWA almost went to the wall as a result of airplane crashes, the grounding of the new Constellation, and a pilot strike. Hughes, through the tool company, put $10 million cash into the airline and took back notes. But these notes were convertible into new common stock and gave him the power to name the majority of TWA's directors, i.e., he took control of TWA. The following year he exercised the option, raising the tool company's stockholdings to 73 percent, and treated TWA as a subsidiary of the tool company. The Civil Aeronautics Board (CAB) approved Hughes's control, complimenting his technical and financial contributions to aviation, but also taking note with some anxiety that TWA was heavy with debt. Hughes preferred big debt. At that time the only source of large private placements, as the long-term loans are called, was the handful of large life insurance companies led by Prudential, Metropolitan, and Equitable. The principal lender to TWA was Equitable.

Equitable came into TWA for the first time in 1945 with a loan of $30 million, increased in 1946 to $40 million. The securities put up for it by TWA, called "debentures," gave Equitable a kind of veto over TWA financing, so when Hughes financed the airline and took control that year, he had to get Equitable's permission, and to get permission he had to agree to further conditions, or "loan covenants."

Owners and lenders normally cooperate in a bargaining relationship. The stake of an owner who wants control of his property is self-evident. The stake of a lender, however, requires formulation. Lenders seek either as much return as they can get with adequate safety, or as much safety as they can get with adequate return. Concern for safety naturally leads to a concern about the way the borrowing company is managed; this is translated into certain veto powers over management, and, in the extreme case, into a demand for absolute control.

The airlines have typically yielded to the superior bargaining power of the lenders, and at the time that Hughes took control of TWA he was no exception. The price of Equitable's agreement was Hughes's agreement that if TWA defaulted on payments to Equitable, the tool company's stock in TWA could be put into an Equitable-controlled voting trust. The seed was planted there.

Equitable, accordingly, throughout the 1950s kept watch on Hughes's direction of TWA, and Hughes kept watch on Equitable's appetite for covenants. Broadly speaking, Hughes exercised his control over TWA informally, leaving the detailed management to the executives and reserving only the major problems for his own decision. There were many criticisms of Hughes's control of TWA's management: a succession of presidents, long leaderless interludes between presidents, his personal assumption of responsibility for aircraft, his retreat into nocturnal telephone contact with his executives and others.

However, from the standpoint of the large lines of management, Hughes thought about the right subject matter for TWA. He concentrated on routes, equipment, and financing. As a stockholder, he resisted stock dilution, loan covenants, and loss of stockholder control. After the Hughes Tool Company took over in 1947, he participated intimately in helping TWA meet its increasing need for aircraft, the assistance extending even to the purchase by the tool company of planes for the airline. TWA's chief engineer and designer, Robert Rummel, represented the tool company as well as TWA in relations with aircraft manufacturers.

In January 1956 there came a turn in TWA's affairs. Ralph Damon, who had been president for seven years, died. Hughes did not replace him for a year; in the interim the airline was operated by committee. Carter Burgess, a former United States Assistant Secretary of Defense, became president in January 1957. He left in December of the same year, having never laid eyes on Hughes, and the office remained vacant until July 1958, when Charles S. Thomas, a former Secretary of the Navy, came in. No explanation has been given for the two interludes, totaling twenty of the thirty months following Damon's death. Though at all times there appears to have been a high order of second- and third-tier management in TWA, the lack of continuity in the presidency was widely recognized in and out of the company as a serious deficiency. Combined with TWA's running losses in the three years 1956 through 1958, Hughes's style of management scared the lenders.

After Damon's death, whether or not there was a president in office, Hughes himself took over the main policy decisions on what had become the key issue of equipment financing. He had the will to stake his fortune on the outcome of the jets, and to try to have his way while staving off the conditions that lenders wanted to impose upon him. He had considerable financial and technical capabilities for this task. With his personal interest in flying and in aircraft design, he had explored jets and jet concepts, sub- and supersonic, in the very early fifties. Wellwood Beall, who led the 707 development when he was chief engineer at Boeing, credits Hughes with knowing the subject.

In an attempt to reduce the scale of jet financing to manageable proportions, Hughes tried to develop a single dual-purpose jet design that would serve TWA's special need to fly both transcontinental and transatlantic. He explored the possibility of going into manufacturing himself—at first, in 1954, in cooperation with Convair, and later, in 1956, through the tool company. Whether these moves were feints or bluffs to stimulate more competition in the aircraft industry or real threats is not clear. At any rate, they were dropped. In February 1956, four months after Pan American and American, two of TWA's chief competitors, had placed their first orders with Boeing, Hughes began placing his first orders through the tool company for a fleet of sixty-three jet aircraft with two companies: thirty-three 707s from Boeing and thirty 880s from Convair. Although the contracts were made by Hughes Tool, they were assignable to TWA. Deliveries were scheduled for 1959 and 1960. The total commitment came to more than $300 million, including spare parts and engines. As this sum was too large for the tool company to finance by itself, Hughes was destined to have to come to some kind of long-term financing arrangements for the delivery period, then three years away.

These turned out to be hard years for the domestic airlines and the Hughes Tool Company. Two things hit the tool company at once: the severe general economic recession of 1957–58 and a decline in oil drilling which reduced the market for its oil tool bit. As for the airlines, their rate of growth declined in the recession. With TWA running in the red, the tool company, despite its own setback, not only put down some money on its commitment for the future jet fleet and substantial sums for the airline's current needs, but also gave support to further TWA equity financing. In 1957 TWA made a common-stock offering to its stockholders, underwritten by the tool company, which enabled them to buy one share for each share they already owned. This raised new equity capital of $43 million. The tool company took up about $35 million of the issue, slightly enlarging the proportion of its equity interest in TWA.

Despite this and other financing, TWA needed $12 million to meet its payroll during the first quarter of 1958. This sum was obtained from Bank of America and Irving Trust on a ninety-day note guaranteed by the tool company. It was renewed once, and on July 1, 1958, Hughes asked for another renewal. The two banks were agreeable, but here Equitable asserted one of the prerogatives of its existing loan indenture. It seems that Equitable would not consent to an extension of the bank loans unless Hughes set up a long-term financing plan for TWA covering the $300-million jet commitment, but the discussions were inconclusive. Among the subjects that came up was the possibility of a voting trust for Hughes's stock in TWA if the long-term financing were not completed within ninety days. Just why the discussions failed is not clear, but the day before the bank loan became due, the tool company paid the $12 million. This still left up in the air the problem of financing TWA's jets.

THE FIRST GAME

The preliminaries ended and the game took shape on the eve of the delivery of the first Boeing 707 to TWA. The delivery was due in January 1959; fourteen more were scheduled to follow at intervals during the next seven months and still more—Convairs as well as Boeings—in 1960. Someone had to pay for them one by one. TWA did not have the money. Hughes, despite his vaunted wealth in Hughes Tool, had only limited cash resources, enough to make a start. The normal financing of the whole jet program by banks and insurance companies was two years late, owing to Hughes's mysterious procrastination; and with time now running out on the clock of deliveries, he soon had to settle on a long-term financing plan or take the consequences. Nevertheless, as there was a gain to be made by whoever participated in the financing, and the nominal objective of all parties was to find the best deal, the game—despite the signs of strategic conflict—could be expected to be essentially cooperative. The central difficulty, and perhaps the overriding characteristic of the game, however, lay in the fact that certain information needed to describe the game as well as to play it was lacking.

A good many realities—in effect, rules of the game—had emerged in the preliminaries. The potential participants would negotiate over how much equity and how much debt would go into the financing, and at what rates, and under what conditions. Each party was in the game by his own consent; each could withdraw from any arrangement deemed unsatisfactory. There were restraints in the indentures and covenants attached to TWA's present loans. The rights of the minority shareholders would have to be respected, even though they were not present as strategic players. The Civil Aeronautics Board had a responsibility for the public interest in the airline, which the players would have to recognize.

To divide prospective gains in this game cooperatively, it is necessary to get some line on the values of the participants. Least known in this respect was Hughes. No one, with the possible exception of Hughes himself, knew for sure what Hughes wanted. The game was remarkable in this respect. Most real games, as noted, are to some extent short on information about the players or what life holds. But here was a game in which the leading player had vanished during the preliminaries, rarely, it turned out, to be seen again to the present time (1974). He was represented by agents, for the most part by the debonair Raymond Cook, a corporation lawyer and negotiator of remarkable strategic acumen, who had an old family tie to Hughes: his Houston law firm—Andrews, Kurth, Campbell & Jones—had represented Hughes's father before him. Hughes also communicated on occasion by telephone with some of the other players, his banker, Ben-Fleming Sessel, of the Irving Trust Company of New York, for one. Yet his true values in the game remained as obscure as his person.

Although games of incomplete information are a relatively

undeveloped part of game theory, some order has been introduced into them. One approach is to adopt the side of a player whose identity and values are known. Since you know one side but not the other, you think of the plausible possibilities on the other side and list them as if the opposing player were several (possible) player-types and you make a subjective estimate of the chances that any particular type is the real player. Then you proceed to play against each of these types as you would in a regular game. I adopt a similar ordering procedure but do not attempt to pursue the theory into its further reaches.[1] Instead, I shall later go on to describe how the real players went about attempting to clarify the information about Hughes and Hughes about them.

The players opposite Hughes puzzled over what he was up to without being able to settle firmly upon anything. But one could imagine Hughes in a variety of guises, any one or more of which could plausibly represent the real player, as follows:

THE MASKED PLAYER

I. Hughes wants a cooperative deal. But what kind of deal does he prefer, and how much does he prefer one kind to another? Three are possible:

> 1. Standard airline financing with banks and insurance companies, with details about rates, time periods, the ratio of debt to equity, indentures, and covenants to be negotiated.
>
> 2. A long-range leasing arrangement whereby a company owned by Hughes would buy the airplanes and lease them to TWA (with possible tax and depreciation benefits to him).

[1] This is the theory of John Harsanyi of the University of California (Berkeley), who has devoted his principal efforts to games of incomplete information. Different approaches have been made by other game theorists. One of these is to play against the unknown other side in a series of episodes, playing for points, and at times yielding points to take short-term losses in the expectation of long-term gains. Each point is played as a separate game.

3. Participation in TWA financing by aircraft manufacturers who wanted to sell jet aircraft to TWA—their money to supplement the senior loans with a second-mortgage type of financing as part of the purchase deals: this would give Hughes altogether 100-percent financing; that is, he would operate TWA entirely on other people's money.

II. Hughes is not playing cooperatively. He prefers to play one-sided strategies. In this case, he will not be interested in the values of the others but only in how his strategies work in relation to theirs. If all sides play this way, each will be interested only in the payoff to himself (contrary to the concept of cooperatively dividing their mutual gains, which would require each to understand the values of the others). As the number of players is larger than two and yet not large enough to correspond to the classical economic model, there is no theory for this way of playing which could be put to practical use. That is to say, they would not be able to play a single strategy through a long sequence of moves, but would have to play in short sequences with pauses to review the information.

III. In either case—cooperative or non-cooperative—Hughes wants no settlement at the time of the beginning of the game. He is stalling in wait for chance events which he expects will favor him. One of these might be a change in financial costs (equity or interest rates)—a single percentage point up or down translates into millions of dollars. Another chance event, an inevitable one, which Hughes may be waiting for is the actual performance of the new and untried jet aircraft, which perhaps he expects to be superior to the prevailing conservative expectations of the lenders: the better the performance, the stronger TWA's position would be and the more favorable the terms Hughes could expect from the lenders, especially as regards his financial guarantees of TWA's debt.

IV. Hughes doesn't know his own values and is agonizing over coming to a decision. His vision may also be colored by emotions of pride, anger, fear, distrust, and the like, all of which have been attributed to him.

V. Hughes doesn't know the rules of the game and is using up time trying to find out what his choices are.

VI. Hughes has ceased to be a strategic player. He is no longer rational or has withdrawn from the game for unknown reasons (the notion that he was incapacitated or a captive of unknown parties or dead arose later in Las Vegas and seemed to be refuted by his telephone interview from the Bahamas with several members of the press who had known him personally, and by his meeting with the American ambassador in Nicaragua. Reports of his last years which appeared after his bizarre death in 1976 failed to clear up many of the Hughes' mysteries.)

VII. It's a strategy game and Hughes is bluffing. His presence in the game is known only through agents. Perhaps he does not let them know what he wants or what game he is playing, especially his strategies. Perhaps they do not have the authority to negotiate and conclude a deal. Perhaps each agent represents a single Hughes strategy: in that case, Hughes, by setting aside an agent or agent's position, or firing him, or causing him to quit, can thereby shift from one strategy to another; that is to say, by randomizing his agents he is randomizing his strategies to prevent anyone from finding out his actual strategy.

VIII. Hughes is playing some combination of the above variations.

IX. Hughes doesn't want to participate voluntarily in any financing deal. He wants to create favorable conditions for selling the airline.

X. Hughes keeps a secret. This possibility is a catch-all for any surprise that may turn up. It is also a reservation for what one may never know.

THE OTHER PLAYERS

The other strategic players, though more visible than Hughes, were not quite an open book. As institutions, the in-

surance companies, banks, aircraft manufacturers, and investment bankers and brokers had well-known values; and their
agents—usually the top officers in dealings with Hughes—as
fiduciaries represented these values. But of course agents, as
individuals, also represent to some extent their own interests,
associations, values, temperaments, and temper, and have
some fiduciary leeway for the exercise of their judgment.
And so, opposite Hughes there was an area of the unknown
which, though narrower than he presented, posed for him too
in some degree a question of incomplete information.

There is no useful way to canvass the unknowns among
the player-agents at the outset of the game. But the values
which bound the institutions are fairly easy to describe.

Investment bankers and brokers, though competitive, are
nominally neutral and catalytic, in contrast to the other
players who had strategic interests.

Among the aircraft manufacturers, Boeing, having the lead
and prospering, would want straightforward buy-sell deals
with TWA or with Hughes for TWA. But Lockheed, in trouble with its then technically ailing prop-jet Electras, needed
the support of contract sales and would certainly not be
averse to side angles to get them. Convair (General Dynamics) had a good jet airplane for domestic use in its 880s
and an intercontinental prospect in its larger planned 990s,
but with only two firm customers, Delta Air Lines and
Hughes, it too could be interested in an angled deal.

The lenders in general, as noted, were in business to lend
with a strong emphasis on their security. They would also
want to maintain their historical customer connections. The
western-based Bank of America, not only the major bank for
Hughes Tool but also the lead bank for Lockheed and Convair, would be Hughes oriented when it could escape
conflicts of interest. The eastern-based Irving Trust Company, as Hughes's personal banker and as lead bank for
TWA, with an officer, Ben-Fleming Sessel, on TWA's board
of directors, would likewise be Hughes oriented. He was
their biggest customer.

Any of the major insurance companies, whose business was

long-range financing, could be expected to appear in so large a financing as TWA required. Equitable of course was at the center, owing to its position as historical lender to TWA. It would like to have—and had the traditional claim on—TWA's new jet business, and it could be expected to share so large a business with another insurance company. Its most urgent business, however, was to protect its existing loans on TWA's obsolescing piston aircraft. This would be a key factor in the game, for these loans were in the form of mortgage bonds which in the event of a TWA bankruptcy gave the insurance company no effective remedy. It had a right to repossess the airplanes—when the court permitted—but distress sales of piston aircraft offered little security. As the piston fleet obsolesced in competition with the forthcoming jets, its value would decline. Indeed, one could imagine a bankruptcy sale in which the market for piston airplanes was limited to marginal buyers: freight carriers and charters. At a sheriff's, marshal's, or trustee's dumping sale, let us say they went for $10 million. Equitable would then have a preferred claim on $10 million and would have to line up with the other common creditors for the remaining $20 million of its loans. Equitable's chances to collect its full claims were essentially no better than TWA's future earning ability (i.e., ability to sell tickets). Hence Equitable's fall-back position, below which it would not willingly go, was to bail out its $30 million in TWA; and to this end it would employ all the force it had in indentures and covenants. Its range of values, top and bottom, thus was clear.

THE ACTION

The first general problem of the game was, of course, to narrow the range of information. One or another of the players would make tries at getting a deal based upon one or another of the assumptions mentioned above. Each try was an event and a revelation. As event, it might resolve the game then and there. If it did not, as revelation, it would narrow the choices. Thus the game in this phase would be dynamic, in the form of a series of subgames.

■ An investment banking firm, the First Boston Corporation, on a monthly retainer from Hughes, undertook during the later months of 1958 to prepare a long-range financing plan for TWA. Such arrangements are customary when someone is seeking financing either by a public offering or a private placement. The retainer normally pays for the time it takes to become familiar with the players and the numbers involved—the preliminaries. The result of this try was cloudy and frustrating. First Boston withdrew in January 1959 without revealing what kind of plan it had worked on. Its head, George Woods, was reported as saying he would not do business with a man who would not meet him face to face. Pique at Hughes's invisibility may have been the whole story. But about the time First Boston withdrew, a New York investment banking company, Dillon, Read—with other New York investment bankers in the background—started work on a TWA plan. The event had one clear consequence: further delay with the clock running.

■ Boeing delivered TWA's first 707 on time in January 1959, and more would soon follow. Though unprepared financially to buy its own airplanes, TWA was well prepared with trained flight and maintenance crews to operate them. TWA began to put its jets into transcontinental service and immediately started to make money domestically. It looked like a profitable year for TWA.

■ Hughes paid for the first Boeing plane and leased it to TWA.

■ After this first delivery, Equitable moved to block TWA from paying Hughes Tool any more rent money for airplanes, which it was able to do under the rules of indenture. Equitable pressed the Hughes forces for a plan that would either take Equitable out or would give it an enforceable security—day-to-day leasing did not provide any long-term protection.

■ The tool company continued to deliver the planes to

TWA on lease, but the rent, though accruing, was not paid.

◼ Dillon, Read put forth a long-range plan involving the leasing of aircraft to TWA by a separate company set up for that purpose, which would be a wholly owned subsidiary of Hughes Tool. There was a widely held presumption that Hughes himself favored it. Leasing aircraft to airlines was not new, and indeed would become commonplace—even the insurance companies would become lessors to airlines. In the Dillon, Read plan, Hughes would have to guarantee the debt one way or another, since TWA's credit was not then sufficient for the whole financing. Equitable, always apprehensive, was reputed to be opposed to the leasing plan, but did not formally say it would not participate in it. The insurance company was never required to accept or reject it.

◼ The president of TWA, Charles Thomas, in an unusual outbreak of independence on the part of a TWA officer, rejected the Dillon, Read leasing plan. Leasing aircraft, though conventional now, may not then have been well understood. One might have thought that if Hughes strongly favored it, he would have overruled or fired Thomas, but Hughes was not ready to turn Thomas down for his judgment. He is reported not to have insisted on the plan because he too became disenchanted with it for various reasons when he thought it through. Even the depreciation benefits to Hughes were not certain under tax regulations.

◼ It was now May 1959 and Hughes was getting into a financial bind. Owing to Equitable's block, so long as there was no long-range financial plan, he would have to go on buying airplanes for TWA and receive in return neither cash nor a negotiable resource. Hughes maneuvered. He defaulted on progress payments to Boeing on 1960 deliveries and at one point released six Boeing Intercontinentals back to Boeing, thereby permitting Boeing to pass the delivery rights over to Pan Am. This move relieved some of the financial pressure on Hughes, giving him more time, and reduced the size of TWA's long-term financing needs, possibly making feasible some other kind of deal.

◼ Hughes then, in the autumn, turned to the potentially

interested manufacturers, Lockheed and Convair, for both of whom the sale of jet aircraft to TWA represented a way out of their own troubles. Hughes apparently saw the economic force that might propel them and their bankers into a coalition with him and TWA, to their mutual benefit. For him and TWA the benefit could be measured by comparing such a deal with a standard financing plan. In a standard plan, the senior mortgage loan would come to about two thirds of the value of the aircraft. On this they would be paying a certain rate of interest, and they would expect to earn enough to pay the interest plus a few points more in profit. In the manufacturers' plan, on the other hand, TWA-Hughes would be borrowing the full 100 percent of the value of the aircraft: the two thirds put up by the senior lenders and one third put up by the manufacturers. As the one third would be in effect a second mortgage, it would cost a point or so more in interest than the standard rate and yet would still yield a few expected points in profit on the manufacturers' as well as the senior lenders' money. When business is good, the extra return on capital invested in such a "leveraged" company goes to the holders of the equity stock. The equity holders also take the risk. In bad times, the risk is that the large interest payments could not be met and the airline would go bankrupt. So in sum, the proposition was that Hughes-TWA would get the loan and the manufacturers would sell their aircraft to TWA.

This plan, however, would add to Hughes's current commitments a new one of $400 million for Lockheed Electras and a second round of the larger Convair 990s. Since the manufacturers did not have the money for the deal, they would have to get it from the banks. The deal hung in the balance for a while as the banks studied it. On the one hand, the manufacturers, for their financial health, needed to sell aircraft, and on the other hand, the assumption that TWA would sell all of its tickets was risky. The bankers finally decided the deal was too risky and denied the manufacturers the money.

■ In late 1959 Hughes, still maneuvering, employed a

combination of engineering and planning rationales to persuade Convair to rotate his unfinished 880s to the end of the production line, which would slow down deliveries he could not pay for.

■ One might wonder why Hughes did not seek the wherewithal to bail out Equitable and remove its block against lease payments to him from TWA. But here Hughes was double blocked. He was told by all that if he did not keep his historical lender, he might have trouble borrowing from other insurance companies. This did not only go for Hughes, nor was it in the rules. It is a custom in the lending business and it works both ways—for lender and borrower—as we shall see. Of course, a time may come for a change of lender, or borrower, but it was not the time for Hughes.

■ Chance did nothing for Hughes one way or the other during 1959 on the standard costs of financing, but it favored him on jet performance which was far above the standard expectations. That would help Hughes when it came to a deal, as it would relieve the tool company of the need to guarantee the prospective loans to TWA.

■ But Hughes had no deal as the year came to an end and he faced the prospect of having to pay for more deliveries to TWA in 1960 while his money and credit were running out.

■ The initiative shifted from Hughes's agents to the lenders. Since Hughes was nearly out of cash, unable to collect the rent TWA owed him for the leased aircraft, heavily in debt, and in need of more short-term money for jet deliveries in 1960, it was the bankers' move. There is stretch in the judgment of bankers, but somewhere there was a stop, for Hughes could not go on indefinitely without a return on his investment, and the banks had economic limits. The stop came suddenly and with a jolt. Irving Trust about the first of March 1960 shut off further credit to Hughes for the purchase of airplanes.

■ In the crisis that followed, Dillon, Read brought out a standard financing plan for TWA, which they had prepared earlier and held as a standby. It was the kind of plan that would satisfy the banks and insurance companies. Equitable, of course, was in it and its head, James F. Oates, brought in a new participant in Hughes-TWA affairs, Harry C. Hagerty, a top officer of Metropolitan. The two insurance companies agreed to share a long-term loan to TWA. Irving Trust, represented by Ben-Fleming Sessel, who had long dealt with Hughes, came in as the lead bank for a group of banks that would take up the shorter-term loans.

■ TWA's board of directors, including President Thomas, faced with fiduciary obligations to the minority shareholders, came to life independently of Hughes and voted approval of the plan. They also threatened to resign if Hughes did not agree. Hughes agreed.

■ The whole play narrowed down to the Dillon, Read plan, and here one must follow it step by step to its surprising outcome:

All parties first agreed in principle on the outlines of the plan. The insurance companies would provide $160 million in senior financing (that is, with first claim on TWA for the money); Hughes, through the tool company, would get his money back for the airplanes he had delivered to TWA, together with the rent money TWA owed him, and he would provide TWA with $100 million in junior financing (that is, money subordinated to the senior claims) and a revolving fund for TWA of $50 million.

That part was simple and easy, a formula. Tougher matters were negotiated during the next few weeks.

TWA needed funds immediately for further aircraft deliveries. And Equitable, of course, demanded that its now remaining $27 million loan on TWA's piston props be paid off as an integral part of the whole deal. There was no dispute over these matters. The banks agreed to put up money for the aircraft deliveries, through an interim credit to TWA of $40 million. TWA's debt to Equitable, due in 1969, was converted to a short-term obligation maturing with the bank loan. Then came the clincher. The lenders required Hughes—through the tool company—to guarantee both of these obligations. They were to be paid the day the Dillon, Read financing plan was to be closed, a date that got moved around a little and extended from June 30 to July 21, 1960. Although Hughes Tool had net assets of at least several hundred million dollars, they were not liquid, and so this guarantee would put Hughes in jeopardy if the deal was not closed on the appointed date; failure to close the deal could threaten imminent receivership or bankruptcy for Hughes Tool and TWA if the deal was not closed on the appointed date.

Among the covenants put into the plan was the condition that if *after* the deal was closed an adverse change of management took place, in the opinion of the lenders, they could demand a voting trust—but with the proviso that ninety days were first to be allowed as a period for Hughes and the lenders to obtain a mutually satisfactory new management.

The parties to the deal approved this plan in late March and early April.

Equitable and Metropolitan signed their letter of intent—the so-called "commitment letter"—which, though not enforceable, was conventionally honored.

The papers were drawn in May.

About mid-May Hughes guaranteed the new bank debt and the old Equitable debt accelerated to the near current due date.

Then came June and strange events.

Sometime that month Thomas requested of Hughes a management contract with TWA. Hughes resisted and there was some bargaining. Eventually Hughes offered Thomas the alternative of a contract with Hughes Tool. Thomas resisted that.

Late in the month the bankers, without approving a Thomas contract with TWA, said the financing plan could not proceed until the Thomas matter was cleared up.

Early in July the insurance companies, banks, and TWA signed the so-called "Bond Purchase agreement," but they introduced a new condition: if, in the opinion of the lenders, an adverse change of management took place *before* the closing, they were not obligated to proceed with the plan. At mid-July, about a week before the closing date, Thomas told

Hughes that he would resign if he did not get a TWA contract.

As Hughes was inscrutable, and so for that matter were some of the lenders at this stage, one should pause here and look around at what might happen.

The potential consequences of anyone's moves were clear.

Begin from Hughes's side: it was his move.

Hughes has a choice: to give Thomas a TWA contract or accept his resignation.

If he gives Thomas the TWA contract, Thomas will not resign, there is no change of management, hence no issue. The deal goes through.

If he accepts Thomas' resignation, the lenders have a choice: to go through with the deal or to call the resignation an adverse change of management and pull out.

In looking forward to these possibilities, Hughes could adopt the point of view of standard decision practice, that is, he could try to guess what the lenders will do—the probabilities, as it were. The late hedge taken by the lenders, giving them the right to pull out before the closing, could be interpreted as a threat to do just that if Thomas resigned; or it could be a sign that they were uncertain; or the hedge was a mere formality and they would proceed to close the deal in the spirit of good faith that had seemed to prevail from March into June, when the deal was negotiated. So there is a chance they will pull out, or proceed, and if they are uncertain, Hughes can try to persuade them to close the deal and, after it is closed, to invoke the ninety-day rule for finding a new and satisfactory management—all chances, and if Hughes is thinking along these lines, he can take the risk according to his lights. If he loses the gamble, he has further alternatives: the chance of some other deal and if that fails, the chance that he will lose control to a voting trust.

The assumption underlying this approach is that the lenders are predictable by some sort of guesswork probabilities, like dice except that the chances of this or the chances of that, and so on, would have to be subjective. It is a common way of thinking, but is one-sided and not at all game theoretic.

At this point the game looks as though it may have taken a non-cooperative turn, and so a one-sided view may be the appropriate one. We have seen above how it might have looked to Hughes from the point of view of standard decision making, with chances of this or that happening. But if he looked at the situation from the point of view of a non-cooperative game, he would not try to predict what the other side would do but rather would look at their possible strategies. The simple realities remain the same but we now see what may happen as action and reaction.

Recall that Hughes has a choice to give Thomas a TWA contract or to accept his resignation.

If he gives Thomas the contract, the game ends with the Dillon, Read plan put into effect.

If he lets Thomas resign, the lenders have two choices: a deal or no deal.

If it's a deal, the lenders afterward have the further choice of letting Hughes alone appoint another president or of declaring an adverse change of management and invoking the ninety-day rule for arranging a mutually satisfactory new management; and if they fail to reach agreement on a new management, the lenders—assuming their grounds have been defensible—may invoke the rule that a voting trust shall take over control of TWA. All of this is by agreed-upon rules.

If it's no deal—i.e., if the lenders pull out under the rule that they can do so if they judge that there has been an adverse change of management *before* the closing—they can then foreclose on Hughes or give him time to find another deal. Suppose they give him time, for which, as we shall see, there are good reasons. Hughes now can seek an alternative source of financing, that is, he can go back to playing a cooperative game with other parties, including perhaps some of the present parties. If he can find another deal, the game is over.

He can give up control of TWA, and accept the lenders' voting trust, and the game is over.

He can resist the voting trust but let it happen and lay the grounds for litigation.

If he takes the litigation route, the lenders have a choice to yield to Hughes's conditions or to counterlitigate.

If the lenders control TWA and counterlitigate, chance makes a move—what the courts will rule. Three outcomes are possible: Hughes wins, Hughes loses, or the result is indefinite as time passes without a final court ruling.

If Hughes wins, he takes control of TWA (and he must arrange a financing deal).

If Hughes loses, a voting trust controls TWA and Hughes remains the beneficial owner of most of the company's stock.

If Hughes loses, the voting trust controls TWA, and Hughes sells out his TWA stock.

If the result is indefinite, Hughes remains beneficial owner or sells out his TWA stock.

That, after a fashion, describes the game as it might have been imagined at mid-1960 after Thomas offered his resignation.

But perhaps one of the various possible outcomes needs comment, namely, Hughes's selling out. As a possibility it was not remote even then. If he could not keep complete control of the airline he might prefer it. But selling would not be easy for one who owned so much stock in one company, whether he or a voting trust controlled the company. He could hardly get out at a good price without a wrangle. The stock-buying public would more readily buy him out if it believed that his management was derelict and he was forced out. One can only say at this stage that if the seeming worst came to worst for Hughes and he lost control of the airline, it would not be the end of the world for him, but rather a new game in which he would not be bereft of prospects, and such prospects could influence the present game.

What actually happened is that on the day of the scheduled closing, July 21, 1960, the Hughes Tool Company announced Thomas' resignation as president of TWA. The lenders declared this to be an adverse change of management and withdrew from the deal. Hughes attempted to persuade them to close, make the management declaration afterward, and give him the then prescribed ninety days to arrange for a new president—to no avail. No one will ever know for sure just how Hughes or the other players appraised the situation and its potential consequences at the time, but some things are obvious.

The lenders had long been irked by Hughes's procrastination in coming to the negotiating table and by his management record. A Thomas contract with TWA would interpose a quasi-independent manager between them and Hughes. A Thomas resignation could confirm their worst fears.

As for Thomas, he bargained from what appeared to be a new-found strength, and as he and Hughes split not over the monetary benefits but over the question whether the contract should be with TWA or Hughes Tool, the issue for Thomas appeared to be his independence. Such a motive was plausible. Hughes, as noted, rarely if ever saw the directors and officers of TWA, communicated with them according to his whims, gave them little authority over anything but routine operations, and left them in uncertainty about his strategic policies; and he also on occasion carelessly injured their pride of person as well as of office. Thomas, feeling apparently that he was the butt of such treatment, could very well insist upon a contract that would give him some protection from it.

Hughes's stated position was that he did not think a TWA-Thomas contract was good for TWA (nor, it seems, did the TWA directors), and he is said to have resented having to bargain with Thomas under the gun of the financing deal. Hughes, also on the record, was loath to give contractual independence to his managers.

What Hughes thought of the lenders at the time is another unknown. One could hypothetically set forth a number of possibilities. These can be simplified by selecting only those that were actually stated later, if that is permissible for an observer writing in the present time. In the game following this one, Hughes would assail the agents of Metropolitan for conflict of interest in having overlapping directors with Pan Am, TWA's chief competitor. And, for what it is worth, Hughes would also accuse the lenders of encouraging Thomas to resign; and contrariwise the lenders would accuse Hughes of forcing Thomas out. But at the time it was impossible to say who was pulling the wool over whose eyes, if that was what was going on.

Once again the information was incomplete, and it was not even clear what kind of information would have made it complete. On the face of it, each side failed to understand the other's management values until an unforeseen incident—the side game ending in Thomas' resignation—brought out the incompatibility, which was enough to put an end to a cooperative game. On the other hand, if their later accusations reflect anything real at the time, the Thomas incident was not accidental, leaving the implication that either or both of them were playing a strategic game along adversary lines.

Whatever the causes, the remarkable thing is that a deal of such magnitude should turn on the resignation of a professional manager. As for the consequences, one does not know how far ahead, in moves to come, the players really looked. But the game had become pretty tight and they didn't have to look far to see well into the "game tree" described earlier. And now that Hughes had moved to accept the resignation and the lenders had moved to scrap the deal, the latter could foreclose on him or could sit by while Hughes negotiated elsewhere, and if he failed to find the money, take over from him.

■ The lenders did not forthwith foreclose on Hughes, but they tightened the noose by ordering TWA to refuse any further airplane deliveries from Hughes, and called their short-term loans for September 1—not much time for Hughes to look for another deal. That this would be his doomsday was not, however, altogether credible, for to carry out the threat the lenders would have to foreclose on TWA as well and that would put everybody—lenders, TWA, and Hughes—under the scrutiny of the courts; and putting airlines in bankruptcy was not considered good public policy. Hughes could count on this inhibition for a while as each side held TWA in hostage. But only for a while. TWA could not last much longer with no president, no more airplanes, no financing plan.

■ As matters stood at the beginning of August, Hughes thus had at least one month and perhaps another one or two, to look for other sources of money. He made a logical move for what it was worth. If it was Hagerty of Metropolitan who led the forces against him—and there was good reason to think so as he was known to take the hardest line against Hughes, and he didn't need the deal as much as Hughes did —Hughes would get rid of Hagerty. He persuaded the others, who held the power over him, to be patient while he tried to raise the money to take the place of Metropolitan's in the dead deal. To this end he persuaded Sessel of Irving Trust to work up a so-called "Bank Plan."

■ While this plan was in work, Hughes, not having any cash, persuaded Convair to shut down its production line of 880s which he was committed to take delivery on. Convair could have refused, finished the fleet, and put the airplanes in storage with interest on the money running against Hughes. But Convair chose to yield to Hughes, and lost the "learning curve" that is essential to the efficiency of aircraft production. Convair's acquiescence in this expedient was later charged as a factor in the disastrous multimillion-dollar loss suffered by Convair's parent, General Dynamics, in 1960–61, which sent that company out of control.

■ The first of September passed, and though the lenders made no move to collect their money, TWA was now in default and could be foreclosed on at the pleasure of the lenders.

■ The Bank Plan took shape in September and turned out to be a new version of the old manufacturers' plan, with

General Dynamics participating, along with the banks and Hughes and Equitable (to the extent of its $27-million standing loan). The plan called for a fast repayment of General Dynamics which Hughes didn't like, but he agreed to the plan. Prudential—long-term lender to General Dynamics—then stepped in and blocked the deal.

■ The failure of the Bank Plan sent the banks and Equitable back into cooperation with Hagerty of Metropolitan for the only available long-term money. Hagerty's condition again was a voting-trust takeover, and so that was the end of Hughes's potential membership in a lenders' coalition. The game now visibly changed in character. It was now clearly a two-person, non-cooperative, strategic game: the lenders v. Hughes. The stake was control of TWA. In such a game it was no longer necessary for either side to understand the other's values. They only needed to know one another's strategies, and these were fairly clear.

■ Hughes's strategic situation for the time being seemed to have deteriorated into disarray. His tool company, besides being committed to TWA's past-due obligation of about $54 million, also owed Irving Trust $15 million, past due; and Hughes himself owed Irving Trust $11 million on a personal note secured by all of his stock in the tool company, which was coming due on October 31. This personal note threatened the centerpiece of his empire, for Hughes had allowed himself to become insolvent; the lenders could soon foreclose on everything. Early in October they proposed to do just that, but held off for a few more weeks while Hughes made a few more desperate efforts to find another financing plan on his own. Then once again they threatened him with a choice between bankruptcy or a voting trust for TWA.

■ Hughes gave in and attempted to strike a bargain. He asked for the right to take over the loans to TWA at some future time without having to pay premiums. It was a concession the lenders could make, though premiums are common on buying back such loans, the rationale being that premiums enable the lender to take the refunded money and buy the safest security, U. S. Government bonds, and come out with the same net proceeds in the end. The banks and Equitable were reported to be willing to consider the concession—i.e., to charge low premiums or no premiums—so that Hughes could readily buy back control of the airline in the future if he got enough money. But Hagerty demanded that Hughes pay a 22 percent premium if he bought back the notes, which would be a considerable block against Hughes's ability to recover control. The other lenders joined Hagerty in the demand.

■ Hughes threatened legal action—the first intimation of a latent new game.

■ On October 25 the banks began offsetting the cash balances of TWA and Hughes Tool against their loans. And yet they still hesitated to throw TWA into bankruptcy.

■ Hughes made feeble tries at reviving the kind of deals that already failed.

■ November passed without apparent event. The lenders then set a final deadline of December 31, 1960, for their takeover or a receivership for TWA and Hughes Tool. The threat was now credible, owing to the lateness of the hour and the exhaustion of other alternatives. A new bit of uncertainty arose as Hughes then randomized an agent. On December 2 Raymond Cook, who had conducted the major negotiations throughout, announced that he no longer represented Hughes (he never revealed whether he was fired, or resigned, or left by agreement with Hughes). His disappearance was at least consistent with the fact that the cooperative policy he had represented had been abandoned. His place was taken by a well-known Hollywood lawyer, Gregson Bautzer, who had represented Hughes on occasion in the past, including a current effort to revive a deal with General Dynamics and one of its principal stockholders, Henry Crown.

■ The last maneuvers were touched with comic desperation as Bautzer alternately appeared and disappeared, while Raymond Holliday, the tool company's agent, waited on his authority for the signing of documents. In the last hour of the last day, with a document still unsigned, the lenders closed out the proceedings and took over TWA with a voting trust. With the noblesse oblige of victors, they took no advantage of the unsigned document which happened to be one needed by Hughes.

THE SECOND GAME

THE PLAYERS

- Howard Hughes, his lawyers Raymond Cook and Chester Davis, and other agents.
- A coalition of two insurance companies—Equitable and Metropolitan—and a number of banks led by Irving Trust; members of a voting trust appointed by the lenders to control TWA; directors and officers of TWA elected by the trustees and led by Ernest R. Breech (chairman) and Charles C. Tillinghast, Jr. (president); several law firms, and in particular the late John Sonnett of Cahill, Gordon, Reindel & Ohl.

Having taken control of the airline away from Hughes, the lenders set up a voting trust for ten years. Three voting trustees were created, one to be named by Hughes, two by the lenders. The trustees were to nominate new members of the TWA board at its next meeting.

Yet even this Draconian end of the first game did not preclude joint arrangements between the opposed parties in TWA; for Hughes still owned most of the airline he no longer controlled. Hughes and the lenders together assembled the wherewithal to finance TWA's jets.[2]

[2] The banks provided a credit of $72,200,000 and the insurance companies put up $92,800,000 (called "Series A" notes), both secured by equipment mortgages. Hughes received $55 million in cash and $100 million in TWA's subordinated notes, in settlement of the airline's debt to the tool company and to pay for the jets; the notes were to be paid later by the sale of debentures which would be converted to equity. Hughes and TWA paid off their old debts. And in a complex series of transactions, Hughes trans-

Under the new rules, the voting trust would dissolve and Hughes could recover control of the airline if any one of three things happened: either Hughes, with Civil Aeronautics Board (CAB) approval, bought out TWA's debt to the insurance companies (Series A notes, plus premiums), to which the voting trust was tied, or TWA itself redeemed the notes (paying a smaller premium), or the CAB invalidated the voting trust. Only the first of these events could Hughes initiate unilaterally, but the possibility of his return to control was there if he could find the money and get CAB approval.

Ernest Breech was in Detroit in December 1960, cleaning out his desk at the Ford Motor Company, from which he had just retired as chairman, and thinking he was going to go crazy with nothing to do, when he got a call from Grant Keehn, then vice president, later president, of Equitable. Keehn asked him to become one of the voting trustees of TWA. At first Breech demurred, though he agreed to go on the board; later he was persuaded to become a trustee for three months, when, he said, Keehn told him it was "his duty to the nation," and he ended up as chairman of TWA in April.[3]

One of Breech's first actions as trustee was to declare that he would cooperate with Hughes. In New York in January 1961, the day before the meeting at which the TWA board was to be reorganized, Breech said to Holliday and Maynard Montrose, a board member from Hughes Tool Company: "You can tell Howard not to worry as long as I'm here. I am working for all the stockholders and his interest is our interest. I want his suggestions, through you."

But Hughes apparently was not interested in such senti-

---

ferred title to the airplanes to the airline, furnished it with credits, and guaranteed its net working capital at $10 million until the last of the Convair 880s was delivered. Aircraft deliveries resumed in January 1961.

[3] Irving Olds, who died March 4, 1963, was the other trustee from the lenders' side. The Hughes trustee was Raymond Holliday, vice president of the tool company.

ments, however well intended. When the TWA board convened the next day, not enough Hughes-designated directors showed up to provide a quorum, thus making it impossible for the trustees to elect the new members. The trustees—with their majority of two to one against Hughes—responded by calling a stockholders' meeting the following month, where they voted the Hughes stock and elected a new board including six Hughes men.

Breech found a new executive to run TWA. That was Charles C. Tillinghast, Jr., who was at Breech's old company, Bendix Corporation, in Detroit. Tillinghast was agreeable to becoming TWA's new president if he were given an employment contract and if Breech became chairman. He got a contract similar to the legendary one Breech had secured at Ford; among its unique features, it enabled him to retire with pay if Hughes brought about the termination of the voting trust (a provision to which Hughes objected).

Things might then have subsided for a while, but at the same meeting at which Tillinghast was formally elected president, the affairs of Hughes and TWA took another sharp turn. The board authorized an independent study by the firm of Cahill, Gordon, Reindel & Ohl, to ascertain—in the mild-mannered corporate language for rough stuff—whether TWA had any legal claims arising out of the corporation's past history. As Breech explained it, the point was "to determine if, for the protection of the board, we should sue anyone, not just Hughes. As a director you're just as guilty for not bringing suit as if you had contributed to the damage."

Early in May, Tillinghast and the Cahill, Gordon lawyers discussed the possibility that TWA as a corporation might have a cause of action of an antitrust nature against Hughes, the man who still owned the vast majority of TWA stock. Tillinghast says he then pondered "whether as a matter of business judgment it would be wiser to enforce any such rights or to let bygones be bygones and get on with rebuilding the airline."

This was the first occasion Tillinghast had to try to think through the kind of game he would play. Not only would a suit by TWA's management against Hughes create a largely non-cooperative legal game and thereby complicate the issues, but in pursuing it, Tillinghast, his board, and inevitably in train the voting trust and the lenders would have to condemn Hughes for his past performance in guiding the airline. Impressing a court was not the only problem; there would be side effects. The contention would create the public impression that Hughes's return to control, if that should happen, would be detrimental to the airline, with repercussions on TWA's stock in the market and doubtless other consequences not precisely foreseeable. A suit, of course, would also create a new set of alternatives for Hughes. How deeply Tillinghast thought this game through in his imagination he hasn't said, but making the try is what a game is about.

Within a few weeks it was clear that bygones would not be bygones. On taking office in April 1961, Tillinghast and Breech adopted an aggressive, expansionist business policy for TWA. By May 1 they had put in an order for twenty-six new Boeings at a cost of $187 million and were negotiating new long-term financing of $147 million with Equitable, Metropolitan, and now also Prudential. Ever wary of the return of Hughes, the lenders imposed the condition that they could, if they chose, demand immediate payment of the new loan if the voting trust were terminated.

Hughes saw the proposed new covenant as another move to block his return to control; and the tool company notified Boeing that it disputed the power and authority of the Breech board to make the deal: TWA should buy the airplanes the tool company owned and had on order from Convair. Prudential saw too much trouble ahead and pulled out of the deal.

About this time Hughes engaged Chester Davis—a New York lawyer known for his flair, dash, and infinite energy—who left his firm to set up a sort of ad hoc law firm for Hughes (it later became a regular law firm with other clients). Davis, on the one side, and the late John F. Sonnett of Cahill, Gordon, on the other—both brilliant legal warriors—began warming up to engage one another in what would become one of the most spectacular and expensive jousting matches in legal history. And in August 1961 Raymond Cook reappeared in New York as co-counsel and negotiator for Hughes.

Meanwhile, Tillinghast received a report from Sonnett, who had conceived the legal case against Hughes. His "theory" was that the Hughes Tool Company was a supplier of aircraft and financing and that it excluded other suppliers from the market (to which Chester Davis for Hughes counterposed among other things the "theory" that the tool company and TWA were not separate markets but an integrated unit of parent and subsidiary, and so there could be no exclusion). Sonnett now advised the management that TWA had a duty to bring an antitrust suit against Hughes. Tillinghast was still studying this advice when Hughes offered to subscribe to and guarantee a $100 million issue of new TWA common stock on condition that the voting trust was terminated. The TWA board rejected the offer. Instead, they filed suit against Hughes in the Southern District of New York, asking not only for treble damages but divestiture of Hughes's stock. A new and different kind of game thereby was superimposed on the economic one.

Spokesmen for Equitable said afterward that they were "horrified" at the idea of TWA's suing Hughes; they said they saw only "suffering" and no benefit for the insurance company. These expressions may not have been as disingenuous as they might seem. They had not used this legal threat—either not having seen it or, having seen it, rejected it—in the first game, and perhaps for good reason: under the conventions, a big lender doesn't sue or provoke such a suit against a big client if he can avoid it. But their creature could and did, and there was "suffering" of a sort in the consequences. About six months later, when Hughes filed his answer to the TWA board, he also set forth counterclaims against the lenders, and everyone in the TWA financing was embroiled in fiercely spoken and costly litigation.

As in other phases of this bizarre conflict, the suit pitted the directors who had no proprietary stake in TWA against the tangibly interested Hughes, organization men against an eccentric individual, big financial institutions against a billionaire heretic of business, and lenders against an owner. Hughes's adversaries attributed devious motives to him, going back years. They directed hot words against his shadow and his defenders replied in kind. They were all honorable men, distinguished in business, finance, and law, and they freely called one another power seekers, lawbreakers, mismanagers, manipulators, self-dealers, monopolists, conspirators, and, by innuendo, thieves. "Let me state it now," said Sonnett to Davis during the pretrial proceedings. "You have asked for it. I did not recommend a suit charging Hughes with being a thief because I thought it wasn't in the interest of TWA."

The game divides here into two levels, legal and economic, and, though related and eventually convergent, they are better seen at first independently.

Despite its complexity, with suit spawning suit and countersuit, the legal contest can be reduced to certain lines. The TWA board entered two suits against Hughes, one in the federal courts charging antitrust violations, the other in Delaware state court charging mismanagement (the latter was a side threat and remained inactive but latent). The federal suit charged that Hughes, when he had control, had taken advantage of TWA to serve his own interests, particularly in connection with furnishing and financing aircraft for the airline. He was charged also with interfering with the new management after the voting trust was set up. The suit, as noted, sought treble damages and an order to Hughes to divest himself of his TWA stock, i.e., the removal of Hughes from TWA affairs.

Hughes's defense was that in running TWA he acted in the interest of the airline, which was a non-consolidated subsidiary of his wholly owned Hughes Tool Company; that TWA suffered no damage caused by him; and that he had done nothing in violation of the antitrust laws. He also pointed out that his actions concerning TWA had been approved by the Civil Aeronautics Board, a key point that would get lost for many years.

Hughes countersued the Equitable and Metropolitan life insurance companies, Irving Trust, and a number of financial executives as individuals for conspiracy to seize control of TWA and monopolize the lending in violation of the antitrust laws—a charge that, of course, they denied.

Tactical uncertainties aroused suspense. Who would be required to depose first, Hughes or his opponents? It made quite a difference not only because the deposer is technically on the defensive but also because these onerous proceedings could last a year on each side. Second, could Hughes's opponents find him to serve a subpoena? Finally—the whole case could hang on it—would Hughes come out of seclusion to meet his opponents face to face across the table or risk losing the lawsuit by default.

Hughes won the right to be the second to depose, whereupon his lawyers held the floor for a year, in "discovery" proceedings, questioning numerous parties in and around TWA. Meanwhile, a squad of ex-FBI agents employed by the TWA-lender side failed to penetrate Hughes's security; no subpoena was served on him. Nevertheless, the time came for him to show up or not show up in person. He did not show (and also declined to produce certain documents). He seemed thereby to indicate one of two things, either his confidence in his lawyers' opinions that he was immune from antitrust attack, or his reticence to appear in public whatever the cost. The district court ruled him in default, dissolving his counterclaims against the lenders, and, while holding the question of the divestment of his stock in TWA in abeyance, ordered a special hearing to determine the amount of damages he would have to pay for the alleged antitrust violations.

Hughes's lawyers appealed the court's ruling, principally on the narrow grounds of jurisdiction (to which the court limited them), contending that the issue belonged not with courts but with the CAB. They lost the appeal in the Second Circuit Court on the grounds of his default. The Supreme

Court turned away further appeal at that time and a Special Master was appointed to assess damages. Though Hughes's lawyers contended there were no damages to compute, the Special Master in 1968 computed about $45 million worth, which, trebled under the law, came to $137,600,000, plus costs and running interest (this involved rewriting TWA's history, but it appeared that when a party responsible for a corporation has not denied an allegation of antitrust violation, his alleged wrongs and mistakes, or appearance of mistakes, can be monetized, tabulated, and charged to him). Hughes again appealed to the higher courts. But meanwhile the economic action took place elsewhere.

While they met as adversaries in court, the two parties all along also met privately and negotiated; their subject matter: the economics as well as the control of TWA. The economics were dynamic in the extreme.

When the Tillinghast management moved into TWA in 1961, the airline was suffering from troubles remote from Hughes. It lost about $40 million that year, including both operating losses and write-offs of piston aircraft. And despite two fare increases, crisis spread across the entire airline industry as it lapsed into another recession. One reason for this was that the big jets were too good and there were too many of them. As they came on the line, the airline leaders quickly jumped to the conclusion that the jets would ruin the industry unless it was reorganized: they said there were too many airlines competing on too many routes; something should be done to reduce the competition.

As it turned out, this pessimistic vision—reflected in TWA's stock declining to 7½ a share in 1962 from its historic high of 35⅛ at the end of 1960—mistook the growing pains of the jet age for a deeper malady. But before this became apparent, the industry almost got reorganized. A worried CAB indicated that it would welcome mergers. The airline leaders snapped up the suggestion and began negotiations aimed at creating a new structure of stronger monopolies.

For TWA, two merger schemes were put forth, one by

Hughes and the other by Tillinghast, and, of course, the twain never met. In 1960, when he was still in control, Hughes had proposed merging TWA with Northeast, reasoning that the Boston–New York–Florida route would take the then traditional seasonal red ink out of TWA's first quarter. Hughes persisted with the idea even after he was out of TWA's management, eventually buying a controlling interest in Northeast to hold it for that purpose.

Tillinghast's proposals had greater scope and were less concerned with the survival of TWA as an independent institution. He began talks with the heads of various airlines in 1961, "exploring," he said, "the patterns of the industry and seeking what to do defensively." At first he favored a merger with Eastern. When Eastern balked at getting involved with TWA's international routes, Juan Trippe offered to help out by buying those routes for Pan American; the overture started preliminary talks between Tillinghast and Trippe on a TWA–Pan Am merger. They were encouraged by the announcement in January 1962 that Eastern and American had agreed to merge. It appeared that, if the CAB approved, this merger would set off a consolidation of U.S. trunk lines into four or five nationwide systems. During the spring of 1962 Trippe and Tillinghast met often in a restaurant in New York's Grand Central Station to bargain over the fusion of their fleets into a single U.S. flag carrier. This would be a close variant of Trippe's lifetime dream of pitting a U.S. "chosen instrument" against the largely subsidized airlines of other countries, an idea blocked years earlier when Hughes had obtained for TWA a transatlantic route parallel to Pan Am's.

The two men bargained in a continuing atmosphere of red ink and the prospect of retrenchment. In the course of 1962, TWA put twenty of the new fan jets into service and revenues rose somewhat to about $400 million, but the company lost about $6 million. A later analysis showed that an upward turn had actually begun in the second half of 1962, but it didn't help at the time. TWA met a strike threat at the peak of the travel season and had to make payments to Eastern

Airlines under an industry mutual-aid agreement when that line was struck. And the projections TWA made for the last four months of 1962 and the first four months of 1963 indicated that the company could be in default on its senior debt because it could not fulfill some of the requirements specified by its loan indenture. In January 1963 TWA's "profit budget" for the new year contained no provision for buying any new equipment.

Tillinghast and Trippe signed an agreement to merge TWA and Pan Am in December 1962. If matters had gone as they planned, there would be no TWA but a new operating company called "Pan Am World Airlines," with Trippe as chairman and Tillinghast as president. The operating company was to be a subsidiary of Pan American, which would become a holding company. The acknowledged purpose of this arrangement was to prevent Hughes, who would be the largest shareholder of the combined airlines (with 29 percent), from gaining control. Trippe, of course, was slated to be the boss. The big lenders presumably were agreeable.

Hughes did not formally take a stand at the time, but in the lawsuit his lawyers complained about the merger. They cited the fact that Trippe was a member of the board and finance committee of Metropolitan Life and that two other Pan Am directors were on Metropolitan's board. Metropolitan and Equitable together had the power to appoint and remove the trustees who designated TWA's board. So Hughes considered the proposed merger as another action to get rid of him.

In March 1963 the TWA-Pan Am merger was blocked by the CAB, which deferred it indefinitely, "at least until the questions regarding the power to vote the [TWA] stock [owned by the Hughes Tool Company] have been clearly resolved." Tillinghast vowed, "We will pursue the matter with single-minded attention on furthering the interests of the employees and stockholders of TWA, consistent with the public interest." But chance events ran over everyone. The airline recession lifted as the "superboom" in the national economy began. The CAB signaled the end of its merger mood on June 20, 1963, by rejecting the American-Eastern merger. In October 1963 TWA and Pan Am terminated their agreement.

TWA recovered in 1963, with a rise of $73,504,000 in revenues—to $476,533,000—and profits of $19,840,000, as compared with the loss of $6 million the previous year. In 1964 the airline business went soaring. TWA's traffic went up 25 percent for the year instead of an expected 16 percent. Its scheduled available seat-miles rose 13 percent and its load factor (percent of passenger capacity actually sold) rose three points higher than projected. Its total revenues rose 21 percent, profits 86.5 percent, etcetera, etcetera. It was a new day for TWA and for all airlines.

An understanding of what this promised for the future of the airlines must start with the misreading of the signs by the industry itself, the CAB, the stock market, and practically everyone else. In the late fifties and early sixties, the rate of growth in passenger travel fell below expectations, just as the radical transition to jets was being made. The debt burden was heavy. Then, as more and more of the pistons were phased out, airline executives for the first time realized the true and growing efficiency of the new jets. The passenger break-even point dropped at about the same time that more people unexpectedly began flying. The ratio of these two elements created the sharp reversal. For TWA in 1964, each dollar of revenue above the scheduled passenger break-even point contributed 91.5 cents to profit before taxes.

This economic phenomenon resulted from the airline industry's peculiar cost structure. Fifty percent of its costs are fixed—i.e., aircraft and other equipment, maintenance base, terminals, offices, etc. Another 40 percent of its costs—fuel, crews, etc.—are sticky in the short run once a schedule of operations has been set. The remaining 10 percent are the only costs that vary with the volume of the business in the short run—food, insurance, reservations, ticketing, etc. Hence, with all the schedules established, a rise in the business above the break-even point—as happened in 1964—is converted automatically to almost pure profit.

What this also proved, however, is that the big swing is reversible. It can go either way. Even without a recession in the economy, the airlines could again find themselves in their own private recession. All they would have to do is produce too many seat-miles—the basic airline product—for the amount of actual business; then the "load factor" would recede toward the break-even level, the big profits would evaporate, and red ink could rise as fast as the black did in 1964.

The price of airline shares rose to new highs in the middle sixties, reflecting the turnabout but not its potential reversibility; and in the airlines boom TWA did better than the others. From the fourth-largest United States airline in scheduled revenue passenger-miles, TWA moved up to become second only to the giant United. Tillinghast forecasted revenues of $650 million in 1965 and $1 billion in 1970. Only one cloud showed ahead: another round of new equipment—including the jumbo jets and possibly supersonic aircraft (SSTs)—and their financing, in the late sixties and early seventies. Tillinghast dealt with the problem in a long-range plan.

Actually, Tillinghast faced a situation very like the one Hughes had faced in the mid-fifties: bigger and more expensive airplanes and the need of vast sums of money to finance them. The ticklish questions were not only a matter of standard decisions—number of seats for projected revenue passenger-miles, etc.—but also again of the interactions of airlines, airplane manufacturers, and lenders.

Two strategic subgames were played here. One engaged the airlines themselves. They did not then compete on price (most of their fares were set; the charter angle was not highly developed; and the international cartel with its fixed prices was for the moment stable). But they did struggle for shares of the market. They competed, for example, for frequency of service on the main runs, notably New York–California. Tillinghast wanted to increase TWA's share. American was a leader in frequency of flights. And the size of United's orders for new planes suggested still more of the same. Matching frequency against frequency brought the "load factor" in the New York–California runs well below the average for the total airline systems, although being long haul these runs were still the most profitable. No airline could drop out of these interactions without yielding position, and none yielded. The consequence: big orders for new airplanes by all major airlines, based in part on the frequency game.

The other subgame engaging the industry, Tillinghast, and the sidelined Hughes as observer raised some deeper questions of strategic corporate management. Boeing technically could not stretch the 707 into a larger airplane and was threatened with a stretched Douglas DC-8. Boeing's reply was the 747 (the "jumbo"), a radical jump in size, support facilities, traffic handling, and costs. There were doubts in TWA and elsewhere about the economic effect of the jumbo jets in the next round of new equipment. The peculiar interplay of surrounding forces, however, took precedence over these doubts. Some of TWA's competitors put in orders for the 747 jumbos. If Tillinghast's technical staff worried enough, as they did in some measure, about the possible overproduction of seats, a standard decision might call for a different (not quite so large) airplane from a different airplane maker. But Tillinghast had also to worry along other lines: if he were right in such a decision, TWA would prosper while his competitors suffered; if he were wrong, TWA would suffer while his competitors prospered. But the chance of being right or wrong wasn't the only question. The further question was the effect of being right or wrong *alone or in concert* with the other major airlines. This was no ordinary decision. To be wrong and alone was a nightmare. But to be wrong if all the airlines were wrong, that would be a different story. With the airlines, manufacturers, and lenders in the same boat, there could be no reprisals; the CAB, as regulator, would doubtless come to the rescue of the industry with higher fares; routes could be rearranged less competitively; appeals could be made for subsidies, or mergers; and so on. So perhaps in some measure did each airline decision maker consider this game. The solution they found was to cluster their future orders centrally around the jumbo jets, in a coalition of sorts, Tillinghast joining in after initial hesitation.

Hughes opposed Tillinghast's long-range plan but not for the equipment or amount of money ($1.8 billion) it projected. He opposed the mode of financing. Tillinghast wanted more equity and less debt for the first five years of the plan; Hughes wanted more debt and no increase in equity. The difference again lay in Hughes's long-standing bias in favor of using debt to give greater leverage to his common stock.

They displayed these differences operationally in March 1965 in what looked like a trial run for the larger issues. In setting up the financing for his five-year plan, Tillinghast forced the conversion of $38,500,000 of TWA debentures, of which Hughes held $30 million. Hughes opposed this action on the ground that by putting more equity into being it would dilute TWA's stock. He had the option to take cash for his debentures, a move which would have blocked Tillinghast's plan. But Tillinghast threatened to go to the market with an equity offering if Hughes insisted on cash. Their lines of thought were quite clear. Hughes saw in the move a reduction in per-share earnings on TWA stock, and he held earnings-per-share as the explicit criterion of success (the stock market, too, had begun to make this its immediate preference). Tillinghast, on the other hand, did not make earnings-per-share an explicit criterion but held that this popular ratio was a derivative of return on investment in the long run. He had also come to believe that the presence of a large strategic private owner of a public service corporation like an airline was not in the public interest. Hughes believed, contrariwise, that TWA's management, representing only 0.3 percent of the airline's stock, found it easy, under the trustee agreement, to fall into a lender-oriented policy for the future. (Hughes also suspected that Tillinghast was trying to cut his potential power by equity dilution.) This difference in values between manager and owner would have a big influence on the play of the game.

Thus Tillinghast preferred coalitions of professional airline managers (along with passive shareholders), airplane makers, and lenders, on the grounds that they gave the best payoff in the public interest as well as the corporate interests in the long run. Hughes held that dealing the strategic owner out put not only him but also the other shareholders at a disadvantage. Thus the second game extended some of the major issues of the first one.

In the issue at hand—bargaining over the conversion of debentures to equity—Hughes found it in his interest to yield to Tillinghast's threat to go to the stock market. Hughes took stock, not cash. The significance of the episode was not immediately evident.

From the beginning of their negotiations with Hughes, the main line taken by Breech, Tillinghast, and Sonnett was that there could be no settlement without a solution to what they called "the Hughes problem in TWA." Hughes, they said, must divest, or submit to a limited voting position, or agree outright to a continuation of the voting trust. Hughes, on the other hand, while ostensibly fighting for control, was ambiguous. The two positions on the surface seemed to be irreconcilable, but the information as usual was incomplete.

Hughes created a mild surprise late in 1963, after TWA's stock had begun to rise, by selling $81 million worth of TWA debentures and warrants which he had received in 1961 in partial settlements of TWA's debt to Hughes Tool. The event had the marks of a significant move in the game. There are seldom single motivations for anything; two were important here. One was that Hughes at that time carried a heavy bank debt and was under pressure to liquidate some of his holdings to pay down the debt. The other was that his stock market consultants advised him that should he ever want to sell a large number or all of his TWA shares, he would have difficulty doing so owing to what they called a lack of a "seasoned market" in TWA stock—meaning in part that the market was too thin. There was little stock out and it was lightly traded. With more shares traded, the TWA market could become liquid. Hence the sale of the debentures and warrants was essential if he had it in mind to sell out. The way was now open if he chose to take it.

The big moves were not long in coming. After the sale, Hughes still owned more than three fourths of TWA's outstanding stock. A few months later, in 1964, Hughes's agents began to discuss the possibility of his selling part of this stock; and early in 1965, they astounded everyone by raising the possibility of his selling all of it, voluntarily.

In the iffy atmosphere of the subsequent discussions, it was difficult for anyone to believe anything for sure. Was there really a price on Hughes's presumed long-standing passion for control of the airline? The opposing lawyers discussed the subject hypothetically, running through an imagined game. One might suppose that a game should be either cooperative or non-cooperative, but, as noted, there are often forces present that lead or drive players, in a nominally non-cooperative game, to worm around the rules to find a way to cooperate. We have seen that, owing to their mutual interest in the well-being of the airline, the players here had never been entirely opposed except on the issue of control. Now for the first time they tangled with the problem of including the control issue along with the others, and the interconnections between them, in a negotiation. The first thing they had to do was to find out more about what kind of a game they were in. Even the rules and their consequences—for a deal—were not self-evident, and so they began by exploring the rules.

The central question was whether control itself could be bargained: could Hughes trade off voluntary divestiture against a settlement of the damage claim and thereby end the litigation? After thinking this over together, the opposing lawyers agreed that there was an impasse, with Hughes's lawyers making the point at least as strongly as the lawyers for TWA's management, despite the fact that the impasse rested mainly on a danger to TWA's management. A package settlement, they concluded, should not be made because it would seem to trade the withdrawal of the alleged damages for the Breech-Tillinghast tenure in control of the airline, thereby opening the possibility, under the rules of corporate law, of a stockholder suit against the management in which they would have to prove that they got something of value for the stockholders, namely, freedom from Howard Hughes —and this was an intangible that was not subject to appraisal.

They found a way to get around the difficulty and this led to the playing of the imagined game. Here again they explored the possibilities together, playing a game which needs classification but is not uncommon among opposed lawyers. The lawyers did the staff work and the talking, but Hughes and Tillinghast were said to be calling the shots, Hughes, as usual, reputedly by telephone. They tried to find their way together through sequences of moves and countermoves to reach two complete coordinated strategies, one for each, which in their interactions would be mutually satisfactory—a hybrid of cooperation with some strongly non-cooperative assumptions: no trust, for example, was one of the latter.

They saw that they could terminate the litigation safely in a simultaneous settlement of damages and divestiture by setting a target date for the sale of Hughes's stock, say, six months off, and in the interim obtain protective approvals from the CAB, SEC, and the courts which could not realistically be challenged by any third party. But under this procedure, Hughes would have committed himself to sell without knowledge of market conditions at the time of the sale. If the price of the stock was to be *at market*, TWA's stock would almost certainly have declined during the interim period as prospective buyers waited for the dumping, and Hughes would end up being taken for a ride. On the other hand, if the price were fixed and the stock did not reach the fixed level on the appointed date, Hughes would not have been obliged to sell, and Breech and Tillinghast would have been stuck with a compromise damage settlement that was difficult to change—while failing to solve their "Hughes problem." Tillinghast urged an agreement hedged with contingency provisions in case Hughes didn't sell, but this idea fell through because Hughes refused to accept certain proposed restrictions on his voting his stock. This run-through ended in a failure to find joint strategies that were mutually satisfactory, but they had uncovered part of the structure of the game.

They broke off these negotiations in the summer of 1965. In July of that year the CAB, after study, but without hearings, ruled that Hughes could take control of TWA if he disposed of his interest in Northeast and other conflicting interests. Tillinghast threatened that he would fight this, and more potential litigation loomed if Hughes acted on the CAB ruling.

Shortly afterward, in September 1965, Hughes's agents requested the broker-underwriting firm, Merrill Lynch, Pierce, Fenner & Smith, to prepare for the sale of 1,363,636 shares of TWA—precisely the number of shares that Hughes had received in the forced conversion of TWA debentures in March of that year.

This move had strategic depth, whether as feint, bluff, threat, or a further exploration of the game. The putative sale would yield him just about enough money to buy in the Series A notes, dissolve the voting trust, and take back control of the airline; with his remaining 5,221,301 shares constituting a clear majority of TWA's outstanding stock. To retake control he would have to get CAB and perhaps court approval. Although Hughes had received the CAB's opinion that he could resume control under certain conditions and meeting their conditions was not impossible (Hughes sold his interest in Northeast Airlines that year), Tillinghast's threat to move against it could entail several years of litigation before the regulatory body. And once back in control, Hughes would have a messy legal problem in the damage suit which he could not unilaterally call off. But Hughes had the option to take this route, and it was a threat to TWA's management.

The move also had the earmarks of a probe; and it did elicit some interesting information. While in conversation with the Hughes forces, Julius Sedlmayr of Merrill Lynch offered the opinion—said to be unsolicited—that the market was strong enough to absorb the sale of all of Hughes's stock. In December Hughes himself called Sedlmayr about this proposition. They discussed the state of the market and whether people in Wall Street would react favorably to Hughes's getting out of TWA and whether this in turn would affect the price of the stock. Hughes learned—or had it confirmed—that news of his departure, far from putting the stock down, which would normally be the case, would in this situation put the stock up. Sedlmayr told Hughes that Merrill Lynch was bullish on airlines and that reports from its sales staff indicated that it could market all the 6,584,937 shares.[4]

From then on, the day-to-day action of the market became an important element in the game. At the year's end TWA stock closed at 63½, a little off from its high of 71⅝ that year.

But then, in January 1966, Hughes's agents returned to the negotiating table to make another surprise move. They proposed to TWA's management that TWA offer to buy back from the lenders the critical Series A notes and refinance them at lower interest rates; and Hughes offered to pay out of his own pocket the $3,250,000 repayment premium required of TWA. The effect, of course, would have been to set aside the voting trust. But Hughes did not ask for a resumption of absolute control; all he wanted, he said, was a voice on the board, and he even offered to assure the continuity of

---

[4] As this was a prediction based on observations of market behavior in relation to a price mechanism, it reflects standard economic theory and is sufficient to the occasion if there are no coalitions or strategic players. Hughes, too, is attempting to predict, in particular how the market will react to his selling under various conditions. Thus the stock market represents only passive players in this game.

Tillinghast's management. He proposed to accomplish these ends by putting one half of his stock in a new ten-year voting trust and voting the other half himself. This would have enabled Hughes to vote slightly more than one third of TWA's total outstanding stock.

The offer met with a wall of suspicion and skepticism—hardly surprising. The main objection of TWA's management was that Hughes's proposal would give him working control of TWA. With Hughes voting 37.5 percent of the stock, the voting trustees voting the same amount, and scattered shareholders voting the balance of 25 percent, the management expected that Hughes could pick up some of the scattered votes and enlarge his position. They also thought it possible that the trustees voting Hughes's stock might not want to oppose his wishes as the beneficial owner. Furthermore, it was evident that TWA's management would then be in the awkward if not wholly inconsistent position of welcoming Hughes back to its board while still opposing him before the CAB and the courts. Again they had played a game and again reached a dead end.

But why had Hughes made a bid to share the control of TWA? At first sight, the move suggested that he was still interested in staying in TWA. Can one believe that the owner-manager conflict which had been so well-defined in previous negotiations could be resolved on all major issues—debt-equity and the like—with both parties inside of TWA's board? Or more explicitly, could Hughes be satisfied without attaining the dominance that Tillinghast feared? And if Hughes didn't attain that dominance, if his views did not prevail, would he have wanted to stay on?

Another reading of the move is more plausible. If he had succeeded in bringing about a voluntary sharing of control, the legal battle would have lost its force. With harmony apparently restored between Hughes and TWA management and Hughes no longer labeled a menace to the airline, the stock market could have been expected to respond with a higher price-earnings ratio on TWA's stock (compounded, perhaps, in Hughes's view, with the stimulation of a TWA-

Northeast merger). As a peaceful stockholder, Hughes would have been inhibited from selling his whole block of stock at once (it would have had a depressive effect on the price of stock). But he would have been in a position to market it in pieces at times of his own choosing—something he could not do to best advantage without settlement of the control issue (i.e., while "the Hughes problem" hung over TWA). Thus the January 1966 move with its two possible outcomes—to share or not share in control—appears to have been a factor in determining not whether Hughes would leave or stay in TWA, but whether he would leave slowly or suddenly.

Tillinghast's rejection of Hughes's offer to share control ended the last of such maneuvers. For Hughes the whole game was reduced to a simple choice: hold his TWA stock possibly for years without control or sell out all at once and leave TWA. The damage suit would continue in either event, but with this difference, that if he kept his TWA stock and had to pay damages, he would be paying them with one hand (Hughes Tool) and receiving back three fourths of them with his other hand (TWA), whereas if he sold out and had to pay damages, he would have to pay all and receive back none.

If he chose to stay, he would leave his large investment in TWA, now highly valued, by historical measures, in the market, in the hands of others during the impending new equipment-financing cycle in the airlines. He had, as noted, no apparent disagreement with TWA's equipment policy, but in matters of debt, equity, and mergers his and Tillinghast's values parted, pointing to wide disagreement in policy. On the other hand, if he chose to sell out, he would have to compare his TWA investment with the value of the money put to use for other purposes.

All through early 1966 airline stocks were going strong, TWA's moving up steadily to a high of 71⅝ on February 10. In mid-February the market started down. It dropped considerably in mid-March and TWA sold as low as 57¾. At this point Hughes called off the sale of the 1,363,636 shares.

But the market started up again. On Monday, April 4, TWA closed at 75¼, another record high. Tuesday, Hughes's agent, Raymond Cook, dropped the bomb. In telephone calls to TWA and Merrill Lynch, he announced that Hughes proposed to sell all his TWA stock.

The following day, at a regular meeting, the TWA board moved quickly to authorize the registration statement for the sale of the stock (the process was expedited by the fact that a statement had already been drawn up for the partial sale). When the directors also declared the second dividend of the year, Raymond Cook saw to it that the stock-sale date was ex-dividend (the Hughes people do not overlook small numbers while dealing in large numbers). Both Hughes and TWA agreed to wash out a remaining proceeding before the CAB, thus making it clear that Hughes had no more strings on the airline, though TWA still kept the pending damage claim against Hughes.

On April 8, while the market was closed for Good Friday, the registration statement was filed with the date tentatively set for May 3, and TWA announced the offering.

On Saturday, Merrill Lynch sent a telegram to about 400 underwriters, inviting them to participate; the allocation of shares was to be specified later. Over Easter weekend, Merrill Lynch contacted six major firms to invite them into a "special bracket" of underwriters. Five came in: Dillon, Read & Company, Inc., the First Boston Corporation, Kuhn, Loeb & Company, Lazard Frères & Company, and Lehman Brothers (Morgan Stanley stayed out). Almost all of the 400 underwriters (including twenty-two foreign firms) responded affirmatively. Merrill Lynch had earmarked half the offering for group sales—i.e., in blocks of 10,000 shares or more. The institutional buyers indicated an immediate demand for about one million shares in blocks that size, from which one could conclude that the stock market would be glad to buy Hughes out.

Under the formal rules, neither seller nor buyer was committed until the day of the actual sale. But before filing, Merrill Lynch had advised Hughes, in the language of Wall

Street, that if he had any doubts he should not start the action, since subsequent withdrawal, after the financial community got well into it, would make any future offering difficult or impossible. There would be no resentment, however, if he withdrew because the market weakened or the price of TWA stock dropped substantially. As the date of the sale approached the only worry among the participants was whether Hughes would think the price was right. They would be uncertain about that until the last minute, and so they settled down to watch the market.

On Monday, April 11, the first business day after the announcement, TWA stock sold off to as low as 76¼ and closed down a point at 79⅜. But on Tuesday it rose seven points, and three days later it reached a high of 96⅞, then drifted off in succeeding days to a trading range of 85 to 88.

Merrill Lynch kept in touch with the underwriters, adjusting allocations of stock among them. For its own accounts, Merrill Lynch sold 1,400,000 shares (900,000 more than its original allocation). Most of the underwriters' orders would be good if the offering price was around 85, but some of them would not be executed if the price were 90. So there was talk about a discount: for example, selling at 85 if the market were 87.

On May 2, the day before the sale, the market movement of TWA stock made everyone nervous. It traded at 89¼ in the morning. In late afternoon it was down to 87½. Five minutes before the closing it was at 87¼. One minute before the closing it was at 86¾. At the bell it was 86. Hughes had lost about $20 million in paper profits in one day, most of it in the last five minutes.

After the market closed, the broker-bankers at Merrill Lynch were worried about Hughes's reaction to the last market action, as they and Raymond Cook began their final negotiations; at one time Cook went into the next room to talk to Hughes on the phone, and for a while the deal looked shaky. They finally reached an agreement. The sale would go through, but there would be no discount, on the grounds that the market drop had already, in effect, provided one. The price was negotiated at 86—the closing market price—with an underwriting spread of $3—that is, the underwriters paid Hughes $83 and sold at $86. Of the spread, $1.75 went for selling commissions, 80 cents for risk, and the balance (15 percent of the total spread) went to Merrill Lynch as the management fee. The deal was cleared with Hughes at 4:30 P.M. At 11:00 P.M., the word came, ostensibly from California, that Hughes had signed his approval of the terms of the sale.

The lawyers worked in Merrill Lynch's office on the price amendment to the prospectus until 4:30 A.M. of May 3. One group of lawyers then hurried off to Washington, D.C., by taxi with a copy for the SEC, whose approval of the price amendment was required before the sale. By 8:45 A.M. all the underwriters, in person or by proxy, had signed the underwriting agreement in Merrill Lynch's New York office. Meanwhile, Sedlmayr for Merrill Lynch, Raymond Holliday, senior vice president of the Hughes Tool Company, and James Kerley, senior vice president for finance of TWA, convened in Merrill Lynch's office in Newark. All parties then signed, at 9:30 A.M. Merrill Lynch, having kept an open wire to the lawyers who had taxied to Washington, filed the price amendment with the SEC. Two minutes later, at 9:45 A.M., it became effective. Fifteen minutes later the New York Stock Exchange opened, with TWA stock at 86½. The Hughes offering was oversubscribed, and at 10:25 A.M. the books were closed.

Merrill Lynch at that moment became the No. 1 underwriter of 1966. The twenty-seven-year Hughes era in TWA ended. Tillinghast had achieved his objective. Where TWA formerly had one shareholder with 75.16 percent of the stock, it now had over 25,000 new shareholders. And Hughes got $550 million in cash.

As it turned out, it was a coup. Hughes had sold his TWA stock close to its all-time high; not long afterward the stock began a decline that took it down below $10 a share in 1970 and it sold below $5 a share in 1974. There is no way to tell whether Hughes was brilliant or lucky in getting out when he did, though there can hardly be any doubt that he, and his agents, got out of the game all of the worth that was in it.

The lawsuit continued on—all told for eleven years—and in December 1972 Hughes sold the oil-tool division and name of the Hughes Tool Company for $140 million, seemingly in anticipation of an adverse Supreme Court decision on TWA's damage claim which, with interest and costs, then came to $180 million. But in January 1973 the Supreme Court ruled that, despite his refusal to appear in his own defense, he was immune from the damage claims—on grounds his lawyers had raised in his original defense, namely, that the CAB had approved of the actions on which the claims were based.

9

WALT DISNEY: TURNING A CAREER OF ART AND BUSINESS AROUND AN IMAGINARY GAME

When Walt Disney got into a financial jam in 1940–41, his banker, the Bank of America, worried about his new experimental film, *Fantasia*, insisted on having the film cut and edited to conventional standards for the market. Walt balked and threatened to get another banker. It was a game. Its outcome changed Disney's career in art and business.

THE PLAYERS

- Walt Disney
- Roy Disney
- Bank of America
- Walt Disney's imaginary banker

As artist and businessman, Walt Disney lived two lives, one before, the other after *Fantasia*. On the occasion of his troubles in producing that film, he and his brother Roy engaged in a real game with a banker, and for one instant Walt imagined a more elaborate game which he could win. It was a fantasy, and when he understood that, he changed his future course as an artist. One result today is the emergence of Walt Disney Productions as one of the largest and most successful corporations in the United States, with revenues of more than $400 million in 1974. If it qualified as an industrial corporation instead of an entertainment enterprise, Disney's company would rank around number 300 on *Fortune*'s list of the 500 largest. No other artist, not even Charlie Chaplin, who once owned a substantial share of United Artists as well as his own production studio and all of his films, has turned his genius into a comparable financial asset.

Although Disney set it all up for the way it came out, he did not live to see the full dimensions of his business success. Indeed, most of his business life was made up of one financial crisis after another, with the worst in 1940–41, just when his reputation as an artist and innovator had reached new heights. He was in debt and under water financially—in a word, broke—and the turning point came over *Fantasia*, which is important to understanding Disney before and after.

A few months before Walt Disney died in 1966, the author had a long talk with him about his art and business in his studio office in Burbank, and also talks at that time with his brother, Roy Disney. Two years later, the author had another long talk on the same subject with Roy. This story brings together selections from those talks. I use their first names not as a sign of familiarity but to distinguish the brothers. At sixty-four, jaunty in muted California colors, Walt lifts his eyebrows high, looking half surprised, half amused, and speaks in a voice that ranges between the high of Mickey and the low of Goofy.

WALT: *We were having a lot of fun with* Fantasia. *Like the Bach abstractions. I said all I can see is violin tips and bow tips, like when you're half asleep at a concert. Tschaikovsky—what color is it? I said gold, somebody else said green, but I won. It was gold.*

I got my neck stepped on for Fantasia. *We didn't have enough time. The bankers got panicked.* Fantasia *was never made to go out in regular release. I had planned it for special release with wide screen and stereophonic sound. Then Europe fell in the war, we had trouble, and I had to let it go conventional. With the bankers and the war and everything I had to go standard, but I already had my sound. They couldn't take that away. I was asked to help cut it for regular release. I turned my back. Someone else cut it.*

McDONALD: Have you ever thought of doing another one like it?

WALT: *I decided I would never do another* Fantasia. *I had the wind taken out of my sails.*

Walt explained that after *Fantasia* (and after World War II) he decided to diversify "like any business." That meant, for one thing, less concentration on the medium of animated film on which his entire career to that time had been based. In this connection, he also interpreted the development of his animated art from the beginning as experiment and a kind of diversification. It was of course the results of these experiments that first made him world famous. From Mickey Mouse's first appearance in *Steamboat Willie* in 1928 to *Fantasia* in 1940, Disney's work had been a progression of novelties in animation film art. He had been one of the first to make a film with sound (1928), one of the first to use color (1932), the first to make an animated feature-length film (*Snow White* in 1937), and the first to use stereophonic sound (*Fantasia*). Each of his creations displayed his desire to do something new, and the Disney style—full, detailed, smooth, naturalistic—came to dominate the field of animation. There was, as we shall see, a radical difference in his experiments after *Fantasia*. What was the force behind the experiments that first made the Disney name and led up to the *Fantasia* affair?

WALT: *I got trapped with the mouse. I started with him. He was a big hit, so I was stuck with the character. But Mickey couldn't do certain things—they would be out of character. And Mickey was on a pedestal—I would get letters if he did something wrong. I got worried about relying on a character like the mouse—you wear it out, you run dry.*

I wanted diversification. We got Pluto and the duck. The duck could blow his top. Then I tried Pluto and Donald together. The stupid things Pluto would do, along with the duck, gave us an outlet for our gags. I made the Silly Symphonies, *which weren't based on any of these characters. The theaters only wanted Mickey, so I said you can't have Mickey unless you take a* Silly Symphony. *Then I made* The Three Little Pigs *and the theaters were bicycling prints [i.e., one theater would show it and run the print over to another].* The Three Little Pigs *cost $22,000 and the banker said, "Walt's costs are running away from him." It grossed a quarter of a million.*

We touched on the source of Disney's comic sense. Like many great comedians Disney talked about his art soberly.

WALT: *I don't know where my comic sense comes from. I've been sort of a ham all of my life. When I was young I used to impersonate Chaplin and win prizes. I'd do his walk. I'd go to amateur nights and win two dollars. Another kid and I worked together and his father rehearsed us. Drawing was a sort of release. I went to art school when I was fourteen years old, Saturday classes. When I was in high school in Chicago I went to art school three nights a week. My first job as an artist getting paid for the stuff was when I was eighteen, at an advertising agency. I was their flunky at $50 a month. In February 1920 I answered an ad. A film company wanted an artist first class. The first class didn't bother me at all. On my own I had a set-up, selling to the guys doing the oil journals. My work was printed. That's how I got into this business. One thing that saved me was that I was pretty good at gags, at copy. Some copy would come to me and it was icky. [Walt screwed up his face.] The old man would say throw it to Disney. The gags saved me because my art didn't hold up. There was an ad for a car top to be done over. I did "Hi, old top, new car?" And the guy in the car says "No, old car, new top." Gags like that.*

The perennial question put to Disney is what his role was in the making of his animated pictures.

Motion picture art is usually cooperative. Chaplin, with his own script writing or improvisation, musical composition, acting, and cutting or editing, was exceptional, though even he needed other hands to help put together a film. It is well known that Disney was a cooperative film maker, with a team of gifted animators, notably Ub Iwerks in the early days. How did Walt see his film making?

WALT: *Animation is the hardest way to make a picture. It is the most demanding storywise. It takes time. There are not too many good stories. Graphics are only one thing. I am interested in story and music. They are very important. Boy, when you get the story. When you get that everybody bounces. In animation it's what to draw, not just the ability to draw. It isn't just drawing the darn thing, it's thinking about it and giving it personality. I was into technique before I should have been. I needed more life. You've got to learn to draw. I needed more drawing. I painted portraits. I painted one of my sister-in-law and she didn't speak to me for months. In the studio we have had an art school; we put all the arts together. You've got to let the boys go, but don't let them get off till they learn the fundamentals. Then let them go. I knew what my boys needed. I always had a hundred students. No, I didn't teach. I had four instructors, in composition, life, animal anatomy, and locomotion—the study of action and reaction. It was needed for this medium. The trouble is they all wanted to draw beautiful pictures. I went in for locomotion, not static. It's like pulling your hand across your eyes: the fingers elongate. And when something stops—a woman stops—the skirt goes on. When a mouse stops, his tail goes around. I used to put in my entire time with the artists until they got better.*

If Walt as artist had an agent, it was his brother Roy. But Roy was more than an agent. He was dedicated solely to Walt. They were a lifetime team, with Roy taking care of the financial end of the business.

ROY: *I've been with Walt since he was a baby. I guess he bought a motion picture camera when he was about fifteen, for $300 which he saved laboriously from his paper route. He never played as a boy. Always worked. Art work. He drew a barber a cartoon for a haircut. He never deviated from that interest. All his life he couldn't wait to get to work in the morning. He came to California with* Alice in Cartoonland, *which was mostly live. It was about a little girl who would go to sleep and dream in cartoon. That was in the early 1920s. The company we had in Kansas City folded and Walt got a print of his* Alice in Cartoonland *from the referee in bankruptcy. That's what Walt peddled here and sold for a series. We hired an actor for $35 a week and I thought what a waste of dough. Years later we spent millions on* Alice in Wonderland. *Seven hundred dollars on* Alice in Cartoonland. *Business was a damn nuisance to him. When the banks closed down in 1933 we had about 200 employees. I panicked. What would we give these people? We got a $10 gold piece for each employee and three days later Congress declared gold illegal. Walt said quit worrying, people lived before banks; if they use potatoes for exchange we'll use potatoes. That's his great basic philosophy of life. He won't stop living. In 1934 we really got started. A film cost of $20,000 returned about fifty, sixty, or seventy. We got on our feet—$100,000, $200,000, $300,000 a year profit. The depression of the thirties was our heyday, a glorious time in a small way.*

The Disneys' company was indeed small compared to the major Hollywood producers, and so were its products: ten-minute cartoons. Theaters ran them as supplements to their regular long feature films. But while the Disneys were earning their first big money in the Depression with the mouse and the duck and the sillies, the market for motion pictures was beginning to change, and the Disneys saw that.

WALT: *The short subject has always been the short end of the stick. You were always what they could do away with. In the thirties came double bills [two features on one*

*program for the price of one ticket]. They wouldn't monkey
with short subjects. The handwriting was on the wall. In
1935 I went to Europe with my brother and saw them
bunching five or six of our cartoons together. So we got the
idea of trying a cartoon feature. The feature was an experiment. The history of this business has been experimentation
and taking a chance.*

The feature, of course, was *Snow White*. The Disneys
staked everything they had and went into debt to produce it
on a make-or-break budget of $1.3 million on the blind
chance of surviving and getting a return on it. Their distributor then was United Artists, which was owned by Douglas
Fairbanks, Mary Pickford, and Charlie Chaplin.

WALT: *I was a protégé of Mary, Doug, and Charlie in
United Artists. They took us under their wing. United Artists
said sell it like a Fred Astaire [i.e., in advance]. Charlie, who
was a good friend, said don't do it. Don't sell it until you've
had a chance to show it. Our bookkeepers went over to get
all his figures. Afterward when we had such a big success
Charlie came over and studied our books. Charlie then
hadn't gone sour on the world. He was more fun than a barrel of monkeys. Charlie really changed [Walt didn't live to
see Charlie change again in old age]. I could never understand. I've had a hard life. I've worked since I was ten years
old. When I look back on it, I appreciate it. My family
wasn't poor but they were not wealthy. I found a work pattern and I have a guilty conscience if I take a day off.*

Walt didn't take a day off or give his money a day off
when after the immediate fabulous success of *Snow White*—it
grossed about $4 million in the United States and about the
same abroad in the first round—he took its net earnings of
several million dollars and plunged them into the studios at
Burbank ($3,800,000) and, with a staff of more than a thou-
sand artists, animators, story men, and technicians, produced
in rapid succession, at a cost of $2 million to $4 million each,
several animated features: *Pinocchio, The Reluctant Dragon,*

Dumbo, Bambi, and *Fantasia,* all wondrous stories and fantasy impressions uniquely executed in the new Disney medium. Others were in early stages of work.

Although *Bambi* and *Fantasia* failed at first to pay off financially, this prolific outburst of creation brought Disney a new distinction as storyteller as well as comedian. In addition to enhancing his world celebrity and bringing him more Hollywood honors, the new work, together with the earlier comedies, also brought him to the attention of serious critics of films. Putting aside some critical reservations, they established Disney in the high reaches of film art along with such other masters as his friend Chaplin. His fellow cartoonist the great English political satirist, David Low, paid Disney this remarkable compliment:

> I do not know whether he draws a line himself. I hear that at his studios he employs hundreds of artists to do the work. But I assume that his is the direction, the constant aiming after improvement in the new expression, the tackling of its problems in an ascending scale and seemingly with aspirations over and above mere commercial success. It is the direction of a real artist. It makes Disney, not as a draftsman but as an artist who uses his brains, the most significant figure in graphic art since Leonardo.

Mere commercial success did indeed elude the Disneys so inundated with fame. For it was at this moment in the early 1940s that the Disneys once again crashed, not quite into another actual bankruptcy but not far from it, and Walt met the crisis of his lifetime in his art as well as his business. First, their heavy debts and loss of foreign markets forced them to go public to raise money. Until then theirs had been a private family-owned company. Now Walt Disney Productions issued 155,000 shares of preferred stock which was convertible to common stock. At $25 a share, they raised $3,500,000; and both Walt and Roy made employment contracts with the company. Their public shareholders could not long have been very happy as the company's fortunes continued to decline and the stock dropped to $3 a share. Nor was Walt, who in that period had his encounter with the bankers over the release of *Fantasia*. One day Walt played a game with the bankers. It was a bargaining game in which Walt imagined a new player. Roy reported it.

ROY: *Our markets were burning up in the war, our stock went to pot, we owed the Bank of America $5 million. It was a case of progressive seduction. The bankers had gone as far as they could and they lowered the boom. We got wonderful consideration at Bank of America. The velvet glove. Mr. Giannini [Lawrence M. Giannini] said give the boys a chance to market their pictures. The ordinary fishy bankers would have wrapped us up. We had expenses of $60,000 a week. Joseph Rosenberg, who was our contact at the bank, went in to see Walt. Walt told him, you damn bankers, you loan an umbrella on a sunny day and want it back in the rain. Actually it happened to be raining. Walt said, I'll take my account to another banker. Joe came to my office and told me what Walt had said. He laughed and said, there are no other bankers. Walt is over his head in debt.*

This encounter apparently was Walt's first conscious brush with an interactive game of business. Roy had always taken care of such matters and had shielded Walt from them. For Walt everything theretofore had been the artist on one side and his vast audience of children and adults on the other: "experimentation and taking a chance." Roy had seen to it that Walt could do what he wanted out of his own inspiration. Now their financial predicament threatened to bring outside control over the editing of *Fantasia*, and to escape it he wanted to get into the game, get another banker and form an alliance with him. It was only a gesture in which he imagined an interaction that would free him. As all games are largely imagined we can reconstruct his gesture as a game in the kind of drawings that game theorists put on the black-board.

Disney has a traditional banker, Bank of America. He wants to borrow money, the bank wants to lend it. Both stand to gain by cooperating. They bargain over the terms for dividing the gain. The terms in the past have included Walt's freedom to edit, but the banker, worried about the security of the investment, wants to change the terms. The implication is that there has been a change in the values. Yet, in that new situation, if there is no other banker who will put a higher value on Disney's business and yield the value of editorial control to Disney; if there is only the old alliance of Disney and Bank of America, they have still the best possible deal, that is, they are in the core of the game. The core here also corresponds to the standard of behavior—that is to say, the traditional banking arrangement. The play may be shown by a line that represents the range of their mutual gain (the angle of the line here is of no significance; it could just as well be flat). The further up the line they go, the more Disney gets; the further down they go, the more Bank of America gets:

This is a two-person game in which the two players can obtain the gain if they can agree on how to split it. Each has veto power over any proposal. They can settle by some kind of bargaining over the split.

Disney and the Bank of America are stuck in the bargaining. In the picture of the line, Walt could view it as follows:

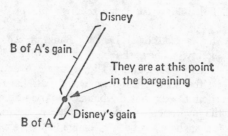

But Walt and the banker evidently have a difference in perception. The banker thinks Walt is getting more than Walt thinks he is. In any case, they are at an impasse.

Walt now wants to give up this game and go to a three-person game, with a second (imagined) banker in the picture.

If in fact the second banker put a higher value on Disney's business, which he might do if he foresaw the enormous future value of Disney's inventory of animated films, then the second banker could be expected to bid higher for the business than the Bank of America could bid, according to the value it put on Disney's business. The game itself would then have a higher value, and with two bidders, we would have something like the farmer game which we have seen: the business would go to the second banker on terms better than the Bank of America could offer, unless there was a standard of behavior that resulted in a coalition of the two bankers against Disney. In either case, however, the game would turn on the difference in the values of the two bidders.

But let us suppose a different situation, namely, that the two bankers valued Disney's business equally and that, as Disney hoped, they independently competed for his business. The line above still describes the potential gain to be divided between Disney and the Bank of America, but another line describes the same gain to be divided alternatively between Disney and his imagined banker (assuming at the moment that banker coalitions are not allowed). Disney quite reasonably expects a higher bid from the second banker:

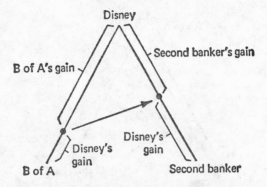

But the Bank of America will now overbid the second banker, and the second banker will again overbid the Bank of America, and this will continue on and on. Indeed, in this fantasy of strict competition, Disney uses his veto power to act like a dictator. He gets all the gain:

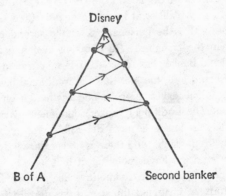

Disney has got himself into the core of the game but it is an unrealistic one. He needs one of the other players. So to bring about a coalition, he grants one of the others—say the Bank of America because it was the traditional banker—a little of the gain.

231

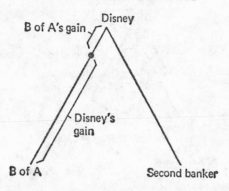

Thus the game ends with a quite different distribution of benefits: Disney gets his deal with the Bank of America and he edits *Fantasia* as he wishes.

But Disney has imagined a society in which bankers cannot cooperate by forming a coalition to bargain as one with him. In the letter of the law in the United States this is true. But in the fuzzy realities at least two qualifications should be made. One is that the personal risk of the second banker is greater than the first one's. He is taking over a deal which the traditional banker has rejected. If Disney should fail and the bank should lose, the fact that the traditional banker had rejected the deal makes the consequences harder on the second banker. The traditional banker's judgment—whatever its consequences in losses—is more defensible. His judgment is tested only in hindsight, and there is no contrary judgment in the background, no finger pointing at him.

Then there is also the competitive feature which might take the form of imagined threat and counterthreat: if I do this to him, he will do it to me. Let sleeping dogs lie is a custom in areas of industry, if not among banks.

One may also take note here that cooperation among banks is encouraged by law. The states impose loan limits by statute. The rule allows a range for interpretation, but beyond some limit, one bank cannot handle the large loan and so must spread the risk among other banks (and insurance companies typically reinsure their large risks).

Thus, in effect, the role of the traditional lender is characterized by standards of behavior which can in some degree influence the outcome of a borrower-lender game.

However, to model a sharply different game from the strictly competitive one pictured above, let us suppose that Disney now imagines that the game is taking place in a society that imposes no restrictions on banker coalitions.

Disney's hope of playing the two bankers off against each other lies in his being able to break up their potential coalition. A lot of possibilities open up here, one of which is that the bankers do form a coalition to act as one in the bargaining. We get a different picture:

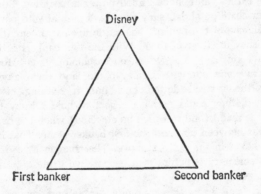

If the first banker and the second banker form a coalition, they must reach agreement on how they will split their gains from the joint bargaining with Disney. Let us say there is a standard of behavior that allots the second banker 10 percent for not bidding. The first banker, as the traditional banker, gets 90 percent of their gains. We still don't know how they come out with Disney, but we could get this picture:

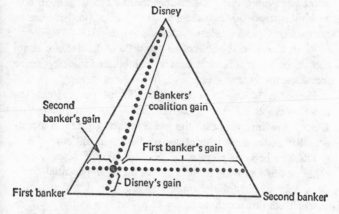

Thus we see that the two bankers, who alone lacked power in the earlier game, have gained power in coalition. Both the banker coalition and Disney now have mutual veto power, if the alliance of the bankers holds firm against potential offers by Disney to either of them. With the two bankers acting as one, we are back to a two-person bargaining game. How the bankers come out with Disney could land them anywhere along the vertical dotted line, but, if nothing else has changed, they could perhaps expect to hold Disney to the gains he made (and to which he objected) when the bargaining was between him and the first banker alone. That is how it is shown in the picture above. The triangle thus displays the elementary structure of a cooperative game.

Had Walt been able to produce a second banker under conditions of no coalition, the direction of Disney's work life thereafter must surely have continued at least for some time more or less along its then current course. As it happened, the Bank of America was right about the situation: there were no other bankers. If there had been, Roy himself—despite his sympathy with the Bank of America's view of the matter—doubtless would have looked into the game for an outcome more satisfactory to Walt; for Roy loved his brother and fostered his directions, even finding sometimes that Walt's risks were better than his own cautions. But on this occasion, though Walt would never forget it nor lose his disrelish of bankers, he yielded. He had little choice. The Bank of America kept the Disneys alive, for which Roy was grateful. Walt, with a stiff upper lip, walked out on *Fantasia*, leaving the cutting and editing to the bankers, and changed the course of his career.

ROY: *Success is hard to take. Walt had moved with his own creative talent on his own bent. Business was a damn nuisance to him. After Snow White, he wanted to make two animated features a year. We couldn't sustain it. We grew like a mushroom and operated uneconomically. The war, plus overloading, and a failure to study the market, put us down. Every creative fellow is so concentrated, he doesn't like to think through the market. Walt was that kind of guy until he learned his lesson. Afterward he got very conscious of market studies. He learned fast.*

Thus Roy put his finger on one aspect of the change that was to come in the direction of Walt's vision. The Disneys would go so far into market studies as to take Gallup polls of public taste. Roy saw this change purely in business terms. In terms of art, it was revolution. The clue to this may have been provided by David Low's extravagant comparison of Walt and the Renaissance painter, sculptor, musician, architect, engineer, scientist, and philosopher, Leonardo da Vinci. The contemporary painter-critic Louis Finkelstein mulled this over (in a private communication to the author) along the following lines.

Disney and Leonardo had in common that they were both interested in art and nature. Both were fantasists and interested in fun and games; Leonardo even made three-dimensional, mechanically animated lions and lizards—the sort of thing that Disney would later do at Disneyland—and like Disney, he liked to lead festivals. But these similarities may be relatively incidental. The real question is whether you view Disney, at the time Low made his observation, as an individual or collective artist. Low implies that to him Disney was then an individual artist, for Leonardo was one of the first artists in history to conceive of art as having an aesthetic message independent of a social, moral, or religious message. Before Leonardo's time, art was conceived not as "art" but as a social function. The "artist" was an artisan; not an individualist creating out of his personal consciousness but an anonymous worker transmitting the prevailing values. His ideas were the collective ideas of his time, his aesthetics—sublime as they might be—were instrumental. The classic example is a cathedral builder. Low seems to say that Disney was not such an artisan but an artist.

The question raised by Finkelstein is a subtle one, for Disney, before 1941, did reflect his culture, yet at the same time, as Low suggests, he looked inward for his muse; his shop produced such individual personalities as the mouse and the duck; and he put the mark of his style on his retelling of old tales. The change of direction in 1941 was not exactly to that of a "cathedral builder"; but henceforth Disney did not trust his personal vision. He looked outward, to the market, to complete his sense of his culture as the way to survive in business. So transformed, the new Disney reflected three historical stages of art, that of a workman in his natural culture, an individual (the Disney style), and a student of the entertainment market. He became the artist as businessman.

ROY: *We got audience reactions to rough-cut film. Eventually we went too far in marketing research on audience reaction, polling with a synopsis of stories in the story stage. The polls couldn't lick the questions of the frame of mind the polled person was in, or the argumentative guy; the poll built up his ego and got answers accordingly.*

The outcome of the game of 1940–41, however, not only had the effect of altering Walt's aesthetic vision. It also eventually taught both Disneys that animated film—then their whole stock in trade—would not alone be capable of satisfying their ambition to go on with a growing as well as a viable business.

But none of this happened immediately; indeed, for the Disneys, as for almost everyone, the next four years were an interlude of war-oriented activity; and to help make ends meet they planted two acres of the Burbank studio land in alfalfa, which they harvested and sold. Government contracts for films helped reduce their debt and they came out of the war ready to pick up the pieces and start anew.

ROY: *After the war we came out like a bear coming out of hibernation. We didn't have any fat on our bones. We entered a new period. Any good product would sell. The pipelines were empty. But in 1948 and 1949 we were in the red. Walt stuck to his idea of feature animation through thick and thin. We had about $700,000 invested in two properties:* Peter Pan *and* Alice in Wonderland. *They were started before the war and were on the shelf. I said, Walt, let's forget them, take them as a loss. He hit the ceiling. We could have picked up half the investment in tax money in that period and to me it would have been a life saver. He made both of them ultimately. I'm afraid if I'd been running this place, we would have stopped several times en route because of problems. With this tenaciousness of his, Walt does a lot of things that surprise us all.*

WALT: *It was quite a job to pull the organization together after the war. We tooled up for theatricals. There was a helluva'n inertia to overcome. It took a hunk of dough to decide to go. When we did decide, let's go and get the dough somehow, we had three unfinished projects to get out,* Alice in Wonderland, Peter Pan, *and also* Cinderella. *I said we're going to do them and get the money somehow. I'm telling you, when you've gotta go down and get the money from a banker, it's a tough one. Now [1966] they're standing around saying, Disney, don't you want some money? Not then. I just said we're gonna go. It got us back in business.*

ROY: *In 1950 we took off. It was* Cinderella *year.*

Cinderella was heartening to the Disneys, as it proved that there was still a large public for animated features. The wartime public had shown little interest in animation; they wanted live action, a circumstance that had left the Disneys worried. *Cinderella* grossed over $4 million in domestic release alone and the Disneys for the first time since *Snow White* were prosperous again. *Cinderella* was also the sign that all their old animated features could be rerun and so had "residual value" in the vault. They knew then for sure that with caution they could pursue more animations but they also saw the limits of the medium in their future. *Fantasia*, for example, rerun in Walt's full original version, would become very successful; even the hippies would adopt it as psychedelic art. On the other hand, Walt would make another first-run flop, *Sleeping Beauty*, which was the main cause of a huge drain on profits when they wrote off $6 million in 1960. But high budgets and risky outcomes were not the only problems of animation. Roy observed that they practically had a monopoly of feature animation. Walt talked about the problem that this posed and what it led to.

WALT: *With the organization growing, you couldn't do it all with cartoons. There is a saturation point for any kind of product. We became our own competition. I didn't want to saturate the market. It is tough to compete with yourself in animation. We have many animated features, all with residual value. That means we can release two every year and not repeat in several years. Furthermore, it takes talent to make an animated picture. I've had a team. I wouldn't be any place without a team. I could have tripled my animation staff but it would come down to a few handfuls to give the quality we demand. I decided I'd rather make what I've scheduled myself: one every three years. I decided I had to diversify like any business.*

Thus, as Roy said, Walt learned fast from the splurge and catastrophe after *Snow White*. Entertainment displaced animated films as the Disneys' broader concept of their business, and within this sphere they proceeded to run the gamut of diversification: short nature films, live-action features, television, their own film distribution company (about which Walt said, "It's always tough when someone distributes other products with yours. You never know what deals are under the table to sell another product"); they got out books and music and licensed merchandisers to use the Disney name and characters; they attempted to set up a gigantic alpine recreational complex at Mineral King in the Sierras (resulting in a bitter protracted struggle with the environmentalists of the Sierra Club); in 1955 they opened Disneyland itself, the first creation after the mouse and the duck and the animated features that added comparable luster to the Disney legend, and followed it a few years later with the beginnings of its complement in Florida, Walt Disney World—an extraordinarily prolific twenty years of diversification from their new start after the war. Each new creation emerged from Walt's inventiveness and remarkable nerve in putting imagined projects into being.

WALT: *We did the nature things. I had to grow with that. When* Bambi *first went out, we didn't get the negative costs back. But out of the experience with* Bambi, *we made the decision to go ahead with the nature things. We sent crews out to get the animals in the wild to help the animators study. If we could stalk and capture nature, that's what we wanted. Our animals were always tricky things. We knew our own anatomy; we wanted to get closer to animal anatomy. I started a school. The animals would sit and munch hay or eat leaves but there was no action. Then we sent the men out and we studied how they do things. It tied in with* Bambi. *I wanted dignity. That's how we got into the nature things.*

I didn't have the opportunity to try live action until I had the problem of getting money out of Europe. We had money impounded in England. I got my feet wet then on live action. I struggled with it. I kept playing around. I couldn't decide what kind of live action I should do, what would please that big family. I never make anything for children but I

*make it so that children can enjoy it. I never made anything
for children until the Mickey Mouse Club and that was for
mid-teens.*

The Disneys made many live-action pictures with moderate box-office success before they hit the jack pot with *Mary
Poppins,* Hollywood's No. 1 "grosser" in 1965. But the fact
that their fortunes were always dependent on the uncertainties of box office led them to look further afield for new
things. The project they counted on the most to serve as their
escape from risky film life was, of course, Disneyland.

WALT: *I started designing Disneyland—it was a pet of
mine—with my own money, borrowed on my life insurance.
The bankers are fellows who don't understand your business,
my problem all along. It was the same thing again with the
amusement park. They were against it. Had their foot right
on our neck all the time. I couldn't get anywhere in the company [i.e. Walt Disney Productions, which had public stockholders and banker relations]. I started it on my own in the
barn. Then I brought in a staff of three people, including an
art director and a draftsman from Twentieth-Century. They
had a layoff over there, so I was able to get them.*

*I had the idea of Disneyland before the war. I was casing
all these amusement parks. My wife said, if you're going to
go to another amusement park, I won't go with you. I went
to zoos too. This was in the late thirties. I was taking my
daughters around. The places were never clean. They
couldn't touch anything. I couldn't get my wife to go with
me any more. There was nothing for the parents to do but
eat with the squirrels.*

For Disneyland, Walt himself designed a train (one of his
hobbies) and with his team, the streets, rides, and features.
He also got into three-dimensional animation with sound and
came up with the fanciful technical term for it, "audio-
animatronics." This is an electronic system for coordinating
voice and movement of lifelike imitations of animals and humans. It causes artificial alligators to rise and spout, ele-

phants to rear and roar, and Abraham Lincoln to rise from a chair in costume and give an address with gestures.

WALT: *Imagineering is the first stage, then engineering. The Lincoln kind of thing is a whole new field for us and, oh boy, things are moving fast in that field. Progress in outer space has changed the whole darn thing in three years. Servo valves do all the activating of the mechanisms. Miniaturized. I can put it in the fingers. Why, I am reaching the point where I could actually make one of these characters play the piano. I don't caricature everything. I like to be serious. With the pirates I was caricaturing. They were for fun, like the Tiki room. I have other animals, a raccoon, an owl, that talk, and two bluejays. With Lincoln I wanted respect, dignity. He stands close inspection, he looks you in the eye. I like to do historical things because once you program them, you won't have to change the program. I could do a stage play, might do it in Florida. I like to do American stories. I would like to do the Washington story, what happened to the Continental Congress. It's a terrific American story. I would like to do the story of the Louisiana Purchase when they bought that little city of New Orleans with peripheral property.*

Walt accompanied this last remark with hand gestures and a broad smile, signifying a Disney gag. When the Disneys went to Anaheim, California, to set up Disneyland, they ran out of money buying land and so couldn't get all they could have used; and perhaps also they did not quite foresee the reciprocal effects of the project with others on adjacent land. They bought a 240-acre orange grove and later another forty acres, and as Disneyland drew its crowds and the town of Anaheim grew rapidly, they got hemmed in with no control over their surroundings. This brought them some disbenefits and none of the benefits. Having suffered that annoyance, the Disneys got interested in the subject of "peripheral property." When Walt dreamed up the Walt Disney World for Florida, the brothers kept it a secret until they had quietly bought up forty-three square miles near Orlando, an assembled tract twice the size of Manhattan island, for about $5 million—one of the great real-estate coups of our time. "If anyone tries to get close to us they're going to be at least ten or twelve miles away," said Walt.

ROY: *Movies are Walt's chief love, with animation and animals more than live action. Everything we've done seems to grow out of movies. The park is almost an extension of that idea. We are trying to get good family entertainment. Walt is self-educated and every picture requires a lot of research and study. And when you see one of our pictures advertised, you are open to like it. You may not like the particular picture but you know it will be clean.* [In Disney language, "clean" means not only family movies but scraping the chewing gum off the streets of Disneyland every morning.] *Everything in the park has educational application. Walt tries to give it something. He never talks down to kids. Seldom do we do small-fry stuff that's not uplifting. The park is for the old and young; most of those who come are adults; presidents and kings and queens come. Walt's image before the world is one of great respect and confidence.*

Disney's art and the culture it reflects, remarked on variously by so many critics and commentators, have been rendered by a perceptive fan of his in the succinct observation: Disney made mechanical things into humorous art forms under the influence of our culture and was not so serious in comedy as Chaplin. This seems quite accurate and corresponds with Disney's own distinction between his serious and his caricatured figures in audio-animatronics. Certainly Disney's comedy characteristically trips the light fantastic, and his storytelling when not comic remains fantastic. His comedy is serious only in the sense that comedy is a serious art. But some say there is an aesthetic statement in his art forms and a message in his ideas of dignity and clean entertainment.

WALT: *I don't like the idea of message. I'm happiest when what we do pleases a lot of people. The public is our customer. The respect we've built up with the public is something we've established and imbedded in the organization. You build a story. Any writer who wants to crawl off in a hole somewhere is stupid. He has no sounding board, no new ideas. I don't crawl off in any hole. I talk, bounce it. I change my mind. The worst thing is for anybody to get off too much thinking about art. He'll never become an individual. He's got to let himself go, be himself. Don't try to be something you're not. Audio-animatronics, for example, is a new form. I don't care if you want to call it art. In films it's O.K. to do that ivory tower stuff. It's for the film festivals. But the big thing is to reach the masses. It is a mass medium. This thing of art, art, art. I don't know if I call what I do art or not. Time is the judge of art. There are a lot of crimes committed in the name of art. It swings with the times. I don't think that sex and violence are entertaining. I don't go to the theater to be depressed. There are too many things to be depressed about.*

Hamlet?

WALT: Hamlet *is a different world, I don't think of it the same way.*

Walt made fine distinctions here, that between violence in Shakespeare and violence for its own sake, and that concerning the language of his profession. In shying away from the word "art" as a working term, despite and perhaps because of its laudatory implications, he seemed to feel that it might restrict him from doing what he wanted to do; and if it did not restrict him, it could lead to the disappointment of those who talked the language of David Low. "Art" is a big word, subject to several meanings, and many persons whose professions are not specifically designated as art have, like Walt, eschewed the term, especially when trying to do something that has not been legitimized in the modern tradition called "art." Yet, in the very broad sense in which the word is also used, it seems that most of what Walt did, for better or worse, is encompassed by the word "art." It seems to be the judgment of time and a lot of people that his is not the "Pop Art" of the galleries but a unique kind of popular "Pop Art."

On the business side, after a lifetime of making money, losing it, worrying about it, Walt at last got out of debt with some "keeping money," and indeed in his last years became a rich man. He got it in salary, in his stock ownership in Walt Disney Productions, from financial participation in his company's films and from royalties on the use of his name, the latter two being corporate arrangements that are conventional in Hollywood. But it was not his good fortune to realize the full payoff, which came later. Although no one apparently at the time of these talks had any notion that Walt had not long to live, he and his associates had on their minds the fact that he would reach the conventional retirement age of sixty-five in December of that year, and that sometime in the fairly near future the company, which was based on his talent, would be trying to go on without him. Concern about that was in the air at the time not only because it is the kind of thing stockholders think about, but also because Walt's eventual disengagement from active guidance of the studio was an operational problem for both of the brothers.

WALT: *Can management produce Disney product after Disney? That's the sixty-four-dollar question. We're hoping we can. As well as I can, I'm untying the apron strings—until they scream for help. I've got some teams I'm building up. I've got individual producers I've been training. Jules Stein [founder and chairman of Music Corporation of America] said if you knock off, the company will make more money than ever before because you won't be there to spend it. Well, we are getting diversified. There is a two-year timetable in Florida after the preliminaries, three or four years is more like it. We are imagineering it now, how it should be, what it should be.*

ROY: *Whenever Walt is out of this business some people think that it will probably fall apart. But when you have a pool of talent like we have in boys coming up, you will have a good batting average. Any company is going to grow and expand or shrink. It is true that after Walt goes, if we don't get on and keep our life, we are going to shrink. But if that were to happen, it would take a long time. We have a marvelous floor under us in our film library, and we have diversification. That's why we are excited about Florida and Mineral King. We have dozens of bright boys around here. We don't have any doubts that the company can go along without the presence of Walt's inspirational leadership.*

The "floor" that Walt left under the company was indeed remarkable. In his lifetime, apart from Disneyland and the initial stages of Walt Disney World, he produced, directly or as executive producer, and stored in the company's library 497 short subjects, 21 animated features, 56 live-action motion pictures, 7 "True-Life Adventure" features, 330 hours of the Mickey Mouse Club, 78 half-hour Zorro shows, and 330 hours of other TV shows. Their residual value was incalculable. But the future remained the question. Two years later, in January 1968, the legacy of Walt's inspiration still dominated the company and the means of perpetuating it were uppermost in the minds of Roy and his associates. E. Cardon Walker, then executive vice-president, later president, said, "Walt left us twenty years work to do."

ROY: *After Walt was gone, the price of our stock went up because of the value of the inventory. People thought we would sell it. But no. Then they saw the value of the going company. The key point in our diversification is that only 42 percent of our revenue now comes from motion pictures. The big new thing is the Florida project. Walt developed the team at Disneyland that can carry it through. I expect that after it is opened, along with other things, the proportion of our revenue from motion pictures will be only about 15 percent. We will at last be really diversified and no longer resting on the success or failure of one picture, as we were in the fifties. Our aim is to get stability by doubling the revenue. The long-range concept is an on-going recreation-entertainment business oriented to the family and education.*

10

OFF-TRACK BETTING ON HORSERACING: THE EFFECT OF A NEW PLAYER IN AN OLD COOPERATIVE GAME

For the old and new strategic players, the object of the off-track betting game is to get all they can out of the business of horseracing and divide it satisfactorily among themselves. What they want includes the horseplayers' money, an increase in the popularity of racing, and the maintenance of New York's supremacy in the sport. The payoffs are available only in coalitions, which must be reorganized since the new strategic player, OTB, entered the game.

THE OLD STRATEGIC PLAYERS

- New York State
- New York State racetracks
- Horsemen (owners and trainers)

THE NEW STRATEGIC PLAYERS

- New York City, represented by its Off-Track Betting Corporation (OTB)

THE NON-STRATEGIC PLAYERS

- Horseplayers

the track, any decline in track business—unless compensated for—is translated fairly soon into smaller purses for horsemen. And since smaller purses leave the owner less return, this translates eventually into smaller salaries and fees to trainers and jockeys and lower prices for breeders. Thus, all horsemen—breeders, owners, trainers, and jockeys—feared OTB and registered outrage at its intrusion into the old sport. Some traveled from the horse states, notably Kentucky, to join New York horsemen in the struggle with the monster. The harness and thoroughbred people, who heretofore had never been especially friendly with each other, started meeting together. OTB's gathering enemies insisted that, as it was set up, it was doing more harm than good and would not realize its own aims.

Horseracing, pure, simple, and entrancing, is a game of chance. Breeding horses is a game of genetic chance. Skill in breeding the best sires to the best dams refines this chance: the best way to get a winner of the Kentucky Derby, Preakness, or Belmont Stakes is to breed a champion or champion-producing mare to the winner of one of those classics or their foreign equivalents. Racing a horse entails some random chance of untoward events. Stumbling, brushing, bumping, lack of racing room, getting a horse's tail caught in the gate or his teeth knocked out, a horse's indisposition on the day of a race, and a thousand others affect races. Conditioning a horse well for a race brings it up to its best chance, and winning races reveals the great unknown—which horses are the best.

Betting on horses is a game of horseplayer against horseplayer. One racing fan may bet his favorite number or numbers associated with his children's birthdays. A handicapping horseplayer, on the other hand, will try to get away from blind chance by predicting, from data on past performance, how the race will be run; as a bettor, he may compare his own judgment about a horse's chance of winning with the consensus on the odds board. Owners and trainers will make some judgmental decisions and follow certain sporting codes in deciding which horses to enter in which races; jockeys make all sorts of tactical decisions during the running of a race. Yet in the main, the rational view is that racing is a game of chance. Horses race in what appears to be a probabilistic world, expressed in the "morning line," the prerace line of prices worked out by experts and published in newspapers and the daily programs at the tracks—though it is not clear whether the "morning line" predicts the behavior of the horses or the horseplayers.

The sport also has some uniquely attractive qualities in its color and romance, the myths associated with horses, the traditions of sportsmanship for groom, trainer, jockey, and owner, the suspense of animal and man in a race. It is a special racetrack world with special and indefinable appeals to horsemen and horseplayers alike.

When all that is said, it also remains true that the *business* of horseracing is not, in the main, a game of chance but a game of strategy, in which many different parties, each seeking to maximize his own advantages, find their interests to be intertwined. Indeed, "horse trading" itself is a synonym for bargaining; and the horsemen bargain with each other over the sale of horses and the marketing or bartering of stallion and mare services. Beyond that, they negotiate and bargain with the racetracks, threatening to go to one track instead of another for a better deal and joining in boycotts to get the purse level up. Racetracks, state governors, the legislatures of the racing states—all these, too, negotiate and bargain in their peculiar way, part political, part economic, with the horsemen and one another. (One of the peculiarities of the states has been that while they are in principle concerned with the well-being of the sport on which some of their revenue depends, they typically construe their interests as being short-run, getting what they can here and now, and shrugging off the future.)

It is characteristic of a strategic game that when a new player sits in, it becomes a new game. And when New York City came to share in the benefits of horse-race gambling, it introduced a radically different kind of player into the game.

The old players—horsemen, racetracks, and the states—had been dividing the spoils in a game whose rules had become pretty well agreed on for over thirty-odd years.

There was, however, one element of instability in that arrangement, and it was fairly important. The economy of racing is based on the "takeout"—the percentage deducted from the betting "handle" before the winning bettors receive their payment. Some of the takeout goes to the state, some to the industry. Arguments about who gets how much of it have tended to be accompanied by much tugging and hauling, boycotts, factional conflicts, splits among the horsemen, and lobbying by the tracks. But when one or another participant in this process succeeds in getting more for himself, it is usually not at the expense of another participant. The extra money is provided, instead, by increasing the total takeout. Or, stated another way, the money is provided by the horseplayers. Since they are themselves non-strategic players, they have nothing much to say about what percentage they are charged for the privilege of gambling. They are stuck with a take-it-or-leave-it proposition.

Until the mid-1940s, the takeout on thoroughbred racing was 10 percent, with the state taking 5 percent, the track the other 5. In 1946 Mayor William O'Dwyer got local governments into the game and the takeout was raised to 15 percent, a hike that horseplayers bitterly dubbed "the O'Dwyer bite." But O'Dwyer and his successors did not have the political power to hold on to the extra 5 percent and in a few years had to yield it to the state—which thus wound up doubling its share from 5 to 10 percent. This division remained stable until 1967, when dissatisfied thoroughbred horsemen, under pressure of rising costs, demanded higher purses and struck—the action was dubbed "the millionaires' strike." More precisely, they shut down Aqueduct by refusing to enter any horses. NYRA said it couldn't pay more out of its 5 percent share and remain solvent. The state, refusing to yield any of its 10 percent, resolved the impasse in 1968 by raising the total takeout to 16 percent and allotting the extra percentage point to the horsemen and track.

The state, one might notice, wears two hats when it participates in these discussions: it is a player with an interest in the game—and the arbiter of the game. As player, it took care of its own interest; as arbiter, it transferred an additional payment from horseplayers to the industry. This division of spoils also proved unstable. In the spring of 1971 the state again resolved a crisis at the track by raising the takeout. This time it went to 17 percent.

An additional hidden tax on horseplayers has been levied in recent years under the euphemism "breakage." This term originally referred to the fact that the track would not pay out odd pennies, which were declared to be a nuisance. The tracks now pay out only at prices divisible by 20 cents and "break" to the lower amounts. With betting tickets sold at a minimum of $2, a payoff of $2.39, to take an extreme example, will break back to $2.20; thus, in this case, about half the horseplayer's winnings are kept from him. On ordinary win, place, and show betting, breakage averages out to about one percentage point, making the total takeout about 18 percent. Each percentage point in New York State as a whole at the time of the arrival of OTB was worth about $16 million. As matters stood in thoroughbred racing before OTB, the state was taking out 10 percent, the track 4 percent, the horsemen 3 percent, with special arrangements for dividing the breakage. (The harness tracks' split is made along roughly the same lines.)

The last two added percentage points seem to have been a factor in a decline in traditional betting. The racing industry worried that it had gone beyond the most that it was prudent to charge the horseplayer. Collectively, of course, all horseplayers must lose. Still, there is a question about how fast they are willing to lose and still come back.

In the efforts to extract more from the horseplayer, the racing industry was also approaching another limit of sorts. Tracks in metropolitan New York, in common with many elsewhere that are under continuous pressure from the state, had increased the *quantity* of racing nearly to its limit in races run per day and racing days per year. The harness tracks run all year round except for a brief rest at Christmas. Some of the horsemen would like to continue year round but many others believe that to be unsound; as it is, the number and quality of thoroughbreds in action drastically decline late in the season.

With the takeout apparently as high as it could go and the racing season about as long as it could go, neither the state nor the industry could discern a way to get substantially more revenue from racing. Indeed, the increasing economic pressures on the racing industry left many horsemen persuaded that the state might have to take *less* than its 10 percent. But the city had a way to raise racing revenues by going outside the tracks.

Actually, New York City had been trying for some years to get off-track betting legalized, on the grounds that it would enlarge the betting market and take the business away from illegal bookmakers, relieve the city's strained budget, and reduce its need to call upon the state for revenue aid. The city's budget analysts had dreamed of taking in $200 million a year from off-track gambling revenue. The city held a referendum on off-track betting and buried the moral qualms of a minority under the favorable votes of the majority (the takeout is a "regressive tax," taking a higher percentage of the income of the poor than the rich). Despite the referendum, the racing industry still opposed the city, as it had for years, and was confident that it had done so successfully again in 1970.

But then, in the last days of the 1970 legislative session in Albany, the lawmakers came under especially heavy pressure to aid the city, which was projecting a budget gap of $630 million. With scarcely any warning, the legislature passed the city-supported bill to make off-track betting legal. The law also gave other municipalities in the state the right to set up their own off-track betting agencies under certain conditions. In New York City itself, OTB would be run by a new public-benefit corporation with a board of directors appointed by the mayor. All the traditional equilibrium between horsemen, racetracks, and the state was suddenly shot to pieces.

The racing industry was horrified by the new rules. They provided that the city would have a takeout of 17 percent on off-track betting—betting, the industry noted bitterly, on *its* races. Part of the 17 percent was allocated to horsemen and racetracks, but their slices were far thinner than those they were used to getting from on-track betting. Specifically, 0.5 percent of the OTB handle went to the state, 1.5 percent to the tracks and horsemen. The remaining fifteen percentage points could cover the OTB Corporation's operating costs and profit. The first $200 million of profit would be divided roughly eighty-twenty between city and state; beyond that point the split would be fifty-fifty. Furthermore, although the law provided compensation to the industry for damage "on account of" OTB, it offered no way of gauging the extent of OTB's responsibility.

The percentages were bad enough, in the industry's view, but its deeper grievance was the mandate that the OTB Corporation had to act as a separate player. OTB was not just another device to extract money from horseplayers. It was the operator of a betting business specifically designed to maximize the city's interest, even where that collided, as it surely would, with the interests of the horsemen and tracks. All this was hard enough to take—and then came Howard J. Samuels.

Mayor John V. Lindsay found in Samuels a man who would not be bashful about exercising the new player's prerogatives. Samuels had managed to lose some New York political campaigns and still emerge a hopeful in politics. Many politicians thought it was folly for him to take on the job of running a "book-making" operation—he was soon nicknamed "Howie the Horse"; but after a year of making the front pages, he observed, with a hopeful's smile, that he had become one of the three best-known political personalities of that time in New York (along with Nelson Rockefeller and Mayor Lindsay).

Samuels' appointment was not simply an exercise of political patronage. He had solid business credentials as a co-founder of Kordite Corporation, in Macedon, New York, which among other things developed Baggies. He and his brother Richard started the company in 1946 on $25,000 of borrowed capital; eventually it was sold to Mobil Oil Corporation, with a payoff of several million dollars for the brothers, and Howard for a time served as a vice president of Mobil.

For all his own aggressiveness, Samuels could not push the other players in the off-track betting game too hard, for in the last analysis all the players were interdependent. Samuels, the horsemen, the racetrack owners and operators, and New York State itself—all had choices that were limited by the others' choices and all had to negotiate and bargain to attain their economic objectives. Samuels needed not only horse races but also the cooperation of the horsemen and the tracks; in particular, he needed some revision of standard racing procedures. For example, a good many OTB customers place their bets on the way to work—i.e., at eight or nine in the morning. But at these times some information critical to horseplayers—for example, on entries, scratches, jockey changes—was unavailable. Most of all, Samuels needed televised races, which proved to be tremendous bet producers. In addition to needing cooperation from the tracks and the horsemen, Samuels had to be careful not to hurt them to the point where his own gambling device, the racetrack itself, was hurt.

The tracks and the horsemen had some bargaining counters that Samuels could not ignore. Racing plants, for example, often have considerable value for alternative real-estate uses, and *in extremis* a track operator may just decide not to make his annual application for a racetrack license. Horsemen can take their stables elsewhere; and racetrack unions actually do strike. The tracks and the horsemen could also retaliate against OTB in court or in the state legislature, where they seemed to have a fair amount of influence.

Acknowledging the inequities in the rules of the original bill and wanting to stave off an industry coalition against him, Samuels tried to bargain separately about the takeout and its apportionment with spokesmen for the different tracks and the horsemen. But from their point of view, more than a new division of the takeout was at issue. The very presence of the intruder, with his special priorities and independent powers, limited the traditional powers of the industry and forced them to deal with him about the entire economics of racing. By now they became reconciled to legalized off-track betting as a new way of life—except for the harness tracks' taking one last (and lost) shot at OTB in court, in an effort to get the basic law declared in violation of New York State's Constitution. But their preference was somehow to get rid of the new player and resolve the economic issues of off-track betting among themselves. With this in mind, the major branches of the industry began to meet quietly in August 1971.

Meanwhile, however, one part of the racing industry, the New York Racing Association, also explored the possibility of coming to terms with OTB. The NYRA is a non-profit corporation (technically, it seeks to make enough money to pay for capital improvements), whose purpose is to foster thoroughbred racing and provide a source of public revenue. It was finding the going tough even before OTB appeared; its handle had been growing but attendance was showing a downward trend, and with increased costs and heavy debt-service charges, it lost money in 1969, 1970, and 1971. After building the great new Belmont plant in the mid-1960s at a cost of $31 million, it was unable to meet horsemen's demands for larger purses, the upshot of which was the state's intervention to hike the takeout by two percentage points.

It seems evident, in retrospect, that the NYRA had deluded itself in the 1960s in thinking that it could build Belmont, maintain its August race meet at Saratoga (the mecca of thoroughbred racing, despite the normally lower attendance and handle of an upstate track), raise horsemen's purses, and at the same time avoid a still higher takeout. The association plainly needed additional income from some such source as off-track betting. If the NYRA had sponsored off-track betting itself several years earlier, it might easily have secured control of the game. Now, with the city's OTB intruding on its province, the NYRA would have trouble over control, and its future was further compromised by the threat of "encirclement" of its metropolitan tracks: prospective new tracks to the north in Connecticut and to the west, across the Hudson River, in the Jersey Meadows, and perhaps to the east in Long Island. Clearly the NYRA needed a deal of some kind.

In the midst of its growing difficulties, the association got a new chief executive in Alfred G. Vanderbilt, a dedicated racing man who had long been a force for change in racing in the councils of the Jockey Club and the NYRA itself. He studied ways to make racing more attractive to the ordinary fan; but his management had not come up with anything that had the potential of state-wide off-track betting with televised races—a huge new market, still virtually untapped by thoroughbred racing. Recognizing the accomplished fact of OTB and not sure whether the new player would be overthrown, Vanderbilt's posture toward it was ambivalent.

Others, too, among them the New York horsemen and representatives of the state, were wavering. But the time had come for all the players to reach a resolution of the game. The situation seen at close range was muddy, with various players at cross purposes and numerous subgames going on between upstate and downstate, small tracks and large tracks, harness racing and thoroughbred racing, different unions, and the like, but the essential outlines can be set down.

Before the game began, the prevailing coalition of state, tracks, and horsemen had drawn its entire gains from on-track horseplayers and divided it between its members. That gave them a standard for comparison in the new game. The old players also were saddled with their tradition of rejecting the legal off-track market and that tradition still carried weight in the minds of many of them. Hence, it was not surprising that from the beginning of the new game, when the 1971 legislation created OTB as a new independent player and authorized it to exploit the off-track betting market, some of the old players held hopes of getting the off-track rule of law rescinded entirely, that is, of abolishing not only the new player but the legal off-track market as well. But, as noted, the main and growing tendency of the old players was to accept the legal off-track market as a new fact of life.

The three principal issues in the new game then settled down to who would control off-track betting, how that market would be exploited, and how the gains would be divided. The control issue could be negotiated within limits, but not, of course, to the point of getting OTB to leave its seat in the game voluntarily. Control was not an issue in a vacuum. It was tied to the economics of exploiting the market and dividing the gains. To get the economics of the game straight, however, it is useful to set aside for a moment the potential, if not imminent, political game and deal first with the economic game in its own terms.

It is important to notice that each of the old players—state, tracks, and horsemen—could gain nothing by going alone; only the new player could make any gain by himself, and that only a small one from taking bets on out-of-state races. With this slight exception, all potential gains in the game had to be made by cooperative arrangements between the players. If one were going to model a cooperative game in the abstract, one would go through the exercise of identifying all possible coalitions and the worth of each of them. Thus, in this game, the potential coalitions and their values were as follows:

State-Tracks	worth nothing
State-Horsemen	worth nothing
State-OTB	worth a little
Tracks-Horsemen	worth a lot
Tracks-OTB	worth a little
Horsemen-OTB	worth a little
State-Tracks-Horsemen	worth a lot
State-Tracks-OTB	worth a little
State-Horsemen-OTB	worth a little
Tracks-Horsemen-OTB	worth a lot
State-Tracks-Horsemen-OTB	worth a lot

This formal display of the potential coalitions in the game, including the impractical and ridiculous ones, serves to emphasize that only the tracks and horsemen are productive of racing, and only they and OTB are productive of a betting business. The state is not productive of much directly (though indirectly, its public services benefit racing); it mainly exercises its power to tax and take a large cut in the profits. Obviously, the coalitions that have any economic value above OTB's small fall-back value are these:

Tracks-Horsemen
State-Tracks-Horsemen
Tracks-Horsemen-OTB
State-Tracks-Horsemen-OTB

As the state is not going to leave the game and has the power to take a cut, the realistic coalitions come down to just two:

State-Tracks-Horsemen (with off-track betting but leaving
    out OTB as a player)
State-Tracks-Horsemen-OTB

Each of these two coalitions would have a different value and yield a different payoff to each of the players. The questions of which of the coalitions represented the higher value in money and sport, how their members would divide the gains of their cooperation, and which coalition, if either, was stable, formed the central economic problem of the game. Although this model suppresses the strategic details of the game and the subgames within the camp of each player (each camp, in fact, represented a complex coalition), it gives in overview the decisive outlines of the game. Everything had to come down to resolving it in terms of the value and stability of these coalitions.

There was a time in November 1971 when the NYRA appeared to have found common ground with Samuels. Its vice president (later president and chief executive), John H. Krumpe, came out of an executive session at a convention of the Thoroughbred Racing Association (the national organi-

zation of thoroughbred racetracks) saying that the NYRA expected to reach an agreement in principle with OTB "within
three weeks" and suggested that the two might together take
their combined proposals as a package to the legislature. But
this alliance never developed. Instead, the alternative efforts
—to bring the industry together and squeeze out OTB—
gathered force. In March 1972 the conflict between the racing industry and OTB exploded, with the sudden appearance
in Albany of an industry-supported bill proposing that a new
state operating board take over off-track betting and also proposing a new apportionment of the gains.

The governing board envisaged in this bill, made up
largely of racing-industry people, would run off-track betting
throughout the state. It would have the power to determine
the number and location of a municipality's betting shops,
the system's communication and transmission systems, the
kinds of wagers permitted and their minimum and maximum
amounts, the race meetings on which wagers would be accepted, off-track business hours, the conditions for televising
races, and the like.

One result of this arrangement would be that the industry,
through the board it would dominate, could divide the betting market along whatever lines it saw fit. For example, it
could decide to limit betting away from the track to exotic
bets—the kinds that appeal especially to long shot or lottery-
minded players. Exotic bets, which had become an important
fixture of off-track betting, and increasingly of on-track betting as well, had taken the form of the "Exacta" (or "Per-
fecta"), the "Triple" and the "Superfecta," in which, respectively, two, three or four horses are picked in order of finish.

All parties, including Samuels, had agreed on promoting
exotic betting, and applying a 25 percent takeout to the
"Triple" and "Superfecta"—the idea being that the bettor
wouldn't notice the deeper gouge because the winning
payoffs are so large—as much an occasion as $10,000 or more
for $2 tickets. There was also talk of taking $1 bets on races
of this type and attracting the numbers players: a prospect of
finding *new* money to divide. But whereas Samuels' OTB

was taking all kinds of racing bets (he would even have liked to expand to all-sports betting), the industry wanted to limit OTB to exotic bets alone—with the traditional win, place, and show bets accepted only at the track. The industry hoped thereby to keep the regular racing fans coming to the track. (Samuels did not rule out OTB's eventually specializing in exotic bets, but preferred to consider the matter after he had more off-track experience.)

The industry-supported plan would also change the payoffs to all the players—the municipalities, the state, the tracks, and the horsemen—and would allot to each municipality a specific share rather than the profit it received under the original OTB bill. The plan assumed that the takeout would remain at 17 percent plus breakage on standard bets and it assigned 6 percent to the state operating agency for its own expenses. All other payoffs would vary with the kind of racing and the volume of business. On the basis of Samuels' projected volume of betting for 1972–73, the tracks and the horsemen of the NYRA, who then received a total of 1.5 percent, would be allotted double that, split fifty-fifty; and the state and participating municipality would divide the remaining 8 percent 3.2 to 4.8. That 4.8 percent contrasted with 7.6 percent that New York City would get under the then prevailing arrangement if OTB, according to plan, brought operating expenses down to 6 percent. So the city would be a substantial loser under the proposed new rules.

Samuels looked for a compromise. He wanted the city to retain control of OTB, but he was willing to revise the scheme of payoffs to make them more favorable to the racing industry. The extra money would be generated mainly by the high-takeout exotic bets. In addition, Samuels proposed a sliding scale on standard bets at the thoroughbred racetracks during the following year, which he expected would average out to about 2.5 percent for tracks and horsemen—not too far from the industry's own proposed figure. He also told the thoroughbred horsemen that if they and the NYRA cooperated with OTB, OTB would guarantee them $2 million more in purses in 1972 than they got in 1971. And he did not overlook the state itself, offering it a 1972 guaranteed minimum payoff equal to about 1 percent, paid monthly.

The only group that responded at all sympathetically to Samuels was the Horsemen's Benevolent Protective Association, an organization of owners and trainers of thoroughbreds. ("We try to keep all the avenues open," said its New York president, Eugene Jacobs.) With the industry supporting a specific alternative to New York City's OTB, Samuels countered by taking his proposals directly to the legislature. The economic conflict had escalated to a political battle and the scene shifted to Albany.

Although politics is a different kind of game, political agents cannot safely ignore the underlying economics they deal with. A political decision contrary to the sound cooperative interests of the players would leave unsatisfied coalitions, and in that unstable situation these coalitions could be expected to return again and again to attempt to upset the political coalitions. As it happened, the legislature could not resolve the issue, although Rockefeller seemed to favor the industry solution. The upshot was a governor's commission which then spent the better part of a year trying to resolve the problem with a recommendation. The commission came to be called the "Delafield Commission," after its chairman, Charles B. Delafield, a former executive of Consolidated Edison Company of New York.

During the year of its work, all of the parties continued to play the game before the commission, presenting more or less the views described above. In March 1973 the commission issued its report, analyzing the situation and resolving it more or less along the lines of the industry's preferred solution. The commission viewed New York racing as an important industry in a time of crisis, with the main threat coming from uninhibited off-track betting. A minority of two commissioners called for total abolition of off-track betting. The majority held in favor of an integrated state-wide off-track system, much muted by restrictions. Among the restrictions proposed were a surcharge on standard off-track betting (win, place, show) and a gradual phasing out of this kind of betting; and an off-track emphasis on exotic betting, with an increase in the takeout from 17 to 25 percent (plus breakage). In sum, an off-track market substantially reduced in size by limited offerings and higher prices for gambling. Payoffs to the tracks from off-track betting would be increased by a new formula for division; payoffs to the city (or cities) would be indirect through revenue sharing at the pleasure of the state legislature. A single state superagency would supersede existing agencies and control all racing and off-track betting. New York City's OTB would be abolished.

As one would expect, the industry hailed and the city (and cities) deplored the Delafield report. Samuels, Mayor Lindsay, and other city officials denounced "a state takeover" and said they would fight. Delafield himself, upon being asked whether he thought his proposal would hurt the city's interest, said, "I'm not principally interested in the city. I'm interested in the viability of horseracing."

After the Delafield report, the issue became thoroughly politicized. The political interplay over OTB is not the subject of this story. Perhaps the fact that OTB provides local political patronage jobs played a part in the legislative proceedings, but if so, only one part in numerous cross currents in the legislature. In any case, in May 1973, the legislature, to the surprise of many, rejected the three-player coalition and adopted the four-player coalition. OTB won and the industry lost the political battle.

In rejecting the main force of the Delafield report, the legislature adopted a number of its details, which had been more or less unopposed. One was a state superagency with control over all racing and gambling, including the state lottery; state-wide integrated off-track betting, with no restrictions on the types of bets taken and no surcharges; the jump in the takeout on all "triple" betting; an increase in the off-track payoff to tracks, horsemen, and the state; and an experiment with a lower takeout on all standard bets. The legislature also extended the racing season the last notch, to all year round and seven days a week; reduced admission taxes; eliminated mandatory minimum admission ticket prices; and made some rescue provisions for the ailing NYRA. Most of the rest was left to the new state racing and gambling board.

This conclusion of the game was approved by Samuels and other city officials and denounced by Delafield as leading "to the end of the glorious sport of horseracing as we once knew it." The harness industry complained bitterly. George Morton Levy of Roosevelt Raceway said: "They seem to have taken the extra monies out of our hide." But Krumpe for the NYRA, though he expressed some dissatisfaction with the division of the off-track payoff, said he could live with OTB: "I can say it is now in our interest under the new law to make OTB successful." And *Bloodhorse,* a Kentucky magazine that speaks for many of the powerful forces in thoroughbred racing, especially on the breeding end, and which had backed the industry's fight in New York, concluded optimistically: "For the first time in the three years since off-track betting was legalized in New York, there are reasonable grounds for believing class racing in New York can survive."

This game ended, as games do in the real world, with the start of a new one. As the players in relative peace resumed their bargaining over the division of the horseplayers' money, the conditions changed. Samuels left OTB to make another try for the Democratic nomination for governor (and lost). Lindsay left the mayor's office, to be succeeded by Abraham D. ("Abe") Beame who, treating the horseplayer as a political derelict as well as a caricature of the consumer in the hands of a monopoly, laid a 5 percent surtax on his own city bettors, which with compound breakage would take out from a quarter to a third of the money they bet. But then the outlook for the horseplayer brightened with the entrance of still another strategic player into the game. Across the Hudson River in New Jersey, a few minutes from Manhattan, a new sports complex, including a racetrack, started up, and Krumpe left the NYRA to run it. In response, Bertram D. Sarafan, chairman of the new New York State Racing and Wagering Board, told the New York *Times* that the state would do "whatever it takes to meet close-range racing competition from New Jersey. If it becomes a difficult situation, we'll have to make our tracks more appealing. We'll have to lower the parimutuel tax, cut admission prices, and offer cheaper food." But the skeptical horseplayers wondered, could New York and New Jersey get together?

11

THE COMMUNICATIONS SATELLITE:
A TEN-PLAYER COOPERATIVE GAME

The game played around the communications satellite is a good one for its display of the interaction of coalitions. The objective of the players is to divide the potential benefits of the new technology that relays a signal in space. It is a rather large game in which the players are free to cooperate in groups. Ten players in a cooperative game present the horrendous prospect of more than a thousand potential coalitions, from among which the players were to try to choose the best ones. The number is large enough to give pause even to a mathematical game theorist, but the real players here valiantly engaged themselves in the game regardless of the peril of wayward outcomes. As supply and demand, though present, were not determining, and the players could seek agreeable partners, the outcomes were highly indeterminate. Furthermore, as this is not a market game centrally involving an exchange of goods, but an intercorporate affair, it is not certain to have a stable economic outcome.

For better or worse, the central game to be described here was actually played to a finish in the course of one year, ending in the spring of 1971. Afterward the commissioners and staff of the Federal Communications Commission (FCC) deliberated and ruled on its outcome. The results would be felt in subsequent games which continued on at various levels—economic, legal, and political—as the new satellite communications industry began to come into being in the United States in 1974.

various government bodies, federal and state. To gain its ends, it employs its established positions, arguments, controlled information, allies, bargaining, and a box of technological, economic, and political strategies. It has an ongoing powerful position, which each succeeding management inherits. Anyone who likes power likes AT&T—unless his interests happen to come into conflict with it. Other corporations and government on occasion do come into conflict with it, as it cuts a wide swath through the economy and its ambitions in communications appear to be limited only by the resistance it meets.

The United States historically carved the field of communications into three parts, giving mail to the government-run Post Office Department, teletype and telegram to Western Union,[2] and the telephone mainly to AT&T. (This was in contrast to Great Britain, for example, where all three were placed in a single government-owned entity.) In the United States, AT&T moved out from the telephone network to handle the transmission over distances of the first nationwide radio networks, which it still does. AT&T expanded again to take on television distribution. This gave AT&T the handle to expand the concept of its business from telephone to all telecommunications.

What each new management of AT&T gets as a birthright is the telephone. The core of AT&T's monopoly power is the accepted policy that there may not be telephones of different companies in one house. There is only one company and its connections with an exchange or switch point. From this sanctuary, AT&T ranges far and wide geographically, through switch points interconnecting with other switch points through short and long lines. It also ranges out with its product policy. Its famous Bell Laboratories has worked brilliantly on the frontiers of science and technology. Its sub-

[2] Western Union, at one time a single company, in 1963 was divided into two companies, Western Union International and Western Union Telegraph Company, the latter confined to domestic business and now the principal subsidiary of Western Union Corporation.

sidiary the Western Electric Company manufactures communication equipment, mainly for Bell System Companies—$7 billion worth in 1973 (although only a subsidiary company, Western Electric is the twelfth largest industrial corporation in the United States). There is always some confusion in the motivation of a public utility, for whom an increase in profits is likely to bring a reduction in rates. Limited in the profit it could get from a telephone, AT&T consistently widened its field of activity to any form of communications. It of course laid claim to the satellite.

AT&T was heavily committed to investment in an international cable program when the National Aeronautics and Space Administration (NASA) put up the balloon satellite, Echo 1, in 1960, proving that the technology for communications satellites was about ready to be applied. But Bell Labs had long been working in this field and had a satellite of its own in development, as did others in the aerospace industry. The then chairman of AT&T, announcing its forthcoming satellite, said that year, "We are ready to do the job," and it looked then as though the great Bell Labs was coming through with the winning technology for its parent company. Before AT&T got the first commercial communications satellite into space, however, Congress moved to block it from a complete capture of satellite communications.

Congress has the responsibility to worry about monopolies and occasionally does. The imminence of an AT&T communications satellite in flight set off congressional hearings aimed at passing a law. Launching a satellite, of course, is a government monopoly. The biggest single element on which the satellite depends is the booster, a technology that was developed with public monies. The key to the satellite itself lies in structures of light weight relative to the strength of the boosters. The communications satellite was developed by both the government and private industry, notably Bell Labs.

Congress also had to face the fact that the aerospace industry wanted an opportunity to provide its technology to the communications field. Otherwise Congress' deliberations mainly revolved around the satellite's tremendous international power—its domestic potential then being hardly realized. The question was whether to give this new power to a government agency, to give it as a monopoly to the common carriers, meaning mainly AT&T, or to give it to a competitor. The difficulty of giving it to a competitor was that one had to be invented.

Here was a remarkable situation which is becoming endemic in the United States, of a largely government-sponsored technology representing a convergence point of billions of dollars of research, needing to be given to someone to put it into operation. Much of the debate ran along classical lines of government ownership versus private enterprise. But there was no qualified private enterprise available that was not a monopoly.

For AT&T, capturing the satellite presented an unusual strategic problem. Through its advanced research and development AT&T had usually controlled technological change in its field at its own pace. The communications satellite was the first major piece of technology since World War II to come into its system from some other source. AT&T had to absorb the satellite as it would a foreign body. The challenge to AT&T was how to adapt itself to a technological force which it did not generate.

The congressional debate on the satellite was still unresolved when AT&T, in its 1960 annual report, featured the satellite and summarized its argument to Congress.

Our business, the report said, "is a growing business (the main value of satellites for commercial communications is that they promise to provide large numbers of worldwide channels to meet further needs)." Profits on satellite investment were some years away, hence "the importance of regulatory commissions allowing overall earnings that create financial strength and encourage look-ahead action." The combination of cable, short-wave radio, and satellite, the report argued, would increase dependability of service. It concluded with the recommendation that ownership and operation of the United States portion of a worldwide satellite communication system should be given exclusively to the

American international communications companies (which would be mainly AT&T).

But Congress ruled otherwise, and in 1962 wrote a new Communications Satellite Act, creating the company known as Comsat. Congress designed Comsat as an institutional coalition of the contending forces. It gave the company an ambiguous monopoly specifying international operations, and a dual and conflicting mission. On the one hand, it was to make a profit for its shareholders and on the other hand, to give support to the nation's foreign policy, which included fostering communications in areas of the world that are unprofitable. Half of its capital of $196 million was subscribed by a number of international and domestic carriers and half by individual investors. The carriers elected six directors (three from AT&T, which took a 29 percent interest in Comsat's stock); the individual stockholders elected six; and the President of the United States appointed three, with Senate approval. Comsat was required to report annually, not only to its stockholders but also to the President and Congress, and came under FCC regulation. It was the nation's "chosen instrument" for international communication by satellite. It was a carrier for other carriers—the phrase "carriers' carrier" came into vogue—but it could also provide service to the government and to "other authorized users."

Comsat's ambiguous charter threatened rivalry to AT&T and the other U.S. ground carriers in international communications and opened a new market for the aerospace industry. AT&T had lost a round, but was not fazed. Its chairman commented, "This action, we are happy to say, strongly reaffirms the principle of private business enterprise under public regulation." (*Annual Report, 1962,* p. 11.) AT&T hadn't got exactly what it wanted out of the "standard of behavior" called "regulated private monopoly" but the standard had held firm for the satellite.

Thereupon the struggle in the United States over the international space signal centered on Comsat. The new company sought to compete in the market for communications services on the ground, and the ground carriers, led by AT&T, sought to isolate Comsat in space as a sort of wholesaler to them. "No competition in the communications market on the ground" was their battle cry.

Another significant event had occurred in 1962. NASA put the first experimental commercial communications satellite system, AT&T's Telstar, into orbit. AT&T paid a fee for the launch and altogether had probably $100 million invested in its satellite. The apparent success of Telstar, a very considerable achievement at the time, made it appear that AT&T's satellite technology would dominate the field. But AT&T was fated to lose another round in an area where it seldom loses. Comsat let out to the aerospace industry contracts for other satellite designs. One of these was a "synchronous satellite" called the "Early Bird," made by Hughes Aircraft. It was launched on April 6, 1965, and bit by bit, as the experimental results came in, everyone began to realize that a communications revolution was indeed in the making.

Telstar was a system of as many as eighteen satellites moving through space at medium altitude and tracked by expensive ground station equipment. Early Bird was a single high-altitude satellite orbiting synchronously with the rotation of the earth so that it was seemingly stationary and in constant line of sight of one third of the earth's surface. Being in effect stationary, it required no tracking equipment. Just three synchronous satellites spaced out over the Atlantic, Pacific, and Indian oceans would form a complete global system. One would be in sight from any point on earth and relatively inexpensive ground stations could be in touch with it.

The synchronous satellite relays a signal with some unique economies. It has relatively large capacities; even the smallest proposed system for the 1970s could transmit simultaneously twelve television programs to as many stations as want to pick them up (the signal spreads out on its return to earth and can reach all stations within a circle whose diameter is 9,000 miles). It is insensitive to distance, and so can transmit a signal—telephone, TV, or electronic data—from New York to Honolulu at the same cost as from New York to Newark; and its transmission costs are not affected by the number of receiving points. Higher-frequency satellites are also expected to come along in the late 1970s with unprecedentedly massive capacities and low cost per information "bit."

Soon after the Early Bird proved itself, this type of satellite became standard for commercial satellite communication. It reduced the investment requirements for a system (leaving Comsat overcapitalized); it eliminated central gateways, bringing remote areas of the world directly into the mainstream of global communications; it internationalized TV; and it opened the way to domestic satellite communication within each nation. International satellite negotiations around the Early Bird, unlike the two-sided negotiations between parties at either end of a cable connection, became multilateral, with direct contact between all nations with ground stations.

As the new and enhanced prospects for the satellite promised an even bigger game in the future, they intensified the immediate struggle in the United States for controls. The carriers' strategic objective continued to be essentially simple and steady: no matter what specific issue comes up, block Comsat from becoming a competitive force. As this position was in conflict with Comsat's individual shareholders, carrier directors on Comsat's board sometimes found their position there untenable and left the board room when the subject came up.

For a while they fought Comsat over the ownership and physical control of ground stations. Comsat won, temporarily, and the battleground shifted to markets. Two big consumers of satellite services, both in government, provided the central issues to be resolved.

NASA proposed to build its own satellite system for the Apollo project which it was then designing. Comsat objected and claimed the right to provide NASA with its system. AT&T, confronted with two objectionable outcomes—government ownership of a satellite system or Comsat with a customer—took the lesser evil, joining forces with Comsat against government ownership. Comsat got the NASA lease;

and the road immediately divided again. Comsat saw the lease as a precedent for direct sales to "other authorized users" and prepared to enter the market. The carriers saw the lease as exceptional. The test came soon, when Comsat found another customer, the Department of Defense, and the basic issue was joined.

Government contracts are a big prize in their own right, and the Department of Defense is the biggest of all buyers of international communications. Add to this the issue in principle: could this new public utility, Comsat, sell international satellite service in competition with AT&T, ITT, Western Union, and RCA? If it could, then it could also sell to broadcasters, the press, private corporations, and others. AT&T and the other common carriers made their key move before the FCC on the Department of Defense contract, opposing Comsat's right to compete with them and claiming that they should be inserted as a link between Comsat and the customers who would use the service.

In a game of this kind, the participants provide the FCC with their rationales for dividing the potential benefits in a way favorable to themselves, each claiming also that his "solution" of the game satisfies the public interest. The moves and countermoves are words. But coalitions of participants also alter the number and kind of alternatives presented. The learned staff of the FCC studies the alternatives presented and their rationales, and perhaps introduces its own. The long-standing criticism of regulatory bodies, even when they are not simply biased, is that they depend too much on the alternatives provided by the privately interested parties; that they are not creative enough in providing their own alternatives on behalf of the public interest. They also have a problem of analysis. Whether the staff and commissioners make a good decision in the public interest depends on how well they are able to measure the payoff to the public in the possible outcomes of a game. One may have doubts because of the inherent difficulty, in the present state of knowledge, of spelling out who gets what in the hard economics of the possible outcomes. And there may be pressures through

Congress and the White House for apportioning the benefits in other ways.

On June 23, 1966, the FCC ruled that Comsat could provide circuits only to the common carriers (except for the government in "unique circumstances"). This was the first battle that AT&T and the other common carriers had won and it virtually won the war. It made Comsat a common carrier's common carrier, that is, a wholesaler to AT&T and the others, and so buried Comsat's satellite system in the prevailing cable and microwave systems.

No judgment about the wisdom of this decision will be hazarded here; suffice it to say that it appears to have been simply a decision by convention, following the tradition, espoused by the carriers, that a new communications technology should not be allowed to reach the "retail" market in competition with old technologies and their establishments. The outcome—blocking Comsat from the market—together with the earlier events in which Comsat came into being and satellite technology developed surprising new capabilities, set the stage for the much bigger game on the domestic scene, where the triumphant old convention would receive a shock.

When the Early Bird proved that a domestic communications satellite technology was both practical and imminent, the American Broadcasting Company, on September 21, 1965, startled the communications industry by applying to the FCC for a permit to put up a domestic satellite of its own. ABC's proposal was far more radical than anything Comsat had put forth—it suggested nothing less than a free market in domestic satellite communications, thereby striking directly at AT&T's theretofore unchallenged domestic monopoly. ABC's bid appeared whimsical, to say the least, to the carriers, especially to AT&T, which carried network broadcasting through its terrestrial system. The carriers had complacently planned in due course also to annex the new technology at home as a common-carrier privilege.

Perhaps it was a whim—ABC is no longer seeking to own a satellite—but it had the powerful effect of raising, operationally, on new ground, the question of whether the new technology should be open to all qualified comers who saw it as an opportunity for competitive business. If ABC got a domestic satellite, why not satellites for any qualified party, carrier or non-carrier: Western Union, GT&E, the other national networks, educational TV, and large corporations and associations such as banker groups, hospitals, press associations and large publishers, General Motors, Ford, IBM, General Electric, Standard Oil (New Jersey)—the list runs on of institutions whose internal and external communications—telephone, video, and data, including computer links—are substantial enough to justify at least sharing a piece of a satellite system through ownership or lease.

A competitive domestic satellite presented an even more formidable threat to the telecommunications monopolies than the international one, owing to the great volume of domestic communications. Hence, it again became especially imperative for AT&T to try to capture the space signal at least at its earthly origin and destination, and bury its economic benefits in the old systems. ABC's bid thus brought about an even sharper conflict than Comsat had between the dominant economic doctrine of the United States, according to which the benefits of a new technology should be spread freely at a competitive price wherever the demand calls for it, and the marginal doctrine of legal monopoly, according to which the new benefits should be blended into the economies of the old.

In 1965 the FCC, recognizing the implications of ABC's request, opened a "docket" on the whole issue of domestic satellites, inviting interested parties to come forth in August 1966—and here began the preliminaries to the game of this story.

Comsat, of course, immediately claimed jurisdiction over all domestic satellites. AT&T sparred with Comsat, laying the foundation for opposing its claim, while leaving the question open and advancing a proposal for its own system; and for a moment it looked as if the center of the domestic satellite issue lay between them in a rerun of their game over the international satellite. Quixotic ABC, however, was then joined by a more formidable newcomer, the Ford Foundation, which bid for an independent satellite for all TV broadcasting—a scheme for leasing satellite service to the commercial broadcasters and using the profits to support educational TV. A nice game got going, with AT&T negotiating a downward price for its services to the networks and offering gifts to educational TV (which might have the effect of blocking Ford). AT&T also began to show signs of willingness to back Comsat as a monopoly wholesaler in domestic space. But before this game could be resolved, it was stopped.

As the issues accumulated before the FCC and that body appeared to falter, a new force descended on all parties. President Lyndon B. Johnson appointed a White House task force and directed it to consider whether Comsat should get a domestic monopoly, and, if so, as an independent or as a captive of the ground carriers; whether the ground carriers should be given a monopoly in space; or whether the satellite market should be opened to competition. The panel's report, in 1968, dodged the resolution of the main issues with a proposal for a pilot system to be operated experimentally by Comsat. President Richard M. Nixon, however, set this report aside and appointed his own task force. This group strongly urged the FCC to adopt a policy of open skies. It got results.

On March 24, 1970, the FCC opened the prospect of a new era in domestic communications with a "report and order" inviting both common carriers and non-carriers to apply for authorization to construct and operate domestic satellite systems. Applicants could act "either individually or jointly," that is, they could cooperate if they chose to. The commissioners also solicited comments from all interested parties on how they thought the affairs of the new medium of communications should be organized: whether satellite systems should be specialized or "multi-purpose" or both, how wide open "open entry" should be, and specifically what role AT&T should play. They allowed, at least formally, for a continuation of the discussion of monopoly, and, mindful of their continuing responsibility for the health of the nation's communication system and the common carriers that operated it, they differentiated public toll services, which would in any case remain monopolies, from specialized or private-line services which hazily formed the prospective market for competitive satellite communications. The commissioners said, in effect, let's imagine we have a new industry here on the fringes of the public telephone system: What can it do? Who should be in it and under what conditions? How should it be set up? What does each applicant propose to do?

It was apparent that the largest impact of a new philosophy of regulation would be on AT&T. Most of the physical plant of communications in the United States, including practically all long lines, was in its hands; and by the same token, most of the potential users of the satellite were its customers. AT&T had justified its advances beyond its telephone sanctuaries by citing not only its generally good performance but also the principle that economies of scale serve the public interest. But now this case, as it applied to the periphery of the company's business, was called into doubt.[3] Domestic satellites posed a unique threat to AT&T inasmuch as the capabilities of satellites provided an unparalleled opportunity for competitors with only moderate capital resources to buck AT&T's billions.

The question was who besides the old players would have what it takes to bid for a satellite. One passage in the commission's statement, however, was particularly inviting to interested parties outside the earlier arena of satellite affairs and was widely taken as the sign that a new climate of regu-

[3] Both AT&T and Western Union were being challenged on the ground as well as in space. Ambitious enterprisers, e.g., MCI Communications Corporation and DATRAN, asked the FCC for authorization to sell private-line services to corporate and other customers on ground microwave systems. The common carriers called it "cream skimming," but in May 1971 the FCC made its historic "specialized carrier" decision which recognized a fundamental distinction between the natural monopoly of public telephone service and private "customized" service. The FCC had made specific grants to specialized carriers before this general decision, which participants in the satellite affair took as one of the signs that a new regulatory philosophy was imminent.

lation had arrived and that a new industry was in the making. It read:

> The most important value of domestic satellites at the present time appears to lie in their potential for opening new communications markets, for expanding the beneficial role of competition in the existing markets for specialized communication services, and for developing new and differentiated services that reflect the special characteristics of the satellite technology.

THE GAME NARRATED

Soon after the FCC issued its invitation, a number of parties, old and new—AT&T, the broadcasters, Comsat, GT&E, Hughes Aircraft, RCA, and Western Union—started walking around to one another's offices to talk over their mutual interests in satellites. From beginning to end, this walk-around was to be the principal feature of the game; for, having leave to act "individually or jointly," the participants sought cooperation to improve their prospects in the imagined industry of the future. As might be supposed, there were some surprises among those who showed up to talk.

AT&T's three major "captives" seized the opportunity to loosen or break their ties with the company they called with wry affection "Ma Bell." Western Union (1974 assets, approaching $1.5 billion), long moribund and substantially locked into AT&T's long-lines ground system, saw a new and glittering life in doing a large part of its business via satellite. GT&E (1974 assets, approaching $12 billion), the No. 2 telephone company, most of whose long-distance business was carried by AT&T's system, saw the way to establish a link of its own between its scattered local operations. The three major broadcasting networks, jointly the largest single consumer of communications services except for the government, saw satellite competition as the means of increasing their bargaining power in their long-standing efforts to reduce the prices they paid to AT&T for distributing their programs.

Two other companies turned out to have rather novel interests. Hughes Aircraft (1974 sales, estimated to be about $1.2 billion), which had been a pure hardware company, was interested in putting up a satellite system to be used as a medium for specialized cable-TV programming in which it wanted to pioneer. RCA's subsidiary Global Communications Incorporated (Globcom), an overseas carrier, gave RCA little claim to a domestic communication position; but having purchased an Alaskan communication system from the U. S. Air Force in 1969, it definitely had its foot in the door and now proposed to expand its services to the conterminous United States.

For Comsat, the game loomed as the severest test of its expansive ambitions.

Thus, a lot was at stake for these companies, and with a lot of uncertainty. The size of the prospective private-line market was itself uncertain—some gave it the round number $1 billion a year for the late 1970s—and since quite different notions could be expected about the best way to exploit satellites, the prospect contained the possibility of several different kinds of markets. The first out-of-pocket stake would not be great for these companies. The cost of an application, with its technical, legal, and other attendant fees, would run between $100,000 and $1 million, depending upon the amount of effort a participant wanted to put into it; and an applicant would not be committed to construct a satellite system. Thus the immediate objective was to get authorized under the best possible conditions for the big stakes of the future.

A major element in the emerging game was the potential satellite traffic already controlled by the broadcasters and the common carriers—AT&T, GT&E, and Western Union. Every player's calculations about the economics of satellite operations had to begin with some notions about the potential volume of traffic; the players with access to traffic clearly had an edge. Hence, much of the early conversation involved soundings on possible deals about traffic. In the beginning these contacts were too fragmentary and ephemeral to be called negotiations. The players were getting their bearings.

Even with no traffic nailed down, John L. Martin, Jr., Comsat's assistant vice president for domestic and aeronautical satellite systems, expressed unqualified determination to enter the domestic skies: "If licensed, we will put up a system with or without committed traffic. Our system takes two and a half years to build and we'll be selling our services during that time." At least one other player, a network executive, believed him. "Comsat may go up," he said, "without us or anyone else. It's their lifeblood."

Comsat's elegant and spacious offices in downtown Washington suggest a relaxed blue-chip sort of life; but in fact a number of considerations were pressing hard on its executives in 1970. One was their uninvested capital. They had been given more money than they needed for their international operations, mostly because the original capitalization was based on the low-orbit satellite of the early 1960s, which, as noted, was superseded by the less expensive geostationary satellite; thus the company had more than $100 million that had to be put to work somewhere (not that this liquid asset has been exactly a misfortune in an era of high interest rates). Comsat's managers also saw the company's role in the international satellite system diminishing in the future. Its potential growth, they believed, lay in the domestic field.

In line with its objective of gaining a monopoly of the domestic skies, Comsat set out in the spring of 1970 to obtain the largest potential building block for its multipurpose system. That prospect, of course, was AT&T. Comsat discovered happily that the giant company preferred to lease satellite space rather than to have a system of its own at this time. AT&T said it was interested in leasing because Comsat had expertise in satellites and was willing to assume the risk of launching and operating them. It also appeared that AT&T did not want to deny the federally sponsored satellite corporation a place in the game—and it could hardly be overlooked that AT&T owned 29 percent of Comsat's stock. However, there proved to be a large problem about an AT&T-Comsat deal. Comsat hoped to lease its channels to *all* carriers and to conduct a communication business of its own from its one large satellite system. AT&T's preference, on the other hand, was to be the sole tenant; it wanted an entire system dedicated exclusively to its own use and in its full control—a so-called dedicated lease. And so the two companies came to an impasse in these early discussions.

Other players also resisted Comsat's lordly ambitions. As common carriers, Western Union and RCA themselves wanted to invest in a satellite system. Both of them explored with GT&E the possibilities of cooperative arrangements. James Clark, GT&E's vice president for communication projects, said, "Each of us was searching for the most attractive and viable approach to satellites." But despite the evident advantages of combining satellite traffic and sharing the costs of a single system, cooperation presented obstacles, notably, that prospective partners would constantly be in competition with each other for the private-line business. And so these early soundings also came to nothing.

Hughes Aircraft wanted to own a system for its prospective cable TV (CATV) business, but since this would not support a satellite by itself, some sharing arrangement seemed preferable to it too. Hughes saw Western Union and RCA as prospects; both of them turned out at the time, however, to hold the position that only carriers should own systems. And so Hughes went in search of a prospect that could lease and support a substantial part of its system, with a few channels to be left over for its own experiments in CATV programming. Paul Visher, pilot of Hughes Aircraft's satellite affairs and an influential figure in the game, had his eye on a new kind of service, "not competitive with network programming, which is based on the mass audience, but providing the audience with a large number of program choices." His aim was to create a series of special-interest offerings—one channel for children's programming, one for theater and other performing arts, one for hobbies and instruction, and so on. The problem was to get there on some economic basis.

Sharing ownership was excluded by Hughes's inability to find a partner, and building a satellite just for its own purpose would have required a fairly sizable investment at a time when there were no proved revenues in the venture. Alternatively, Visher could try to find a customer to share in the use of the system. Like so many others, he looked to the networks.

The networks were widely considered to be one of the best prospects as tenants of satellites, especially after AT&T in October 1969 made a stiff increase in its price for network service—from about $55 million to $75 million a year for the three combined. The networks had for some time been gradually giving their distribution business in isolated areas to less expensive carriers, and by 1970 these were supplying network transmission to about one third of the affiliated stations. Now the networks had still more incentives to cut their distribution costs, and the satellite seemed promising. Allen Cooper, NBC's vice president of planning, reduced the complexity of the network's position to a single observation: "We are looking for reliability, quality, and economy. We're satisfied with AT&T on the quality and reliability."

Although the networks were not yet clear on what their satellite requirements might be, they were expected to use three channels each. (Eventually they would write detailed specifications asking for eleven full-time channels and twenty-two channels for use on football weekends.) At first Visher thought that a deal with the networks would materialize before long; but then he got the feeling, as in time everyone did, that the networks were not really in a hurry to do business. Which left Hughes Aircraft feeling that its prospects for a deal were pretty slim.

These early conversations, in the spring of 1970, could be fairly relaxed because there was no specific deadline for anyone to meet. But in July, Western Union suddenly filed for permission to operate a system of its own. The company proposed to put up twenty-four primary and twelve backup channels, considerably more than it needed for its own business; however, it hoped to attract others, notably the networks, into its system. The FCC responded to the filing by setting a deadline of December 1, 1970, for all applications. The pace of the activity quickened and the players found themselves under greater pressure to make their plans firm.

Another participant arrived. This was MCI Communications, a ground-based "specialized carrier." MCI made a deal with Lockheed Aircraft Corporation, which had a prototype satellite of its own design and wanted to take a crack at Hughes's dominance of communication-satellite hardware. Together the two formed MCI Lockheed Satellite Corporation. This company hoped to find its principal market in private lines, for which the large forty-eight-channel Lockheed satellite was especially adapted. (The satellite was designed in part to beam signals to small earth stations, e.g., on the roofs of downtown buildings, and so to avoid the need for long and expensive ground interconnections with larger stations.)

Perhaps because of the new pressure to make a deal and perhaps also because AT&T had begun to show some interest in buying a system of its own, Comsat gave in and accepted AT&T's terms. But Comsat then decided that it would put up two systems. One would be used to meet AT&T's demand that it be a sole tenant, with complete control over the system's use. At AT&T's disposal would be two satellites (one of them a backup), with a total of forty-eight channels. The other system would be under Comsat's own control. Its size was unclear at this point, but the company was plainly thinking big and wanting to line up all the rest of the prospective satellite users. In trying to negotiate with these prospects, however, Comsat faced certain large perplexities, especially around the so-called "fill factor." Like the load factor for commercial aircraft, the "fill" is critical for a satellite's economic viability. No one of the remaining customers could fill the system Comsat projected; and so, in negotiations with prospective customers, the company did not want to set firm prices—but prices contingent on the final fill factor. These contingencies soon became a critical element in Comsat's efforts to sign up GT&E as a satellite tenant.

The deal was possible because GT&E was by now committed to leasing, rather than owning, a system. The owner of a satellite system has a lot of money at risk: first, because the satellite may not have a successful launch; second, because it may not last as long as expected in space. Launches are performed, for a considerable fee, sometimes as much as $25 million or more, by NASA; and in the event of a launch failure, the satellite owner also loses the bird itself—which may have cost another $10 million or $15 million. And while most of the parties looked to a seven-year life per satellite, no one really knew what to expect; the oldest satellite in use in 1970 had been up just five years. GT&E did not want to assume the risks of ownership on top of those associated with a new technology. Hence GT&E's decision to lease.

The question was, from whom? As the December 1, 1970, deadline approached, GT&E was down to two prospects: Comsat and Hughes Aircraft. Comsat offered eight channels, at a price rumored to be about $1 million apiece—provided that the fill factor was high enough and also provided that it got a monopoly grant from the FCC. Hughes offered GT&E a much simpler deal: eight channels at a firm price of $900,000 per channel per year. Both offers specified that backup facilities would be continuously available; however, Hughes made no secret of the fact that it was planning to use these facilities for its own programming—i.e., it was gambling that its technology would be reliable and that GT&E wouldn't need to use the backup, at least for a while.

This expectation was one reason that Hughes was able to underbid Comsat. Said Paul Visher: "We are highly motivated to make the system dependable since we are the primary beneficiaries of its reliability." GT&E came to an agreement with Hughes just before the deadline.

As it turned out, the companies need not have hurried. Upon receiving requests from the other aspirants, the FCC extended the deadline, eventually to March 15, 1971. But the price that Hughes Aircraft had given GT&E now became a major piece of information to other players, for whom it got to be a pricing guideline of sorts. Some players, in fact, were attracted by the price and went to Hughes to lease a couple of channels. With GT&E signed up, however, Hughes was no longer looking for customers.

One of those turned down by Hughes was a newcomer to the game, Western Tele-Communications, a major supplier of transmission services to the television networks in the Rocky Mountain states. After failing to get a lease from Hughes or anyone else, the company got some technical help on satellite systems from North American Rockwell and ended up filing for a system of its own. The system involved two twelve-channel satellites; searching for customers, Western Tel began sounding out the networks and also some cable-television operators.

The Hughes-GT&E deal also appears to have had an effect on the Comsat-AT&T contract, which carried a somewhat higher price per channel than GT&E was to pay Hughes. After this price became known, AT&T with marvelous flexibility reassessed its requirements upward—and renegotiated the price per channel downward. In March 1971 AT&T and Comsat refiled for a larger system of two twenty-four-channel primary satellites and one backup.

Comsat's own system appeared also to have been affected by the Hughes price. In order to justify its monopoly argument, Comsat had to be able to meet that price for its own system. To do so, it relied, in part, on the economies associated with volume purchasing and filed for three twenty-four-channel birds. Comsat considered this sizable system to be optimal—but the larger the system, of course, the greater the fill problem.

Meanwhile, RCA and Western Union were also talking about cooperating. For RCA's top management, which was then suffering severe losses on its computer operations (later abandoned, in a $250-million write-off), any major investments in new technologies obviously involved considerable risk. Yet the company was adopting a quite aggressive posture: it was planning to integrate a new satellite system with its existing Alaskan network—and planning to serve the lower forty-eight states and Hawaii besides. If the company had been willing to stay in Alaska, RCA and Western Union might have made a deal. But Western Union did not want to help bring RCA into the lower forty-eight states, where it would be competing for the private-line business. Not being able to figure out how to divide the market, the two companies finally abandoned their efforts to strike a deal. Western Union stayed with its original filing and RCA filed for a system of its own.

One more applicant materialized late. Fairchild Industries, which had a contract from NASA to develop a communication satellite, decided to enter the game with it. The satellite was vast, with 120 channels, and the two-satellite system the company proposed was by far the largest of them all. The key to Fairchild's approach was AT&T. Ninety-six channels on each satellite were specifically designed with that company in mind, with Fairchild's managers pointing out, hopefully, that AT&T's growth alone could take up that capacity in two years. AT&T, however, argued that the technology was unproved and therefore unacceptable. This left Fairchild with only a hope that the FCC might come to view its system as the most economical—and persuade AT&T to adopt it.

At this point, after a year of gathering information, some players that had ready blocks of traffic at their disposal—AT&T, GT&E, and the networks—had decided against filing for ownership of satellites and had instead made their presences felt through alliances, or potential alliances, with other players who *had* chosen to own. On the other hand, seven companies—Comsat, Hughes, RCA, Western Union, Fairchild, MCI Lockheed, and Western Tele-Communications—had worked out their tentative approaches to participating as satellite owners. With their interactions, they had woven their futures into the skein of a single game. Even in what was visible, and a good deal was not at all visible, each player became related to all the others.

THE GAME MODELED

This narrative of the observable events surrounding the satellite suggests that the participants did in fact play a game during the year of the walkaround. The game, however, has more dimensions than straightforward narration can convey. To focus them, one can draw a simple line around the game and describe the area within as follows: a total of 1,023 coalitions of ten or fewer players were possible in the abstract.[4] Out of these they formed only two new coalitions during the course of their reflections, discussions, and negotiations, namely those between AT&T and Comsat and GT&E and Hughes (the old networks-AT&T alliance continued on). In adopting these two new coalitions, the players thus rejected more than a thousand other possible coalitions. The wonder is how they managed to do that. One may also ask the more pointed game-theoretic questions: Were the adopted coalitions, together with the fall-back positions taken by the players who failed to find alliances, the best, from the standpoint of the interests of the players and the public interest? And further, were the adopted coalitions stable? Asking these questions about the satellite game is hardly likely to bring the sharp answers one would like to have. One asks them, nevertheless, because they are important questions to put to any game; in this game they help to define the efforts of the players; and in pursuit of them one may at least discover things that are not otherwise evident.

The problem of working with so many coalitions and their bearing on one another, even if one had clear values to start with, might appear to be insoluble and perhaps would have been had the players not been able to begin with a fairly simple means of winnowing, instead of having to examine them all in detail. Two conditions could immediately be seen

[4] In calculating the number of potential coalitions in a game, game theorists for convenience include single players as if each was a "coalition of one." Hence ten singletons are included in the 1,023 coalitions mentioned above.

to block or inhibit large numbers of coalitions. One of these was technology, the other was traffic.

The players, as we have seen, came into the game with four satellite technologies, distinguished in the simplest sense by their size. Players offering the smallest one (twelve channels) claimed proven performance and immediate production. Those offering the next in size (twenty-four channels), a combination of two of the small ones in a somewhat different configuration, claimed both conservatism and economy of scale. The two largest ones (forty-eight and one hundred twenty channels) lacked the proven performance but promised both economies of scale and innovation. A fifth design, with higher frequencies and a vastly increased capacity and belonging to the next generation of satellites, was latently present in the game, inasmuch as it was the probable choice of AT&T if that player went alone.

It is true that one player, RCA, was ambivalent between twelve and twenty-four channels, Fairchild could split its big satellite into twenty-four and ninety-six channels, and others could make switches if they chose to during the walkaround; in sum, the technological commitments were the choices of the players and were not altogether firm. Nevertheless, the four explicit designs and the one latent one had the effect of restricting coalitions. The scale of Fairchild's limited that player to a key coalition with AT&T and, through its twenty-four-channel split-off, a possible coalition with the networks. MCI Lockheed, likewise, was limited by scale to AT&T and the networks. Such incompatibilities, and various reservations among the others about making switches, eliminated quite a number of possible coalitions.

Even more drastic in eliminating coalitions was the effect of the lock that some of the players had on existing traffic. Of the ten players only four had substantial traffic, three had trickles, and three had none. Any coalition that did not combine sufficient existing traffic to meet the minimum fill conditions for a satellite system was not likely to form. Coalitions could be imagined to form to share the investment risks—without traffic, but counting on market prospects in the future—were it not for the fact that going alone also had prospects. One could safely hazard the surmise that the value of going alone would outweigh the values of joining a coalition that had no traffic, with the result, under the conditions of this game, that none of the latter would form. This consideration did in fact eliminate all coalitions that included only some combination of Comsat, RCA, Hughes Aircraft, MCI Lockheed, Western Tele-Communications, and Fairchild— those with no traffic or only a trickle. To put it the other way round, the only coalitions considered to have real value were those that included at least one player with substantial traffic, namely, AT&T, GT&E, Western Union, or the networks. The pressure in the game thus came down to the six players without viable traffic seeking to align themselves with one or more of the four who had the traffic.

One might wonder why any player with traffic would want a partner. The question is especially puzzling with respect to AT&T, the player who at the start of the game was in possession of most of the business that the other players hoped to obtain and put on satellite; but discussion of this player will be passed here, to be returned to presently. GT&E, as noted, wanted to lease to avoid risks of ownership. Western Union, having only marginal traffic in being to support a system, could use a partner who would bring along some additional traffic. The networks preferred to give their broadcasting business to someone else because they were not in the physical communications business and to get into it would have to take the trouble and risk of forming a joint venture among themselves and learning a new business. It is worth noting here, with respect to coalitions, that the networks, who could fill a satellite system, had no need for more than one partner, though they probably would have no objection to doing business with a joint venture.

Altogether, it seems a fair guess that the conditions of technology and traffic brought the number of potential coalitions down from about a thousand to about a hundred. But the feat of reducing potential coalitions from large to smaller numbers was not appreciably diminished in difficulty by the ease with which the players made the first big cut. Coping with a hundred, more or less, still made a big game.

RCA considered a discriminatory solution: that a carrier should not do business with a non-carrier. If effective, this presumably would have excluded the hardware players Fairchild and Hughes from negotiations; Comsat, MCI, and Western Tel all had a claim to being classified as "carriers." Western Union also considered adopting the discriminatory position—it was the traditional one among common carriers—but dropped it, and as the other carriers did not go along, the reduction of coalitions by discriminatory means did not spread through the game.

Much more effective was the disinclination of the strong players to put the weaker ones into business. This was not discriminatory, as it did not involve the cooperation of the strong players (those with traffic) against the weak, but was simply a negative value that each strong player held and which he calculated when valuing coalitions. A weak player, on the other hand, of course, put a high positive value on an alliance with a strong player. These values were not exactly translatable into money, but as they reflected ways of dividing the future satellite market, they represented a money value.

These attitudes further reduced the number of prospective coalitions sufficiently to bring the entire active game into view. The coalitions that appear to have been seriously considered, discussed, negotiated, or played out in subgames may now be set down in a compendium of the preferences of each of the players, in descending order (e.g., Western Union prefers the networks to GT&E, if it must choose), as follows:[5]

---

[5] The difference in the intensity of these preferences is touched on later, as are also the instances in which preferences are not exclusive, that is, where a player could consider two or more independent deals. The order in which the players are listed here is more or less arbitrary, but seemed to be most convenient for the purposes of this model.

1. WESTERN UNION
   (1) Networks
   (2) GT&E
   (3 or 4) Hughes
   (4 or 3) GT&E-Hughes (Western Union is indifferent
       between 3 and 4)
   (5) RCA (Alaska)
   (6) Comsat (a dedicated lease on the AT&T-Comsat
       model)
   (7) Go alone (i.e., file for authorization alone)
2. COMSAT
   (1) One system: a grand coalition of all players under
       Comsat's aegis, that is, a single Comsat-owned sys-
       tem from which the others would lease. The key to
       the feasibility of this preference was AT&T's will-
       ingness to enter an open system, apart from the
       question of the willingness of the other players to
       join it. A more modest statement of this preference
       would be an open lease to AT&T followed by simi-
       lar leases to any other who would come along.
   (2) Two systems: one, a dedicated lease to AT&T; the
       other, a Comsat system (within the framework of
       this game, the latter could include leases to the net-
       works, GT&E, and others).
   (3) Networks
   (4) Go alone (with one system)
3. RCA
   (1) Networks
   (2) GT&E-Western Union
   (3) Western Union
   (4) Go alone
4. HUGHES AIRCRAFT
   (1 or 2) GT&E
   (2 or 1) Networks (Hughes is indifferent between 1
       and 2)
   (3) Western Union
   (4) Western Union-GT&E
   (5) Go alone

5. MCI LOCKHEED
    (1) AT&T
    (2) Networks
    (3) Go alone
6. WESTERN TEL
    (1) Networks
    (2) Hughes or any other player with a viable system (a lease)
    (3) Go alone
7. FAIRCHILD
    (1) A grand coalition of all under Fairchild's aegis, with AT&T the key (very like Comsat's first preference)
    (2) Networks
    (3) Go alone
8. AT&T
    (1) Comsat (a dedicated lease)
    (2) Go alone (with a change of technology to higher frequencies)
       (Note: In either case AT&T also wants to keep GT&E and the networks in line.)
9. GT&E
    (1) Either Comsat or Hughes
    (2) Western Union-RCA
    (3) Western Union
    (4 or 5) Western Union-Hughes
    (5 or 4) Go alone (GT&E is indifferent between 4 and 5)
10. NETWORKS
    (1) AT&T or any of the other candidates

A peculiar thing about these preferences is that at first glance they are one-sided. Each player decided on his preferences independently, and so they appear to mean only that a player sees a benefit for himself in certain coalitions. On second look, however, it is apparent that no player could exercise his preference for any coalition (other than the fiction of "a coalition of one") on his own. Each player had to find other players who were willing to cooperate. It would scarcely be realistic to suppose that a player would go so far as to negotiate with another if he did not believe that the other would also see a value for himself in the potential coalition (whether or not either of them is deluded about the actual values). One may assume, therefore, that any coalition here represents one player's idea of *mutual* gain with someone else.

In point of fact, of the twenty or so explicit coalitions here, a half dozen are not reciprocated anywhere among the preferences of the desired partner. One can see the dreams of grand coalitions disappearing in AT&T's refusal to enter any system not exclusively dedicated to and controlled by AT&T. RCA wanted to get together with Western Union, but Western Union would consider only RCA (Alaska), and so on. The natural surmise in such instances is that the rejecting party has figured that he might do better not only in another coalition but also if necessary by going alone.

The potential coalitions with the networks kept up the hopes of several players but had little effect on the actual formation of new coalitions owing to the fact that the networks, though negotiating, remained throughout poised in indecision, far from a satellite settlement.

But these matters were not self-evident at the beginning of the game; they were discovered in the course of the walkaround. Attention finally centered on only a handful of coalitions:

Comsat-AT&T (with a dedicated lease)
Comsat-GT&E
Western Union-GT&E[6]
Western Union-Hughes
GT&E-Hughes
Western Union-GT&E-Hughes

[6] Western Union remains in here despite its early independent filing because its presence was still felt; its agents continued to be active and under the rules could always amend their filing before the final deadline.

To interpret the influence of these coalitions upon one another and how their interactions were resolved, one first needs some sense of the value the players put on going alone. This is a difficult piece of information to obtain, but one must make the try in order to establish the starting point for ascertaining the gain to be made in coalitions. Fortunately, in this game there is a plausible way to decipher the values of the players alone and in coalition.

Let me set down first the approximate values which, as I see them, the players realized by going alone, after which I shall explain the observations. The minimum value of anyone going alone I give arbitrarily as 1. We are only concerned now with a few of the players, but I include a figure for each of the ten, as follows:

PLAYERS	VALUE OF GOING ALONE
Western Union	3
Comsat	1
RCA	1
Hughes	2
MCI Lockheed	1
Western Tel	1
Fairchild	1
AT&T	2
GT&E	1
ABC-CBS-NBC	1

This rough estimate of the players' individual values is undeniably hazardous, doubly so since it has important consequences. From it, together with the ordering of the preferences of the players given above, one can derive the approximate value of various coalitions and their pressures upon one another.

At this point, therefore, in support of these estimates, I introduce some observations about the specific values of the players. They were multifarious. Making money of course was the nominal objective of all the players, and it had a number of operational aspects. Among them were the extension of communications services from ground to space

(AT&T, GT&E, Western Union, RCA, MCI, Western Tel); viable traffic to justify a satellite system (the urgent need of at least five of the players); the sharing of investment, equipment, and risk (desired or needed by several players); protecting a present investment (RCA-Alaska); corporate diversification (RCA, Hughes, Lockheed, Fairchild); new uses for existing product (all the satellite hardware companies); corporate image (Western Union); getting to market first (several players, but especially Western Union).

The value of power and control was evident especially among the large traditional carriers, and was the dominant issue in a side game between GT&E and AT&T.[7] Fear of the economic strength of actual or potential competing satellite systems was endemic. The strong players, as noted, put a high value on avoiding the encouragement of a potential competitor, though because of other desires they could not entirely avoid it. Comsat was concerned with institutional expansion and the employment of its idle capital. The traditional carriers rated highly their long-run market position. Conversely, the newcomers, who were looking for a position at the start of the new industry, put the stress on their short-run position. The ambitions of the executives were a force both in the new entrepreneurial creature companies set up for the occasion and in Western Union. Political values counted as usual with AT&T and to some extent with Comsat. And for all, the value of getting authorized by the FCC was basic.

Melding these values is psychological alchemy. Yet, one needs some means to express the combination of values that enables a player to make a choice when that choice is not impulsive or random. The problem is much simplified when one considers only the value of going alone in this game (the values of coalitions are more complex). Certain values then become prominent. Going alone, as noted, meant prospects (the chance of favorable rulings, a seat in the next game, etc.). For these prospects only authorization was needed, and

[7] This side game between GT&E and AT&T, which was not directly involved in the walkaround, will be discussed later.

any player could get authorization by persuading the FCC that his application satisfied the public interest. Hence, for going alone I simply give any player the minimum value of 1. Seven players get only this value, five of them—Comsat, RCA, MCI Lockheed, Western Tel, and Fairchild—because they have little or no traffic in hand with which to establish a going satellite business. GT&E gets 1 because of its aversion to the risk of going into space alone, which was based not on any lack of resources but on the possibility that the risk might be held contrary to the public interest (its telephone subscribers might have to pay for any failure in the launching or in satellite life in the sky). The networks get 1 because of their aversion to going into a new business.

The other three get more than 1 because of their unique postures. Hughes gets 2 not only for its prospects for favorable rulings—which could be among the hopes of any player—but also for its negotiating position in future deals with its new service and limited back-up satellite requirement. AT&T gets 2 because it has the traffic to fill almost any satellite system and has in prospect a higher-frequency larger-capacity system that it could bring into being a year or two later than the proposed systems (AT&T itself questioned the economy of the proposed satellite systems as compared with ground systems). Western Union gets 3 because of the very high value the company places on the satellite as the key to transforming its present dull image into a glittering one and because of the value it places on getting to market first with a satellite system as the means of overcoming its marginal traffic base.

If the reader prefers to remain skeptical about these ratings and the order of the players' preferences for coalitions, as perhaps to some extent one should until someone discovers better ways of observing real-life games, I suggest that the ratings be accepted as a hypothesis. If they are accepted at least on that basis, they provide a means of looking into how a coalition game may be played, which, in economic game theory, is the heart of the matter. There are curious things about the satellite game, as we shall see, that this approach will disclose.

First of all, we now have a clear rationale for understanding why the players summarily rejected hundreds of potential coalitions—they could see at a glance that the payoffs did not come up to their fall-back values—and we can proceed to look closely at the interactions of the coalitions that the players themselves intensively studied and negotiated.

Take AT&T and Comsat. It is easy to understand why AT&T preferred to go alone rather than to accept Comsat's proposal for AT&T to put its traffic on Comsat's system: Comsat in that event would have a viable system to start with and could go on to sign up GT&E and others in one powerful satellite system competitive with AT&T. The coalition, therefore, one may say, offered AT&T a value of much less than the 2 it gets for going alone. Why then did AT&T offer the limited deal by which it leased a "dedicated" system from Comsat? Its principal stated reason was Comsat's experience; and one can also see a minor gain through AT&T's 29 percent ownership of Comsat. The values here are difficult to gauge. The mammoth corporation, seemingly about to lose its virtual monopoly of the private-line business but still in possession of that market as it stood and concerned with the problem of keeping as much of it as it could in face of an uncertain number of newly legitimized competitors, had every reason, on economic grounds, to ally itself with no one. Yet it gave Comsat a partial boost into the business. Although the net gain for AT&T is not evident in hard economics it becomes more understandable in other terms. Consider the social-political situation. Comsat, as we have seen, was born of a compromise with the common carriers, principally AT&T. The compromise was worked out in Congress, and AT&T bought Comsat stock and took a position on its board of directors, where it still had its three members. Refusing outright to yield anything to Comsat in the domestic field would hardly seem to be the right spirit toward a company it helped to start and continued in part to direct. If this line of thought is meaningful, one may interpret AT&T's proposed deal with Comsat as based in part on social and political considerations.

We have seen in the earlier narrative a good many of the interactions between Comsat, GT&E, and Hughes. They need only a few more observations. Comsat was seeking a monopoly, either by the edict of the FCC (included among its prospects) or by its power to sign up the field voluntarily. It had established a price in its AT&T deal, which it could not undercut in dealing with others. It could not lease to GT&E at a lower price than it had to AT&T without putting AT&T in violation of the public interest for paying more for the same type of service. In addition, as we have seen, Comsat's monopoly ambitions led to its choosing a large satellite system which GT&E did not have the traffic to fill. Hughes, seeing that Comsat was frozen into its price and contingencies, moved in with a lower price bid and no strings, which it was able to do entrepreneurially on the basis of its economic circumstances. Comsat in turn not only could not make a satisfactory counterbid but had to lower its price to AT&T so that AT&T would not be in violation of the public interest. This game hardly needs modeling in detail, owing to the great disparity in the competing coalitions. The interactions in another subgame, however, are worth looking into both for their own sake and for their consequences.

WESTERN UNION, GT&E, AND HUGHES

This game, which can now be fenced off, was also a cooperative one. The cooperative economic game of two or, more especially, three or more parties, which is common but not always differentiated in real life, is in modeled form almost the pure invention of game theorists. Its decisive actions are all contained in the simple lines of coalitions, their values, and the forces that move players to form them.

Consider the cooperative interactions in the game between Western Union, GT&E, and Hughes. Each player, as noted, comes into the game with a value he can achieve by himself without cooperation. He is interested in thinking about joining a coalition if it promises more than the value of his going alone. The peculiar value of a coalition for each of these players is the *additional* gain that derives from his participation in it, over and above the value of his going alone. The total net value of any coalition the players might form is the sum of these additional gains brought to it by each member. Hence, the coalitions that may form determine the amount of new wealth to be divided. A player, of course, may not necessarily expect to obtain from a coalition the same amount that he brings to it. How the players will divide the pot, so to speak, and which of the several potential pots they will divide, will depend upon how their various potential coalitions interact.

Four coalitions are possible among these three players:

> Western Union-GT&E
> Western Union-Hughes
> GT&E-Hughes
> Western Union-GT&E-Hughes

What is each of them worth? There is a way to put a value on them. We know the fall-back value of each player, and we know the order of their preferences for coalitions. We don't know exactly the intensity of their preferences: just how much they prefer one to another. But with the background of knowledge of what is driving them into coalitions or repelling them from them, we can make a judgment which should not be too far off.

Take the coalition of Western Union and GT&E. On the scale that gave a minimum value of 1 to any player for going alone, Western Union got 3 because of the high value its managers put on a new satellite image for the old company and on getting to market first, which they believed was feasible with their present traffic. They could do even better, however, in coalitions that reduced their risk without creating a new competitor. Like most of the others, they put a high value on an alliance with the elusive networks, which was sufficient to provide any weak or marginal player with a going satellite business. Their second preference, an alliance with GT&E, was almost as good and did not exclude the networks, whom they could go on courting. Alliance or no alliance, GT&E was going to be a competitor anyway, and by taking on GT&E's traffic, Western Union reduced or eliminated its risk of going alone. It seems reasonable to say that Western Union saw an additional value of 2 for itself in this coalition. Combining this with its fall-back value of 3, Western Union sees a total value of 5 as its contribution to the coalition.

GT&E, on the other hand, sees this coalition in a different light. It has some positive value for GT&E inasmuch as GT&E, too, is interested in reducing its risk. But it also has for GT&E the negative value of strengthening Western Union as a competitor. GT&E prefers not to be the instrument to put Western Union safely in business. Balancing the positive and negative values, GT&E sees a small gain in the coalition, which is reflected in the order of its preferences: after Hughes and before the coalition of all three. It seems reasonable to say that GT&E sees a gain of .5 in this coalition. Combining this with its fall-back value of 1, GT&E brings to the coalition the value of 1.5.

Thus, the sum of the values that each member brings to this coalition is 6.5. When they come to consider how to divide this sum, neither party, of course, would accept less than what he could get by himself. So what they would really have to consider is the net value of the coalition after subtracting their fall-back values. As Western Union has a fall-back value of 3 and GT&E of 1, they have to subtract 4 from their total sum of 6.5 in coalition. That gives them a collective net gain of 2.5 for their cooperation; or, one could say, that is the amount of new wealth available to divide in their coalition.

A similar examination of each of the four potential coalitions in this game shows the net value of each of them:[8]

[8] I reached the estimates of the values of the three remaining coalitions as follows:

Western Union-Hughes

Western Union is indifferent between forming a two-player coalition with Hughes or a three-player coalition with Hughes and

Western Union-GT&E	2.5	(with Hughes getting a coalition value of zero)
Western Union-Hughes	3	(with GT&E getting zero)
GT&E-Hughes	5.2	(with Western Union getting zero)
Western Union-GT&E-Hughes	1	(with all three sharing the gain)

GT&E, and sees only a moderate gain in either which I estimate as a plus 1. So Western Union, with its fall-back value of 3, brings a total value of 4 to either coalition.

Hughes, on the other hand, sees a substantial gain in a two-player coalition with either of the other players, which I judge to be at least equal to its fall-back value of 2. In coalition with Western Union, I give Hughes a gain of 2, which with its fall-back value of 2 enables Hughes to bring a total value of 4 to a Western Union-Hughes coalition.

The total value of the Western Union-Hughes coalition is therefore 8, and the combined net gain of the two players in coalition is 3.

GT&E-Hughes

Each of these players has a first preference for a coalition with the other in this game. I give GT&E a plus 3 here because of the intensity of its preference over other alternatives. As GT&E gets 1 for going alone, it brings a total of 4 to this coalition.

Hughes has a slight preference for GT&E over Western Union, and so I give Hughes a gain of 2.2 in coalition with GT&E, which with its fall-back value of 2, enables Hughes to bring a total value of 4.2 to this coalition.

The total value of the GT&E-Hughes coalition is therefore 8.2. GT&E's fall-back value of 1 together with Hughes's fall-back value of 2 add to 3. The difference between 8.2 and 3 gives them a combined net gain of 5.2 in coalition.

Western Union-GT&E-Hughes

The value of Western Union's gain in this three-player coalition as noted is 1. Western Union's fall-back value is 3, and so it brings a total value of 4 to the coalition.

GT&E, not wanting to put both Western Union and Hughes into the satellite business, sees no gain in this coalition. Having a fall-back value of 1, GT&E brings only that value to the coalition.

Hughes, for reasons given, also sees no gain in this coalition, and hence brings to it only its fall-back value of 2.

The total value of the three players in coalition is 7, and since their combined fall-back values come to 6, the net gain of the three in coalition is 1.

This little model suggests, at first sight, that the game actually ended as one would expect, with GT&E and Hughes forming a coalition around the highest payoff: 5.2. But the stability of this coalition, or its lack of stability, in the model, is not immediately open to the eye. A game-theoretic analysis promises discoveries.

But first a comment on the validity of the numbers in the model. The most one can claim for the entire description of the game in this story, and especially for the values assigned to the players alone and in coalition, is plausibility. This condition is neither better nor worse than an observer or player usually meets in real life. But game-theoretic analysis has its own ground: it is logical. In an effort to make the distinction between the plausibility of the description of the game and the logic of game-theoretic analysis as sharp as possible, I handed this model to the mathematician-game theorist William Lucas of Cornell and asked him the following question: Assuming that the values in the model are valid for the game and that they could be transferred among the players, did they find a "core" of stability in the game? Specifically, is the GT&E-Hughes coalition stable?

Lucas looked at the four coalitions and the numbers attached to them and made some calculations. The following is a paraphrase of his analysis, and to put the suspense where it belongs—on his reasoning—I start with his conclusion:

The GT&E-Hughes coalition in the model is almost but not quite stable. If you examine the mutual interdependence of the four potential coalitions of at least two players in the game, you can see that there is no way that GT&E and Hughes can divide their gain between themselves without Western Union intervening to break them up by offering one or the other an inducement to leave the coalition and join Western Union.

Consider the reasoning: the value of the GT&E-Hughes coalition is 5.2. When they come to divide this amount, each member of the coalition must receive as much or more than he could get in coalition with Western Union. The value of GT&E's potential coalition with Western Union is 2.5. Hence, GT&E must get at least 2.5 out of the coalition with Hughes. If it gets less, Western Union can make GT&E an equal or better offer, which could lead GT&E to leave Hughes and join Western Union.

Turn now to Hughes's view of the matter. If GT&E takes 2.5, that leaves Hughes with 2.7. If Hughes takes any more than that, GT&E falls below 2.5 and goes over to Western Union. But why should Hughes take only 2.7 when its coalition with Western Union is worth 3? Western Union could make an attractive offer to Hughes and one could expect Hughes to leave GT&E and go over to Western Union.

Thus their difficulty is that to be really stable, GT&E can take no less than 2.5 (giving Hughes 2.7), and Hughes can take no less than 3 (giving GT&E 2.2).

Western Union's threat derives from the fact that the combined value of the potential coalitions Western Union-GT&E and Western Union-Hughes (5.5) is greater than the value of the GT&E-Hughes coalition (5.2). No matter how they divide the 5.2, Western Union can break up their coalition; and so in the mutual interdependence of these coalitions, the GT&E-Hughes coalition is inherently unstable. But it missed by so little—only .3, the difference between 5.5 and 5.2—that one should expect that its members could make it more stable with a side payment to Western Union.

Now look again at the relations of all three players. The value 5.2 can only be achieved through the cooperation of GT&E and Hughes. They are in coalition and must decide how to divide 5.2 not just among themselves but among all three. Neither can ask for too much without the risk of breaking their coalition. Let us say they could satisfactorily divide the amount 4.9, giving 2.7 to Hughes and 2.2 to GT&E. We have them make this division for the following reason:

If Hughes were to receive less than 2.7, then the payoff to GT&E and Western Union would total more than 2.5. As 2.5

is the most they can get in their own coalition, it is the most that their coalition can enforce. If they try to get more than that, Hughes can block them simply by not cooperating. Hughes could defect and offer to form a new coalition with Western Union.

If GT&E, on the other hand, were to receive less than 2.2, then the payoff to Hughes and Western Union would add to more than 3, which is more than they can achieve in their potential coalition, hence more than they can enforce. GT&E could defect from its coalition with Hughes and join a new one with Western Union.

Thus we can see how to divide 4.9 of the 5.2 which was originally available for division: GT&E and Hughes get 2.2 and 2.7, respectively. Their problem comes down to how to divide the remaining .3. This amount does not represent a claim to very much power but it is enough to lead one to expect that perhaps the GT&E-Hughes coalition would give something to Western Union to lessen its ability to intervene or find some other way to reduce the amount that Western Union could offer either of them to upset their relationship.

With .3 to be divided between the three of them, imagine the situation as a segregated region of the game. As any two-player coalition inside this region can upset any other coalition, it is hard to expect any strong stability there. Two players might get together to split fifty-fifty and deal the third one out—perhaps GT&E and Hughes, as they are already in coalition, would be able to do that. Or the three of them might split in some equitable way, such as .1 for each, which would give a final payoff of 2.8 (Hughes), 2.3 (GT&E), and .1 (Western Union). This has some merit over the fifty-fifty split, for if Hughes and GT&E split .15 and .15, they end up with a payoff of 2.85 and 2.35. As Western Union gets nothing in this arrangement, it can return to its original coalitions worth 3 and 2.5 and come up with a lure of .15 to offer either of the other players. It's not much but it's stronger than the .1 Western Union would have to work with, under the equitable three-way split, to make its own gain and pay off a partner to defect from the GT&E-Hughes

coalition. With each player getting .1, Western Union might be willing to settle, if only because further effort could result in failure and the loss of the .1.

Thus Lucas concluded his observations on the satellite game model, with a side payment to Western Union as a reasonable stabilizing compromise.

As it happened, Western Union got no side payment in the walkaround, nor did it threaten to upset the GT&E-Hughes coalition. Several explanations are possible. The values in the model may be disputed; or the weighted figures may be too broadly approximate to pick up a true discrepancy of .3. On the other hand, if the discrepancy was realistic in the sense that it gave an intimation that some coalition work had been left undone, it is possible that the players just didn't sense it. Even if the values were correct and known clearly to the players, it would be reasonable to surmise that the coalitional discrepancy was not open to intuition but required a somewhat formal game-theoretic analysis to isolate and identify it.

And so, to sum up, the walkaround, which began with 1,023 potential coalitions, was concluded for the moment with three coalitions in addition to the five players going alone. The old AT&T-networks coalition remained intact and two were new: AT&T-Comsat and GT&E-Hughes. But the walkaround game was not yet quite finished.

By March 1971 all of the players had filed their positions with the FCC. They presented the results of the walkaround and also their proposals, which they had been invited to make, for new arrangements and rules for the next game. Before the FCC ruled on the game, however, an event occurred which put an extension on the walkaround.

The commission's staff of experts in its Common Carrier Bureau studied the game as it had been played, criticized its economic results, and made new proposals. Usually such staff reports are confined to the commission. But in this case the commission, instead of accepting or rejecting all or part of the staff report, chose to circulate it among the players for their comment. Thus, the staff report, while it represented a recommendation, was not presented as an order. The players had a free choice to accept or reject it or to amend their own play of the game in light of its criticisms. As the staff is a learned and influential group of analysts, however, the players could not prudently ignore it.

The staff's criticism of the AT&T-Comsat coalition was so sweeping as to constitute a change in the rules and had better be reserved for the question of new rules which will be discussed below. Its criticism of the GT&E-Hughes coalition, however, was economic and came within the prevailing rules. Its main point was that Western Union, by going alone, was taking a risk excessive enough to constitute a failure to satisfy the public interest: "In addition to offering specialized terrestrial services, Western Union furnishes public message telegraph and other essential public services which could be adversely affected by an improvident investment of substantial size in domestic satellite technology (assuming it could obtain the necessary financing)."

Western Union had to meet that challenge on its merits, apart from the staff's ideas of what should be done about it. But the remedies proposed by the staff were also interesting and had to be considered. The staff proposed that Western Union should take a safe haven in the GT&E-Hughes coalition, making it a coalition of three. The staff also thought it would be even better if options were given to RCA and Western Tel to join the coalition, making it a four- or five-player coalition.

When Western Union, GT&E, and Hughes came to ponder the staff's criticism and remedies, they concluded that adjustments were called for in their previous resolution of the game, and so they resumed negotiations. Two things then became immediately clear and were agreed upon by all three players: they accepted the bureau's criticisms as valid but rejected the remedies.

GT&E and Hughes, in again rejecting the three-player coalition, had only to reiterate their previous objection that that coalition contained a very low payoff for them. Hughes's ob-

THE COMMUNICATIONS SATELLITE

jection was primarily economic: putting two primary satellites in front of its backup satellite nearly doubled the risk
that the backup would be called upon to deliver its service to
a potentially disabled primary. Hughes could calculate that it
was 90 percent confident, as it were, that it would have free
capacity on its backup satellite for over four years, if there
were one primary and one backup. With two claims on the
backup, it could estimate a drop to two years, hardly long
enough to test its cable TV program and product. Hence,
aside from any other details of the staff's proposal, Hughes
was strongly motivated on hard economic grounds to avoid a
three-player coalition.

GT&E's motives were different. The FCC staff wanted the
three players to share the *ownership* of the proposed coalition's satellite system, which was contrary to GT&E's preference for leasing to avoid risk. However, the staff's remedy, as
noted, was not obligatory, and if it had been, the FCC would
have been taking responsibility for the risk: any GT&E losses
would go into the rate base and would be paid for by its telephone customers. GT&E's principal objection to a three-
player coalition, even one that contained its desired lease,
was, as noted, that it did not want its traffic to serve Western
Union's ends. They were, after all, competitors for the private-line market, and the ultimate payoff to the participants
in the new industry would be conditioned by their number
and strength. Hence the very low value that GT&E continued to put on the three-player coalition.

Western Union's first preference we know was for a coalition with GT&E, its second for one with Hughes, and its mild
third for the three-player coalition. But now, having also to
consider concretely as a prospect—one that had always been
there among the possible rulings and that the staff had made
explicit—that the three-player coalition might be enlarged to
four or five, Western Union, too, feared it. Like GT&E and
all the common carriers, Western Union did not want its
traffic to serve the ends of RCA and Western Tel. This realization may have had the effect of reducing the value of the
three-way coalition to the players, but as that value was al-

ready very low, the change had no real effect on the game.

Thus, when the three players came together to renegotiate they were very much aware of the interrelation of their potential coalitions. Except for Western Union's abdication from a potential three-player coalition, they still held to their original preferences. But the GT&E-Hughes coalition could no longer take for granted that it was perfectly stable. If Western Union could not meet the public interest by going alone, it had reason to bring pressure on the others for some sort of new arrangement. Neither GT&E nor Hughes wanted to give up their coalition. So, in that box, what did they do? They considered making a side payment to Western Union to bring its independent position into line with the public interest.

Although the values in the game were not as readily transferable as simple money, the players found a way to attack their problem, as follows. Western Union had filed for three twelve-channel satellites. One of these had no bearing on this subgame. It was there in case Western Union could get the networks. It was no trouble for Western Union to strike one satellite from its system, but that pro forma gesture did not resolve Western Union's problem. The two-satellite system still contained too much risk to satisfy the public interest. Hughes provided the solution.

Presumably with the assent of its coalition partner, Hughes met with Western Union and negotiated to reduce Western Union's risk. They settled by sharing booster risks and spare satellites on the ground. The new arrangement thus hooked Western Union into Hughes's technology and expertise in the space segment of its system. Western Union also received the benefits of economies of scale in the building of satellites, which resulted from the traffic that GT&E was bringing to Hughes. Consequently, Western Union not only satisfied the public interest through risk sharing, but also gained the strength to resist other coalitions, such as those with RCA or Western Tel, which it preferred not to enter.

Hughes gained in the arrangement by a reduction in its costs.

GT&E lost a little, to the extent that its coalition with Hughes aided the presence of Western Union as a competitor in the new industry.

Although this event could quite clearly be interpreted as a side payment to Western Union, I would not want to say that it corresponds exactly to the division of the .3 in the model. Yet it is curious that the scale in the model—.3 in relation to a total value of 5.2—is about right for the reality. The model showed that in forming coalitions the players had almost but not quite satisfied their interactive economic interests and that Western Union had left some small power which it could exert on the other two players. The Common Carrier Bureau also found the coalition results wanting; and the players resolved the problem with the side payment.

But the differences between the solutions suggested by the model and the one actually adopted are also interesting. In the real end game, Western Union got a side payment corresponding to all of the benefit represented by the model's .3. This was not excluded from the extreme possibilities in the model, had there been some strong standard of behavior to justify it. For the division of the .3 was a very open and essentially unstable business, the resolution of which could take any form that economic or social convention decreed. The players did not perceive such a solution until the Common Carrier Bureau introduced a standard of public interest, which as it happened usurped the entire .3 or its real-life equivalent. To manage this, the players departed somewhat from the lines indicated in the model. There the coalition of GT&E and Hughes was held stable by a division of 4.9 into 2.2 and 2.7 respectively. In reality, the maneuver by which the coalition made the side payment to Western Union required GT&E to take a little less and Hughes a little more in their coalition, a stand-off that presumably left the total value of the coalition intact. The redivision between GT&E and Hughes, in which GT&E yielded, say, a value of .1 and Hughes gained .1, did not appear in the model because the tangible form that the side payment would take did not appear. When it did appear in reality, some of the values in the coalition turned out not to be transferable. At least, so far as one knows, there was no way for Hughes to make an adjustment to compensate GT&E.

Two points remain, and they are not small. Discrepancies between the model and reality could readily be attributed to variations somewhere in the approximate values assigned to the players and their coalitions. This is a problem not of game theory proper but of the soundness of one's observations; and some say that reality is too complex for one to extract reliable measures of value from it. There is no doubt that a small revision in the values given in this game could wash out anything like a magnitude of .3 and bring about a different outcome. The significant point about the analysis of the game, however, is that a change in the numbers to some other numbers would have no effect on the *mode* of analysis. For example, if GT&E and Hughes had had 5.5 to divide in coalition, they could have divided 2.5 and 3 and been immune from the pressure of Western Union. With more than 5.5 to divide, they would have encountered a larger and larger "core" of stability within which they would have had to bargain or haggle over the division of the excess. And even so, some force of custom or tradition might have appeared from outside their own hard economics to demand a cut for Western Union.

The other point is that a very different interpretation could be given to the intervention of the FCC through the Common Carrier Bureau. The interpretation here has been that the bureau was only the catalyst of the action in the end game and played no strategic role. One could argue with that. The vibrations set off by that intervention in the minds of the players could be conceived as reactions to threat. The threatener must needs be a new player in the game, i.e., there is a change in the rules, a new game. This, too, could be accommodated. So long as there is a game, there are ways of going at it. In this instance, one would need to end the game with the walkaround, instead of tacking an extension on it as we did here, and start a new game with a new model containing the FCC as a new player.

As it is, the model and the analysis of it here somehow gave a suggestion, for whatever it is worth, of the unfinished business to be cleared up in the coalitional relationships of the players.

The satellite game now moved to new ground.

AFTER THE GAME

The walkaround was a game of consent, negotiated for the most part intently but coolly on the basis of the economic strengths of the players. It was followed by a maelstrom of social and economic proposals, emanating from the same players, for designing the communications satellite industry, introducing new rules, and enforcing them by fiat.

The FCC should organize the industry around a Comsat monopoly, said Comsat, for only we have no conflict of interest in space; all others should be disqualified as equipment suppliers, potential users of satellite services, or ground-based carriers.

"We feel we're the David to the Goliath [AT&T] in this arena," said Fairchild's space man, Melvin Barmat. Representing a hardware hopeful, he objected to the continuation of Comsat's history of procuring satellites from Hughes, and he called upon the FCC to dissolve the deals between Comsat and AT&T and between Hughes and GT&E. But he, too, thought Goliathlike. Multiple systems are wasteful and inefficient, he said, making the standard argument for monopoly, which Fairchild needed to fill its gigantic satellite.

The other participants were not sympathetic to these aspirations.

Bar Comsat from the domestic skies, said Western Union, and MCI Lockheed echoed the demand. Comsat, they both said, is ridden with conflict of interest, with AT&T directors on its board and international obligations incompatible with a domestic system.

Block Hughes from freedom to price its cable-TV programming services, said RCA and Western Union; all should be under common carrier regulation.

What right, demanded Western Union, has RCA to introduce its international carrier, RCA-Globcom, into the domestic field?

The prime target of the players, however, was AT&T.

Western Tel worried that AT&T might take unfair advantage of its competitors.

Hughes proposed that AT&T's use of satellites be limited to telephone toll messages, at least for two years; and also, said Hughes, bar AT&T from leasing channels to anyone else.

Western Union was sterner: bar AT&T from owning a satellite system, at least initially, and when it leases from others, limit its business in space to toll message telephone service.

MCI Lockheed went still further: bar AT&T altogether from space during the initial stage of the industry, and when the proper time comes to let AT&T in, require it to lease from others, but not from Comsat, which, as noted, MCI Lockheed would bar unconditionally.

Behind this outpouring was the widespread feeling among the potential participants that it was not realistic to assume that anyone could get established in the private-line market in the presence of competition from AT&T. They feared not only the company's overwhelming size—its interstate long-lines in 1974 represented about an $8-billion business with a 10 percent yearly growth—but more pointedly, its ability to subsidize its competitive services out of its monopoly services.

With competition in communications, the issue of cross subsidy acquired a new dimension. Regulated rates are based on investment costs. Satellite aspirants asked the key question: what costs do you allocate to what services? If monopoly services can be used to subsidize competitive services, competitors without monopoly services are at a disadvantage, perhaps, they thought, hopelessly. The absence of verification of AT&T's long-lines costs had long been a frustrating issue before the FCC, leading some to wonder whether the FCC could really regulate AT&T. Furthermore, contrary to the myth that a regulated monopoly can only employ one pricing system, AT&T uses three modes of pricing. One—the conventional one for a public utility—is to price on a fully allocated basis, with every cost built into the dime. Another is to price according to what the traffic will bear; for example, not on what it cost but on what people are willing to pay for a call from New York to San Francisco. A third is the price for encounters with a competitor or rival, called "incremental pricing," as it is based mainly on the cost of a new service. In its renegotiations with Comsat during the walkaround, AT&T had given a dramatic demonstration of its flexibility in filling and so maximizing the economies of satellites of different sizes, while the uncertainties of fill plagued the viability of other systems, raising among some participants the specter of premeditated disaster for them in the new industry. MCI Lockheed put it most vigorously: "Open entry is no entry. If you let AT&T run with it now and then try to unravel things, it will be too late."

The Department of Justice, exercising its responsibility for antitrust angles, also put in for some rules to restrict AT&T's power in the satellite market. Its lawyers proposed to bar both AT&T and Comsat from the networks' business in space, so as to allow that business to bring into being an additional viable satellite system. But they pointed out that barring AT&T from providing specialized services by satellite was not an escape from the issue of cross subsidy. If AT&T was cross-subsidizing its terrestrial systems, it could threaten the viability of others' satellite systems from the ground. But the mystery of AT&T's internal operations returned again unexpectedly from a new quarter.

AT&T itself had approached the question of restrictions delicately. The FCC, said the company, should authorize any applicant who had sufficient technical and financial resources and who could show that its system served the public interest. The tone of expression was mild but it did not contravene AT&T's long-standing view that AT&T serves the public interest best. AT&T at first proposed to rule out no one in particular. But Richard Hough, president of the company's long-lines division, observed: "You don't put your cards on the table before the hand is played." He soon turned one card up.

The Common Carrier Bureau provided the opportunity. The bureau challenged a number of the arrangements made in the walkaround. Citing the close ties between AT&T and Comsat, it questioned whether the two would really compete, whether possible large domestic losses would affect Comsat's global obligations, and whether GT&E's satellite system would cost more and be less efficient than its prevailing arrangements with AT&T's long lines. Its conclusion: Comsat should serve AT&T or the others, not both; and both Comsat and GT&E should make further showings demonstrating that their satellites would not adversely affect the public interest in their present systems. AT&T, apparently touched to the quick by GT&E's proposed intrusion into its basic control of long lines, seized upon the bureau's question to GT&E and suddenly attacked the No. 2 carrier's right to a place in the skies. The traditional quietude in the central sector of the communications industry exploded.

The issue of AT&T's control of long lines was indeed a sensitive one. GT&E had few facilities of its own to interconnect its widely scattered local services; that function, as noted, was performed for it by AT&T's Long-Lines Department. The communication satellite provided an unparalleled opportunity for GT&E to connect its interstate traffic—between California and Florida, for example—with long-haul links of its own. GT&E would also transmit by satellite calls originating in its own territories and terminating elsewhere—it would pass them along to AT&T at the point in its own network that was closest to the number being called. GT&E stated its motive in a few words: "These trunks would provide diversity of routing and reduce the frequency of nonavailability of circuits to GT&E customers." With about 10 percent of U.S. telephones and a faster growth rate than AT&T's, GT&E thought it should be a partner in the nation's basic long-distance toll network. Against that, AT&T contended that it would be difficult to connect GT&E's satellite service with the basic long-distance system without increasing costs to the public.

Some of the players watching this contest rather obviously rooted for GT&E. The federal government itself seemed to like the idea of having another strong entry in the long-lines business. The FCC would gain a deeper understanding of how the toll system worked; it would have what spokesmen for the White House (Office of Telecommunications Policy) called a "significant and singular yardstick against which to measure the performance and economies of AT&T's long-lines network." The other companies were interested in learning about long-lines economics for the rather special reason alluded to earlier: they wanted to know more about the extent to which AT&T, as they suspected, might be subsidizing one service with another.

There was no doubt that GT&E's proposal threatened AT&T's exclusive control of the national telephone net, and that AT&T had strong reasons to resist the invasion. Not the least of these reasons was the fact that AT&T moves the long-lines money around its system to maximize its return in ways that are obscure to outsiders, including the FCC itself. A GT&E satellite link would open up this long-lines profit box. Such exposure could limit AT&T's maneuverability within its system.

With the Common Carrier Bureau questioning the soundness of a GT&E satellite link in the national toll system and AT&T directing a full-fledged technical attack on GT&E as a harmful interloper, the pressure was on GT&E to make a satisfactory showing that its satellite was in the public interest. The fight, however, was strategic as well as technical. If GT&E fought back hard, long, and intensively, it might eventually force AT&T also to make a broader and deeper showing of the workings of its control of the national toll system. The balance of threat and counterthreat was delicate. Long-distance telephone is not only AT&T's but also GT&E's most profitable business. Although AT&T was in control, the two had a coalition of sorts which provided the high payoffs. GT&E's proposed satellite link would give GT&E a share in the control, suggesting a possible redivision of the payoffs. It seems a fair presumption that both companies knew that in a fight to the finish, that is, to full disclosure, they would give up secrets of their profitability, that is, the very means by which they escaped the paradox of public-utility motivation according to which higher profits meant lower rates. Who then had the upper hand? Or did either?

AT&T apparently hoped that the FCC would cut short the fight and simply rule against GT&E. But it was not a simple situation for the commission, which was torn between two of its responsibilities: on the one hand the commission had to protect the national toll system, which AT&T contended would be disrupted by a GT&E satellite link. On the other hand the commission desired to learn more about how that system worked. Furthermore, if the commission took GT&E's satellite traffic off the market, that would shrink the new industry that the FCC was preparing to launch and increase AT&T's power in that industry, which pointed to a frustration of the commission's aims.

These issues gave GT&E some leverage against AT&T and gave both of them some choices. If GT&E chose to threaten a fight to the finish, which its posture suggested, AT&T could threaten joint "suicide" (not quite sensible but common enough in industry), offer a negotiated deal to share control of the national toll system, threaten reprisals in other areas, or open up some other "down card." AT&T and GT&E played this game in private, but one can muse over its possibilities.

One possibility was that AT&T and GT&E would reach an impasse in their "division of revenue settlements." They, and other independent telephone companies, divide the long-lines revenue pool in proportion to the capital that generates the service. The capital thus is the measure of the division. AT&T could refuse to allow GT&E to put its satellite earth stations into the revenue division. If GT&E could not put them in, no revenue would come out—in which case GT&E could not profitably build a satellite system. How strongly each was committed to such a collision course depended on how much GT&E valued a satellite system and how much AT&T valued its control of long lines.

The game-theoretic question to be asked here is whether the two great telephone companies were playing non-cooperatively or cooperatively. If they were playing non-cooperatively and with irreconcilably opposed interests, they would probably end up in court. But if they were playing co-operatively, they would aim to wrap up all the above threats and counterthreats and angles and interests in a negotiation, look for their core of economic stability in coalition, and, somewhere within that haven, strike a bargain. As members of a regulated industry they would then together seek to persuade the FCC to approve their solution.

Although this game, however the two companies chose to play it, was not part of the main line of the walkaround, its resolution would have a substantial effect on the new satellite industry. Quite simply, the question was whether GT&E would bring its substantial traffic into that industry inside or outside the AT&T system.

THE RULE MAKER (FCC)

When a regulatory body confronts issues of the kinds described here, it decides them by a voting mechanism, and the decisions are binding on the parties involved. One tends therefore to think of such bodies as rule makers, and indeed they are. But behind the rules they make are their "solutions" to the games played before them; the rules reflect these "solutions." Such was the case when the satellite game came before the FCC.

Regulation is itself one broad solution to a game (among others are government ownership or the free market). Not long ago the accepted standard for the economics of communications in the United States was regulated monopoly. In the changing social philosophy of the past few years this standard still held for the local public telephone system but not for long lines or private lines by ground microwave or satellite. An FCC decision on the satellite that reflected this change would entail a reorganization of a substantial part of the communications industry, which was not easy.

On June 16, 1972, the FCC finally laid down its first set of rules for the game. Broadly, it ruled for "multiple entry," i.e., satellite competition for private-line business. The commission, in its ruling, said that it generally shared its staff's concern about AT&T's "strength and dominance" and about cross subsidies that might eliminate competition at the outset; it also agreed to limit the relationship between AT&T and Comsat. But the commission disagreed with the staff's effort to solve the problem of fill by proposing coalitions based on similar technologies. Instead, the commission authorized all the qualified players, acting either independently or in coalitions, to operate communication satellites. There were, however, some conditions attached to this ruling—e.g., carriers would have to show that their existing customers would not be burdened by any of the changes. And special restrictions were placed on some of the companies.

Comsat's and AT&T's expressed intentions were fettered most by the ruling. The commission rejected the joint Comsat-AT&T proposal. Comsat instead was offered a choice between two quite different concepts. First, it could function solely as a "carrier's carrier"; this would mean that it offered no services of its own and would be restricted to leasing channels to other carriers. According to this concept, it could serve AT&T, but only on the same terms it was offering to other carriers—an arrangement something like the one that AT&T had earlier rejected. Second, Comsat could proceed with the multipurpose system it had applied for, serving both carriers and private customers; but in this case it would have to get along without AT&T's business.

The commission gave AT&T a choice between leasing from Comsat (or any other carrier) on these terms and, alternatively, developing its own system. In either case, during the first three years after its system was put in operation it would be pretty much limited to basic telephone service, private service for the Department of Defense, and emergency service. This could give the newcomers an opportunity to get established in private lines. But at some point during the three years, the commission said, it would consider altering this arrangement.

Other elements of the decision:

■ GT&E would be required to make additional showings of the potential benefits and detriments of its proposed system. If its deal with Hughes were finally authorized, GT&E's satellite services would be restricted to the same functions as AT&T's.

■ Owing to the "distance-insensitive" feature of satellites, rates for service to and from Hawaii, Alaska, and Puerto Rico would become comparable to those within the forty-eight conterminous states.

■ All of the other applicants were authorized to go up with only minor restrictions. The commission requested all participants to declare their intentions within thirty days— i.e., by July 25, 1972. They all had, of course, the right to appeal.

In view of the conflicts among the players and the complexities involved in setting up a new industry, it is not surprising that the vote on the rulings as a whole was close (four to three). The commissioners agreed unanimously upon the standard that a competitive satellite industry in private-line services would best serve the public interest. Their disagreement centered upon the social and business standards that should govern competition. The majority held, as most of the players did, that the big participants, especially AT&T, would have to be restricted to avoid the likelihood that open competition would actually result in unregulated monopoly (one of the commissioners, Nicholas Johnson, expressed only a slight preference for even restricted competition over regulated monopoly). The spokesman for the minority, Dean Burch, objecting to the fetters on AT&T and Comsat, set forth the opposing standard: don't penalize success. "I find this an ironic twist indeed," he said, "that 'success' is to be penalized rather than rewarded and that economies of scale must be foresworn as inconsistent with a theoretical model of pure competition [for traffic, he noted, 'that is mostly a gleam in some speculators' eyes'].""

The judgment of the majority may have implied a hankering for "pure competition," but none of the markets imagined by any of the commissioners met the criteria for a classically pure market. Both the majority and minority were talking about markets that would be guided by judgments of value, strategies, coalitional groupings, and social norms, i.e., they were game-theoretic markets. Their vote made rules for the next game.

THE NEW GAME

We have seen the players in the walkaround seeking profitable coalitions in a game with a minimum of regulatory rules; and the FCC questioning, qualifying, and approving or denying one or another of their solutions. Although the FCC initially gave the players only thirty days to declare their intentions, and Western Union declared that it would proceed immediately, the others asked for and were given more time, about a year as it turned out. During that period of time they played a new game, the dissatisfied reorganizing their coalitions, and all submitting further filings and counterfilings. The FCC, on October 26, 1973, approved, except for a few details, the new arrangements along with those they had approved earlier.

I shall give only a brief account of these events and their consequences as the new industry came into being with the launching of Western Union's satellite—the first to fly—in the spring of 1974.

Recall that the players in the walkaround were as follows:

AT&T
Comsat
Hughes
ABC-CBS-NBC
Western Union
GT&E
RCA

MCI Lockheed
Western Tel
Fairchild

AT&T now agreed to sell its Comsat stock, thereby removing the conflict of interest between the two companies. Comsat in turn, to avoid the objection that it might cross-subsidize among its different operations or harm one with the other, formed a wholly owned subsidiary, Comsat General, for domestic operations, with up to $200 million in capital. As a result of these changes, the FCC allowed Comsat to set up a separate system for AT&T.

MCI Lockheed then also withdrew its objections to Comsat and AT&T and made a deal with Comsat for joint ownership of a satellite system. They set up a new separate company called CML, each parent company owning one third of it.

The technical rationale for CML was that Comsat had knowledge of satellite operations and financial resources lying fallow; Lockheed had aerospace knowledge; and MCI had knowledge of the domestic communications market. But CML ran into strategical and other difficulties. AT&T moved to block MCI as a specialized carrier from interconnecting with AT&T's local services. The FCC directed AT&T to provide them. AT&T appealed to the courts, and a federal court in Philadelphia ordered AT&T to comply; but AT&T said it just couldn't, technically. So MCI's future became cloudy. Lockheed, on the other hand, was having more than enough financial difficulties of its own in the aircraft business, and was not in a position to put more money into CML. The new little company announced another move to circumvent AT&T's block. As noted earlier, the currently standard frequencies for satellites require local interconnections to reach the end customer—a stronghold largely monopolized by AT&T—but higher frequencies, a more advanced and still developing art, can dispense with interconnections and reach the customer directly from satellite to rooftop. CML now proposed to come down to twenty-four channels, at less capital cost, using higher frequencies to jump over AT&T's blockade. To get the financing CML could go to the public equity markets or could merge with still another partner. But as Western Union led the industry into space, CML was stalled; it had not yet even contracted for its satellite system.

Hughes made no further moves in this period, except to set up a wholly owned subsidiary corporation, separate from its satellite manufacturing operations, to handle its proposed programming distribution business on the backup of GT&E's twenty-four-channel system (enlarged to twenty-six channels). But the outcome for Hughes in this game depended on what happened to GT&E.

The networks appeared to withdraw their threat to go to a satellite system, or let it subside, when they got a payoff in substantially lower tariff rates from AT&T, which may have been their preferred outcome all along.

Western Union, which got the jump on everyone with its satellite system aloft, quickly filled its first bird. It had an option on a third one if there were sufficient demand for its services. Western Union was disappointed only in failing to get the right to serve the Hawaiian market on a permanent license. The old company thus got the first real business as well as the ornament it wanted.

GT&E received approval of its satellite system from the FCC, along with favorable indications that it would get the coveted Hawaiian link. But AT&T made new moves to block GT&E from getting into space, as we shall see.

RCA, after looking so weak in the walkaround, surprised the other players with an aggressive move in technology at a total projected cost of about $100 million for the system. RCA proposed to build its own twenty-four-channel satellite (two with the backup), and to pay for an enlarged (Thor-Delta) booster which, by putting up more capacity at less cost, would give it a more efficient system than the one Hughes was offering. In the business, it was looked upon as a sporty proposition, with risks that the booster would blow up, that the satellite would not last more than two or three years, and that the market would not provide enough traffic for it in competition with the others. There was also the strategical uncertainty of whether AT&T would block RCA's interconnections as it had MCI's. But the system had prospects; among them, perhaps it could take NBC's business away from AT&T.

There were other strategical possibilities in RCA's proposed move. The FCC granted RCA the Alaska link and for a starter RCA rented space in a Canadian satellite put up while the U.S. satellite game was in progress, though RCA also has the right to its own equipment. Although RCA's Alaskan communications business was not profitable by itself, it might be made so if the investment were tied into AT&T's national network with the customary rate averaging, which would enlist the lower forty-eight states to subsidize Alaska. Viewed as a threat, RCA's proposed twenty-four-channel system for the whole of the United States could conceivably bring AT&T to the negotiating table on the Alaskan matter.

MCI Lockheed, as noted, disappeared into CML with attendant uncertainties.

Western Tel retreated to lease space in another system.

Fairchild, which had long since given up its 120-channel satellite, merged its interests in communications satellites with Western Union International to create a new corporate player called Amsat. Amsat bought three twelve-channel satellites from Hughes on a contract guaranteed by Fairchild and then ran into trouble. Short on financing, it slowed down the contract. Western Union International dropped from 50 percent owner of Amsat to 19 percent, with Fairchild picking up the 31 percent to become 81 percent owner, and then moved from there to 100 percent. Eventually Amsat, lacking funds, terminated the contract with Hughes, an event which took the new company out as a hardware-owning prospect. Amsat laid the blame on AT&T because of its tactics on interconnections. It then leased three channels from Western

Union for $6 million a year—a nice deal for Western Union which had space to spare.

Thus the number of active individual and group players in the game as prospective owners of satellite systems at the outset of the new industry in the spring of 1974 came down to five:

    AT&T-Comsat
    CML
    GT&E-Hughes
    Western Union
    RCA

All together, counting the shaky and the firm, they proposed to put up a total of 194 satellite channels. As AT&T's seventy-two channels and GT&E's twelve primary channels would be barred by FCC rule from the private-line business for three years, 110 channels would be putatively available in the private-line market. Of these, the participants could fill about thirty for sure, leaving about eighty channels to be filled in the open market—an enormous capacity potentially overhanging the new communications industry.

The private-line business—on the ground, of course, before Western Union went up—totaled a little over $1 billion in 1974, and about 90 percent of the business was in the hands of AT&T. The new industry would be playing largely to capture what it could of the growth in this business—and so the health of the industry would depend upon how much growth it could stimulate through the new technology. Thus even if strategical uncertainties could be set aside, the industry would still be dominated by the uncertainties of this market. But strategical uncertainties could not be set aside; indeed they dominated this on-going game more than ever.

Through all the years of struggle over the satellite, AT&T had not been fooling. That the volume of the prospective growth in private lines was modest beside AT&T's super-billions in assets and revenues was not the point for the big company. No profit, however slight, was to be overlooked, but the main point was that its treasured monopoly must be defended in every place where it was threatened, even on the fringes, not to speak of the inside of its sacrosanct long-lines network. Yet the FCC had legitimized competition on the private-line fringe and had granted GT&E the right to a long-lines satellite system.

But that was not the end of the road. In 1972 there had come a change inside AT&T. From 1967 to 1972 the company had been guided by its chairman and chief executive Haakon Ingolf Romnes. He was succeeded then by his vice chairman, John Dulany deButts, a man, it appears, with a new policy. For all the vigor of Romnes' leadership in AT&T's struggle for supremacy in communications, he had seemed to be prepared, under the pressures, to yield a modest amount of private-line business so long as the company retained its economies of scale and freedom to compete. It was not a weak policy by any means; indeed, as viewed by potential competitors in private lines, the adoption of that policy would lay them low. But the new management soon adopted a more militant policy with a frontal attack against competition in any form under any conditions. They threw the block operationally against interconnections. They went before the regulatory bodies of the individual states to block the new industry at every point. They took the FCC to court to block its October 1973 rulings. And they threatened to go to Congress.

For all this and more they lost the support of the White House, which had sought a measure of competition in private lines. But the great immediate impact was at the economic level. Blocking the interconnections of fledgling private-line companies threatened to starve out those seeking equity financing. Some could be driven out by state-by-state legal costs while AT&T fought for free, its costs reimbursed out of revenue requirements. And taking the FCC to court over the GT&E satellite put GT&E in a position of risk whether it went into space or endured delay.

The coalitions began circling again.

GT&E abdicated its satellite position in the sky for a lesser one on the ground, pulling out of its alliance with Hughes, and entering one with AT&T. The new AT&T-GT&E coalition took GT&E out of satellites and thereby out of the main line of AT&T's national system and gave GT&E three earth stations, one for each of its major concentrations of local traffic: California, Florida, and Hawaii. These earth stations would use AT&T's satellite system.

CML fell apart, with Lockheed and MCI prepared to retire from the game.

At the same time, a new player came in: IBM. IBM is a powerful company, perhaps powerful enough to take on AT&T, and it had the incentive. IBM is in the business of big computers, and big computers stationed in different parts of the country—as, for example, airline computer systems—need cheap communications between them. The satellite relay signal could reduce such long-haul data costs.

IBM first approached Hughes after GT&E pulled out of its Hughes lease, wondering if Hughes would be interested in a jointly-owned satellite system. But for Hughes this meant a big investment in the communications data business. With interest rates at historic highs and AT&T to fight all over again, Hughes declined.

IBM went to the ailing CML and offered to buy out Lockheed and MCI, thus setting up a new force: Comsat-IBM.

The putative new industry now took the form of four principal entities:

AT&T-Comsat
Comsat-IBM
Western Union
RCA

The struggles over the satellite between these players and others promised to continue throughout the seventies and into the eighties. But it would again be a new game. For an answer to the impasse between AT&T's absolute opposition to competition and the government's insistence on competition as a yardstick for regulation came from the Department of Justice which, in late 1974, opened an antitrust suit aimed at breaking up AT&T and taking away from it, among other things, its treasured long lines. One might think at first sight that this could be the end of AT&T, and well it might be in the end. But by itself the suit will hardly bring relief to AT&T's aspiring competitors. The suit is expected to take many years and to cost tens of millions of dollars in legal fees. But AT&T's legal fees—by custom if not by rule—are normally reimbursed out of its tariffs at cost to its telephone customers but not to its stockholders; and its assets are expected at least to double in ten years. So on this course AT&T could still make all the gains it could possibly make for a decade and let the future take care of itself. The other remaining players have that condition to ponder in the new game, and one may expect action on all fronts, economic, regulatory, legal, and political. Although the regulatory, legal, and political games over the satellite are subject to their own peculiarities—bench rulings, lobbying, legislative coalitions, voting, and the like—which are very different in character from economic games, nevertheless the ruling bodies will need to understand the underlying economic interactions described here and carry them out as well as possible to their payoffs in the public interest, if they are to reach a stable resolution of the satellite game, as it turns out, the whole communications business as well.

12

SEARS, PENNEY, AND WARD:
ONE-, TWO-, AND
MANY-SIDED GAMES

The great merchandisers Sears, Penney, and Ward have created for their business a common corporate model which with variations reflects how the modern corporation in general is designed as a game. The chief distinction of their model is the way it guides billions of dollars' worth of merchandise from its origins to store counters and catalogues. It also provides for different ways of playing the many games in which these companies have made their colorful histories.

THE PLAYERS

- Sears, Roebuck & Company
- J. C. Penney Company, Incorporated
- Montgomery Ward & Company
- Other merchants

Only recently have the old and still leading general merchants Sears, Penney, and Ward met substantially on common ground—full-line department stores competing in major markets—after putting in most of the present century in markets divided either by territory or lines of goods. Together they sell about 12 percent of the general merchandise sold in the United States—more than $20 billion worth in 1974. But their individual fortunes have varied widely. Sears has always led, by a little or a lot; it now does more than half the combined business of the three. A transformed Penney has gained rapidly to account for about a third of it. The once powerful Ward almost collapsed some years ago and, though still trailing, has struggled back to life through strenuous games.

Many of the major decisions taken by these merchants through this century have been of the kind described in this book as one-sided. They have treated as nature all that appeared to them to be naturelike, notably the movements of the population; the technical aspects of distribution, especially the economies of scale inherent in moving large quantities of standardized goods; the future level of the economy; and the like. Knowing their primary wants—mainly money and survival—they made choices, for better or worse, based upon formal predictions or guesswork concerning such matters.

All that was not naturelike they treated, in the language of this book, as a game. Working from a more or less common corporate model, they often played the game as if it were one-sided, each party, for example, laying down its strategic policies and plans calculated to meet the apparent strategies of competitors and to reach the desired end.

But they did not overlook the cooperative approach to games that could better be played that way. Relations with suppliers, for example, required their negotiating and bargaining; shopping centers made it necessary for them to agree upon close-range competition; raids on management—mainly on Sears's—were common among them and were sometimes permitted, sometimes blocked; they sought the discriminatory allegiance of customers through store and brand loyalty; one of them—Ward—chose a voluntary merger to avoid takeover; and so on, as the following story will show.

• • •

SEARS

Sears is the nation's No. 1 retailer—selling almost everything but food, liquor, and automobiles—and the envy of all other merchants for making success for a long time look easy in a business that has not been easy for all. One way to describe Sears's success is to say that it got there early and made few big mistakes. It went with the country, often anticipating where the country was going and serving the needs of the time. It was at first a catalogue business selling mainly to farmers by mail before there was an automobile. When the automobile brought farmers to town in large numbers in the 1920s, Sears went into the retail store business in a big way. It opened 324 stores between 1925 and 1929, mainly in the larger towns and cities, with tools and fishing tackle out front. It was primarily in the hardware business, with economy dresses, overalls, and a few other clothing staples on the side.

Consumer hardware all but disappeared during World War II and so Sears compensated by offering more clothing. It hired Mary Lewis, a then famous New York stylist and merchandiser who had been at Best and Saks Fifth Avenue, as a consultant, mainly on sportswear for women. She worked with suppliers to add style to Sears's economy clothes and actually succeeded in making some farm clothes (e.g., denim pants) fashionable. Sears let up on soft goods after the war to exploit the booming appliance market, and when that tapered off in the fifties, went back to soft goods, again talking fashion and selling even mink stoles. In short, Sears went middle class, and was now in the full-line department-store business, with private brands, and a service organization supporting its sales. Along the way, diversification: the sale of insurance, for example, which fitted into its distributive organization.

The overriding decision at Sears after World War II was to expand in anticipation of a long period of national prosperity, and again to go where the country, or at least the new middle class, was going: west, south, and to the suburbs. Sears plotted the population movements, picked the best new locations, often before the people got there, set up its big free-standing stores, majestically isolated while other retail businesses clustered in shopping strips, and then later moved into shopping centers when they became the shoppers' new way of life. Because Sears concentrated on metropolitan centers, it linked its stores in large groups which benefited from common distribution centers and—a key function—from common metropolitan advertising. To get skilled manpower and womanpower, it developed an intensive training program for college graduates, promoted its people from within, from selling floor to store manager to headquarters. And it set up a profit-sharing fund for employees which bought Sears's stock, as a result of which the employees came to own more than 25 percent of the company's stock.

These were classically one-sided decisions, based upon the management's very good observations of their business and its surroundings. But the more subtle aspects of Sears's progress are found in the design of its corporate game model which has given the company its operating force and control.

At the base of this model are the stores and catalogue outlets across the country. Above them are regional and territorial executives who control the general management of the stores in their jurisdiction. Also above the stores on another stem is Sears's merchandise headquarters in Chicago. There a special management group makes and executes merchandise policy for the stores and catalogue and controls the purchase and manufacture of the goods. And still further up in the hierarchy, above both the territorial and the merchandise managements, is the top corporate management that makes policy for the whole company, with its different lines of business and its social and political environment.

Sears's corporate model thus corresponds rather closely to the general four-level corporate game model described in Chapter 2.

At the first level the managers and staffs of the stores and catalogue outlets conduct the day-to-day transactions in the consumer markets on the basis of policy rules laid down from above.

At the second level are the two different management groups over the stores, one governing general store policy in regions and territories, the other governing all aspects of the flow of merchandise. For the executives at this level the store rules are not fixed but variable. Indeed, they make rules for the stores and in doing so make strategic policy for them over time.

At the third level, the top corporate management rules the scope of the business, that is, the kinds of business Sears will engage in—including participation in the ownership of manufacturers—along with its financial and other general policies.

The fourth level is non-economic: the rules of the game as derived from political life, which Sears, along with all corporations, attempts to influence to its advantage through the political game.

The distinctive feature of Sears's game model is its control of the merchandise. Retailing through a chain of hundreds of stores is a considerable exercise in such control. A single "Class A" store—i.e., a full-line department store—may have annual sales of $30 million or more. Altogether, Sears in 1974 was operating about 300 complete department stores, about 400 medium-sized stores, and about 200 hard-goods stores; and a dozen catalogue order plants serving about 2,500 local outlets. The first simplification lies in the recognition that although that is a lot of different businesses to open up every morning, it is also in certain respects just one business. The merchandise displayed in the stores, of course, varies somewhat by region—splashier clothing in the Southwest and California than in New England, for example. But despite such variations, the stores are unmistakably Sears in design and management and also in merchandise—$11 billion worth in 1973. All of these goods are controlled from one point in headquarters. Sears thereby takes full advantage of the technological facts that producing large quantities of goods with standard specifications reduces the cost of manufacture and further that channeling the distribution of the goods in an orderly way to numerous controlled outlets likewise reduces costs. Every Sears store manager is a captive customer of a single "seller," namely, Sears's merchandising department in Chicago and its branches in a number of other large cities. All merchandising decisions, down to the specifications and price of each item, are made in Chicago. This department creates the product, assigns it to a specific place in the catalogue and a specific counter in the stores, and also provides the stores with a "syndicated service" of display materials, advertising designs, and selections for special promotions. The merchandising vice president, who oversees this operation, has generally been regarded as the No. 3 man in the company, after the chairman and the president.

The merchandising department has numerous divisions—fifty or more at any time—each representing a category of product, such as plumbing and heating, infants' wear, automotive accessories. Each has its own supervisor, an executive whose sales volume will run anywhere from a few million dollars (notions) to hundreds of millions (appliances). Each has some freedom for decision and each is monitored by a general departmental executive. As buyers, these supervisors differ from the traditional department-store buyers who shop around among suppliers and deal with them at arm's length. Sears's buyers are responsible for the design of the product, which they may develop themselves, and for factory production. This takes close work with manufacturers, designers, and Sears's central staff of engineers, distribution and marketing experts, and financial people. When they have settled on a program for a year, each supervisor then maintains a watch on the flow of goods, which he may increase, reduce, or shut off.

This kind of arrangement, which enables Sears to merchandise its own brands at low cost with quality controls, rests on close and usually long-term supplier relationships which are quite unique in American business. One usually observes intercorporate buyers and sellers struggling over information about each other's position, with costs often held as a trade secret. Sears negotiates on the basis of open information on the part of the suppliers. It makes most of its purchases on a "known cost" basis. That means that Sears is privy to the manufacturer's production data. Sears may even provide engineering and other technical assistance. Nobody "sells" Sears. The first cost it cuts out of a supply contract is the selling commission. Sears thus has great power in the arrangements, but that does not deter suppliers from a willingness to cooperate to get in on its great volume.

Sears has gone even further into the supply side. A considerable volume, at one time almost a third, of Sears's products have not been really bought at all, but manufactured by companies in which Sears has had an equity of from 9 to 100 percent. Sears is, in fact, one of the largest manufacturers in the United States.

The centralization of merchandising in Sears has one counterbalance in the decentralization of the administration of the stores and store groups. It is the store in the end that shows the profit or loss; and it takes considerable skill, and considerable training to get the skill, to run a store. Store managers are prized people in the organization, much coveted by competitors. The store units and their managers are tied back into Chicago through several territorial organizations. Each territory is headed by a vice president who is corporate oriented—assured by the fact that he sits on the board of directors and is eligible to succeed to the high command.

Thus, the Sears model permits several ways of playing the game in accordance with different phases of the business. There is a great deal of one-sidedness in the merchandising department's approach to the consumer markets; it makes predictions, for example, about how various goods are expected to sell. At this level, one might interpret any particular large merchandise market as behaving somewhat like the standard economic model: a large number of sellers in free competition, bound by the exigencies of market prices. It is possible that in many markets Sears is the most efficient distributor of hard goods and so sets limits on the prices of other sellers. But one can't push this line of thought too far. Sears does not appear to regard a specific price for an item as automatically given. At the store end of the model, the manager is bound by rules from on high—i.e., by limited choices—as regards the selection, promotion, and pricing of merchandise. This looks like a strategic game played one-sidedly against the known strategies of discounters, standard department stores, and other general merchandise chains. Sears knows each of its major markets microscopically—from distances between their own and other competing stores to the external benefits of locating a store in a shopping center with the give and take of traffic between stores from which all benefit by their combined "draw." Sears is not out to get all the available business in a market, but just the business—kind and amount—that makes a store profitable. The store rules are the strategies of the central merchandisers for this non-cooperative game.

On the supplier end, the game is cooperative: individual interpersonal deals, negotiations with fairly complete information at least about the suppliers, resulting in cores of stability. Sears is par excellence a corporation designed as the model of a game.

PENNEY

J. C. Penney has long been the No. 1 merchandiser of soft goods in the United States and is now second only to Sears in general merchandising. It has grown enormously in recent years—to sales of over $6 billion in 1974—but has not made as much money as its management would like. The measure is Sears. Penney's profit as a percentage of sales has been below Sears's. One outstanding reason for this is that Penney in recent years got into a new game, and for a big, old company, a new game, with its new players, new rules, and need for new strategies, takes time and costs money.

From 1902 to the early 1960s Penney was a dry-goods chain selling mainly staples: practical clothing for the family, work clothes, shoes, notions, piece goods, some housewares.

By the 1950s, its 1,700 yellow store fronts on the Main Streets of the country had a look of Americana. And in fact its business was growing obsolete. Customers were moving away from its old locations, and in its new ones it was not competing well with department and discount stores. Its costs rose, its profits declined.

In 1957 William M. Batten, an assistant to the president, wrote a memo to the board of directors about the problem under the innocuous title "Company Merchandising Character." The board adopted it and made Batten president, later chairman. His experience is revealing.

Batten, the son of a West Virginia storekeeper, is a gentle, persuasive man with a soft voice who first went to work for Penney in 1926 as a part-time clerk. He didn't like it. "My father's general store gave me enough of that kind of business, or so I thought," he says. But after graduating in economics from Ohio State his thoughts went back to retailing. In 1935 he again took a job in a Penney store and by the early fifties was a vice president of the company and Penney's long-range planner. In 1954, at a company convention, he began asking the question, "What kind of company do we want to be?" Later he wrote an influential memo in which he argued that population growth was concentrating in metropolitan areas, incomes were rising, and the buying power of consumers was being attracted toward merchandise that represented "'want' rather than 'need' . . . In such a market, style and fashion play a more important part in creating sales than does utility."

Batten asked for a study of the problem. His request was granted and it took him and a company team four years to complete the study. They formulated Penney's past policy as selling a limited number of merchandise lines for cash in retail stores. They proposed instead a change to the broader concept of a distribution business for goods and services. This meant, specifically, designing and building new, modern, full-line stores mainly in new locations, entering the catalogue business, and seeking diversification—in general outline what Sears was doing.

The concrete foundation of the new policy was a new type of Penney store. Most of the early Penney stores were in small- and middle-sized markets in towns and farm areas; in the 1950s Penney had started to move into metropolitan-area shopping centers with larger soft-goods stores. The new markets, however, pointed to the need for much larger and more complete stores. Sears, as noted, had led this movement, mainly with "freestanding" stores, while most of the big merchandisers until the late 1950s went to strip or L-shaped shopping centers. As luck would have it, Penney made its big policy change when shopping centers, too, were undergoing a major change from strips to so-called "regional" centers. The new shopping centers were large—500,000 square feet or more, with a mall—and designed to include both big department stores and small specialty and service shops. The main direction of Penney's new policy was to put big full-line stores in these new centers. The company went to work on a prototype store in King of Prussia, a suburb of Philadelphia. After the planning was done, it took eleven months to build the store and four more to equip it with fixtures and merchandise. When it opened in August 1963, the Penney of the future went on display. The first of a succession of such full-line stores, the King of Prussia store was timed by Penney and by providence for the long economic boom and new styles of the 1960s. In pursuit of its customers, the traditional merchant of the blue collar had gone middle class.

Besides fashion departments, Penney now sold major appliances, paint and hardware, auto accessories, sporting goods, furniture, cosmetics, and electronic equipment. And it leased out concessions for beauty salons, fine-jewelry counters, restaurants, and photographic studios. Its appliances were made by General Electric's Hotpoint division under the Penney label, "Penncrest." Auto centers were opened adjacent to stores in shopping centers, displaying, among other things, sporty car accessories and motorcycles. Meanwhile, Penney also started an experiment in Wisconsin with a separate group of unique quasi-discount supermarket stores called "Treasure Island." And in a very daring move,

Penney for the first time entered the formidable catalogue field.

To get the specialists it needed to fill out its forces, Penney raided other companies—Sears, Ward, department stores, credit companies—and with these specialists as a nucleus, began training its own corps of specialists. Penney also had to pay heavily to finance its future, and at the same time it had to live in the present, with profit enough to support the projects and satisfy the shareholders with a return year by year. Led by Batten, Penney made it. Ten years after the King of Prussia store opened, Penney had more than tripled its sales, with more than half the business in about 300 full-line stores, the rest in about 1,300 soft-line stores, 23 Treasure Islands, the catalogue, and several diversified operations—all together, one of the most gigantic transformations ever made in American business.

Batten made some observations on the transformation and the nature of the game in an interview with the author:

> The longest-range decision in business is the kind of company you want to be and the kind of business you want to be in. The decision we made on this was, of course, the biggest decision in the company in modern times. In the 1920s Sears and Penney talked merger. Sears then specialized in hard goods and Penney in soft goods. The decision was not to merge. Sears decided on retail stores and expansion into soft lines. That gave Sears hard, soft, and catalogue. Penney stayed retail and soft until 1958 when we started the countermove to go into hard lines and catalogue. Penney was between Sears and Ward on expansion after World War II when Ward knocked itself out of the market, but Penney took thirty years to respond to Sears's move.

The outlines of Penney's corporate model resemble Sears's, not so much as a result of imitation as of a common rationale. The four-level structure of rules and rule making common to most corporations reappears, along with the feature of central merchandising control. The top management deals with the rules of society (for example, "truth-in-lending" legislation); top management also decides what business the company will be in, which, as noted, is its biggest economic decision. The next levels of management make policy over time in their spheres: the stores, the catalogue, other lines of business. And at the first level the store manager operates with some flexibility under the corporate rules. To quote Batten again:

> A John Smith store is not a J. C. Penney store. When we put in a new manager, he needs to have a good knowledge of what a Penney store is and the areas where he can use his imagination. When I join a company, I give up some things and gain some things. If you want to run a business any way you please, you go into your own business. In a big organization, you take strength from its strength but give up what you solely think is right. You have to accept the policy or procedure until you persuade the top management otherwise.

Penney, like Sears, negotiates and bargains with suppliers, though unlike Sears does not buy into them. Batten expresses the concept of a many-sided cooperative game here when he says, "We have responsibilities to from eight to ten thousand suppliers. We do not want to overpay them nor to drive them to the wall. We are careful not to exploit our market power. They are entitled to a profit for their services." And, on the other hand, when he turns to the retail market, he expresses the concept of a non-cooperative game with competitors. In this game, he again takes the one-sided view, playing against an environment consisting of the strategies available to the others. Thus, as in Sears's game, Penney brings several kinds of solutions into play.

Batten discussed the kind of things he finds subject to direct observation as the basis of decision.

> Conclusions about the number of people, the demographic structure, etcetera, we regard as sure things. But suppose we have a decision to make on putting in a

new department in a store. You have certain hard facts: the size of the present market, its trend, expectations about the future, information about who's getting the business now and how they're growing, who the customers are and where they are likely to shop if given a reason. You want to know how much of this merchandise is being marketed now, what is the awareness and alertness of the competition, their ability to meet the market, and to have an appraisal of your own minuses and pluses and what advantages you have over the existing competition. Do you have something new? A new approach? A running start? And what are your disadvantages? Your weaknesses?

He differentiated Penney's operation and posture from those of others:

We have our own pricing and sales promotion policy and in that sense we are indifferent to the competition—that is, we must be eternally alert to what the competition is doing but must never let the competition run our business. We want to run our kind of business and hope it is pleasing to a large market. We don't want a "me too" operation. We want to be distinctive and not copy anyone. The customer separates us from all other stores.

We observe the competition carefully in regard to their quality of merchandise, pricing, and their way of presenting it. We make these observations not to copy the competition but to know it. We also watch their advertising and total public relations program. Public relations is not big in the formal sense but is significant in the behavior of every sales person.

We study the kinds and locations of competitive stores, their philosophy of location, and the kinds of tenants they like to be identified with.

"Indifferent" is a significant word—"indifferent to the competition"—in Batten's remarks above, from the game theory point of view. The player in a non-cooperative economic game has no malefic attitude toward his opponents. In real life we may even find him wishing his competitors well, as an act of social grace. But in playing the non-cooperative game, he is indifferent to their outcomes. He is governed only by how his side may fare, in accordance with his own "individual rationality." This appropriately is in contrast to his concern that suppliers make a profit and that shopping center tenants be compatible—both of which suggest the mutuality of interest that characterizes a cooperative game.

Then he moved to the interactions, non-cooperative and cooperative:

> How will the competition react to your entry into a market? What is the arithmetic on the cost of entry? You have limited, selected strategies and attach numbers to them. What if the worst happens? What would it cost you? We may test a new department in one store. We set it up where the odds are not too favorable, trying to find out what true life is, where the competition is rough and all the odds are not for you. It is a mistake to try five spots where there is no tough competition. The test wouldn't answer how you would do where there is more competition. We test against the best competition.
>
> Let's talk about a specific market. It already has shopping facilities. A new shopping center is going to be built. If we decide to go in, the competition will react. We credit the competition with being aggressive and alert, protecting their vital interest. So we try to determine their capability for reacting. We look at them and the new center. Would the new one be a logical expansion for them, or are they two and one half miles away and not in position to open a new store here?
>
> We like our best competition to be with us in some centers, particularly in a big center, a Sears, a Penney, and a department store to provide shoppers with the opportunity to shop. If there are to be only two major stores, it's better to have a department store plus a Sears, a Ward, or a Penney. But if there are three, it's

better to have one department store and two of the others. The Penney merchandise is not the same as the others. We have more soft goods. Small shops make their leases contingent upon the shopping center getting two or more big ones, for the traffic. We may have to choose between going further into one area to round out our market penetration or going into a new shopping center where it is a question of now or never.

So there is competition for locations and cooperation of a sort in coming together in shopping centers. Once a site is settled upon, however, other uncertainties arise. Batten elaborated:

We have our own strategies. Although we are conscious of the competitors' known capability, we are also aware that they have plans we don't know about. We think what we would do if they did something.

The strategy of many discount stores is to try to locate near a big-name store to feed off its traffic. We're pretty predictable on site locations. The ingredients are not too mysterious. There are advantages in being unpredictable in regard to a loss leader. But we are an open book with regard to space, location of goods, advertising, and past behavior. We see patterns in regard to items, price of pants, etc. We do study surprises. Competition credits you with seasonal knowledge; they don't expect you to be foolishly unpredictable. We can't sell overcoats in the spring. So there are limits on unpredictability. If a store manager is on his toes, he has a line on what the customers like. This will be promoted and it narrows the field again. It doesn't mean you can't surprise the competition. But they can react quickly. They find out what the public is buying and so on. So the initial surprise is good for two or three weeks. The name of the game of merchandising is marketing. It differs from development of a new product or long-range research and development where maybe you can enjoy two to five years advantage by being unpredictable to the competition.

Batten described Penney's strategy of fending off the competition and getting the loyalty of the consumer for the quality and price of its goods over time:

> In our pricing policy we advertise and promote at regular prices. But our policy is competitive and flexible. We will meet local competition. Our analysis would probably show that the first reaction of the competition would be in price. This and how we would in turn react to it would be wrapped into our numbers. It is important to decide what you want to be, and this is justified in the market and not just whimsical. Under our policies we can't come out and say "ten percent off or fifty percent below wholesale." If we get hurt in price competition, we play our own strength harder. We are competitive, anyway, in price. Our policy is for the course of a year. I could say we are competitive without "sales." We have a low price every day. The extreme opposite policy would be to have a sale every day and say, "Here's something at three dollars that is worth five dollars." We think consumers are smarter than that. The consumer is entitled to the best values and prices. I keep coming back to the company, knowing its objectives and what it wants to be. This is the fundamental decision.

WARD

Montgomery Ward, as Batten accurately put it, "knocked itself out of the market" after World War II. No rival, no competitor, had anything to do with it. One man alone, its then chairman Sewell L. Avery, the cantankerous hero of business opposition to President Franklin D. Roosevelt's administration, did the job with one standard-type but erroneous decision after the war. He predicted another great depression and folded Ward's tent in wait for it. Had it come, Ward and not Sears might have been No. 1 merchant of the century, and Avery would have been twice the hero of business.

Ward, like Sears and Penney, is one of the few really traditional American corporate institutions: it was a hundred years old in 1972. First the business was limited to the catalogue for farmers, then, along with Sears but in different locations, it also became in the 1920s a chain of retail merchandise stores. It was No. 2, but close to Sears, with sales that for a long time ran about three fourths of those of the leader. But as noted, their stores did not compete. While Sears went to the cities, Ward went to the farm belt and put hundreds of stores in towns and a few middle-sized cities: Fort Worth, Kansas City, and Detroit. Like Sears, it started with hardware and in time added soft goods. Like Sears and Penney, it had a corporate game model built around central merchandising.

In 1955 the financier Louis E. Wolfson raided Ward in a proxy fight aimed at wresting control from Avery. By then, Avery's bet on a depression was a long-lost cause, much to the advantage of Sears, which ran loose in the new markets without competition from its natural rival. Ward's sales had been static at about $1 billion for ten years while Sears's had tripled to more than $3 billion. Ward showed higher earnings as a percentage of its sales than Sears, but it was profit at the expense of growth. Indeed, Ward was becoming more bank than merchant, with over $300 million in cash and total current assets about level with its net worth. But raiding old companies was not well received in business, even by shareholders. Wolfson lost his bid for control. The struggle, however, resulted in Avery's retirement, and the company was taken over by the man who led the fight against Wolfson, John A. Barr, a lawyer and Ward's vice president and secretary. There was hardly a top merchandise executive left in the company; Avery had fired most of them during the years of contraction and liquidation.

Having come to power in defense of the previous power, Barr began a course of verbal courtesy toward his old mentor. In his first report as chairman he wrote: "For Montgomery Ward & Co., 1955 was a year of progress." Barr did try valiantly to turn the company around. He had about 570 stores, none of which had been rehabilitated since the 1930s; the youngest store in the company was fourteen years old. Barr knew what he had to do, which was to follow Sears into the big markets with new full-line stores. He engaged merchandising men and a brilliant young location theorist, Howard Green, who would have considerable influence on Ward's store strategies for some years. Between 1958 and 1961, Barr started up about sixty new stores, but Ward was not easy to turn around. The 500-odd old stores were a drag on profits, while the new ones took time to pay off. In the sluggish economy of the early 1960s, with disaster for Ward impending, Barr went to look for a Sears man to take over.

That turned out to be Robert E. Brooker, president of Whirlpool Corporation, Sears's largest supplier, which was partly owned by Sears. Brooker had also been a vice president and director of Sears. With these credentials, he was one of a small group of available people with both the corporate experience and talent in mass merchandising that Ward required, and so he had considerable bargaining power and the ability to use it when he was asked to take over Ward. Seldom has the treaty between shareholders and management been more explicitly expressed than in Brooker's arrangement with Ward. Seldom has the influence of the values of management had more explicit effect on the affairs of a corporation than it had on Ward during Brooker's efforts to bring the company back.

Brooker was able to ask for and obtain effective control of the company. He then assembled a new team of experienced mass merchandisers, recruited from several sources outside Ward, notably from Sears. Their talents, too, were special, scarce, and in demand. To persuade them to change their careers and take the risk, he offered them a share, so to speak, in his control. He and his fellow managers pledged themselves to work together along the lines of an agreed-upon mass-merchandising policy during the years it would take to turn the company around. The new management took up key stations in all phases of the business and in effect transplanted the Sears system to Ward.

Brooker very early presented to the board a plan of expansion that contained expectations of raising Ward's earnings per share regularly year by year. He and his team took both cautious and unavoidably risky courses to fulfill these expectations. They played a number of strategies in the merchandise markets, revolving mainly around expanding in old markets and invading new ones. Like all corporate managers, they dealt with the two kinds of uncertainties of games: those in which the information was incomplete but could be approached with the tools of observation and standard analysis; and those involving the counteractions of competitors and of other outsiders that could not be predicted. Eventually, they suffered a serious setback when a conjuncture of events occurred in which both of these types of uncertainties turned out unfavorably at the same time. In 1966 Ward's earnings collapsed again.

This reversal threw Brooker into a new game. With the shareholders unhappy, Ward became a prize candidate for take-over. An overt raid could have opened up a conflict between the values of the stockholders and those of management. Responding to this situation, Brooker drew up a strategic plan with many facets. Owing to the essential importance of his management associates to the operation of the business and their mutual commitments to maintain continuity, Brooker was in a strong position to defeat any rude effort at take-over. But he decided to try to avert the threat by choosing his own partner in a merger. He found that partner in Container Corporation, then a $463-million manufacturer of packaging and paperboard.

In 1970 Brooker discussed with the author how he took over the ailing company, deployed it into new markets, defended his control against take-over, and brought it into a merger with a partner of his choice. His judgments of both Wolfson and Barr were well tempered:

> Wolfson, I think, intended to run the company well . . . Barr brought a lot to the company and kept it alive during a very difficult period. He made the basically sound decision to initiate a program of new stores in new locations . . . But he could not resolve the problem of maintaining profits at the same time. Eventually, to eliminate the cost of new store openings, his management decided to cancel the new-store program. Ward's profits declined badly in 1960. Its earnings per share were $1.07 in 1960, as compared with $2.28 in 1959. And early in 1961 it looked as though earnings per share were going to drop to sixty cents for that year. If that happened, he would have been very vulnerable. So he went about making a sound arrangement and worked a way out for the company.

McDONALD: How did Barr happen to come to you about the problem?

BROOKER: *Early in 1961 Barr went to see Ted Houser, a former chairman of Sears, to ask for recommendations for the top job at Ward. Houser recommended Ed [Edward] Gudeman, who had once been merchandising vice president at Sears, and myself. Since Gudeman was then with the Commerce Department [he was Under Secretary of Commerce in the Kennedy administration], Barr came and talked to me. I had been at Sears from 1944 to 1958 and was then president of Whirlpool, which I helped to organize in 1956 and which, as you know, is a major supplier to Sears.*

Q: So Barr recognized that he needed a Sears man to put Ward on the right track?

A: *Yes. He wasn't a merchandising man and had never thought of himself as one. He knew he had to find someone, attract someone, who knew mass distribution.*

I studied Ward's situation as well as I could from the out-

side and concluded that I could do something constructive with it over a period of time if I had control. When I came into Ward I bought 29,800 shares for one million dollars, a sum that represented about half of my estate. Thus, as probably the largest individual shareholder in the company, my identification from the beginning was with both shareholders and management.

Q: What did you work out with Barr to give you control?

A: *It was expedient for Barr to reorganize the board and transfer power. Before I agreed to come to Ward, Barr and Phil [Philip R.] Clark, who was chairman of Ward's executive committee, agreed that I would have authority in management. And they also agreed that I would name four new board members. The board would be expanded by two and the two eldest men on the board would resign. And there were two others who were both seventy-two and had agreed to retire in five years. One thing I knew was that I had to have a board with marketing experience to whom I could acknowledge any mistakes I might make as we went along. Ed Gudeman became one of our directors when he left the government in 1963.*

Q: When you took over with effective control and a free hand, what was your strategy for Montgomery Ward?

A: *Well, first of all, internally we had to recognize that Ward had been structured for small stores supplied by distribution centers. We had to eliminate the distribution centers and go to the big stores. We also had to reorganize to get away from some department-store concepts that were being practiced at Ward. The big thing here was a new procurement policy, which would be part of a complete mass-merchandising system extending from the suppliers at one end to the customers at the other.*

Externally, I suppose you could say that our strategic situation was the opposite of Sears's. Historically, Ward had been in small towns, and it had not substantially moved into the new markets. Many other competitors had come into these markets, including expanding department stores, discounters, and Penney, which was then going to new full-line stores. We were at a strategic disadvantage in almost every major market. It is very difficult in this business for a latecomer to build up a viable position in a major market. Several advantages go to the one who has been in a market for some time—customer loyalty, volume to carry the load, greater exposure, and so on. We had to pay the price of invasion. We not only had all those old stores to replace, we also had to get into the new big markets with new big stores. We had to do something every year and yet not have such losses.

I should mention here that I found Ward's condition to be even worse than I had thought. The fourth quarter of 1961 came in better than expected, so that earnings per share were $1.13, six cents above the earnings of 1960. But even though I'd studied the figures carefully before I came, there were a lot of things about Ward that I didn't know when I first arrived. The figures weren't that good. The reason that performance had looked good for 1959, in my opinion, was that Ward had lacked a concept of merchandise control—especially a system of aging inventory and writing it off. Ward had a system, but it was not enforced. To get control of our inventory we had to get an internal-audit function into operation. This took time. To have changed it in the short run could have thrown Ward into a loss position. This made matters more difficult but did not alter the basic situation or the general strategical concepts I came in with.

Q: What were the most important decisions you had to make?

A: *In general, the most important decisions are about people. I don't think, by the way, that I spend the majority of my time making decisions. It's the groundwork that takes the time. I have made decisions largely on the policy level, at least in getting agreement on what the policy is to be and who the people should be.*

351

Q: You say the most important decisions are about people. One often hears that said ritualistically. What do you mean by it?

A: *I mean that turning Ward around was not a one-man job. To form the kind of organization that was needed to put the company on its feet I had to bring in a lot of people at all levels, and that involved management commitments. There were probably from a hundred to two hundred men who played a very significant part in the comeback of Montgomery Ward, men experienced in the different phases of the business, of whom twenty or thirty were key individuals. There were some good men already at Ward. But I had to go outside to get many of the people I needed, a good many from Sears. They made a commitment to me to join and stay with the company on the basis of a concept of mass distribution that we agreed to follow. My commitment to them was that we had board support to continue this program and that we could make it on our own.*

You have to understand the unique qualifications of this particular management for overcoming Ward's weakness at that time in mass-merchandising organization and in market position. There's Ed [Edward S.] Donnell, who became president of Ward under the new setup. I brought him over from Sears, where he was group manager of the Los Angeles district. He had marketing experience and knew how to organize metropolitan markets. In Ward he provided the leadership on how large stores should be prototyped and architected the metro-district concept for us. Or take Jim [James] Lutz and Dick [R. L.] Abbott, whom I brought in for merchandising. Lutz had been president of McCrory [Corporation] and he became the top merchandising man here. In the mass-merchandising business, the merchandising vice president is next to the president in rank—his is the key spot in the company, covering buying, merchandising, advertising, display, and catalogue. Dick Abbott, who had been head of a chain of music stores, is now head of our New York office. In the course of developing the merchandising opera-

tion, we also brought in ten or twelve men at the department level. That was enough, because they then became the pace setters who showed the others how. John Marchese, who was assistant to the vice president in charge of factories at Sears and is now head of procurement at Ward, brought three or four men along to work with him in that area. And there were others who had a distinctive role in the new management.

Since Brooker had been vice president for manufacturing at Sears, I asked him whether that experience had served him in any particular way in reorganizing Ward. The merchandising schemes at Sears and Penney, as we have seen, are very like; so was Ward's, with variations. Although Brooker's discussion concerns organizational details, I include it here because of what it reveals concretely about mass merchandising and Brooker's high operating authority. Again we see the corporate game model with cooperative supplier relations at one end and store management by corporate rules at the other end.

BROOKER: *Well, I had a concept of procurement different from Ward's. I was brought up in a company with the basic philosophy that you worked with your sources and had commitments with them. You agreed to take a substantial part of their output and schedule it so that they would get economical operations. You don't ask the manufacturer to gamble on the variables that go into his operation—the cost of raw materials, labor. You expect him to be responsible and efficient, of course, but you give him a base so that he can achieve the efficiency. To do that you have to make contracts with him, and longer-term contracts.*

Under Mr. Avery's system, a buyer wasn't able to make a commitment. He'd talk to a source and ask for a price on twenty thousand units, and then if he didn't need all of them, he had no responsibility to take them because he had no contract. Ward had a lot of good people, but management had never given them the authority to make commitments. When a promotion was planned, a buyer would offer the goods he had available. He could overbuy or underbuy, but he couldn't replenish.

The key to mass merchandising, as I conceive it, is controlling the flow of goods to the market. Mass merchandising is a combination of procurement, promotion, and advertising, or relating catalogue space and pricing requirements, and of retail store operations. There are certain basic items that all our stores have to take. The central buyers determine what these are. The store manager knows he's got to stock a complete assortment of items for every department in his store. A Ward store manager applies the national promotion programs to his local market—he represents the company in that market.

Ward now has about 7,200 sources—less than half the number we once had—and about two hundred of them supply half of all our goods. One major effect is longer production runs, which benefit both the suppliers and ourselves. Take men's work pants. If the buyer tells the manufacturer he's going to need a hundred thousand pairs a year and the manufacturer knows what styles and price lines are needed, he'll be able to run a portion of the order once a month or every six weeks, and that's more efficient. He saves because he is scheduling a larger number of pieces over all, and the quality control is better. We can save a lot in transportation. Hence the real advantage of this type of procurement is its high degree of efficiency.

A notable side effect of this procurement system was that it made it possible to set up our own servicing organization, which is becoming more and more important in hard goods—outboard motors, refrigerators, lawn mowers, and the like. We don't find ourselves having to say, "We can't get that part from the manufacturer." We are also in a better position to set a marketing program. We hold the buyer responsible for the sale of goods. The buyers completely control procurement. If the buyer has to mark an item down to move it through the stores, that depreciation is his responsibility.

Our policy used to be not to be critical if we lost business as a result of lack of inventory. Buyers were criticized only if *they overstocked. So there was a trend toward preventing criticism by not stocking too much. Now we have a performance standard—both ways—for the store and the buyer. Not to have too much or too little. It is quite a responsibility, and it will take years to establish it with the buying organization.*

McDONALD: You mentioned that Ward was at a strategic disadvantage in most major markets. Yet you had to move into those markets, and that was risky. The stakes were high, but your resources were limited. How did you weigh the stakes against your resources?

BROOKER: *A businessman doesn't gamble his company. Maybe in a young, growing company he would, but not one that has eighty thousand shareholders. If failure would take the whole show down, I wouldn't take the chance. We had to make the transition from small stores to large stores without having start-up costs jeopardize earnings. So we had to temper our expansion of stores. You're trying to build a sound basic structure for growth. You want to get a base of good stores, and you want to close your old ones. It is obvious that it costs money to start up a store, but it's an odd fact that it also costs money to close a store. Each small old one you close costs you $30,000 to $40,000 in current expenses— there's always some separation of people, transfers, improvements that haven't been completely written off, accounts that have moved out of town and you can't collect. If you close five hundred stores, that would be $15 million or $20 million; so obviously you've got to phase them out. Both start-up and close-down involve expenses out of earnings—you can afford to go only at a certain rate. When we started, Ward was earning only $16 million. Our resources were limited.*

Q: To get a program of new stores going, you raided Sears for men. The key man here was Donnell. What critical information did he bring over?

A: *The basic concept for big markets—the metro concept—which was centered. . . . That means in a big market you've got to have central management for that market—the same goods in the stores, the same space for them, and the coordinated program of promotion and advertising. We set up a new metro organization with San Diego as a pilot. I had the feeling that only if you pilot something, could you see how it would work for Ward even if you knew how it worked at Sears. And it's easier to expand from.*

Q: Why San Diego?

A: Well, we already had three stores there, each different. Two of them were about 70,000 square feet. The largest was about 130,000 feet. We ran a survey of their inventory stock and found that only one third of it was the same for all three. You can imagine the difficulty in promoting the merchandise of all three. We put an experienced staff into the area and the whole corporate team worked with them on the pilot operation. Ward had been losing money in San Diego before we set up the metro district there in 1962. The year after, San Diego made money and has ever since. We expanded from the pilot model of San Diego. In Fort Worth, for example, we had two stores already and a small one under construction, and another two in Dallas, and we combined those into a metro group. We moved on into other market areas where we had an existing position, and, of course, we also had to move, and with greater difficulty, into areas where we were not established.

Q: With new people coming in and a new structure in mind, how did you go about making an over-all plan?

A: There were also some old Ward men who played a significant role here. Two key men whom I worked with on the plan were Harold Dysart, who was then controller, and Howard Green, Ward's research man, who was expert on store sites. Green and I worked out how fast we could prudently move over all. The programming of store relocations in areas where we already had acceptance was a basic element. This way we'd gain incremental business, which in retailing has a tremendous effect on profits. Once you break even, the plus business is increasingly profitable. Your immediate objective is to build up to the point of increment.

We were able to take all the stores that had been opened, get an experience curve, and apply it to expansion, predicting with some degree of reliability how much it would cost to go one way or another. We found that by relocating an old store that was doing well, that had better than five percent of the market, and that was ranked in the top three in the town, it could be profitable in one year. We had one hundred and ten of these situations in which the new stores could do two and a half times the volume of the old. They had the people, credit, reputation in the town. So by scheduling to reopen these, plus the new stores, plus the metromarket concept, we could maintain a degree of profitability. Howard Green worked out how fast we could move without disturbing earnings. I brought to the board in early 1962 a five-year expansion plan with estimates on how it would affect profits.

Q: How did the competition figure in your calculations?

A: It's useful in this business to think of the competition in categories or kinds of merchandisers, such as department stores, discounters, and the mass-merchandising chains. Today Sears has six to six and a half percent—it may be up to seven percent—of the sales nationally of the kinds of goods we are in. We're under two percent and I think Penney is close to three percent. But the mass merchandisers do not compete nationally. It depends on location. The market shares of the three of us vary a lot from the national averages in individual markets. There is more over-all competition in catalogue sales.

Mass-merchandising techniques are entirely different from techniques of department stores or discount stores. Sears and Ward have about half their business in lines that take professional knowledge to stock the goods. Department stores don't have these people. And the techniques of discounters, I think, are just as different. They do local buying, spot buying, etc., in order to get flexibility—and that doesn't fit our

357

way of doing things. Discounters have done well when they've kept close to their own centers, where they can manage with a lack of system. But as you try to expand, you've got to have a system of national distribution. You have to elect which way you're going to go.

In pricing, of course, we have to be competitive. We shop all the competition and are alert to changes. We keep watch on the credit sales and credit terms of our competitors and the services they offer. When you put your price down, your competitor will meet you. That's not a probability; it's a dead certainty. When you put it up, maybe he will think he has a competitive advantage, unless his costs are high—then he will follow. But going down, you won't be there long alone. Sometimes you can cut prices and hold up sales, if you do it skillfully. But usually if you cut the price on an important item, you won't get a bigger share of the market. Essentially, mass merchandising is planning in advance.

Q: Did a competitor ever retaliate unexpectedly?

A: *One that comes to mind is a saturation test we made in an area with our catalogue. We spent a lot of money mailing catalogues to every family in the area to see how many we could get an order from and would qualify as regulars for our big catalogue. One of our competitors laid a saturation test of its own down on top of ours—increasing its number of circulars on a monthly basis—and destroyed our test.*

The competitor was undoubtedly Sears. Its countermove might seem contrary to the indifference to the welfare of the competition expressed by Batten of J. C. Penney. But it seems plausible to interpret the catalogue countermove against Ward as a strategy which, though punitive, was taken in self-interest. When a corporation plays for position in a market, even at cost to all participants, it is usually for a long-term gain for itself. The incident is obscure, and yet something like it was to happen again, even more disastrously, as we shall see, when Brooker raided Sears for store managers. Brooker himself did not attach too much significance to the catalogue fight, as he made clear when he resumed after the above observation.

BROOKER: *The most important competition, however, is long range. Share of market, of course, is the thing we have to look at. When a market is growing, we try to see how fast Penney and Sears and Kresge are growing. Location is an important element in getting share of market. Competition for locations is basic in this business. Sears was the first to move from the old downtown locations to the perimeters of cities. Ward, starting late and moving largely from towns to metropolitan areas, had to find its locations farther out. Until recently, Sears preferred freestanding stores. Sears was strong enough, especially in credit accounts and good salesmen for specialized products, to go it alone. Today it is coming into shopping centers. We have preferred shopping centers, and so we went ahead of Sears in this respect. So did Penney. Department stores all go into centers.*

If you are going into regional centers in a major market, you can't have a lot of checker playing. You have to have pretty firm convictions to make a decision on a store. Real-estate research can project the growth of a market, but it's not an exact science and there is often an uncertainty about whether the market will build to a certain size in a certain period of time. You usually try to figure out what the competition is doing; it could be wrong to put additional pressure into the market. You could overbuild the market. A normal amount of footage per capita is two and a half to three square feet. When you get up to five square feet, an additional store would be more than a market could absorb. And there's always some uncertainty about whether the people you have running the organization in a market have the ability to put it all together.

Q: What makes you want to join with competitors in a center?

A: *If you're strong, people want to go into a regional*

center with you. Until recently, Sears didn't want to be with us in a center. They didn't want to pull people in for us. But now we've got some muscle. We also go in with Penney and other chains and local department stores. We like to go into a center with two other strong stores, even when they are as competitive with us as Sears and Penney are. The traffic we can draw together is worth more than the business we take from each other.

Q: How do you explore a market area before you invade it?

A: *Take Los Angeles, which became a problem for us. If we're going into Los Angeles, where, say, Sears has twenty stores in a grid, each about ten miles apart, I can be pretty sure that Sears is not going to put another one into that structure. From a practical standpoint, you know you can get customers to go five miles to your store. If Sears has two stores ten miles apart and they put another one in the middle, they'd be transferring some of their own business away from an existing store. So I know that if a center is going up halfway between two of their units they're not likely to put a store in it. We wouldn't expect them to, because if they did, it would tend to diminish their rate of return.*

It is prudent, I think, to expect your major competitors to be sound. I expect them today to be motivated by sound economic practice. From a rational standpoint, given their objectives, there is a limit to what Sears can get. If, in Los Angeles, Sears has from eight to ten percent of the market and if they were given the opportunity to raise it to twelve percent, but in so doing reduce the profitability of the stores now operating, they probably wouldn't consider it. By taking business from their own stores, they would be diminishing their average profit and they'd be taking it away from the most profitable part of their business, which is the incremental business off the top. But if we put a store into the grid, any profit we make is additional. And we know that when we get four percent of a market we can make a highly satisfactory rate of profit.

Q: When you speak of profitability of stores, are you thinking of return on investment?

A: *There's nothing sacred about return on investment. Return on investment can be helpful in comparing the performance of different companies, but in this business it has very little value in operations. If you followed that reasoning far enough, you wouldn't have any stores. And every time you'd close one, your burden would come up—you wouldn't have the base to absorb the burden. I can figure what the return on investment is if I can get sales per square foot. From your square-foot sales, with a standard efficient operation, you know your pretax profit. From your pretax net profit you know what the return on investment will be. If the store is producing $110 of sales per square foot, that tells you what you want to know. The thing is to get the store to produce $110 per square foot. You can't do it for every store, but that's the concept you're based on, not return on investment.*

Q: What was your score card for progress under your plan?

A: *Certain rules of thumb influence a lot of decisions. I am speaking of standards which you can relate, one to the other. Although return on investment is not a useful operating objective, a chief executive has to have a corporate standard of return and he has to know how to make it. If a new store has no prospect of reaching $100 to $125 of business per square foot of selling space, you'd say it does not qualify. In the catalogue you look for sales of $100,000 per page to meet our minimum profit objectives. If delinquencies are over three percent in a market, you don't have control over your collection procedures. If promotional markdowns are too low, you are not being as aggressive as you should be. In a business of this kind there are many such built-in standards for decision.*

Applying the square-foot rule of thumb to our stores, you get this picture of the company. Our average today [1970] is about $80 a square foot—we've brought it up from $60.

Right now, we've still got some old stores that run at $40 to $50 a square foot, and that's pulling us down. Ward still has 233 old stores. We had almost 500 when I came here. Our new stores average $90 a square foot, and as they mature they'll go up. If we can get the average to between $100 and $115, and maintain our margins, we'll be in great shape. Our greatest leverage in improving the company's earnings per share, therefore, is in the maturing of our retail organization—having the right people in the organization and doing the basic things right: service, credit, merchandise, and the image you build, and getting customers' loyalty.

Q: What happened to your earnings per share?

A: The year I joined Ward, you will recall, our earnings per share were $1.13. In the plan of 1962 we expected our earnings per share to grow by roughly fifteen percent a year. That would take us up to about $2.30 a share in 1966. As it happened, we came pretty close to the projection through 1965, but then we ran into unexpected trouble on several fronts and instead of $2.30 we made only $1.24 in 1966 and $1.31 in 1967.

Q: That setback had serious repercussions in the following years. What went wrong?

A: One critical thing was the credit squeeze of 1966. The other was overconfidence in operations. Our plan went reasonably well in the relocation of stores and the development of metro markets where we already had a position of acceptance. The trouble came in metro markets where we were the invaders. Los Angeles and Chicago, for example, were major elements in our slump in corporate profits in 1966 and 1967.

Q: What happened in Los Angeles?

A: After the first three stores, we opened five new stores in Los Angeles in eighteen months. We had to move fast to get choice locations and to reach a level where adver-

tising would pay off. Eight was not enough to make us efficient in that market. At that time we were in the periphery of Los Angeles and didn't have enough stores to advertise profitably in the Los Angeles Times. We committed ourselves to a viable penetration of the market area with eleven stores by 1970 and planned more after that. But by 1966, with a substantial metro complex there, we found the price of invasion was too high. The theory was sound, but the basic mistake was that we just didn't have the muscle to do the job as we planned it. We made the mistake of pushing too fast. Our timing was off. We didn't have the people for the metro organization, and we hadn't yet developed a sufficient group of store managers. The result was that in 1966–67 we were overloaded.

Q: Why didn't you go on raiding Sears's management?

A: *They tightened up on us and we couldn't get the people. We got all we could.*

Q: What happened in Chicago?

A: *We made another mistake in timing there—that's quite clear now. We owned the four Fair stores—standard department stores—in the Chicago market, and we decided we'd convert them to Montgomery Ward stores. We did a two-year study, but we hadn't really realized the magnitude of the job of changing all those people. The department-store people weren't able to function in a mass-merchandising procedure, so it took longer than we had expected. If we were to do it again, I'd do it differently. By training a crew and then bringing it in, you could make the change faster. It would be better to do it that way and take the expense of it before you start operating. But the basic mistake in Chicago and Los Angeles was in deciding that, since we were doing so well on the schedule we'd set up, we could add more on—and it was just too much for us to digest.*

Q: You suggested earlier that your difficulties in 1966 were compounded by the national credit squeeze at that time. Was that an important factor in the trouble?

A: *Yes, the setbacks in Los Angeles and Chicago happened to come at the same time as the credit squeeze, and we had to take an extremely difficult decision on credit. Our financial management had been too confident in relying on short-term borrowing and didn't anticipate the crunch. We had a balance between long- and short-term debt, but we had been expanding rapidly, pushing sales with credit, and we needed to give still more credit to continue expanding. Under our revolving-charge plan, the customer had up to thirty months to pay. We knew that if we cut our terms to twenty-four or eighteen months, our rate of collection of receivables would go up. But the change meant people would have to pay more per month, and so they couldn't buy as much and that would hurt our business. And because of the marginal nature of our business, the incremental aspect at the market level that I have discussed—it would hurt our profits. We had bank lines to cover our commercial paper, but you don't want to use them—they're for one year and basically for protection. When money is scarce and you haven't enough long-term debt and are heavily dependent on short-term, it is prudent not to increase receivables, because that would mean you'd have to borrow more money.*

I had to choose whether to maintain receivables and borrow money or tighten credit terms to customers and lose sales. I consulted several people, and there was a difference of opinion among them on whether we'd squeeze it out if we continued to expand receivables and then we met an economic recession. If we got in trouble, the banks to a degree would have steered the ship. We finally had to use our own judgment on which way to go, and our judgment was that it was better to cut back on credit terms. That subsequently hurt our sales and profits. We were a little too conservative, but at least we were prudent.

These were typical one-sided decisions, except for Sears's reaction to the raiding for store managers. But now we come to decisions with more than one side. I put an extended question to him about the corporate raiding game.

McDONALD: You were in a slump. The prospect of your eventual turnaround was not readily visible. The price of Ward's stock was low. There was a lot of corporate raiding going on, and rumors were circulating that you were a candidate for take-over. What thought did you give to that threat?

BROOKER: *Had we been exposed to a raid during that period, it would have been easy for the stockholders to say that they had expected us to do better and that they wanted a new management. It was impossible to avoid recognizing that we were exposed. It is true that we were behind our planned level of progress, the price of our stock was down, and there were some rumors. Every so often we'd hear that someone was going to make a pass at us, though there was never anyone who approached us directly. This was a problem throughout the business community, and we were no exception.*

You know when you take charge of a company that is in trouble that you may have this problem somewhere along the line. You become most vulnerable when raiders see that you have solved your basic problems and are about to turn around. Some corporate raiders have a feel for a turnaround situation. The art of take-over is to see the prospects of a company before they are recognized in the stock market. That was our problem at that time.

As I thought about it at the time, I could see that some conglomerates, Litton [Industries] and Gulf & Western [Industries], for example, were successful—they convinced managements that it was good to join them. A number of conglomerators—Ling [James Ling of Ling-Temco-Vought], for example—had a sense of timing, had paper, and could buy almost anything. They could borrow to pay cash. But some failed at take-over because they didn't have management [of the target company] in their corner. A raider—as I use the term—tries to divide a company by moving without consulting its management or board.

Q: Would it have been easy for some powerful acquisitor to knock off Montgomery Ward?

A: Not really. We were an inviting prospect, but the management of Montgomery Ward in 1966 and 1967 was not easy prey to anyone. We would have been willing to talk to anyone legitimate if it would have been good for the stockholders. But it would also have to have been good for the management team, because they were under no obligation to stay if the top structure changed. All of them—the twenty or thirty key men—were basically independent people. They didn't have to work at Montgomery Ward. It wasn't a captive management. The people weren't chattels of the company. They were people who had come here, taken the risk, and done well. They'd been successful and could do better in the future and build bigger estates as a result. All this was inherent in the fact that turning Montgomery Ward around was not a one-man job. It was to the shareholders' advantage to have these men running the company.

Most people who are interested in making a take-over want to get the management too. Legitimate people want to arrange an acquisition on a basis that will get management support. If I had been faced with someone who sought management's agreement for a take-over, I would have had to go back to the people I had brought in and see what they wanted to do. That goes back to the commitments I made to them and they made to me at the beginning of my administration. That doesn't mean a tender offer couldn't have won, but if one had come along, we'd have fought it.

Q: How? Did you make a strategic plan?

A: We explored the probabilities of a raid, just like the military, and prepared a good defense. If you are prepared for a raider, his chances for success are only three in ten—the track record is that seven out of ten raids have been unsuccessful. Since the chances are only three in ten, you don't have to worry if you develop strength to meet the raid.

We had a plan all set up—the advertising, the organizational structure. The only worry we had was of somebody's tendering without talking to us first. If they approached us first, we would have had plenty of time to adapt our pro-

gram. It was a good exercise. If you recognize that you have some vulnerability, rather than worry about it, you put your strengths together, make yourself ready to counterattack. You have to have good relations with shareholders to do this and a basically strong, healthy, growing company. But you might be vulnerable for a period of time, and we were.

Q: You resolved the problem in part by merging with a partner of your choice. Was this to gain defensive strength through an increase in size?

A: It is true that increase in size is to some degree a defense against a take-over threat. But our situation gave us other solid reasons to merge with Container Corporation, and there were also other solid reasons on their side. Even before the merger, we were aware that size alone is no barrier to a raider when he is skillful. We also had to have the turnaround.

Q: What interested you particularly in Container Corporation?

A: There were three fundamental reasons that made the merger attractive, in addition to the defensive value of increased size and some compatibility in being together. One was the fact that we were on the road to recovery. When you're in that position, and you still have a low stock price, you know you're attractive to someone who is looking for an acquisition and can afford to pay better than the market price for something he can see in the company that the stockholder hasn't yet seen. Container was exposed also. It had always been a good earner with a low multiple. So we both faced the same threat.

Another reason was that with the acquisition our cash flow would increase. We are allowed to defer some income taxes because of our credit business. With Container's earnings added to ours, we were able to defer considerably more, and that money would be available to either company. The third reason is that we were gaining an experienced top-management man of good age in Leo Schoenhofen [the fifty-

four-year-old chief executive officer of Container Corporation]. Our depth in Ward with top corporate-management experience was one-deep—that isn't very deep. Container was basically one-deep. Now we're two-deep at the Marcor level. That gives us time. There are good people in both companies coming along, but both companies needed time. It takes a period of time in the corporate office to develop a good corporate officer.

Another big advantage, by the way, was that we were both Chicago companies, which meant that Container could keep its base and not have to move people around.

Q: How did you negotiate and reach agreement on the exchange of stock?

A: Obviously, during the period of talking you establish certain criteria that enable you to make an agreeable offer. We wanted to buy at the best price we could and at a ratio that would appeal to Container. But we didn't really have to bargain in the usual sense. We worked out a ratio that they thought was very fair, so there wasn't anything to bargain in it. They tried it out on Al [Albert H.] Gordon, their financial adviser and a member of their board. He gave some practical advice that involved adjusting some of the relationships of the securities but not the ultimate value. In a tax-free merger, more than half of the exchange has to be for equity. For some technical reason, it's not good to have fifty-fifty, so what we wanted was to get no more than forty-nine percent of the Container stock tendered for debentures. Actually we got between forty-one and forty-two percent.

Q: Was your offer near the high end of your range?

A: It was the high end. But we could live with it. We thought we'd be able to handle it.

Q: What in your opinion were the results of the merger?

A: Just taking the market aspect into account, we now have a stronger group of loyal stockholders. And the merger

*has raised the market price—of course, the market also got
new confidence because Ward had re-established itself . . .
And the prospects are very good.*

*On the straight line, Montgomery Ward's rate of growth
will be greater than Container's for five years [from
1970]—after that I think it will be about equal. There's
more room for improvement at Ward. The base is low, you
see. Today we project a sales growth rate for Ward at nine
percent annually compounded for the next five years and an
earnings improvement compounded over the next five years
that is far greater—fourteen percent. The reason for this, as I
have explained earlier, is the maturing of stores, expressed in
high square-foot sales.*

*Marcor is a holding company. Schoenhofen has come into
it, but each company has been able to maintain its own
course. If you want to get a good man, you're going to have
to offer him the top spot in the company, and this had been a
problem in looking around at possible companies. When
Schoenhofen takes over [as chief executive officer of Marcor],
I'll be staying on as chairman of the executive committee,
which between quarterly board meetings determines matters
of policy and is influential in all major capital-investment decisions. I will also be chairman of the nominating committee,
which passes on directors and top management. It's a guarantee that things will go just the way we planned them. That
was the purpose. I don't want to disturb Container and he
doesn't want to disturb Ward. That's the reason Mr. Schoenhofen and I were able to agree.*

Marcor prospered more or less as Brooker expected it to in
the next few years. In fiscal 1974 its sales reached $4 billion,
its earnings $96.7 million, its earnings per share $3.01. Ordinarily, a take-over of a company with such a record, would
hardly be expected, assuming that the stock market put an
appropriate price on the stock. But in that year of extraordinary profits in oil, the Mobil Oil Corporation, employing a
standard take-over strategy, proposed to buy control of Marcor at a premium price in the open market, after quietly

picking up close to 5 percent of the company's stock. To get 51 percent of Marcor's stock, Mobil was prepared to put up about $800 million. And so, after avoiding take-over through all the ailing years, after escaping it by mutual rescue with Container Corporation, and after putting on a high performance in business operations, Brooker and Schoenhofen found themselves in a new one-shot game with the survival of Marcor as an institution at stake. Mobil's move was remarkable in several respects, not the least of which was that it took place at the top of the U.S. corporate world—it helped to place Mobil fifth in rank on *Fortune*'s 500 list, after Exxon, General Motors, Ford, and Texaco. A change of position in the top ten is an event. It raised the question again not just of size, but of social and business standards for take-over which have been unsettled since the conglomerate revolution of the sixties.

13

THE MORGAN BANK:
A MANY-SIDED GAME
WITHIN A ONE-SIDED GAME

The Morgan Guaranty Trust Company of New York—now a subsidiary of J. P. Morgan & Company—met its first crisis of liquidity in 1966. Like any common mortal, Morgan was short of money. To uphold the preeminence of Morgan as banker to corporations, its officers played a game which went to the heart of banking. They played it from a model of their business.

THE PLAYERS

- Morgan Guaranty Trust Company of New York
- Ten thousand corporate customers of the Morgan bank
- The Federal Reserve Board
- Unidentified traders in the money market

It is a rule of the game that a banker's business is normally limited to borrowing short and lending long. This rule follows from the fact that there is one interest rate for short-term borrowings and—usually—a higher rate for a longer term. The banker seeks a profit in the spread. If he can borrow at 6 percent and lend at 7 percent and his costs are less than 1 percent, he's got it made—providing that in the imbalance of time and rates he can maintain a continuous balanced flow of money. Failure to do so has, at times, had dramatic consequences in bank failures and panics, reflected in the homilies "Don't make unsound loans" and "Avoid a run on the bank." Ordinary credit ratings for loans appear to have become satisfactory on the average, though for large customers they differ and the best banks, even the whole money market, can still be stunned by the collapse of a Penn Central—a kind of event common enough to suggest that the banker's art of evaluating corporate games is not highly developed. As for the classic run on the bank, it has been quite well taken care of by federal and state regulation and insurance. Nevertheless, the perpetual central problem of banking remains liquidity. A bank must be to some extent liquid to be able to make a loan. An absence of liquidity defeats the purpose of a bank; worse, it is a sign that crisis impends.

Two such crises, one in 1966 and another in 1969, loomed in the long inflation that began when the monetary cost of the Vietnam war was first expanded without taxation. They were factitious banking crises in the sense that they were engendered and controlled by the Federal Reserve Board, the regulator of the nation's money, in an attempt to control inflation through the instrument of the banks. But they were none the less real for individual banks, even, and especially, for the Morgan Guaranty Trust Company of New York, vintage bank, bank of banks, wholesaler of money, and specialist in lending to corporations. Morgan Guaranty is the last bank one would imagine having liquidity trouble, and certainly, if worst came to worst in the banking system, it would not be the first to—what should one say?—be embarrassed like any one of us? Go under? There was, in fact, talk of panic in Wall Street in 1966, and Morgan did get into enough trouble to cause its president, later chairman, John M. Meyer, Jr., the gray, calm, money-oriented patrician sophisticate one would expect at the head of Morgan, to say that though the fear of panic was overplayed, "an awful lot of people didn't know what it was really like to be a banker until the tightness came along." Even at Morgan a hitch had developed between borrowing short and lending long.

Morgan had an old and, in normal times, unobtrusive pencil-and-paper model of banking, which its officers dusted off in 1966 and put to its severest test. The events of that year also marked the beginning of attempts at Morgan to develop a technically more sophisticated model of its game. But the rudiments of borrowing and lending expressed in the old model brought into view the questions it would have to resolve.

The game. Commercial banking at the retail level does not look much like a game-theoretic game. With millions of small customers on one side and relatively few banks on the other side, the game has been formalized into routines; indeed, retail banking could almost as well be conducted by robots and much of it today is in fact programmed into computers. But if one looks closely at "wholesale" banking, one sees that there is some degree of free choice on either side, interpersonal relations are common, and judgments of value are called for, which robots can't make. Furthermore, the market for large sums of money tends to be occupied by a fairly small number of large traders, especially when money is tight; and large companies typically borrow from a limited number of suppliers of money, if only in the name of administrative efficiency (a variation on the economies of scale common to many industries). In these circumstances, the exchange of money is negotiated and bargained; in short, there is an interactive game here.

The "marrow of banking," to use an expression we shall return to, is a cooperative deal between bank and customer. The customer makes demand deposits at no interest. The bank in return enters into an understanding that it will lend money up to a certain limit to the customer. Both are in the arrangement by consent. Either is free to withdraw—the customer literally to withdraw his demand deposits, the bank to decline to lend or to put obstacles in the way of lending. But these fall-back positions obviously are not worth as much to either of them as the cooperative deal. Two judgments of value in money, one made by the customer, the other by the

373

banker, determine the range of value. Competition—alternative banks, alternative customers—reveals the best deals. A certain amount of bargaining brings a deal to its definite terms.

But the bank also faces the world at large and in this posture takes the one-sided outlook: the bank versus the total environment, including the impersonal money market and the Federal Reserve Board which employs strategies to regulate the conduct of banking on behalf of the nation. Both ways of playing—cooperative and non-cooperative—as we shall see, are linked and played simultaneously. Morgan's model and the way it was employed in the crisis of 1966, as we shall also see, may be understood along these lines.

In the late summer of 1966, when the money men on Wall Street were asking how Morgan would ever make it through the summer and how, if Morgan couldn't, anyone else could, the author visited the famous mound at 23 Wall Street for a few weeks to observe what Morgan was doing. Interest rates were rising; the large money-market banks were squeezed for funds, their time deposits were declining, and they were rationing loans to customers. There was an imminent prospect of the road ending in an actual gap between their lending long and borrowing short. And there was uncertainty about what the Federal Reserve Board would do about it, especially since creating uncertainty was a calculated part of its policy. There was a little history behind it.

It had been a year in which loans expanded enormously. From the middle of 1965 to the middle of 1966, Morgan had expanded its loans by $1 billion, which was an increase of 35 percent; and most of this expansion took place in a brief time in the spring of 1966. The bank had raised the money in various ways, selling certificates of deposits (CDs) which are the bank's IOUs with specific, fairly nearby dates for redemption; increasing its domestic and foreign demand deposits by several hundred million; and selling securities from its portfolio—mainly municipal bonds, on which it took a substantial capital loss. Thus, Morgan played the game at all costs, determinedly meeting its customers' extremely heavy demand for loans. Then a contraction began, in loans, time deposits, and demand deposits, and the value of Morgan's investment portfolio fell below cost. The contraction was accompanied by increasing pressure from the Federal Reserve Board to restrain business loans, which hit Morgan harder than others since the main line of its business was in business loans. All this led to the question of what Morgan could do to meet its obligations and the future loan demand of its customers.

Morgan's monumental style rests in its special relationship with corporations and institutions; it has about ten thousand corporate accounts. It is the fourth-largest bank in the United States in assets and of all banks is probably the largest operator in money markets. It often leads in setting the prime rate of interest. Its operations include trading in government securities (it did about 12 percent of this business in 1966) for its own and customers' accounts and for its correspondent banks and buying, selling, and underwriting state and municipal issues. It is a diversified bank, with an international division and a large trust and investment division. But as it has only a token retail business, it could not grow as fast as Chase Manhattan and First National City banks. It has had to make most of its profit out of the wholesale corporate business, which, as noted, was precisely the kind of business that the Federal Reserve Board wanted to hold down.

Morgan's growth had for some time depended on its time deposits; in the six years before 1966 such deposits had gone up 350 percent while demand deposits almost stood still. These time deposits were mainly negotiable CDs in denominations of $1 million or more. Morgan had always been able to raise money more or less at will by selling its CDs at competitive interest rates. But then the Federal Reserve Board, in December 1965, issued its "Regulation Q," which ruled that rates for CDs could not exceed 5½ percent. This was a kind of price control intended to prevent banks from bidding higher to get more money to make business loans. If the market for money put interest rates for equivalent competing financial paper above the Q ceiling, the banks' own CD paper would become non-competitive and difficult or impossible to sell. That is in fact what happened in 1966. Interest rates went through the Q ceiling. Blocked from borrowing on time deposits, Morgan's officers faced an impasse.

True to form in their non-observance of panic, they studied the rules of the game, including a backward look at how they got where they were in the dynamics of the money market. They traced the large spring 1966 demand for money, which they had failed to predict and which had sent the market rates above the Q ceiling, to an unexpected fiscal action by the United States Treasury. The Treasury one day in the spring had suddenly changed the rules for corporate tax collections, putting corporations on a current basis for delivery of withholding taxes. Corporate treasurers, seeing their ready cash decline, turned to the banks to refill their coffers. That was, anyway, the only rationale Morgan's officers could find to explain the beginning of the uncharted rise in corporate demands for money. It was plausible enough, and as the new tax payments from corporations brought a decline in the federal deficit, it dawned on the Morgan men that the banks had in effect financed the alteration in the federal budget.

The pressure of this demand sent the prime lending rate for money to 5¾ percent, later to 6 percent; and yet the demand for loans continued undeterred. (At that time bankers believed that 6 percent was close to the maximum rate that was "politically acceptable" in the United States.) Savings banks brought their mortgages to commercial banks for money, and life insurance companies came for help when their policy holders exercised their right to borrow at 5 percent (they could easily reinvest it at 6 percent). At midsummer the rising money market, seemingly detached from objective cause and effect, went "psychic."

The consequence of these compounding demands was that bank loans rose faster than deposits. At the same time, since the rates for all competitive commercial paper were above the Q ceiling, the banks as noted could not raise more money by selling CDs. The situation indicated a possible banking crisis along classic lines.

By early August, however, the Federal Reserve Board had still failed in its objective to force corporations to reduce business inventories and otherwise curtail expansion; certainly the higher interest rates were having no such effects. A simple fact of business life then emerged, namely, that rises in interest rates, up to some unknown high point, will not have the effect of curtailing corporate programs. For corporations, in this situation, it is not the cost of money but its availability that matters. And as for individual banks, they were, in the nature of their game, as we shall see, loath to turn away customers of long standing so long as banks could lay their hands on money. Despite the rising rates, business loans continued to rise until mid-August.

Bank loans then at last began to level off as the banks' lendable funds began to dry up. Unable to raise new money with CDs, the banks' time deposits dropped precipitously. The Federal Reserve Board thus was getting results, and by the same token the banks were now in deep trouble. The billions of dollars they had borrowed from investors, mainly corporations, on their CD notes would be coming back for redemption. Hence, the prospect for all banks, and especially for Morgan, that a run-off of deposits combined with the usual seasonal rise in corporate demand for loans for dividends and taxes in mid-September would put more strain on the banks' reserves than they could stand. Morgan was caught between borrowing short and lending long, the banker's nightmare.

At mid-August, Morgan's policy committee of seven top officers met and made some unusual strategic decisions. They got out their model and at that moment played a game in imagination into the autumn, as follows.

The model had two parts. The first part, called "projected flow of funds," described the bank's current demand deposits and the maturing dates of its time deposits; then its loans;

and then a few other items, including its portfolio of long-term securities. The second part, called the "position sheet," described the bank's position in so-called "money-market instruments," a variety of short-term entities which we shall see more of in a moment.

The first part of the model gave essentially a summary description of the rules and the state of the loan-deposit game between the bank and its customers (the securities' portfolio was in there as a backup for loans); that is, it described the limits of the bank's choices.

On the deposit side, the policy committee concluded that it could take some action to get better balances in demand deposits from customers; this was not a standard prediction of the behavior of customers but an evaluation of what could be negotiated. As to time deposits, the committee members as individuals surmised that they could get a good proportion of them renewed with shorter maturity dates. This was based in part on the mutual accommodation expected between borrowers and their traditional lender. But as a committee they concluded that they should assume the worst; that is, that none of their CDs would be renewed but would have to be paid off on maturity.

On the lending side, they surmised as individuals that, contrary to the prevailing view, the corporate borrowing splurge of June and July would have the effect of moderating the usual autumn rise and so reduce some of the pressure. But acting as a committee in the matter of policy, they allowed for the possibility that the seasonal rise in loan demand might take place, with customers coming in to claim the credit to which they were "entitled" by long-standing relationships with the bank. "It may not look too hard for a bank to limit its over-all extensions of credit," said Stuart W. Cragin, chairman of Morgan's credit committee. "In practice, however, a bank must consider the position of credit-worthy customers who have earned some amount of credit by established deposit relationships. This is the marrow of banking."

Thus Morgan had, over-all, two choices. One was to cut its

loans to protect its liquidity. The consequence would be the impairment of its standing relationships with its customers. The other choice was to take extraordinary and costly measures to meet the potential loan demand.

The policy committee chose to meet the demand. They would try to restrain their loans as well as they could by persuasion, but make preparations to meet demands for credit based on "established deposit relationships."

To lend without time deposits would not only be costly; it would also be a test of banking skill. Morgan's managers would have to find new ways to stay liquid. They scoured the far corners of their business, domestic and foreign, for resources that were or could be made liquid, including a transformation of their investment portfolio. The last was accomplished by selling off some of their municipal bonds and converting other municipal bonds and also government bonds from long-term to short-term. On the whole, they took action, on pessimistic assumptions, to establish a position that could ride out the worst that could happen in the months ahead. This was not, of course, the worst conceivable but the worst within practical limits of tolerance. Staying liquid within these limits would ultimately depend on the ability of the bank to maneuver in the day-to-day money market.

Thus, turning to the second part of the model—the position sheet—the policy committee looked at the bank's position over time in the money market. That position would be the ratio of the bank's liquid assets in money (or near-money) and its short-term borrowings. Net borrowings or lendings in the money market involve federal funds (overnight high-interest loans between Federal Reserve banks without collateral), dealer loans, and loans from the Federal Reserve Board. The Board at its discretion makes collateralized loans to banks—as a privilege, not a right—at its so-called "discount window." Such loans, in effect, reduce a bank's reserve requirements; or, one could say, they make up a bank's deficit in reserves. Morgan's net position in these various monies was compared day by day with the bank's short-term holdings (Treasury bonds under eighteen months, short-term municipals, dealer inventory, and various pieces of commercial paper). This balancing act would result in a current average figure, plus or minus, that is, a basic surplus or deficit of liquid resources in hand. For Morgan the figure, of course, would not be random. It was a number set in the first part of the model as a target, and once set, it guided the bank's money-market operators for a period of time. Morgan's money-market department then aimed to strike an average balance corresponding to that number.

The man in charge of this department at Morgan very likely handles more money in the course of a year than any other person in private industry. At this time he was Ralph Leach (later vice chairman of the bank), who, as one might imagine, was another lifelong money-oriented patrician and a virtuoso. His transactions amounted to a billion dollars a day —a volume derived from Morgan's four functions in the money market. Two functions are profit making: acting as a dealer in government bonds and as an underwriter and dealer in municipals. The other two functions represent the bank's internal operations. One of these is performing an advisory service on money-market affairs for the bank's customers, which includes acting as agent for transactions. The other—the maneuvering point in this complex of transactions —is trading for the bank's own account.

That summer, Leach had his target position which, as noted, described in a single number the state of the bank's liquidity. For the critical weeks, the number, of course, was a surplus. He carried a net plus balance of liquid assets for the anticipated loans. In this posture, Morgan's managers waited for the test of actual events.

If the worst happened, Morgan would, on the one hand, be meeting the maximum demand for loans and, on the other hand, liquefying its assets at a loss, borrowing short-term funds at high cost, and appearing as supplicant before the Federal Reserve Board's "discount window" where it would offer its securities and loans as collateral for cash. It can happen that a bank borrows money at a rate higher than it charges for its loans, hoping to make up the difference in the compensating balances (i.e., the customers' demand deposits on which the bank pays no interest). There were, as noted, limits of tolerance on all these things, which had been accounted for in the model. Beyond these limits was "unreality": Morgan would have to put its prime rate for loans up higher than competing rates and in effect be out of the banking business. If the limits of tolerance were approached, Morgan would not go broke or even fail to meet the loan demand. It would simply have little or no earnings to show for being in business. Morgan preferred to risk paying this price to the alternative of denying its customers their normal credit.

Anything beyond the limits of tolerance was unthinkable, except, as one Morgan man put it, "Morgan would not be the first to go."

Some further observations on Morgan's game model can now be made.

At its terminal in the money market, the model was one-sided: Morgan against the whole environment of money, with Leach responding to various chancy events in the market and the strategies of the Federal Reserve Board to maintain the desired liquid surplus.

But imbedded in the first part of the model was a different kind of game, namely, the mutual interactions of Morgan and its customers. Morgan's managers did not have to worry equally about all of its ten thousand corporate accounts. They distinguished, for example, between two kinds of major customers: those with whom they dealt impersonally and those with whom they had valued long-term relationships and dealt with personally.

Their impersonal customers were mainly financial institutions, finance companies (e.g., dealers in government securities), and brokers. These are Wall Street's "sophisticated" traders, oriented to the wide public market for money. The norm of Morgan's relationships with them was understood, if it was ever given a thought, to be that the parties would make whatever deal was mutually profitable at any given moment. If Morgan chose to raise its rates to these customers to avoid making a loan, no harm would come to their future relationships. In a pinch, Morgan could cut off loans to these players and lose nothing but the business at hand, as it in fact did in the late summer of 1966.

But this solution had little merit in Morgan's game with its long-term customers among business corporations. With them Morgan had a continuous relationship of confidence and trust. It was not a rule but it was a norm of the banking business that certain expectations would be met regardless of the exigencies of the moment. Sentiments might be present on either side, but they concerned some unsentimental realities. It is in the nature of the business that bank and customer settle upon a relationship that is beneficial to both. In doing so, they take account of the worth of the customer, the services of the bank, and the like, to reach specific terms for borrowing and lending. The customer places demand deposits in the bank at no interest, which provides the bank with its main lending power. The bank in return provides the customer with a credit upon which he can draw for loans, the amount of which is several times the size of the demand deposit. Loan and deposit each have a measurable value. But in addition to that, over the course of time bank and customer come to put a special value on their historical relationship. The bank also values the long-range potential of any new customer, and on occasion it may court a new customer who represents a way into a new industry. And so they negotiate and bargain and in time become bound by historical ties.

The historical ties create the complication. The game may be visualized by lining up all qualified customers on one side of a page and all qualified banks on the other side. Assume it to be a rule that banks are forbidden to make coalitions of banks (other than certain consortiums to divide large-scale risks) and that the meaningful coalitions are across the market between individual customers and individual banks. Numerous customer-bank pairs are then possible, and customers and banks find some coalitions more beneficial than others. Each looks for the best arrangement (one or more), that is, the coalition that represents the greatest mutual profit in their combined judgment of value. Imagine that the deal is one-shot. All who have found the best one and settled on it are now in the core.

But suppose the circumstances change for a bank or customer and it is now more profitable for one to disappoint the other, even perhaps to seek another partner. One day, for example, in a tight money market, a bank turns down a customer's normal request for a loan; tomorrow, in an easy money market, the customer shops around for another bank. Neither now has trust or confidence in the other. For banks and their impersonal customers mentioned above this is the accepted practice. But for business corporations which are making future plans this adds another contingency—will they be able to get the money when they want it if they have to switch coalitions? Availability of money when they want it looks better to them than a possibly better interest rate or some other advantage.

As for the bank, it, too, would like to know where it stands with the customer in various circumstances.

One way for them to resolve this would be to put a present value on their long-term relationship, so that instead of judging the value of a one-shot game, they would judge the value of a succession of games and arrive at a sum which they would use in determining the one at hand. All sorts of difficulties get in the way of this concept. Looking into the uncertainties of the future, for example, would require numerical probabilities that may not exist or, at best, are hard to see, and risks of commitment that are uninsurable. In sum, it would be difficult to write the contract.

But another solution is possible, namely, Von Neumann and Morgenstern's standard of behavior, in this instance the business norm of the historical lender. It is weaker than a formal contract. It can be revoked, though there are good reasons why it is not likely to be revoked frivolously. This norm is understood to mean that the coalition will be maintained even if one or the other party can do better to leave it for another deal. The price of this stability for the customer is that he will not take advantage of his bank when the bank has difficulties; and the bank on the other hand will not refuse to lend money to the customer even though it may not be convenient or profitable to do so.

In our story, Morgan's crisis of liquidity may be seen as an unexpected situation which put to test the norm of the historical lender. With its corporate business customers Morgan was in the predicament that if it chose not to meet its established commitments, it would weaken if not dissolve the long-standing character of its relationships with those customers. As one Morgan officer put it, if you refuse a loan to one of them, "he will remember it."

But as resolving its problem by adherence to the norm covered numerous accounts, Morgan had more work to do. Its unit managers would attempt to persuade each customer to be modest in his demands for new loans; or persuade him not to draw down on his line of credit but to use it as a backup while selling his own corporate financial paper to a commercial paper dealer. (This suggestion, made by many banks, resulted in the birth of a substantial modern commercial paper market in 1966.) The norm for the customer obliged him to be persuaded to some extent along these lines. The Morgan manager could also point out that the Federal Reserve Board was opposed to the bank's making loans for non-productive purposes (another—regulatory—norm that would hold if all banks subscribed to it, as they well might in view of the discretionary power of the Federal Reserve Board at its "discount window"). But with these qualifications, Morgan had to get ready to pay the price of its solution of the game.

As the actual events went, Morgan did not have to live through the worst of its assumptions. On September 1 the Federal Reserve Board, whose repertoire includes persuasion as well as regulation and money-market operations, relaxed the situation somewhat with a novel turn from traditional practice. It issued a circular offering assistance at the "discount window" to member banks suffering deposit withdrawals. However, it implied that the banks would have to meet two principal conditions: (1) they would have to stop selling municipal bonds from their portfolios and (2) they would have to reduce their loans, especially to business. The opening of the "discount window" somewhat relieved Leach's problem of maintaining a liquid surplus, but the condition that business loans should be reduced was no help to the business bank. Morgan's officers insist that they could have survived, albeit at a cost that would have depleted the bank's earnings, if the seasonal rise in loan demand had materialized in September and none of their CDs had rolled over. But in fact, the month of September passed with no increase in loan demand. As Morgan's officers individually believed, corporations apparently had got enough money in the spring to carry them through their fall dividends and taxes. A proportion of CDs were renewed, the customers, again, accommodating Morgan. For the rest, Morgan borrowed federal funds from member banks of the Federal Reserve and cash from the "discount window"; and so, with the softening of events and relief from the Federal Reserve Board, the camel went through the eye of the needle.

The game was rerun in 1969, with variations including larger magnitudes; but with the lessons of 1966 built into it, Morgan's model worked more smoothly. In 1973 the Federal Reserve Board more or less gave up on using the banks to suppress the expansion of business loans and allowed interest rates to rise to once unthinkable heights, in the hope that at some level of market cost, business would stop bidding for money. High interest rates then paralleled the new high prices for everything.

14

NEGOTIATING POLLUTION:
LARGE COALITIONS ON
SOCIAL ISSUES

On issues of pollution, millions of people may align themselves along a relatively small number of sides, each with similar interests. These sides, some hazy, some clear, become group players in a game, represented by agents or less formal spokesmen. Their struggles are most visible when they seek political coalitions to legislate the issues by majority rule, leaving out dissatisfied groups. But on occasion they attempt to negotiate group interests by the consent of the affected parties, a game that is less visible and less well known, though it has great economic significance for the future. It is a game of coalitions between groups with both common and divergent interests. Its aim: to cut the losses from pollution. Two basic game models, one of a pond, the other of a stream, refine some of the major issues and suggest solutions. An ongoing struggle over oil in Maine brings into focus a representative pollution game in the real world.

Pollution: How do you distribute negative goods in society when there is no market for them? Suppose one thinks about it as a game. Pollution became an active issue in the United States and most industrial nations in the 1960s when a considerable number of players on the receiving end raised the question of their consent. If it had been an inactive game theretofore, one could explain it perhaps as having been resolved in the global enthusiasm for the tradition of industrial creations, qualified by resignation to the consequences in the environment; the dissatisfied raised their voices with only episodic effect from out of the pale. But as the desired goods increased, so did the undesired ones and the sensitivity to them. After a long reign, the old solution—to pollute at will, which the corporate executive usually took to mean pollute or die—became unstable. The dissatisfied groups grew in sufficient number to precipitate a cultural revolution. They overthrew the old standard but could not at the same time raise a new one of equal force. Judgments of the disvalue of pollution came into conflict. Political efforts to obtain legislation that would unseat the polluters and seat the polluted—new rules for a new game—became the quick order of the day. But whatever its merits, law alone would not be enough. For if the political solution were weakly supported by a new social standard or if no underlying core of economic stability based on consent were found, the political solution of the moment would eventually yield to the continuous reordering of coalitions, which is to say it would have little or no stability.

The number of pollution games on earth is infinite, and the energy crisis of the 1970s only sharpens the issues between the conflicting values of industry and the environment. Perhaps one cannot reduce all pollution games to two or three universal kinds, but in matters of air and water, one can see that two—though they are often mixed—are outstanding: the games of the pond and the stream.

Around a pond the polluters and the polluted are typically the same parties. The "pond" is a conception for any situation of that kind: the still air over cities, filled with the chemicals and atomized debris of their residents; the lakes and the oceans (except for their currents); and even in certain respects the band of air around the whole earth.

The stream, on the other hand, is the prevailing winds, and the movement of water through rivers, lakes, and oceans. It has its peculiar dimensions, upstream and downstream, with the polluters upstream depositing their waste on the polluted downstream.

Negotiating pollution around a pond is quite different from negotiating it along a stream. First, look at two game models, one of each, and then at a real game in a proposal to bring oil to the coast of Maine.

THE POND GAME[1]

Ten players surround a pond, each with a factory which needs clean water to operate. Each pollutes with a discharge of dirty water. Let us say money is the measure of value. In their inflow of water, let us say it costs each of them $5 to clean up the mess made by *each* of the others and by himself. Thus, with everyone polluting, each player is paying $50 to get clean water. Collectively they pay $500 to clean their mutual mess in their inflows.

On the other hand, let us say it would cost $10 to clean up the outflow from each factory, that is, $100 for all to stop polluting. The collective diseconomy for their pollution thus is $400. They could save that much if no one polluted.

But suppose for the moment that the players want to play non-cooperatively, each on his own. With such "individual rationality" prevailing, the best strategy for each one, if all others are polluting and can't be persuaded not to, is to pollute. The reasoning is simple: If all others are polluting and I clean up, I pay $45 on the inflow for their pollution and $10 to clean my outflow, for a total of $55, or $5 more than it costs me to join the crowd and pollute.

Surprisingly, perhaps, by the same logic, if all the others stop polluting, my best strategy again is to pollute. For if I clean up, I pay $10 on my outflow plus zero for the others, for a total cost of $10. And if I don't clean up, I pay $5 on my

[1] Adapted from a pond pollution model designed and discussed by Lloyd S. Shapley and Martin Shubik (*The American Economic Review*, Vol. LIX, No. 4, Pt. I, September 1969, 678–84). The adaptation of the pond model and the design of the upstream model that follows reflect discussions with William Lucas in the Center of Applied Mathematics at Cornell University.

inflow plus zero for the others, for a total of $5. Thus I save
$5 by polluting. My pollution in this instance is, of course,
costing the others $5 each for a total social cost of $45 over
and above their outflow clean-up costs—but according to my
principle of individual rationality, I am indifferent to the outcomes of the other players. As noted earlier, such indifference
is a feature of non-cooperative economic games.

So, in sum, if all pollute, I pollute; and if all clean up, I
pollute. I in this case am thinking like everyone, and so, accordingly, we all pollute. How far the results are from the
best that this society of polluters and polluted could obtain
can be seen by comparing them with the results of playing
the game cooperatively.

One could jump immediately to the grand coalition of ten
players which would save their society $400 by cleaning up.
But as more than one coalition is possible, there is something
to be learned by taking them in stages. One player, if he
can't persuade anyone else, as we have seen, would do better
financially to pollute. If two form a coalition it costs them
$10 each to clean up their outflow and $40 each to clean up
the mess of the other eight in their inflow, for a total of $50.
Their cooperative gain: zero.

But if three agree not to pollute their lot improves. They
pay $10 each to clean their outflow and $35 each to clean
their inflow from the seven polluters on the outside, for a
total of $45 each—a saving of $5 each. The outsiders now
pay only $35 each, saving $15 each from the coalition's
clean-up, to which they make no contribution. The members
of a coalition of four pay $40 each (the outsiders $30); five
pay $35 (outsiders $25); six pay $30 (outsiders $20); seven
pay $25 (outsiders $15); eight pay $20 (outsiders $10); nine
pay $15 (the outsider $5); and ten pay $10 each with no
outsiders.

Thus there are increasing returns to scale in the enlarge-
ment of the coalition; each new member contributes more to
it than his predecessors, as more pollution is controlled at its
source and more players benefit from the control. As the

theorists put it, the coalition "can afford to internalize the diseconomy."

One might worry that the last member, or any member, of the coalition could save himself $5 by not cleaning his outflow and paying only to clean his own mess in the inflow. But if he thinks of cheating and assumes the worst about the others—as this model assumes—he sees that they see this too. If the tenth member pollutes and saves $5, so can the ninth, and the eighth, and the seventh, and so on to complete dissolution.

The players in this model negotiate and settle the matter all at once. Since they can imagine the possibilities for defection on the part of anyone, with its consequences, they settle for cooperation in a coalition of ten, which is the best deal for all of them. And since the costs and benefits in the model are symmetrical, the players have no difficulty in dividing the $100 cost equally, $10 each (variations in the costs and benefits to each would, of course, complicate the working out of the solution). The arrangement is stable because no individual or group can upset it with any other offer.

In real life, one would expect a contract with some means of enforcement. And from a social point of view, which is not essential to the above line of reasoning, one can see also that if the society of the game had a standard of behavior against cheating, it would reinforce the straight economic solution.

THE UPSTREAM GAME

Pond and stream make very different pollution games. Suppose the players in the pond model, with the same costs— $5 to clean the inflow of each polluter, $10 to clean each one's own outflow—arrange themselves along a stream, one below the other. Each needs fresh water and each pollutes. Say they are not cooperating. The first player upstream receives fresh water and pollutes the stream for the other nine; the second, for the other eight; and so on, with the following costs for each:

Players	Cost in dollars	
1st	0	
2nd	5	(he cleans only one batch of pollution)
3rd	10	(two batches)
4th	15	(etc.)
5th	20	
6th	25	
7th	30	
8th	35	
9th	40	
10th	45	
Total cost	225	

They should be able to do better than this but they have a problem negotiating who pays for what and what the whole clean-up should cost. The costs described above are what they pay for not cooperating, so no one is going to pay more than that to cooperate. The first player, then, is not going to pay anything, though he could allow others to pay for cleaning his effluent. The second player is not going to pay more than $5—the cost of cleaning up the first player's mess. The third won't pay more than $10, and so on. Now all ten meet to negotiate and play a cooperative game in their minds.

Since the first player is costing the others a total of $45 and has no motive for cleaning his outflow, the other nine could propose to pay him $10 to clean up. Divided equally, it would cost them $1.11 each instead of the $5 each they are paying for his pollution. The same logic would go for the second player, and so it would pay the remaining eight to pay him $1.25 to clean up; seven should pay the third player $1.43—and so on down the line. But when it comes to the last couple of players, the situation changes. The last one won't bother to clean his outflow since it now disappears from the game. (If it didn't, you would have to add more players or give the "wilderness" a value, either of which would change the model.) Nor will the last player pay the second-last one $10 to clean his outflow when he can clean the mess in his inflow for $5. So the second-last player doesn't clean up either.

The negotiation is difficult. Try the concept of equity, which is simpler. Say everyone is responsible to everyone else for clean water. If each cleaned his own effluent, it would cost them $100—but there are a few things in the way of that. The last two players, as noted, don't have to clean up, while the last one pays $5 to clean up the second-last one. So they can knock off $15. The cost of a complete clean-up is not $100 but $85. That much is established. But again, who pays what? The idea of equity is in trouble if eight are paying $10 each while the second-last player pays nothing and the last one pays $5; and they are also in trouble with the rules of the game according to which the first player can't be made to pay anything and the second player can't be made to pay more than $5. Hence, along this line of reasoning, there is no way to divide the $85 fairly among all the players.

Yet if they can find a satisfactory way to distribute the cost, they can make a good deal—the difference between the $225 they are paying and the $85 they could pay, or a net social gain of $140 for cooperating. The description of the game offers no further information on how to narrow matters to a final settlement, but it is possible to lay out some possibilities, as follows:

	FALL-BACK (COST IN DOLLARS TO EACH WITH NO COOPERATIVE DISTRIBUTION)	COST IN DOLLARS TO EACH WITH ONE COOPERATIVE DISTRIBUTION	COST IN DOLLARS TO EACH WITH ANOTHER COOPERATIVE DISTRIBUTION
Players			
1st	0	0	0
2nd	5	5	4
3rd	10	10	8
4th	15	10	12
5th	20	10	11
6th	25	10	10

7th	30	10	10
8th	35	10	10
9th	40	10	10
10th	45	10	10
Total cost	225	85	85

The cooperative distributions above, and any number of others that did not charge any player more than his fall-back cost, would benefit most of the players individually, take nothing from any of them, and give an optimum solution to the pollution problem for this whole society. They are in the "core." But the core, though stable, is somewhat indefinite; as a solution, it offers no further information about the specific way to divide the costs. One could say that the players, having negotiated their way into the core, have agreed to stay there and find some way to settle on the final details of the distribution of costs.

Imagine, now, a trout-fishermen's revolution. All ten players become trout fishermen as well as factory operators (and to simplify matters, let's say they are not fiduciaries beholden to shareholders but owners of their plants). They form a club, one of whose binding ties is the trout fishermen's code against pollution. The costs of clean-up are still the same but the values of the players have changed. Player #1, despite his having his own clean water, might now clean his effluent in obedience to the code. If he lapsed, the others would shun him, even perhaps expel him from the club: the orthodox driving the heretic into line. If he persisted, they might go back to negotiating with him as an outsider and pay him a price for cleaning up.

Likewise, player #9 under the code would clean up, adding $5 to the collective cost, now $90. If the code extended to the wilderness below, as would be likely in this society, player #10 would also clean up, though the benefit would be spread throughout the society. Each member of this society would then be paying a tithe of $10 for global clean-up. The total cost is now $100. It's optimal for the way they value the clear stream. How do they divide the cost? This club might assess each member $10, or it might adopt some other standard for allotting the costs.

THE GAME IN MAINE

The moral, aesthetic, sporting, and pecuniary values of a group of trout fishermen are not too difficult to fathom, but what of a pollution game encompassing an entire state? The relatively undeveloped state of Maine has been offered the prize of oil refineries, and with them the threat of polluting its celebrated sea coast. Since 1967 Maine has not been without an oil-pollution game, with both "pond" and "upstream" aspects, as one oil company after another has proposed building a refinery at one location after another on or near the coast. Because the question is not mainly one of cleaning up existing pollution, of which there is some in spots, but the risk of introducing pollution of large magnitude into harbors and tidal currents, the game has been almost entirely imagined. Yet it has been real enough in interactions of thought, expressed with intense feeling, as it brought into play almost every major economic group in the state. By the mid-1970s oil refining had not yet come to Maine, but the game, or series of games, continued and the players had learned to play it well enough to see the possibility of solutions on terms worked out in coalitions involving such usually polarized parties as oil operators and passionate environmentalists.

First a sketch of the game, the players, and the interests. I call it a "game" in the singular because the people of Maine and their agents attempted to grasp it as a whole, though this whole contains a series of particular games—call them "subgames"—with variations in time, place, and people.

The game was set off when several oil companies made specific proposals to develop deep-water harbors for tankers and build refineries on the state's unspoiled rocky coast. Several groups in Maine stood to benefit, directly or indirectly, from this development. But some other groups could see that their interests were threatened by the possibility of oil spills. The broad problem was reconciling economic development with protection of the environment. A more specific problem was finding a way in which all groups could in some sense be satisfied: by sharing in the benefits of the development, for example, or by getting assurances that damage would be avoided.

One can visualize the Maine coast as running roughly from Kittery at the New Hampshire state line northeastward for about 250 miles as the crow flies, or 2500 miles as the coast zigzags, to Eastport, beyond which lies the Canadian province of New Brunswick. About a sixth of the way along is Portland on Casco Bay—a substantial oil-transfer port which has been proposed as the site of a refinery. About halfway, in Penobscot Bay, is Searsport, which has also been proposed as a site for an oil port and refinery. Still another is Machiasport, about thirty miles from Eastport. There are other harbors along the coast, but these have been the targets.

The principal companies in the game at one time or another and the areas in which they have declared an interest have been as follows:[2]

■ Occidental Petroleum Corporation—originally at Machiasport, then at Eastport.
■ Atlantic Richfield Company—at Machiasport.
■ Maine Clean Fuels (informally associated with Ashland Oil, Incorporated)—at Searsport and Portland.
■ Metropolitan Petroleum Company (a division of Pittston Company)—at Eastport.
■ Gibbs Petroleum Company and a consortium—at Sanford (near Portland).

Although these companies have had in common their interest in oil complexes in Maine, each of them came into the game independently.

[2] Another company, King Resources, is latently in the game in Casco Bay and off shore, but is not dealt with here.

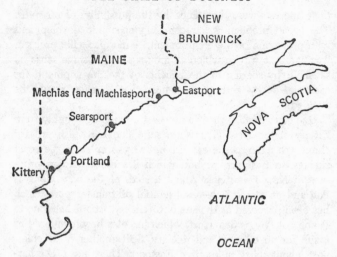

The economic interests in Maine that would be affected by the proposals of the oil companies crystallized into a number of broad sets of participants.

First, there were those who could somehow gain from it:

■ Local businessmen and bankers, whose opportunities have been limited by Maine's relatively stagnant economy.

■ Industries throughout Maine that would gain business from oil complexes; these include the utilities, construction companies, and Maine's two railroads, the Bangor & Aroostook and Maine Central. These groups would benefit from the construction work and the shipment of oil products and in some cases would also benefit from increases in the value of their properties.

■ All the industries in the state that want a nearby source of fuel.

■ The unemployed and underemployed residents, who would benefit from jobs created by new industry.

■ All the residents of Maine as taxpayers, who want new industry to raise the state's low tax base.

Second, there are those who have nothing to gain and perhaps much to lose:

■ The environmentalists, who see in oil the potential for sullying if not destroying the natural beauty of the Maine coast.

■ The coastal tourist industry, which depends upon the preservation of that beauty.

■ Coastal property owners, who see the value of their property threatened by oil.

■ Citizens of some of Maine's local communities, who are apprehensive about changes in the character of their communities that might result from the increasing industrialization.

■ Those industries in the state that are now relying on cheap labor and would be threatened by competition from the better-paying oil business.

■ Lobstermen, clam diggers, and other sea and shore fishermen, who are convinced that oil and fish don't mix and who fear that oil spills will destroy their livelihood —and way of life.

Third, there are oil companies already doing business in Maine, principally distributors and the owner-operators of a pipeline from Portland to Montreal, which is fed by tankers from abroad. These are American, Chevron, Cities Service, Getty, Gulf, Exxon, Mobil, Shell, Sun, and Texaco.

The game owes its origin in part to the immutable circumstances that Maine possesses virtually the only natural harbors in the eastern United States with water a hundred or more feet deep. This resource had no special industrial value in this century until a few years ago, when oil tankers began to outgrow such traditional harbors as those in upper Delaware Bay. Of the tankers on order or under construction in the early 1970s, 85 percent were ships of more than 200,000 tons. Ships of 300,000 tons were already in service and larger ones were forthcoming. A number of different ports on the coast of Maine would be capable of receiving these mammoth ships, whereas no port elsewhere in the East could dock a tanker of over 80,000 tons.

What gave force to the worry about tankers and refineries is the remarkable character of the Maine coast—an area almost as vivid in the national imagination as the Grand Canyon and Yellowstone National Park, and even more prized than these wonders by generations of artists and writers. Although the coast above Portland is only a few hours' drive from centers of eastern population, the industrial revolution has as yet scarcely reached it. The danger of an oil spill from a supertanker is a nightmare to state-of-Mainers: the ravages of catastrophic spills around the world have been shown repeatedly on Maine's television sets, and still photographs of disasters are furnished on call by environmental organizations.

But several opposing forces also bear upon the game. First, Maine is a relatively poor state, with an economy well below the national average. It is heavily dependent on lumber, paper, shoes, farming, fish, and tourism, industries that on the whole—excepting tourism—offer little promise of expansion. The state has no special love for the oil business, but oil has offered the only immediate prospect of a substantial new industry. Governor Kenneth M. Curtis in 1970 put the case for new industry forcefully: "Right now 7.6 percent of the population of Maine are unemployed. In Washington County it's 12.7 percent. You can't sustain rates like that, and an excessive number of our people are underemployed besides. That erodes your tax dollar. You can't plow the roads, keep the schools open. Without tax money, how are you going to clean up the environmental damage that's been done and that will occur in the future? A lot of those who oppose oil projects in Maine are people from other states who made their money polluting other states and now they've come here for serenity. The only answer for Maine is to try to develop industry that's compatible with the environment."

One other major force was also at work. New Englanders have long been dissatisfied with the price they pay for oil products. They contend—though it is disputed—that whatever this price is for the nation at large, they pay more, owing to regional discrimination. So they want New England refineries, which would require the importing of crude oil. When there were quotas on imported oil—a rule of the game at its beginning—they wanted them either lifted or shared.

And so it is not surprising that preliminaries of the game began in Washington, D.C. On September 29, 1967, Senator Edmund S. Muskie of Maine wrote a "Dear Stew" letter to Interior Secretary Stewart L. Udall, which began as follows: "Jack Evans is delivering this letter, together with a letter from Governor Curtis and a memorandum outlining a proposal for a deepwater port and industrial complex in the area of Machias [adjacent to Machiasport], Maine."

John K. Evans, an independent oil promoter, was then operating in the Northeast. The "deepwater port and industrial complex" were his ideas and finding an oil company to implement them was now his mission. Udall was the man to see because, as Secretary of the Interior, he presided over the allocation of oil-import quotas, which were considered essential to both the port and the refinery. Machias is a small town in Washington County at the northeastern tip of the United States. Its fine harbor made it a thriving port in the nineteenth century, but it has long been quiet except for a few skiffs and lobster boats. The whole county had been officially designated a "depressed area" by the Commerce Department's Economic Development Administration.

Senator Muskie's letter went on to argue briefly for Evans' project on the grounds of economic need. He said that the region was "suffering from severe economic dislocation and poverty" and closed with a plea: "I hope it will be possible for the Department to use the authority available to it to permit the location of such a facility in the continental United States." Governor Curtis' accompanying letter briefly set forth a similar argument for assistance in the economic development of Maine. The notion of combining a request for an import quota with a plea about the economic needs of a region did not originate in Maine. Udall had earlier indicated that he would look favorably on such applications, which had some precedents—for example, Phillips Petroleum had got a quota so that it could build a refinery in Puerto Rico.

About eight months later, in June 1968, the federal government received a second ambitious request from Maine. The Maine Port Authority applied to the Foreign Trade Zone Board in the Department of Commerce for a zone in the Machias area; the authority had an agreement with Evans giving him the right to operate in the zone, in which there would be an oil refinery with a capacity for refining 300,000 barrels of crude a day and a deepwater terminal. Foreign trade zones have a unique legal status. They are foreign territory so far as customs are concerned and thus can receive raw materials without having to respect any quota or pay any duty. Only when goods are "imported" from a zone into the United States are they subject to any quotas or other restrictions. A zone had another advantage from the point of view of the state: as landlord, the state would have complete control over decisions affecting the environment.

Two requests had now emanated from Maine: one for an oil import quota and one for a foreign trade zone. At about the same time, Evans also submitted to Udall a "definitive plan" tying the two together. He requested a special authorization to ship 300,000 barrels a day of foreign crude into the zone. He also requested a quota that would let him ship 100,000 barrels a day of refined product *out* of the zone to U.S. markets: 90 percent of this was to be residential heating oil, 10 percent gasoline. The other 200,000 barrels of crude could either be made into residual fuel, which is used industrially, and shipped to U.S. markets since it is exempt from the quota, or it could be refined into some other kind of petroleum product and shipped abroad. The plan was designed to provide New England with industrial fuel and residential heating oil at a price lower than it traditionally paid. The governors of the six New England states immediately got behind the project and declared it vital to the whole region.

An oil refinery almost invariably results in the building of a nearby petrochemical complex, and the Evans plan took note of this prospect. Indeed, it looked forward to the associated development of ore-reduction plants, pulp and paper mills, and ship-building in the Machias area.

The plan also required an operating oil company, and Evans found one in Occidental, which bought out his interest. The company under its spirited chief, Dr. Armand Hammer, had two years earlier made a rich strike in low-sulfur oil in Libya. To obtain an outlet for it, he had bought the European refining and marketing organization of Signal Oil & Gas Company. But Hammer had no U.S. refinery and no quota tickets, and so he had a good reason to seek a deal that would help him get Libyan oil into the United States. From Hammer's point of view, the Evans plan was just such a deal, and it looked like a bonanza. At the time, quota tickets were worth about $1.30 a barrel—the difference then between world prices and protected domestic prices. The return on the investment involved in refining 100,000 barrels a day would be very high, and the move into consumer petroleum products would make Occidental a new oil power on the East Coast.

Occidental emphasized repeatedly that the economic benefits would be widely shared. They included new and higher-paid jobs and production of low-cost and low-sulfur fuel. And, recognizing that environmental interests would be involved, Occidental emphasized that its production of low-sulfur fuel would help fight pollution of the air. The company also committed itself to contribute $7,300,000 a year (20 cents a barrel on the daily quota of 100,000) to an independent marine-resources research fund to serve the interests of New England's marine industries, coastal residents, and environmentalists.

Many of the big oil companies, which saw Occidental's bid as a serious breach in the quota system, fought it from the beginning in Washington. They took their case to the White House, asking President Johnson to turn down the proposal. With pressures from the industry on one side and pressures from New England on the other, Johnson cheerfully let the issue go over to the new Administration. But President Nixon did not move rapidly either. Instead, he awaited the report of his oil task force, appointed in March 1969 and charged with reviewing the whole import program. The task force did not report until February 1970, and when it did, the President overrode its recommendations (a majority had favored ending the quota system and replacing it with a tariff on oil). Thereafter he took no action on the requests by Occidental and the state of Maine for a zone and quota. Hammer's Machias project remained on ice.

Meanwhile, other strong oil companies came in. Atlantic Richfield, in July 1969, announced that it had taken options on land in the Machias area and had tentative plans to build a 100,000-barrel-a-day refinery. The company requested neither a zone nor a quota and so did not have to wait upon the decisions of higher powers, as Occidental did.

Atlantic Richfield's primary concern appeared to be the Alaskan oil that it and Humble (Exxon) had struck, which it wanted to bring to the East Coast. The company viewed the Machias area as the prospective site of a new refinery using some combination of regular domestic, Alaskan, and foreign crude and serving the New England and other eastern markets. After taking options on a refinery site, the company further demonstrated that it meant business in Maine when, in August 1969, it joined with Humble in backing the experimental voyage of the icebreaking tanker S.S. *Manhattan* through the Northwest Passage. The voyage showed that it was in fact possible to bring oil from Alaska to the East Coast by sea, though whether it was practical remained uncertain.

Metropolitan Petroleum Company, a division of Pittston, also announced early in 1969 that it was "actively engaged in studying and planning for its own refinery" and that it owned "a deepwater site on the East Coast which can serve its domestic and Canadian markets." The site was at Eastport and there Metropolitan bided its time.

After these moves, the groups that would be affected by oil projects began to perceive their various and conflicting interests, and the game over the environment began to take shape.

The groups most directly touched by the environmental issue in Maine were the fishing industry (estimates of its annual volume run up to $100 million), the tourist industry (a few hundred million dollars), and coastal property owners (the market value of whose property may be in the billions of dollars). Although Machias lies about fifty miles east of the principal summer-resident areas, the prospect of any oil spill there was viewed as a threat because it is considered "upstream"—the tidal currents run westward from Machias toward Portland, even, fishermen say, to Cape Cod (the prevailing winds are the reverse). The concern of these groups about oil spills at this time was reaching a peak. The *Torrey Canyon* accident off the southwest coast of England in March 1967 was at first regarded as a freak; but in 1968–70 there was a succession of catastrophes—in the Santa Barbara channel, on the Gulf Coast, and off Nova Scotia, where the breakup of the tanker *Arrow* brought the issue close to home for state-of-Mainers. With each report of a major spill anywhere in the world, a shudder ran down the Maine coast. What Mainers feared would come before their eyes in 1972 when the tanker *Tamano* struck a ledge in Casco Bay and spilled about 100,000 gallons of fuel oil.

The Maine Lobstermen's Association had about 600 members. Its leader, Ossie Beal, who lived on Beals Island, a few miles by sea southwest of Machias Bay, was the only official spokesman, but a forceful one, for about 6,000 independent lobstermen on the Maine coast. The association came out actively against the Machias-area projects as a threat to their livelihood and, incidentally, to that of clam and sea-worm diggers, shrimp fishermen, and related interests. Lobstermen, reputed to be about the most independent breed of businessmen in the United States, are a power in Maine.

The coast of Maine, along with the perimeters of the state's 1,200 islands, is almost all privately owned. A lot of it belongs to out-of-state summer residents; the proportion is especially high in the choice areas around Penobscot Bay and Frenchman Bay. These property owners are overwhelmingly opposed to the oil industry's coming to Maine. And it is an established doctrine in Maine that the summer residents, though they have no vote, possess enormous strategic power within the state—in part because so many of them are influential businessmen to begin with, in part because they are substantial taxpayers in Maine, and in part because their economic interests are interrelated with those of so many others along the coast.

Like the lobstermen, summer residents feel that they have nothing to gain and a lot to lose from oil. But many of them have different values from the lobstermen: the very presence of supertankers and a refinery would "pollute" their vision of a summer haven—even if there were clean air and no spills. As one state-of-Mainer put it, "Oil millionaires don't want refineries in their back yards."

Coastal residents give substantial help to environmentalist organizations. More than a hundred such groups are affiliated with the Natural Resources Council of Maine, which, not surprisingly came out in mid-1969 against oil-industry operations on the coast. Although some members of these organizations are intransigent, many have been feeling their way toward compromise. Legislation they have helped draft implied a willingness to come to terms with the forces of economic development.

At the time the first oil proposals were made in 1968, Maine had no effective laws that would restrict or control oil development in order to protect the environment. Indeed, the leaders of the state, so renowned for its natural beauty, theretofore had shown little or no interest in the social cost of industrial development. The state didn't get much of such development after its once great shipbuilding industry declined to its present modest estate. But what Maine got—paper mills along its rivers, for example—it allowed to pollute freely. Its seacoast survived in a natural state by default. No heavy industry saw any way to exploit the coast—except at Portland—until the oil men, with big tankers in mind, recently saw the prospects in deep water and available land.

An unprecedented thing then happened at the capital in Augusta. The generally conservative Maine legislature in 1970 unanimously passed two of the severest environmental laws in the nation; and Governor Curtis, in striking contrast to his earlier role in the Evans proposal, became one of the leaders in establishing the values expressed in the new laws.

With one of these the legislature created an independent State Environmental Improvement Commission, now the Board of Environmental Protection (BEP), to review and license sites for large development projects. When a company now selects a site for an industrial plant, it must apply to this regulatory agency for a permit before it can break ground. But the agency was not set above the battle. Appointed to it were representatives of both industrial and conservationist forces.

In addition to this site act, designed to minimize environmental damage, the legislature passed an Oil Conveyance Act, which required payments for any damage that occurs when oil is brought in by ship. When those responsible for spillage cannot be caught—it isn't always easy to catch tankers that spill oil—the damage becomes the responsibility of the terminal operators. The latter must now pay a conveyance tax of one-half cent on each barrel of incoming oil; the receipts will go to build and maintain a $4-million fund, which is to be spent on research, cleaning up oil spills, and paying damages. Like the site act, the law was promoted by Governor Curtis, supported by Senator Muskie, and passed overwhelmingly with bipartisan support.

Although this "oil-handling law," as it is commonly called, was aimed at proposed new ports, it also applied to existing oil-transfer operations at Portland. That city, it should be noted, is the third-largest crude-oil port on the east coast, owing mainly to its being a terminus of the Montreal pipeline. One meaning of the Oil Conveyance Act was that Maine residents were now refusing to carry the risk of this vast transfer of oil to Montreal. They were shifting the risk to the big oil companies.

405

The ten oil companies doing business at Portland, which, as noted, included most of the largest in the nation, reacted by joining to sue the state of Maine; they argued that the law was unconstitutional. (For example, the complaint charged that the half-cent-per-gallon conveyance tax was really a tariff and thus the prerogative of the federal government.) They saw the Oil Conveyance Act as a precedent that might be followed in other states and lead to a vast and, for them, undesirable reallocation of the social costs of oil pollution.

Important as it was in its potential consequences in Maine, the struggle with the major oil companies at Portland was off to the side of the issue of opening new oil ports with refineries along the coast. Suffice it to say here that the Oil Conveyance Act was upheld in the courts of Maine and in the U. S. Supreme Court. Whether it will have consequences elsewhere remains to be seen.

The first important oil proposal to come up for site approval under the new law had, it seems, little chance for success. An oil-promotion company with some import rights, Maine Clean Fuels, after being rebuffed by the town of South Portland, applied to build a refinery and deepwater port for large tankers at Searsport, in Penobscot Bay, the heart of tourism and recreation on the Maine coast and a special retreat for rich eastern families for more than a century. The hearings at Searsport, however, exhibited some of the issues and alignments that could be expected wherever the game broke out. The oil company set forth among its arguments the usual expected economic benefits and some extras such as a sewage-disposal operation for the town of Searsport, a technology for controlling oil spills, and the production of low-sulfur fuel. It was supported by a railroad company with a terminal at the site, other businessmen, and by the town fathers. Any town that got a big new oil refinery got a dazzling break in property taxes and a prospect of growth in general business as side-effect bonuses which would appear to yield a net gain even after its payment for new roads and utilities, schools, fire and police protection, and other services were taken into account.

But the counterforces were also strong in number and arguments. Nearby towns saw themselves getting the burdens of providing new services without the tax or other benefits. Doubt was raised that many of the present residents of the area were qualified to get the construction or refinery jobs. Lobstermen and fishermen saw operational disaster in normal oil spillage, apart from the risk of a major spill. People in the hotel, recreation, and tourist businesses talked of the incompatibility of oil and water. And, of course, coastal residents and environmentalists overwhelmingly opposed the project for obvious reasons.

After heated, placarded, yet fairly decorous local hearings, the site commission rejected the proposal, but this outcome only proved what had been widely surmised, namely, that an oil project could not buck the center of the Maine coast.

It became apparent, too, however, that many Mainers were of divided mind on the oil issue. A businessman, for example, might want oil for economic growth, be a member of the Audubon Society, and own a cottage on the shore. Groups as well as individuals might have divided interests. Typically, the groups that would benefit from oil were already benefiting in some measure from those "coastal groups"—that is, from fishermen, tourism entrepreneurs, and property owners—on whom the risk of loss might be imposed. A few interests stood to gain from oil regardless of what happened to the others; but many, for example, local businessmen and bankers, stood to lose on balance if the coastal interests suffered a substantial loss. The latter could expect to gain from oil only if some reduction in risk and some provision for compensation were given to the potential losers. Property owners—in land, houses, and business—had both monetary and aesthetic interests, which were often tied together. The rich could be expected to pay substantially to avoid oil, not just because they owned property but because they were part of the community and its way of life which was inseparable from its pastoral setting of land, water, woods, air, and sky.

The large number of different interests with cross representation made it difficult to identify the groups and their interrelationships. For the game to get anywhere the players would have to be grouped into smaller numbers and the issues would have to be more sharply joined. Furthermore, the physical area of the game was so large that it needed a smaller arena where the players could come together to discuss the questions and perhaps negotiate. And most difficult of all, the mixture of monetary, ecological, and aesthetic values, complicated by the problem of the risk of an oil spill, needed some sort of common measure. A cooperative game cannot get far without a sense of the worth of the potential coalitions that could form to attempt to resolve it.

The Maine legislature had gone a long way toward narrowing the game with environmental laws, which expressed the minimum standards of the environmentalists while still allowing the forces of economic growth to proceed. But the site-approval law put oil on a case-by-case basis with the prospect of an endless series of localized subgames no one of which would resolve the general issue of what was the best outcome for the whole state.

Conceptually, one could of course get a drastic state-wide simplification of the million or so players—individuals, corporations, and groups, strategic and non-strategic—by dividing them into three sets: those who quite clearly expect to make a net gain from oil; those who expect only a net loss from it; and those who have straddled interests.[3] Members of the first group, seeing a profit directly or indirectly in oil, would have to offer something positive to members of the other groups to bring coalitions with them into being. The second group (lobstermen, fishermen, coastal residents, environmentalists)

---

[3] One could add a fourth group with no strong interest, though its economic role as a group would be vague. Disinterested individuals, however, would be urged to perceive or adopt an interest, and their sympathies would be important politically, especially in voting.

would have to yield something to the same end. The alignments of the third group would be influenced by these offers, and it would perhaps make some offers of its own. Still to perceive the game and find their way through the maze of potential subcoalitions they needed something more.

It is a remarkable fact in keeping with the legendary wit and wisdom of Mainers that they found a way to meet approximately the severe requirements for an intelligible cooperative game. Governor Curtis in late 1971 put together a "task force" to study the subject of energy, heavy industry, and the Maine coast and to make proposals for policy. He made the usual plea for impartiality, but did not make the appointments that are usually made to such bodies. Instead of calling upon mainly disinterested professionals, he gathered together twenty-six influential individuals, most of whose backgrounds or positions suggested that they could represent the concrete economic interests of heavy industry, transportation, banking, public utilities, trade unions, lobstermen and other fishermen, taxpayers, coastal residents, and the most effective environmental groups in the state. And to these he added a number of key people in related government operations and leading members of the state legislature. In sum, the governor provided a place for the game and brought in real players. He put them literally in one room and let them play the game.

After eight months the task force players and their staff set forth their resolution of the game. They expressed it tantalizingly in a grand coalition on most, but not quite all, of the issues.

The members of the task force had gone at their business in a most orderly cooperative way by coming to an agreement on their alternatives. Starting with the rule of the site law, which stated that *unrestricted* heavy industry—meaning mainly oil at this time—would not be permitted on the Maine coast, they saw three choices open to them.

One choice was to continue to review projects case by case in accordance with the site law (to which they might add

409

improvements in the criteria for judging the appropriateness of sites).

The second was to allow no further development of heavy industry on the coast. This would leave the coast to its prevailing economic development, mainly in the fields of fishing, tourism, vacation homes, recreation, residence, and a sprinkling of light industry, together with some shipbuilding and oil-transfer operations at Portland.

The third was to place heavy industry in one or two zones on the coast. The limit of at most two such zones was fairly natural: no one could imagine enough heavy industry coming in to occupy more than two zones.

They looked at the case-by-case alternative and noted its benefits: flexibility and the dispersal of polluters, population, and employment. They also noted, on the other hand, that it created speculation and uncertainty and prevented the exercise of foresight. They saw no joint benefit in this alternative and rejected it.

Then they considered the question of barring heavy industry altogether from the coast, except what was already there. They agreed that this would bring the least change in the future state of affairs, but they forecast a sharp increase in tourism, recreation, and second-home development (that was before the 1974 energy crisis), more fishing and aquaculture if these were fostered, and a moderate development of retail business and consumer services. They noted that tourism brought its own severe pollution in the forms of traffic congestion and local sewage, plus a good deal of profitless activity (the one-day tourist and the camper). Tourism was on the whole a low-profit business, not to be disdained but not to be relied upon for substantial improvement in the economic level of many groups of Mainers. Light industry and research work were most welcome but probably would be attracted more to the inland transportation arteries than to the coast. Many coastal groups preferred to exclude heavy industry, but as this alternative brought little benefit to others, the members of the task force collectively rejected it.

The third alternative—to set up one or two zones for heavy

industry on the coast—offered the prospect of new benefits: good jobs, tax revenues, and products of high value and profitability, with ecological and social costs measured and controlled. The attention of the members of the task force centered upon this choice for its possibilities of trade-offs between the values of the different groups. A maximum of two zones left 98 percent of the coast free of oil operations, thereby satisfying to that extent the coastal groups while also satisfying those looking for economic development.

They all agreed to adopt this alternative.

The question then was whether to create one or two zones.

They decided with apparent unanimity in favor of two zones, one around Portland, the other far out northeast around Machias. Both had deepwater harbors. Portland was already a fairly well-developed industrial center which could take much more development. The Machias area was in dire need of economic development.

Unanimous agreement went no further.

The majority of the members of the task force concluded that oil should be excluded from the Machias zone "until Maine has greater reason to believe that spillage can be prevented and contained." The reasoning behind this concerned not only the pollution of Machias Bay and tidal currents that run southwestward along the coast, but also the fact that Machias is too far distant to justify a pipeline to take refinery products to the New England market. They would need to be shipped by tanker and barge along the coast. Oil, therefore, said the majority, should be limited to the Portland zone which could economically reach northern New England markets by pipeline.

A "substantial minority" disagreed. They preferred to make the Machias zone eligible for all heavy industry including oil.

Thus the game hung in the balance with dissatisfied groups on both sides.

The task force was not, of course, intended to be a politically effective body like a legislature or regulatory agency. Its voting settled nothing. Nor, as an economic body, was it empowered to write contracts. Yet its members played a significant game in what they revealed about the actual and potential alignments in the state. As real players they made quite thorough analyses, tested their values individually and collectively, and reached both true agreements and a true impasse.

Their official report did not reveal the positions taken by individuals or groups, but unofficial reports from the inside indicated there were few surprises. Arguments were not just exhortations but exchanges of information; and the players took positions corresponding to their interests—no one went against his affiliation. They sought agreements in a mutual interaction. In brief, they acted as they would in a typical large-scale economic negotiation. But in the final split over oil in the proposed Machias zone, the more or less disinterested ones provided the votes that created a majority.

No simple connection can be made between this oil-pollution game and the upstream model described and played earlier in this chapter. The values in the model were reduced to simple money; the costs of pollution and cleanup, and the benefits, were standardized and fully known to all the players. In Maine, the values were mixed, and a medium for transferring them between the groups was not evident. The costs and benefits were not fully or firmly known, and as noted they were complicated by the uncertainties of risk.

The game in Maine, however, had some striking similarities to the model. The players came down to small enough numbers to be manageable. The issues became quite clear to all. The coast, like the stream, had tidal pollution with its peculiar problems for the first, middle, and end players (though there was contention about the facts here). And in Maine the players found a way to combine monetary, ecological, aesthetic, and risk values in a common measure of sorts: they got down to trading with two types of heavy industry (oil and other) and locations.

The potential sources of oil pollution on the Maine coast,

with their associated players, in downstream order, emerged as follows:

1. Machias zone groups.
2. Machias-to-Portland groups.
3. Portland groups.

A polluting Machias zone would pollute itself at a cost presumed to be less than the value of its production of desirable goods. And it could also send its pollution to the players downstream—with or without their consent, depending on the outcome of the game.

For the groups between Machias and Portland, the cost of polluting themselves was greater, in their values, than the benefits of producing desirable goods like oil products.

The Portland zone could pollute itself in some measure (the measure perhaps of its prevailing pollution), with a net benefit and would further pollute little in Maine below the zone, if only because it was close to the state line. Global environmentalists who worried about polluting New Hampshire and other areas downstream were offered a pipeline that kept the outgoing oil products off the seas.

Thus the problem of the polluter furthest downstream in Maine was resolved so far as his own actions were concerned.

The middle area, all agreed, would be closed to heavy industry, hence to industrial pollution. The industry groups yielded the value of economic development in this area, in exchange for heavy industry in the zone at Machias.

To Machias, furthest upstream, they allotted heavy industry because the economic development groups wanted it and because there was little opposition from local groups, owing to moderate tourism and economic depression; indeed, the local population was prepared to welcome industry. And among the natural elements favoring it were available land and cooling water.

Then came the impasse over whether to include or exclude oil in heavy industry at Machias.

As in the model, though for somewhat different reasons,

the upstream polluter in Machias had an advantage. He polluted the others and they didn't pollute him. The downstream players had to offer Machias some value greater than Machias could expect to get from oil. What could they offer? Money would do it since money and oil could be equated, but it would require a tremendous tax on the downstream groups to buy off a refinery. Whether any of the players considered this they did not say. But a minority inside the group representing Machias made it clear that they would accept other heavy industry at Machias in lieu of oil. Had the downstreamers been able to deliver such heavy industry—i.e., make the required payment—it appears that they might have obtained an effective coalition to bar oil from Machias. But as the game went, it seems that the key to the failure to resolve it was the inability of the downstream forces to provide a tangible prospect of heavy industry other than oil for the Machias zone.

The voting in the task force was not binding on anyone and the game ended with the issuance of its report. Viewing the game strictly to this cutoff point, one must conclude that the players came close to finding a core of stability that would have resolved it by the mutual consent of the effective groups involved. If they had found such a core, ratification by the Maine legislature would very likely have followed; the chief function of the state government would have been to provide a mechanism for the enforcement of the agreement.

Having missed the core by such a close margin, the players might yet reasonably have expected the legislature to adopt the report and vote it into law, with a view either to closing the gap at Machias by some means, or to being resigned to a partial core imposed upon the minority. They might have done so simply because the task force came up with the widest agreement they could expect to get in the state as a whole. But the legislature did not adopt the report. It did not formally reject it but by default let the status quo run on. This action, or non-action, is to be explained by a surprise event.

The status quo, as we have seen, was the case-by-case approach of the environmental site law, which had been rejected unanimously by the members of the task force in favor of the zone approach. Under the site law, oil companies were free to apply for permission to build a refinery and harbor facilities anywhere on the Maine coast. Two companies now applied for such permission, each moving strategically along a different course and the legislature took pause.

The Pittston Company, through its subsidiary Metropolitan Petroleum, mentioned early in this story as sitting on a prospective refinery site at Eastport, just east of Machias but outside of the proposed Machias zone, applied in 1973 to the Board of Environmental Protection for permission to build a refinery on that location. That same year the Gibbs Petroleum Company applied to build a refinery at Sanford, near Portland and within the proposed Portland zone.

The forces described in this game then indefatigably reformed and grouped themselves for contests over these sites. The Gibbs project, which fitted into the zone concept most favored by the task force, had some strong local opposition; but the town favored it and environmentalists gave it qualified benediction. But the public hearings for the Pittston project in 1973–74 saw a rerun of previous struggles with a similar lineup of forces for and against it.

The Eastport site had the merit of having a railroad connection. It also satisfied those who were most concerned to do something for the depressed economic state of Washington County (both Machias and Eastport are in this county). And the company was willing to contend with the physical deficiencies of the port, which has fierce tides and is often blanketed in fog. But a refinery there conflicted with another long-standing proposal, the Passamaquoddy Tidal Power Project; and the company faced another hazard outside of Maine: the tanker approach to Eastport ran through binational waters and so would be subject to veto by Canada. But the worst of the company's difficulties, which amazingly popped up after nearly a year of hearings that were expensive for everyone, was its failure to complete the assembly of land for its site. The company started to assemble another one, but its position at best was shaky. All parties put a high value, plus or minus, on the Eastport affair because if a site there were approved, the resulting fact of a refinery in being would change the rules of the game for the foreseeable future.

The inability of the players to bring the game to a conclusion with the task-force report had another consequence to which all games are vulnerable, namely, dynamic changes in the basic conditions of the real world. Uncertainties about the sources of energy swept over the nation and altered the rules of innumerable economic games. We have seen how in the time of import quotas, the federal government implacably blocked oil companies from receiving foreign oil at Machias; and how, for other reasons centering on pollution, coastal groups and various conservationists also opposed oil in Maine, which gave rise to the game described here and its play to within an ace of resolution. The emergence of the "energy crisis" wiped out quotas and brought open season on oil from abroad. The escalation of crude prices by the cartel of oil-producing countries—a type of coalition that comes as no surprise in game theory when the conditions suit—and new pressures for domestic sources of energy, created new uncertainties in Maine. As energy doesn't come easy and pollution doesn't go away, the games go on, but with the prospect of further changes in the values to be gauged, negotiated, and resolved.

15

LEARNING FROM GAMES

I started this book with the observation that modern thought about interactive games has something to add to the long tradition of learning from games, and along that line, I undertook to explore some real games. I shall conclude with a few remarks on how I think this learning may serve to refine one's natural intuitions about matters that may be considered as games—which is where my interest, and I imagine that of most readers, lies.

Interactive games are distinguished by the freedom of choice granted to the players. This element of freedom alone defines their character. One can argue forever whether free will is a distinctive feature or any feature of human thought and action; well-known views hold that man is a behaving mechanism like the universe around him. The view I have taken has philosophical implications which I do not pursue. It's just a common observation that you can get into situations—games here—by fate or blind chance. But once you are in a game in which the players are granted free choice, neither fate nor blind chance will explain what happens if you and the others exercise that choice. This is an arbitrary statement of assumptions, but on the level of what is observable in the world, even so convinced a determinist as the scientist-philosopher Percy Bridgman conceded that the future is not determined in the same sense that the past is. The assumption of free will is compatible with what happens in interactive games: most of the games described in this book would fall apart under mechanistic assumptions.

Make the mechanistic assumption and build a robot to your fancy. There is a fallacy abroad, emanating perhaps from the marvels of the computer, that your robot can be programmed to play any sort of game. Those who theorize about such things, or build them, agree that when one person is playing against nature, with free choice on the player's side but not on nature's, that player can be replaced by a robot which will answer the player's questions. But they would be mechanistic questions: Robinson Crusoe seeking advice on how to satisfy his wants on the desert island; a farmer devising a planting strategy in relation to the weather; a credit manager composing diabolic threats of increasing intensity to thousands of slow-paying customers.

Two robots playing against one another in a two-person zero-sum game—chess, poker, and the like—form a strange case. Each can be programmed with a grant of free choice within a determined system, and within technical limitations can do a good job of picking rational strategies—rational being defined again as a preference for high scores over low ones. If computers could count to a large enough number they could pick the best strategies in a chess game. The outcome, in theory, is ordained, free choice notwithstanding, the first move implying a mate for black or white, or a draw.

Robots can play two-person games of pure opposition because the play of such games rests solely on the rationality of the individual. I don't know what inferences should be made from this odd association of robots with individual rationality. But there is a phenomenon to be noted here. When you go over to a gainful game between two persons or any kind of game with more than two persons and no rule against cooperation, robots can't play them. They are perforce limited to the non-cooperative outlook. The principles of mechanics cannot be extended to groups, where the sharing of gains by bargaining between two persons or by forming coalitions among three or more of them entails a creative effort. Such effort rests not upon individual rationality but upon a common one: what two or more persons can gain together in a mutual interaction. Free choice and mutual values form a combination of human qualities that cannot be imitated in the mechanical universe.

Free choice thus takes one into the question of whether one is exercising a choice in the interests of an individual, a group, or society. Not that the individual loses his own interest in the group. The difference is in the outlook: rawly, whether it pays to cooperate.

But there is a route to travel through a game. We have seen how in taking hold of a game in mind—any game in this book—one goes from what can happen (the description, rules, choices) to what will happen (the so-called solution, usually without the implication of prediction). The question of what will happen leads to what the players want from the game, a matter that may also influence its description.

The act of describing a real game is a demanding enterprise. That's clear, I imagine, from my efforts to gather the facts about games in the real world and to reduce them to the player's choices, and from worries I have expressed about the adequacy of the information: whether there are too many blank spaces and whether the filled spaces will last—that is, whether dynamic changes will alter the game before it is played out. One arrests the Heraclitean flow in a pause of mind, which is either in the nature of human thought or a flaw needing a better theory to correct it.

Yet all is not lost in the flow. That rules of real games hold well enough for steady states of play is an observed fact: you drink a lot of martinis in resolving an intercorporate game under the martini norm, which executives follow in resolving so many of their cooperative games. Corporate policy typically implies repetitive acts in the marketplace.

There are also the one-shot games: an acquisition or merger by friendly negotiation and bargaining, as in the Boise Cascade game, or a take-over as in so many conglomerate raids. The one-shot game is often the mark of a crisis, as it was with Disney and the banker over the editing of *Fantasia,* Ford and General Motors in 1921, J. Paul Getty in California in the sixties. Momentous events in a person's or corporation's history may turn on chance but they seem as often to turn on a single strategic game.

A chief executive normally guides his organization through routines about which he makes no further decisions until he makes the quantum jump: a new policy. Observing this, one is already into improvising a dynamic model. But in the ongoing games of business with their trickling payoffs and changing personalities, the players' intuitions have a corresponding gait which it is difficult to capture in a game model that wants its cut-off and score. And yet when the rules hold approximately for periods of time, one can get a score of sorts which includes the value of playing further games. These results then can be brought into the starting position of the next game. Not all of the rules need to be rewritten, as we saw in the sequence of games over the communications satellite. But one cannot get away from the concept that a change of rules is a change of games. One new player is enough to create a new game, as in the ongoing games for the horseplayers' money.

Granted these ways of adapting games to dynamic change are patchworks, they are no less patchworks in the minds of real players; one can judge for oneself the insights one gets from rough-modeling them. Businessmen and government agents, for example, constantly wrestle with long- and short-range plans. A game puts time on an operational basis: it raises the question of how far forward (and backward) you can go into action and reaction and suggests where the indeterminacy and unpredictableness lie. It also puts chance in its place and relates strategy to rule. If you know the rules, you know the strategies. Furthermore, today's strategy may be tomorrow's rule, as when by strategic choice a company builds a new plant and then has to live with it. But the study of games does not, except in certain simple situations, prescribe specific plans; it points to the nature and location of the strategic problem.

The two big things that emerge from the playing of games are strategies and coalitions. Strategies are a feature of the non-cooperative approach to games. The characteristic model of cooperation, however, washes out the strategic detail for the simplifying view of coalitions, with their conditions of communication, trust, and agreement.

Whoever joins a coalition does so presumably because it promises a gain over and above going alone, and the sum of these gains becomes the value of the coalition. Hence, when you go to coalitions to resolve a game, you want to know the value of all the possible coalitions in the game—in practice, all the significant ones. This list gives you the beginning of a cooperative model, setting the stage for the interplay of the coalitions, in the course of which the players will attempt to choose those that have the highest value and that will have some stability in face of counteroffers from outsiders and threats of members to leave.

And so, from the description of games to their resolution, from non-cooperative to cooperative solutions, and from strategies to coalitions, we get to the high levels of learning from cooperative games. Given the rules, everything else is adjustable, taking the form over time of numerous customs and traditions which distinguish one society from another. The alignments represented by such standards of behavior, a number of which have been described in this book, express common ways of resolving the play of cooperative games in business and the professions and other subsocieties, political and economic, as well as in the whole society. As forms of wide agreement and of people acting in concert, they exert their force across a game. Even the rules of law reflect them, and one can see that if all were made rules, the rule books would bury the participants. Games sharpen the sense that society is to a degree stabilized by its standards of behavior, some of which are reinforced in law.

The act of interpreting standards of behavior by means of games, and, conversely, of interpreting games by means of standards of behavior, has been the big thing in this field of thought ever since Von Neumann and Morgenstern set it forth as *the* solution of games, though it is no longer widely accepted as the only solution.

We have seen game models showing how the chaos of churning coalitions takes over in the absence of standards of behavior. In them someone can always make an offer to break up and reorganize the prevailing alignment; the outs can always overturn the ins, as in political voting games. The coalitions come to rest when a custom or tradition develops and takes hold of them, saying we will divide the benefits along certain lines. The dissatisfied ones may be restive and heretical, but the solution is fairly stable until the revolution: a new standard of behavior, or none and back to chaos.

The model of chaos, however, had a special characteristic: the sum of its payoffs to the players is constant. The players are dividing and redividing among themselves a fixed sum of values—political, pecuniary, or other. Economic games of this kind do exist, as we have seen, but they are marginal. The typical game in the main line of economic life is neither zero-sum nor constant in any sum. It is a trade, which is a constructive thing. A trade creates wealth for the parties to it and increases the wealth of the whole society. With a gain to be made in the game, chaos no longer threatens. Indeed as noted, the tendency of market games is toward stability.

There are various ways of looking at the play of gainful games, among which is the one called the "core," which I described earlier as the most important new insight into economic life developed in recent years.

The best way to see the core of a game is to hold in abeyance one's recognition of standards of behavior in society. The core works in all societies and can be seen independently of such standards; one can return to them after the core is found, if it is there to be found.

Finding the core is the natural way to reach agreement on a deal. As we saw in the play of the game of one seller and two buyers, the seller's reserve price sets a floor, the value of the tradable thing to its owner, the sign of his being "rational" as an individual. He won't sell the thing for less. The game comes to life because the thing is worth more than this value to both of the potential buyers, and more to one than the other. The potential gain in the game then lies between the worth of the thing to the seller and its worth to the buyer for whom it has the highest value. But there will be bidding or negotiating to see who gets it and how the gain is to be divided. Call the buyer of lower worth the "first buyer," the buyer of higher worth the "second buyer." The first buyer can bid anywhere up to the full value of the thing to him. This sets the level above which the second buyer must bid; the outcome, then, one could expect to be a deal between him and the seller at a price somewhere between the full value to him and the full value to the second buyer. Thus the loser influences the winning deal; if the negotiation on price should go below the value of the object to him, he will make an offer, driving the price up to his highest possible bid. Above that bid lies the best deal, and its peculiarity is that its range is contingent upon the loser's highest bid. The winning coalition of buyer and seller cannot do better as a group than to reach their final terms of settlement in that range. It does not matter to the basic deal what price they settle at within the range; if the price is on the high end, the seller gets more of the gain, the buyer less; and vice versa: that, as much as anything, describes the stability of the outcome, for the outcome is the range that expresses their mutual gain. It is sufficient that they have agreed to bargain within it. As a group they can't do better by dissolving and forming another group. They are *in the core* of the game.

The core is a group forming within the whole society. Its "group rationality" lies in the fact that as a group its members get more than they could otherwise. They have the power, by their own consent, to secede from arrangements in which they are not getting all they could, to trade among themselves. There is only one coalition in the core of the game we have just seen, but with more players there could be more coalitions in the core. Theorists observe that market games always have a core because in them there is always an outcome—a distribution—such that no subgroup can do better by withdrawing and forming another coalition around another deal. There are no effective groups left dissatisfied; all have done the best they could. If the whole society reached that state, one could say that the society was rational, meaning that no further gains could be made by any group within it except at someone's expense and that no further gains could be made by society as a whole.

This simple but very interactive model shows the force of purely economic coalitions in mutual interaction, with the best deal *on its own merits* immune from the pressure of alternative deals. It represents a force that is present far, wide, and deep in economic life, either actually or latently. We have seen a number of examples of it in real games. Boise Cascade and Ebasco, negotiating the terms of their merger, are in the core of their game. They have already looked over alternative mergers and have seen, according to their perceptions, that their coalition has the highest value. They bargain across the range of that value to reach the final settlement, and, after agreeing on a point of settlement, face a rebellion on the part of a minority of Ebasco directors. At first sight, one might wonder whether in fact they are in the core: will the minority come up with a better deal for Ebasco, alone or in other coalitions and will it be effective internally in making such a view prevail? Apparently not. All parties agreed to stay with the proposed merger and to reopen the bargaining within the range of value of their coalition. The complaints of the minority are minimized by giving Ebasco better terms in the ratio of exchange of stock. That Ebasco got more and Boise Cascade less in the bargaining exhibits strikingly the stability of the core. The coalition held firm, dominating all other possible coalitions. No other coalitions materialized to make effective offers to break it up. The fact that the deal didn't work out as expected is another story and another game. The parties to the merger found the core and settled there in a one-shot game.

Yet outcomes outside the core of a game do in fact commonly occur, despite the fact that they leave some groups dissatisfied; that is, despite the fact that someone is around who can make better offers. How then is one to explain why an outcome occurs when it could be overthrown? The answer is that coalitions in the core, representing the best deal, do not always dominate everything on the outside, particularly other arrangements guided by the standards of society. The customs or traditions of a society may, of course, favor the best deal; indeed, if the best deal has been concluded, one may presume that it is a part of the social fabric; there are standards for mergers, for example, some written into law, some embodied in custom. Thus, the core of a game, if it exists, is always contained in a social standard. It's when an outcome gets out of the core and is nevertheless stable that one looks for another source of stability in a social standard.

In the model we have just seen of the seller and two buyers, we disregarded the question of what society the game was played in. Now we look at the society and let us say that according to its customs the losing bidder may be compensated. Crudely, it could be a bribe to get him not to bid, which would change the outcome for the others. More sophisticatedly, it could be any arrangement that cuts third parties in on the payoff. Perhaps the first arrangement of this kind was made long ago, and though unstable, it worked once, twice, and so on, gathering the stability of a custom, so that in time nobody gave it a thought: third parties just got cut in.

Assuming that such is the case, we have seen in detail, in the chapter on cooperative games, the difficulty of settling on the amount of the side payment. The higher bidder, having proposed to pay the lower one to withhold his bid, now attempts to negotiate a price below the value of the tradable object to the lower bidder. But so long as the negotiation is below that value, it pays the low bidder to come back in and start bidding again; they are all then back on their way to the best deal in the range between the full values the two bidders put on the object. That's the instability of splitting the gain among the three players in the game. For the deal to work against the force of this instability, a different kind of force must intrude. Society has set the standard that side payments are legitimate. Specifically, custom says the loser gets a cut. The two buyers get together—call it their "coalition"—and agree to split whatever gain they can get out of it by driving the seller to a price below the value of the object to the low bidder. In the three-way split of the total gain, the seller than gets less than he would in the best deal. The arrangement is sanctioned by society and is fairly stable: no other arrangement inside the standard can dominate its arrangement; heretics can attempt to overthrow it from the outside, but presumably there is something in the standard to counter the heretic—until in a revolution the standard falls and, if a new one does not immediately take its place, the negotiating and bargaining begin again from scratch.

From this model of side payments to the loser in formal economic relationships, it is no great leap to the real world of buyers and sellers making deals not in the light of the best deal on the hard economics, but over their traditional martinis, sanctioned by the society of business; oil men receiving a variety of side benefits outside the hard economics of their business; farmers and others getting subsidies, labor the minimum wage; industries set aside to be regulated; antitrust rules written to force sellers to play a non-cooperative game; and so on, through the customs and traditions of economic life.

Some of these arrangements are built into the moral character of the society. Some are shortcuts to a solution of a problem of the public interest, and in that sense efficient. Some only reflect political power which may pass; for not every economic custom is secure. It is holding back some other arrangement which puts pressure on the prevailing one.

The concept of the core too is significant not only at the level of a business deal but also at higher levels of society. Many laws are written to resolve a problem which they do not resolve because they failed to reflect the interaction of the actual groups involved, and so after being voted in they are presently voted out. To get a tax scheme, for example, that people won't vote out, you may have to find the core, in which it doesn't pay anybody to form new coalitions. So it is with energy and pollution and other issues of our time. And in the largest sense, games suggest that the productivity of a society is influenced by such economic arrangements—who gets together with whom to create something—and the results can vary widely on the same technological foundation.

The core and the standard of behavior are not the only co-operative solutions that have emerged from the study of games. There's the view that asks what's a fair payoff to a player in view of his power—the pivotal voter, for example, as compared with the other voters; and likewise, what it is worth to enter a game, determined by averaging the value that all the players bring to a coalition. There is a bargaining concept which has the players minimize the maximum objection of any potential coalition to arrive at the best deal; and there are other solutions, each distinguished by satisfying some of the objectives in a game but not all. It's open season for the exploration of games, the purpose of which is not to say precisely what to do, but to try to understand what's going on.

FROM GAME TREES TO
STRATEGIES TO COALITIONS

The word "strategy" in recent years has come into common use in the language of business and politics. But putting a strategy into effect has practical limits that are not always recognized. A clear view of these limits is given by two examples of the most primitive of game models.[1]

The game, let us say, to begin, has two players, A and B. Player A has only one move, with two choices: to go left (L) or right (R). In either event, Player B in sequence has one move: to go left (L) or right (R). That is all there is to this game.

The first sketch below—called the "game tree" or "extensive form" of a game—depicts the alternating moves of the players in their sequence at the fanning points of a branching tree, shown on the following page.[2]

Player A has the first move. He makes a decision. He chooses to play L or to play R. Let us say he plays L. It is B's move. Because they are playing in sequence, we may assume that Player B knows which choice Player A has played. He knows, therefore, where he is in the tree. He is at the fanning point B in the upper branch, where he now makes a de-

[1] Suggested by Melvin Dresher.
[2] A picture of a real game modeled along these lines appears in connection with the General Motors-Ford game.

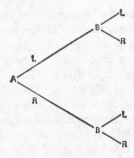

cision about which of his two choices he will play. He plays L or R. End of game.

But suppose Player B wants to make a strategic plan in advance, that is, to make his choice before he knows Player A's choice. The rules of the game—i.e., the choices available to both players—remain the same. But the *strategic* information has changed. Player B has a strategy problem. To make a complete plan he must describe what he can and will do in all eventualities, that is, in view of what Player A can and may do. To make the circumstances clear, let us say that Player B, after making his plan, intends to depart from the scene of the game before the action takes place, leaving his instructions with an agent who will carry them out. To write these instructions—his complete strategic plan—he transforms the above model into another one of a different kind, as follows:

| | PLAYER A | |
	PLAYS L	PLAYS R
	L	L
	L	R
PLAYER B		
	R	L
	R	R

429

This model, called the "strategic"—or "matrix" or "normalized"—form of a game, contains all the complications of information resulting from the matter of who moves first.[3] Player B can now see all the possible strategies he could play in view of anything Player A can do. In this simple game Player A of course can only do one of two things: play left or play right. Player B, however, has four strategies to choose among, each a complete plan described by a row. Each row says what Player B will do in response to either of Player A's choices (and in a developed game there would be various payoffs for the junctures of the two players' choices). He chooses the row he considers best and, handing it to his agent to play, becomes committed to that course. Let us say he gave the instruction, "Play the first row." That would mean that whatever choice Player A made, Player B plays left. Or say he gave the instruction, "Play the second row." That would mean that if Player A plays left, Player B plays left; and if Player A plays right, Player B plays right. And so on. Every game which can be described in a sequence of moves, as in the tree we just saw, can be converted into such a box of complete strategies. The game thus shows that if you know the rules (choices), you can set forth the available strategies. And that's not all it shows.

The strategic model, we have seen, compresses the different possibilities for Player B into one choice described by a row, and in theory the model serves this purpose even in a vastly more complex situation. But there is a hitch in the practicability of this transformation. One will have noticed that in the tree Player B, knowing Player A's choice, had to consider only two choices for himself, whether to play left or right. In the strategic model of the same game, he has four strategies to consider. But give Player B one additional choice at each move, say to play Center (C) as well as left or right, and his available strategies will jump to nine, as follows:

[3] An example of this model with payoff numbers for the opposed players appears in the J. Paul Getty chapter.

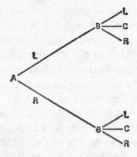

Player A again has the first move. He makes a decision, choosing to play L or R. Let us say he chooses to play L. It is B's move. Because they are playing in sequence, we may assume that B knows where he is in the tree, that is, at the fanning point B in the upper branch, where he has three choices. He makes his choice and the game ends.

But as in the previous game, he wants in advance a strategy for all eventualities which he will leave with an agent, and so he again transforms the tree of rules into a box of strategies, listing them as follows:

PLAYER A

	PLAYS L	PLAYS R
	L	L
	L	C
	L	R
	C	L
	C	C
PLAYER B	C	R
	R	L
	R	C
	R	R

431

Player B now has nine possible strategies, each described by a row. This phenomenon of strategies increasing faster than one's choices is significant, for they continue to increase astronomically, until, as in the example of chess, they go out of sight, and the complications of chess are often exceeded in the real world. Give the computer its due; it can count a lot of strategies and is "learning" to count more. But the problem is not merely one of computing; it is conceptual. There are real games that can be seen in a frame of strategies; and some real games are not as big as they look at first sight. In the General Motors-Ford game, a mountain of facts could be reduced to a few choices, and as I interpreted it, even with chance moves one could see through the simple tree to the scoring points. But if the tree branches out very far into sequences of moves, strategic visibility declines. Real players, unlike robots, typically stop now and then to look back to see where they are as well as forward to where they want to go. Experience and common sense tell them to play a strategic game around a few fanning points, as chess players do. Corporate executives express confidence only in the short run and periodically check their strategic plans with a view to revising them, for the same reason and other reasons too; theirs is not usually a zero-sum game even when there are only two players. Thus a complete strategy for a complex game with only two players is not realistic. The importance of the strategy model is conceptual.

The complexity of a strategic situation, however, gets far worse when one more player enters the game, or several, or many. Although in theory, there are ways of trying to cope strategically with the problem of many players, the main line of thought about games here ceases to be preoccupied with strategies. We meet the fork in the road of thought which divides non-cooperative from cooperative way of playing games. The non-cooperative way is the way of strategies, with their questions about who plays first and the like; there may be a sort of middle ground where players tentatively coordinate their strategies, which we saw in the second Howard Hughes-Trans World Airlines game, where the opposing lawyers ran through several strategic sequences in a warily cooperative effort to resolve Hughes's sale of the stock without either party getting trapped. The characteristic model of cooperation, however, washes out the strategic detail for the simplifying view of coalitions, with their conditions of communication, trust, and agreement.

There is reason to go to coalitions when there are more than two players, if only to obtain this simplifying effect; real players as well as game theorists are attracted to them, I believe, by the force of this expedience. And there are other even more pressing reasons. Gains may be made in coalition that are greater than the gains from strategies, at least by some of the players in many games, and by all of them collectively in economic games.

The most conservative strategy in a game is the so-called "minimax": minimizing the maximum loss or maximizing the minimum gain. It rests on the pessimistic assumption that the players are all-out opponents giving no quarter and that they might find out one another's strategies. Hence each plays a strategy (or a random mixture of strategies) that minimizes the most he can lose or maximizes the least he can gain as a guaranteed outcome. It is conservative because while the outcome is guaranteed, it is less than one could get without such a guarantee; by cooperation, for example, based on trust.

INDEX

Abbott, R. L., 352
  See also Montgomery Ward &
    Company
ABC. See American Broadcast-
    ing Company
Adelman, M. A., x, 91, 94
Advanced Study, Institute
    for, xix
Alice in Wonderland (film),
    225, 237
  See also Disney, Walt
American Airlines, 168, 170,
    173
American Broadcasting Com-
    pany (ABC), 267, 276–
    77, 296, 322
American Economic Review,
    The, 388n
American Telephone & Tele-
    graph Corporation
    (AT&T), 266–329
    passim
  Bell Laboratories, 24, 269,
    270
  Long-Lines Department, 316
    and Telstar, 273–74
Andrews, Kurth, Campbell &
    Jones, 175
  See also Hughes, Howard
Applied Mathematics Center
    (Cornell University),
    388n

Arrow, Kenneth, x, 111
Arrow (tanker), 403
Ashland Oil & Refining, 86, 395
  See also Getty, Jean Paul;
    Pollution, negotiating
Astaire, Fred, 226
Atlantic Richfield Company,
    395, 402
  See also Pollution, negotiat-
    ing
AT&T. See American Tele-
    phone & Telegraph Cor-
    poration
Audubon Society, 407
Aumann, Robert J., x, 120n
Automobile industry. See Ford
    Motor Company; Gen-
    eral Motors Corporation
Avery, Sewell L., 80, 345–46,
    353
  See also Montgomery Ward &
    Company

Bambi (film), 227, 239
  See also Disney, Walt
Bangor & Aroostook Railroad,
    396
Bank of America
  and Howard Hughes, 167,
    174, 179
  and Walt Disney, 220, 228–
    35

Banks, Louis, *xiii*
Bargaining games, 142–65
    See also Boise Cascade Company; Ebasco Industries, Inc.
Barr, John A., 346, 349–50
    See also Montgomery Ward & Company; Sears, Roebuck & Company
Batten, William M., *xi*, 338–39, 340, 341–45, 358
    See also J. C. Penney Company, Inc.
Bautzer, Gregson, 194
Beal, Ossie, 403
Beall, Wellwood, 173
Beame, Abraham D., 264
Bell Laboratories. *See under* American Telephone & Telegraph Corporation (AT&T)
Bendix Corporation, 197
BEP. *See* Board of Environmental Protection, Maine
Bernheim Distilling Company, 13
Betting. *See* Off-track betting on horseracing
Bickner, Robert, *x*
Bloodhorse magazine, 264
Board of Environmental Protection, Maine (BEP), 405, 415
Boeing Aircraft, 167, 168, 173, 174, 179, 181, 182, 198, 207
    See also Hughes, Howard
Böhm-Bawerk, Eugen, 120*n*, 121
Boise Cascade Corporation, *xi*, 142–65, 419, 424–25
    and merger with Ebasco, 146–61
    failure of, 161–65
    See also Ebasco Industries, Incorporated; Hans-

berger, Robert Vail
Boise Payette Lumber Company, 145
"Bond Purchase" agreement, 186
    See also Trans World Airlines (TWA)
Borges, Jorge Luis, 83
Bourbon Institute, 14
Bradford, Peter, *xii*
Bradner, William, *xii*
Brams, Steven J., *x*, 30
Breech, Ernest R., 196, 197, 198, 209, 211
    See also Hughes, Howard
British scotch-whiskey trust, 6
Bronfman, Samuel, 1–2, 6–14
    See also Seagrams *v.* Schenley
Brooker, Robert E., *xi*, 347–70
    See also Montgomery Ward & Company; Sears, Roebuck & Company
Buhagier, Marion, *xiii*
Burch, Dean, 321
Burgess, Carter, 172
Business norms, 135–41
    See also Cooperative games; Game theory

CAB. *See* Civil Aeronautics Board
Cahill, Gordon, Reindel & Ohl, 195, 197, 198
    See also Hughes, Howard
Carson, Lorraine, *xiii*
CATV, 283
CBS. *See* Columbia Broadcasting System
    See also Hughes Aircraft Company
Center of Applied Mathematics, The (Cornell University), 388*n*
Certificates of deposits (CDs), 374–78, 385

435

See also Morgan Guaranty
Trust Company of New
York

Chammah, Albert M., 94*n*

Chandler, Alfred D., *xiv*

Chaos, models of. *See under*
Cooperative games

Chapin, Roy, 66*n*

Chaplin, Charles, 221, 223,
226–27

Chase Manhattan Bank, 375

Chevrolet Company, 35, 36, 43,
44, 48–69
See also Ford Motor Company: *v.* General Mo-
tors

Chevron Oil Company, 397

Chrysler, Walter P., 36

Chrysler Corporation, 33

Cinderella (film), 237
See also Disney, Walt

Cities Service Oil Company,
397

Civil Aeronautics Board
(CAB), 170, 175, 196,
201–2, 204, 207, 211–
12, 214, 216, 219
See also Hughes, Howard

Clark, James, 283

Clark, Philip R., 350
See also Montgomery Ward &
Company

CML, formation of, 323–28
See also Communications
Satellite Corporation
(Comsat)

Coalitions and social issues. *See*
Pollution, negotiating

Cole, John, *xii*

Columbia Broadcasting System
(CBS), 267, 296, 322

Commerce, United States Department of, 349
and Economic Development
Administration, 399
and Foreign Trade Zone
Board, 400

Common Carrier Bureau, 311,
316–17

Communications Commission.
See Federal Commu-
nications Commission
(FCC)

Communications Satellite Act,
creation of, 272

Communications satellite cooperative game, 266–329

Communications Satellite Corporation (Comsat), 267,
272, 275–78, 280–89,
292–96, 298–300, 314–
16, 320–22
and CML, formation of, 323–
28
created by Congress, 272

Comsat. *See* Communications
Satellite Corporation

Congress of the United States
creates Comsat, 272
negotiating prices within, 110

Consolidated Edison Company
of New York, 262

Container Corporation, 137,
348, 367–70
See also Montgomery Ward &
Company

Convair (General Dynamics),
167, 173, 174, 179, 183–
84, 192, 194, 198
See also Hughes, Howard

Cook, Raymond, *xi*, 175, 194,
199, 216, 217
See also Hughes, Howard

Cooper, Allen, 284

Cooperative games, 102–141
and chaos, models of, 116–20
core of, 130–35
and farmer game, 120–30
Morgenstern on, 102–4, 107,
114, 116–21, 121*n*,
123–24, 126*n*, 134–35,
140
and new players, effect of,
246–65

and norms of business, 135–41

and ten-player game, 266–329

See also Game theory

Cornell University, *ix, xii*

Center of Applied Mathematics, 388n

Corporate models, 51–60, 92–93, 122–35, 289–300, 333–41, 342–45, 377–79

Corporate playing, 83–101, 430n

See also Game theory; General Motors Corporation: *v.* Ford; Getty, Jean Paul

Corporate values, 70–82

and chief executive, 78

and combining values, 78–82

and management and shareholders, 76–77

Cragin, Stuart W., 378

See also Morgan Guaranty Trust Company of New York

Crown, Henry, 194

Curtis, Kenneth M., 398, 405, 409

See also Pollution, negotiating: Maine, game in

Damon, Ralph, 172

Davis, Chester, *xi*, 195, 198–200

See also Hughes, Howard

Davis, Morton D., *x*, 30n

deButts, John Dulaney, 327

Defense, United States Department of, 275, 320

De Havilland Aircraft Company, Ltd., 168

Delafield, Charles B., 262–63

Delta Air Lines, 179

Dillon, Read & Company, Inc.,

181–82, 184, 185, 188, 216

See also Hughes, Howard

Disney, Roy, *xi*, 220–21, 224, 227, 235, 236, 237, 238, 242, 245

Disney, Walt, *xi, xiii, xvi*, 420

on art and business, 221–27, 237–44

compared to Leonardo da Vinci, 235–36

and Disneyland (California), 239–42, 245

and Disney World (Florida), 245

films of, various, 220–23, 225–28, 232, 235, 237–40, 245, 420

and imaginary business game, 220–45

and Mickey Mouse Club, 240

Distillers Corporation-Seagrams Limited, 1–14

Dodge Corporation, 33, 34

Donnell, Edward S., 352, 355

See also Montgomery Ward & Company; Sears, Roebuck & Company

Donovan, Hedley, *xiii*

Dostoevsky, Fëdor M., *xxiin*

Douglas, Donald, 168

Douglas Aircraft Company, Incorporated, 168, 169, 207

See also Hughes, Howard

Dresher, Melvin, *x*, 428n

Dubey, Pradeep, *xii*

Duell, Sloan & Pearce, 85

Dumbo (film), 227

See also Disney, Walt

Du Pont, chemical company, 36

Du Pont, Pierre S., 33, 36, 37–38, 41, 46, 61, 64

Durant, William C., 35, 36, 37, 40

Dysart, Harold, 356

See also Montgomery Ward & Company

Early Bird. *See under* Hughes Aircraft Company
Eastern Airlines, 170, 203
Ebasco Industries, Incorporated, 142–65, 424
  and merger with Boise Cascade, 146–61
  failure of, 161–65
Economic Development Administration, 399
  Maine Department of, *xii*
Edgeworth, F. Y., 121, 121*n*
Einstein, Albert, *xvii*
  on criteria of mathematics, *xvii*
Eisner, Florine, *xiv*
Eisner, William J., *xiv*
Environmental Protection, Maine Board of (BEP), 405, 415
Equitable Life Assurance Society of the United States, 167, 171, 174, 180–86, 193–201
  See also Hughes, Howard
Evans, John K., 399–401, 405
  See also Pollution, negotiating: Maine, game in
Exxon Oil Company, 370, 397, 402
  See also Humble Oil & Refining Company

Fairbanks, Douglas, 226
Fairchild Industries, Incorporated, 267, 288, 291–94, 296, 298, 323, 325
Fantasia (film), 220–22, 227, 228, 232, 238, 420
  See also Disney, Walt
Farmer game, 120–29
  model of, 120–34
  See also Cooperative games

FCC. *See* Federal Communications Commission
Federal Bureau of Investigation (FBI), 201
Federal Communications Commission (FCC), 266, 267*n*, 268, 275–76, 278, 280, 286, 288, 297, 300, 312–27
  as games rules-maker, 320–22
  and "specialized carrier" decision, 279*n*
Federal Reserve Board
  money controlled by, 108
  and Morgan Bank, 371–85 *passim*
  and "Regulation Q," 375–77
Federal Trade Commission, 100
Finkelstein, Louis, 235
First Boston Corporation, 181, 216
First National Bank, 375
Fitelson, Anita, *xiv*
Fitelson, H. William, *xiv*
Ford, Henry, *xvi*, 32–69 *passim*, 105
  and "Peace Ship" proposal, 34
  on profits, 34–35
Ford Motor Company, *xii*, *xiii*, 80, 196, 277, 278
  early growth of, 34–41
  and General Motors' market-invasion plan, 41–45
  v. General Motors, 32–69, 370, 420, 428*n*, 430
  and actual game scored, 60–64
  interpretation of, 45–51
  line drawing of, 58
  and second game narrated, 64–69

Foreign Trade Zone Board (United States Department of Commerce), 400

Fortune magazine, *xiii, xviii, xx,* 83, 136*n,* 221, 370

Foster, Doris, *xiv*

Frye, Jack, 170

Galbraith, John Kenneth, *xiv, xix*

Gallup polls, 235

Games, cooperative. *See* Cooperative games; Game theory

Games, corporate. *See* Corporate models; Corporate playing; Corporate values

Game theory
  and abstract models, 25, 27–30, 91–92
  fourth-level, 29–30
  and analyzing conflict, value of, *xxii*
  in ancient Greece, *xvi, xix*
  and bluffing, *xxi*
  and chief executives discussed, 27–28
  and coalitions, large, 386–416
    See also Pollution, negotiating
  and cooperative games, 102–41
  and chaos, models of, 116–20
  and farmer game, model of, 120–30
  and norms of business, 135–41
  and corporate playing, 83–101, 430*n*
    See also Getty, Jean Paul
  and corporate values, 70–82, 83–101

and combining values, 78–82
and economic games, *xxiii, xxiv*
and entertainment games, *xix, xx, xxin, xxvii,* 26
finding choices in, 15–31
and imaginary games, 220–45
  See also Disney, Walt
and interactions, mutual, 1–14
and invisible player, value of, 166–219
  See also Hughes, Howard
and learning from games, 417–27
and management, value of, 77–78
and many-sided games, 330–70, 371–85
  See also Morgan Guaranty Trust Company of New York
in Middle Ages, *xv, xvi, xix*
and new players, effect of, 246–65
  See also Off-track betting on horseracing
and one-sided games, 330–70, 371–85
and rationality, *xxv–xxvi*
and rules of game, 15–31, 319–21
and shareholders, value of, 77–78
and steady-state games, 24
and ten-player cooperative game, 266–329
  model of, 289–300
  narrated, 280–88
    See also Communications Satellite Corporation
and three-part divisions, *xxvii–xxix*
and two-part divisions, *xxv–xxviii,* 32–69

and two-sided games, 330–70

Western thought on, *xxv*

and zero-sum game, 32–69

   See also Morgenstern, Oskar; Von Neumann, John

General Dynamics. *See* Convair

General Electric Company, 277

   Hotpoint division, 339

General Motors Corporation, *xii, xiii,* 24, 136, 370

   early growth of, 33–41

   and Ford market, plant to invade, 41–44

   Oldsmobile Division, 35, 36, 61, 66*n*

   v. Ford, 32–69, 420, 428*n*, 432

     and actual game scored, 60–64

     interpretation of, 45–51

     line drawing of, 53

     and second game narrated, 64–69

General Telephone & Electronics Corporation (GT&E), 267, 277, 280, 281, 283, 285–88, 291–99

   and coalition with Hughes and Western Union, 300–29

   See also Hughes, Howard; Western Union Telegraph Company

Getty, George F., II, 84, 88*n*, 89, 100

Getty, Jean Paul, *xi, xvi, xxin,* 74, 420

   and corporate playing, 83–101, 430*n*

   and Neutral Zone, 87

   See also Standard Oil Company (New Jersey); Tidewater Associated Oil Company

Getty, Sarah C., 85

Getty, Sarah C., Trust, 85

Getty Oil Company, 83, 85, 86, 87, 101, 397

Giannini, Lawrence M., 228

Gibbs Petroleum Company, 395, 415

   See also Pollution, negotiating

Gillies, D. B., 120*n*, 121

Global Communications Incorporated (Globcom), 281, 314

Gordon, Albert H., 368

Grayson, Iris, *xiv*

Green, Howard, 347, 356

   See also Montgomery Ward & Company

GT&E. *See* General Telephone & Electronics Corporation

Gudeman, Edward, 349, 350

   See also Montgomery Ward & Company

Gulf & Western Industries, 365

Gulf Oil Company, 87, 89, 397

Hagen, Grace, *xiv*

Hagerty, Harry C., 185, 192

   See also Hughes, Howard

Hammer, Armand, 401–2

Hansberger, Robert Vail, *xi,* 142–65

   See also Boise Cascade Corporation

Harsanyi, John, *x,* 176*n*

Harvard Business School, 144

Hawkins, Norval, 34

H-bomb, mathematics of the, *xvii*

Higgins, Carol, *xiii*

Hiram Walker Incorporated, 4, 5, 13, 14

Holliday, Raymond, 194, 196, 196*n*, 218

See also Hughes, Howard
Horsemen's Benevolent Protective Association, 262
Horseracing, off-track betting on, 246–65
Hotpoint division (General Electric), 339
Houser, Ted, 349
Hudson Motors, 33, 66n
Hudson's Bay Company, 6
Hughes, Howard, xi, xiii, xvi, 74, 83, 432
    and Bank Plan, 192
    as invisible games player, 166–219
Hughes Aircraft Company, xii, 267, 281, 284–88, 292–96
    and CATV, 283
    and coalition with GT&E and Western Union, 300–29
    and Early Bird, 273–74, 276
Hughes Tool Company, 167, 169–70, 172, 173, 174, 181, 184, 185, 186, 189–90, 193, 195n, 197, 199–200, 204, 209, 215, 218–19
    See also Hughes, Howard
Humble Oil & Refining Company, 96, 402
    See also Exxon Oil Company
Hyatt Roller Bearing Company, 40

IBM. *See* International Business Machines
Institute for Advanced Study, xix
Interior, United States Department of the, 399
International Business Machines (IBM), 277, 328
International Telephone and Telegraph Corporation. *See* ITT
Irving Trust Company, 167, 174, 179, 184, 192–93, 195, 201
    See also Hughes, Howard
ITT, 136
    South American cables, 268
    See also Communications Satellite Corporation

Jacobs, Eugene, 262
J. C. Penney Company, Inc., xi, 25, 330, 337–45, 359
    corporate model of, 340–45
    and King of Prussia store, 339–40
    merchandising policies of, 337–45, 353, 357
Jersey Standard. *See* Standard Oil Company (New Jersey)
Jockey Club, 248, 257
John Hancock Insurance Company, 154
Johns Hopkins University, xiv
Johnson, Lyndon B., 278, 401
Johnson, Nicholas, 321
John Wiley (publishers), 18n
Jones & Laughlin Steel Corporation, 136
J. P. Morgan & Company of New York, 37, 371–85 *passim*
    See also Morgan, Jean Pierre; Morgan Guaranty Trust Company of New York
Justice, United States Department of, 315, 328
    blocks Getty's interests, 96

Keehn, Grant, 196
Kennedy, John F., 349
Kerley, James, 218

King Resources, 395n
  See also Pollution,
    negotiating
Kojima, Nancy, xiv
Kordite Corporation, 254
Kresge & Company, Inc., 359
Kristol, Irving, xiv
Krumpe, John H., 259, 264
Kuhn, Harold W., x
Kuhn, Loeb & Company, 216
Kuhn, Sherman, x

Langan, Pat, xiii
Lazard Frères & Company
    (investment banking
    house), 148, 216
Leach, Ralph, xi, 380–81, 385
  See also Morgan Guaranty
    Trust Company of New
    York
Lehman Brothers, 216
Leland, Henry, 36
Levy, George Morton, 264
Lewis, Mary, 332
  See also Sears, Roebuck &
    Company
Lindsay, John V., 254, 263, 264
Ling, James J., 136, 136n, 146,
    164, 365
Ling-Temco-Vought, 365
Liquor industry. See Seagrams
    v. Schenley
Litton Industries, xii, 365
Lockheed Aircraft, 167, 169,
    170, 171, 179, 183
  See also Hughes, Howard;
    MCI Lockheed Satellite
    Corporation
Low, David, 227, 235–36
Lubar, Robert, xiii
Lucas, William, on game
    theory, ix, xx, xxx, 304,
    307, 388n
Luce, R. Duncan, x
Lutz, James, 352
  See also Montgomery Ward
    & Company

McCormick, Fowler, 83
McCrory Corporation, 352
McDonald, Dorothy, xiii
McLaren, Richard W., 136,
    136n
Maine, Pollution in. See
    Pollution, negotiating:
    Maine, game in
Maine Board of Environmental
    Protection (BEP),
    405, 415
Maine Central Railroad, 396
Maine Clean Fuels, 396, 406
  See also Pollution,
    negotiating: Maine,
    game in
Maine Department of Eco-
    nomic Development, xii
Maine Lobstermen's
    Association, 403
Maine Natural Resources
    Council, 404
Maine Port Authority, 400
Maine Times, xii
Manhattan, S.S., 402
Marchese, John, 353
  See also Montgomery
    Ward & Company
Marcor Corporation, 137,
    368–70
  See also Montgomery
    Ward & Company
Martin, John L., 282
Mary Poppins (film), 240
  See also Disney, Walt
Maschler, Michael, x, 120n
Massachusetts Institute of
    Technology, x
Mathematics, criteria of, xvii–
    xviii
Maxwell-Chalmers. See
    Chrysler Corporation
McDonald, Katherine, xiv
MCI Lockheed Satellite Cor-
    poration, 267, 279n, 285,
    288, 291–98, 314–15

and CML, formation of, 323–28
Menger, Karl, 120n, 121
Merchandising policies
  Montgomery Ward, 347–54, 357
  Penney, 337–45, 353, 357
  Sears, 334–35, 340, 353
Merrill Lynch, Pierce, Fenner & Smith, 212–13, 216–18
Metropolitan Life Insurance Company, 167, 171, 185–86, 191, 192, 195, 198, 201
  See also Hughes, Howard
Metropolitan Petroleum Company, 395, 402, 415
  See also Pollution, negotiating
Meyer, John M., Jr., xi, 372
Mickey Mouse Club, 240
  See also Disney, Walt
Miller, Joan, xiii
Miller, Richard, xiii
Mission Securities Limited, 86
  See also Getty, Jean Paul
M.I.T. See Massachusetts Institute of Technology
Mitchell, David, 147
Mobil Oil Corporation, 90, 97, 137, 255, 369–70, 397
  See also Socony Mobil Oil Company
Models, game. See Corporate models
Montgomery Ward & Company, xi, 80, 137, 330, 340, 345–70
  corporate model of, 356–70
  and credit squeeze, effect of, 363–64
  merchandising policies of, 347–54, 357
  merges with Container Corporation, 348–49

Montrose, Maynard, 196
Mood, Alex, x
Morgan, J. P., 37, 371–85 passim
Morgan & Company, J. P. See J. P. Morgan & Company
Morgan bank. See Morgan Guaranty Trust Company of New York
Morgan Guaranty Trust Company of New York, xi, 371–85
  and certificates of deposits (CDs), 374–78, 385
  model of, 377–78
Morgenstern, Oskar, ix, xviii, xx, xxii, 15, 17, 72, 383, 422
  on cooperative games, 102–4, 107, 114, 116–21, 121n, 123–24, 126n, 134–35, 140
  on game rules, 15
  and treatise on games, xvii–xviii
Morris, Alice, xiii
Moss, Frederick, xiii
Mullen, Barbara, xiv
Music Corporation of America, 244
Muskie, Edmund S., 399, 405
  See also Pollution, negotiating: Maine, game in
Muzzio, Douglas, 31n
My Life and Fortune (Getty), 85

Nader, Ralph, 30, 140
NASA. See National Aeronautics and Space Administration
Nash, Charles, 36
Nash Corporation, 33
National Aeronautics and Space Administration

(NASA), 270, 273, 274, 288
National Broadcasting Company (NBC), 267, 284, 296, 322
National Distillers Products Corporation, 4, 5, 13
Natural Resources Council of Maine, 404
Nault, Marc, *xii*
NBC. *See* National Broadcasting Company
Negotiating pollution. *See* Pollution, negotiating
Neumann, John Von. *See* Von Neumann, John
Neutral Zone (Saudi Arabia), 86–87
See also Getty, Jean Paul
New York Off-Track Betting Corporation, *xi*
See also Off-track betting on horseracing
New York Public Library, *xix*
New York Racing Association (NYRA), 247, 248, 251, 256–57, 259, 261, 264
See also New York Off-Track Betting Corporation; Off-track betting on horseracing
New York State racetracks. *See* Off-track betting on horseracing
New York State Racing and Wagering Board, 264
New York Stock Exchange, 218
New York *Times*, 264
Nicholson, Ronald, *xiv*
Nixon, Richard M., 31*n*, 136*n*, 278, 401
Norms of business, 135–41
See also Cooperative games; Game theory
North American Rockwell, 287
Northeast Airlines, 212
Novick, David, *x*

NYRA. *See* New York Racing Association

Oakland Corporation, 36, 61
Oates, James F., 185
Occidental Petroleum Corporation, 395, 401–2
See also Pollution, negotiating
O'Dwyer, William, 251
Off-Track Betting Corporation. *See* New York Off-Track Betting Corporation
Off-track betting on horseracing, 246–65
and betting percentages, 260–61
and racetracks, various, 248, 249, 256–57, 263
harness, 252
Oil Conveyance Act, 405
See also Pollution, negotiating: Maine, game in
Olds, Irving, 196*n*
Olds, R. E., 35
Oldsmobile Division (General Motors), 35, 36, 61, 67*n*
OTB. *See* Off-track betting on horseracing
Owen, Guillermo, *x*

Packard Corporation, 33
Paige Corporation, 33
Paine, Ralph Delahaye, Jr., *xix*
Pan American Airlines, 170, 173, 182, 191, 204–5
Papson, Magda, *xiv*
Parker, Sanford, *xiii*
Passamaquoddy Tidal Power Project, 415
Patterson, William, 170
Paxson, E. W., *x*
Penney. *See* J. C. Penney Company, Incorporated

Percentages, betting. *See* Off-track betting on horse-racing
Peter Pan (film), 237
  See also Disney, Walt
Phillips Petroleum Company, 86, 100, 100n
  See also Getty, Jean Paul
Pickford, Mary, 226
Pinocchio (film), 226
  See also Disney, Walt
Pittston Company, 395, 402, 415
Pollution, negotiating, 386–416
  and Maine, game in, 394–416
  and pond game, 388–90
  and *Torrey Canyon* accident, 403
  and upstream game, 390–93
Port Authority of Maine, 400
Princeton University, *xii*
Prisoner's dilemma (game), 94n
Prudential Insurance Company of America, 167, 171, 198
  See also Hughes, Howard

Racetracks. *See* Off-track betting on horseracing
Racing and Wagering Board, New York State, 264
Racing Association of New York (NYRA), 247, 248, 251, 256–57, 259, 261, 264
Radio Corporation of America (RCA), 267, 268, 275, 280, 283, 287–88, 290–98, 310, 314, 324–28
  of Alaska, 293, 297, 325
  -Globcom, 314
Raiffa, Howard, *x*
Rand Corporation, *ix*, *x*, *xii*
Rapaport, Anatol, *x*, 93n
RCA. *See* Radio Corporation

of America "Regulation Q." *See under* Federal Reserve Board
Reluctant Dragon (film), 226
  See also Disney, Walt
Remer, Georgiana, *xiv*
Reserve Board. *See* Federal Reserve Board
Ricciardi, Franc, *xii*
Richfield Oil Corporation, 96, 97
Rickenbacker, Eddie, 170
Rockefeller, John D., 83
Rockefeller, Nelson, 254, 262
Rockefeller Foundation, *xii–xviii*
Romnes, Haakon Ingolf, 327
Roosevelt, Franklin D., 345
Roper, Edith, *xiii*
Rosenberg, Joseph, 228
Rosenstiel, Lewis S., *xi*, 1, 2, 9–14
  See also Seagrams *v.* Schenley
Rummel, Robert, 172
Ryan, E. Barry, *xi*

Saks Fifth Avenue, 332
Samuels, Howard J., *xi*, 254–55, 260–64
  See also Off-track betting on horseracing
Samuels, Richard, 255
Sarafan, Bertram D., 264
Satellite communications. *See* Communications satellite cooperative game
Schenley Industries, Inc., *xi*, 1–14
Schenley *v.* Seagrams. *See* Seagrams *v.* Schenley
Schoenhofen, Leo, 367–69
  See also Montgomery Ward & Company
Schwarzhaupt, Emil, 1, 13
  See also Seagrams *v.* Schenley

Scripps-Booth, 36, 56
Seagrams Limited, 1–14
Seagrams v. Schenley, 1–14
  and "Bottled in Bond" labels,
    7–8, 14
  and brands mentioned, 2, 3,
    4, 7, 10
  and sales percentages,
    4–5, 14
  and whiskey compounds, 6–7
Sears, Roebuck & Company,
    330–38, 346, 347–48,
    350, 352, 353, 356,
    358–60, 364
  corporate model of, 333–41
    passim
  merchandising policies of,
    334–35, 340, 353
SEC (Securities and Exchange
    Commission), 211, 218
  See also Hughes, Howard
Sedlmayr, Julius, 213, 218
  See also Hughes, Howard
Seligman, Dan, xiii
Sessel, Ben-Fleming, 179, 192
Shapley, Lloyd S., x, xx, 23n,
    28n, 121, 121n, 122,
    388n
Shell Oil Company, 87, 89, 90,
    97, 397
Shubik, Martin, x, xx, 18n,
    92–94, 121, 121n, 122,
    388n
Sierra Club, 239
Signal Oil & Gas Company, 86,
    401
Skelly Oil Company, 86, 101
  and merger with Tidewater,
    88
  See also Getty, Jean Paul
Sleeping Beauty (film), 238
  See also Disney, Walt
Sloan, Alfred P., Jr., xiv, xvi,
    32, 38–41, 44–49, 55,
    61–62, 64–68, 105, 107
  See also Ford Motor

Company: v. General
    Motors
Smith, C. R., 168, 170
Snow White (film), 222, 226,
    235, 238
  See also Disney, Walt
Socony Mobil Oil Company, 97
Sonnett, John, xi, 195, 199–
    200, 209
  See also Hughes, Howard
"Specialized carrier" decision,
    279n
  See also Federal Com-
    munications Commission
Standard Oil Company, 83
  (California), 97
  (New Jersey), 84, 85, 86,
    87, 90, 96, 277
  See also Getty, Jean Paul
Steamboat Willie (film), 222
  See also Disney, Walt
Stein, Jules, 244
Stevens, Catharine, xiv
Stitzel-Weller Distillery, 7
Stock Exchange, New York, 218
Strategy and Market Structure
    (Shubik), 18n
Strategy in Poker, Business and
    War (McDonald), xx
Supreme Court of the United
    States
  and dealings with Hughes,
    201–2
  and TWA's damage claim,
    219
  upholds Oil Conveyance Act,
    406
Swayne, Elizabeth, xiii

Tamano (tanker), 403
Tele-Communications. See
    Western Tele-
    Communications
    Incorporated
Telecommunications Policy,
    Office of, 317
Teller, Edward, xvii

Telstar. *See under* American
    Telephone & Telegraph
    Corporation
Texaco, Incorporated, 90, 97,
    98, 100, 397
*Theory of Games and Eco-
    nomic Behavior, The*
    (Morgenstern and Von
    Neumann), xviii, xix
Thomas, Charles S., 172, 182,
    186–91
    See also Hughes, Howard
Thoroughbred Racing Associa-
    tion, 259
Three Little Pigs, The (film),
    223
    See also Disney, Walt
Tidal Power Project,
    Passamaquoddy, 415
Tidewater Associated Oil
    Company, 85, 85n, 86–
    100
    and merger with Skelly, 88
    See also Getty, Jean Paul
Tillinghast, Charles C., Jr., xii,
    195, 197–99, 203,
    204–14
    See also Hughes, Howard
Time Incorporated, xiii
Torrey Canyon accident, 403
    See also Pollution,
    negotiating
Trans World Airlines (TWA),
    xii, 166–67, 169–77,
    179–219, 432
    and "Bond Purchase"
    agreement, 186
    See also Hughes, Howard
Treasury, United States
    Department of the
    and liquor duties, 6
    money controlled by, 108,
    376, 379
Trilling, Lionel, xiv
Trippe, Juan, 170, 203–4
    See also Hughes, Howard

"True-Life Adventures"
    (films), 245
    See also Disney, Walt
Tucker, A. W., x, 94n
TWA. *See* Trans World
    Airlines
Tyler, Ann, xiii

Udal, Stewart L., 399, 400
Union Oil Company of
    California, 97, 98
United Airlines, 170
United Artists, 221, 226
    See also Disney, Walt
United Motors Corporation, 40
United States Department of
    Commerce, 349
    and Economic Development
    Administration, 399
    and Foreign Trade Zone
    Board, 400
United States Department of
    Defense, 275, 320
United States Department of
    the Interior, 399
United States Department of
    Justice, 315, 328
United States Department of
    the Treasury
    and liquor duties, 6
    money controlled by, 108,
    376, 379
United States Supreme Court
    and dealings with Hughes,
    201–2
    and TWA's damage claim,
    218
    upholds Oil Conveyance Act,
    405–6
Upstream game in pollution
    negotiating, 390–94

Values, corporate, 70–82
Vance, Eugene, xiii
Vanderbilt, Alfred G., 257
Van Winkle, Julian ("Pappy"),
    7

Vaughan, Samuel S., *xiv*
Vickrey, William, *x*
Vietnam War, economical
    effects of, 372
Visher, Paul, *xii*, 283–87
Von Neumann, John, *ix*, *xvi-*
        xix, *xx*, *xxx*, 15, 17, 72,
        383, 422
    on cooperative games, 102–4,
        107, 114, 116–21, 121*n*,
        123–24, 126*n*, 134–35,
        140
    designs H-bomb, *xvii*
    and first treatise on games,
        xvii
    on game rules, 15

Walker, E. Cardon, 245
Walt Disney Productions. *See*
    Disney, Walt
Walter Kidde & Company, *xii*
Warburg, S. G., 147
Ward. *See* Montgomery Ward
    & Company
Warren, Robert Penn, *xiv*
Western Electric Company, 270
Western Tele-Communications
    Incorporated, 267, 288,
    291–98, 323, 325
Western Union Telegraph
    Company, 267, 268,
    269*n*, 275, 277, 279*n*,

    280, 281, 283, 287–
        88, 291, 292–98
    and coalition with GT&E
        and Hughes Aircraft,
        300–29
    International, 269*n*, 325
Westinghouse Corporation, 136
Whipple, William, *xiv*
Whiteford, William K., 101
Wilkins, C. T., 168
    technology since, 272
Williams, John D., *x*
Willys-Overland Corporation,
    33
Wilshire Oil Company of
    California, 98
Wolfson, Louis E., 346, 349
    See also Montgomery Ward
        & Company
Woods, George, 181
World War I, 34, 37
    and Ford's proposal to stop,
        34
World War II, 4, 8, 80, 170
    consumer shortages during,
        332
    liquor industry during, 4, 8,
        10
    technology since, 272

Xerox Corporation, 24

Zeckendorf, William, 80, 164